# HUMANISTIC PSYCHOLOGY

## A SYNTHESIS

# THE DORSEY SERIES IN PSYCHOLOGY

# Humanistic Psychology

## A Synthesis

C. William Tageson
University of Notre Dame

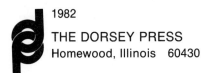
1982
THE DORSEY PRESS
Homewood, Illinois   60430

ISBN 0-256-02742-0
Library of Congress Catalog Card No. 81–70946

*Printed in the United States of America*

1 2 3 4 5 6 7 8 9 0 MP 9 8 7 6 5 4 3 2

To Carol, who lives what this book teaches.

# Preface

The main purpose of this book is to fill a gap in the existing literature on humanistic psychology. I have discovered during the course of my teaching career that there is no single book which summarizes the contributions of this important and growing area of psychological investigation. There are many works by individual authors, some helpful books of readings, and several textbooks for courses on personal growth, but no single source of information on the entire field of humanistic-existential psychology. This book therefore issues from my own experience as a professor of this subject who has attempted, over the years, to synthesize this material for my students, undergraduate and graduate.

It is also a personal statement in that it embodies my own efforts to provide a beginning theoretical synthesis of this movement. That comes, as do most good things, from personal experience. I have been intrigued, since my own adolescence, by the mystery of my own self-awareness and by the subsequent realization that it is this attribute, above all, which distinguishes the human species from all others on this planet. I therefore identify seven major themes or issues addressed by humanistic authors, summarize their thoughts on these themes, and show how they are all unified by the humanistic emphasis on this species-specific attribute: self-reflective awareness. There are undoubtedly other ways in which the views of this disparate set of authors could be synthesized, but the notion of a *proactive* self, aware of its own existence, has certainly been a central, unifying characteristic of this movement. And as a result, human consciousness (and its potential expansion) is beginning to reclaim its rightful place in the discipline of psychology.

From this standpoint, humanistic psychology is presented as an approach complementary to other current emphases. Its many applications, both within and outside the discipline of psychology, are extensively surveyed. Finally, an attempt is made to respond to current criticisms of this movement and to suggest some needed directions for its future development.

Major humanistic authors whose thought is distilled in this volume include: Joseph Nuttin, Carl Rogers, Abraham Maslow, Viktor Frankl, Amedeo Giorgi, Sidney Jourard, Frederick (Fritz) Perls, Rollo May, Charlotte Bühler, Ludwig Binswanger, and others. The book also serves as an introduction to a new movement arising from this emphasis, known as transpersonal psychology. Because of the nature of this work and its subject matter, the style is both objective (in presenting the thought and research of these various authors) and somewhat personal (in presenting my own reflections and conclusions).

It is my belief that this book will be of principal interest as a text or supplementary source book for professors and students (formal and informal) of humanistic psychology and personality theory at the graduate and upper-division undergraduate levels. I suspect it will be of equal interest to professionals and students in other fields touched by the humanistic movement, such as psychiatry and medicine, clinical and counseling psychology, social work, sociology, philosophy, and humanistic studies. And, though it belongs to the academic wing of humanistic psychology, it may be of some interest to the more informed general public, particularly those who have come in contact with the human potential movement.

Initial encouragement for this project came from two former colleagues at Notre Dame, Professors John Meany and Morton Kelsey, and from my colleague and former chairman, Dr. John Borkowski. The manuscript was begun while I was a Visiting Fellow at the Center for Studies of the Person in La Jolla, California. I wish to extend my deep gratitude to the members and staff of that center and particularly to Dr. William Coulson, his wife Jeannie, and their family, to Dr. Carl Rogers, and to Dr. and Mrs. Spencer Johnson for their hospitality, stimulation, and encouragement. Dr. Ellen B. Ryan, as chairman, kindly provided additional time for completing the manuscript. Special thanks are extended to Professor Salvatore Maddi of the University of Chicago, who reviewed the entire project as Consulting Editor of this series; to Professors Robert C. Bennion of Brigham Young University, Arthur Warmoth of Sonoma State University, and Irwin Mahler of Occidental College, who reviewed significant portions of the manuscript; and to my colleagues, Professors Sheridan P. McCabe and George Howard, who reviewed single chapters. Their suggestions, frequently followed, were of invaluable help. I must assume full responsibility for those I was unable to incorporate. Many of my students, too many to mention by name, provided helpful suggestions and feedback on ideas presented in this text.

I wish to thank Pauline Wright for typing initial drafts of many chapters and Linda Guyton for her tireless and efficient care in preparing the final manuscript. My wife, Carol, and my children, Lisa and Erik, put up with me throughout and cheered me along the way. The term *gratitude* does not cover all that I owe them.

**C. William Tageson**

# Contents

1. **Four Trends in Contemporary Psychology** . . . . . . . . . . . . . . . . . .   1

    In the beginning. The rise of behaviorism: *Philosophical roots. Operationism. Neobehaviorism. Limits of objectivity.* Depth psychology: *The dynamic unconscious.* Humanistic-existential psychology: *Origins.* Transpersonal psychology: *Precursors. Altered states.*

2. **Prologue: The Levels of Conscious Experience** . . . . . . . . . . . . . . .  17

    *The role of understanding.* A humanistic approach. Descriptive analysis of conscious experience. Levels of consciousness: *Irreducibility. Culture and human needs. The interpenetration of conscious levels. Knowledge as power.* The dialectical nature of consciousness: *Rychlak's dual model.*

3. **The Major Themes of Humanistic Psychology** . . . . . . . . . . . . . . .  31

    1. Phenomenological approach.   2. Holism: *Goldstein's influence. The experience of consciousness.*   3. The actualizing tendency: *Trusting the organism. The role of consciousness.*   4. Self-determination: *The developmental view.*   5. The ideal of authenticity: *The inner locus of evaluation.*   6. Self-transcendence: *The transpersonal level. Emphasis on encounter. Other viewpoints.*   7. Person-centeredness: *Purpose versus method. A radical approach.* Conclusion.

4. **Phenomenology and the Science of Person** . . . . . . . . . . . . . . . . . .  52

    Scientific paradigms: *Paradigms in psychology.* Philosophical contributions to psychology. Structural phenomenology. Functional phenomenology: *Rogers's self-theory.* Current examples of functional phenomenology: *Kelly's personal construct theory. Rychlak's logical learning theory.* Radical versus moderate approaches. Science and phenomenology: *Coexistence: The moderate approach.* Prediction and control.

5. Holism versus Reductionism ............................. 78

Varieties of reductionism. Biological reductionism: *The behavioral position. The Freudian position. The humanistic position.* Holism. The life-cycle approach. The mind-body dichotomy. The conscious-unconscious dichotomy: *The body as repository. The intimate conscious. The Rogerian approach. The role of self-disclosure.* The self-other dichotomy. Common thread. Mathematical reductionism.

6. The Actualizing Tendency ............................... 105

Needs and drives. Science and teleology. Homeostasis and growth. Historical origins: *The Aristotelian legacy. Carl Rogers's actualizing tendency. Maslow's self-actualization drive. Nuttin's "drive" for self-realization. Other viewpoints.*

7. Self-determination ....................................... 123

Hard determinism: The natural science paradigm: *Hard determinism: The behavioral view. Hard determinism: The Freudian view.* Soft determinism: The humanistic-existential view: *May's concept of intentionality. Rychlak's concept of telosponsivity. Consciousness, health, and freedom. The developmental dimension. Contributions of the humanistic approach.*

8. The Ideal of Authenticity ................................ 146

Behaviorism. Depth psychology: *The Freudian model. The Adlerian model. The Jungian model.* Humanistic-existential viewpoints. Structural orientations: *Nuttin's constructive ideal of personality. Maslow's self-actualized person. Frankl's will to meaning.* Process orientations: *Perls's "free-functioning" organism. Rogers's fully functioning person.* Conclusion.

9. Self-Transcendence ....................................... 183

Nuttin's transpersonal level of experience. Viktor Frankl's will to meaning. Maslow's B-domain. Process theories and self-transcendence. The Asian connection: *Taoism: An example.* Transpersonal psychology: *Classification of altered states.* Self-transcendence and religion.

10. Person-Centeredness: In Research and Therapy............... 208

Phenomenological approach: *Experimenter bias. The cooperative approach.* The principle of self-actualization: *Applications to psychotherapy.* Reemphasis on self-determination. A radical person-centered approach. A new eco-psychology.

11. **Eco-Psychology: Impact on Social Systems** . . . . . . . . . . . . . . . . . . . . **227**

The human potential movement. Humanistic management: *T-groups. From T-groups to organization development.* Humanistic education: *Some historical notes. Organization development in education. The affective matrix.* Humanistic medicine. Humanistic psychology and the law: *Legal education. Law enforcement. Corrections.* Humanistic psychology and religion. Marriage, family, and children. Power to the powerless. Humanistic political science.

12. **Epilogue: Critique and Future Directions** . . . . . . . . . . . . . . . . . . . . . **249**

Cultural revolution: *Toward a broader ethic.* The role of the unconscious: *The problem of evil.* The issue of verification. Further directions for the future.

**References** . . . . . . . . . . . . . . . . . . . . . . . . . . . . . . . . . . . . . . . . . . . . . . . . . . **259**

**Index** . . . . . . . . . . . . . . . . . . . . . . . . . . . . . . . . . . . . . . . . . . . . . . . . . . . . . . . . **277**

# 1 Four Trends in Contemporary Psychology

There are many images that come to mind as I meditate on the plight of the individual in our Western technological society. One in particular haunts me. It is of a pretty Berkeley student standing before a TV camera in the days of the free speech movement, long hair, eyes smiling, wearing a man's shirt, Levis, and sandals. And pinned to her shirt is an IBM card on which is written in bold, black letters: "Do not fold, spindle, or mutilate me!"

This image symbolizes so much for me: the indomitable, youthful, optimistic spirit of the girl rising up against the oppressive impersonality of the modern multiversity. The spirit of man himself, every man and woman, crying out into the maelstrom of social forces seemingly beyond our control: "I am here! Attend to me!"

This cry expresses for me a basic truth about human existence. We are, it appears, the only self-conscious animals in any meaningful sense. As the existential phenomenologists have pointed out, we alone ex-ist; stand out in the world of being, alone in the awareness that we are, capable of reflecting on our own ongoing reality.

I vividly remember the words of a teenaged girl whom I counseled years ago: "Childhood seems like one long dream to me. Only now do I feel really alive, aware to my life!" There was exhilaration in her voice but anxiety, too. Life really began for her, as it does for all of us, in those magical moments of self-awareness.

So much stems from such moments: a sense of the mystery of existence, so quickly lost as we grow older and find ourselves caught up in the daily routine of survival. In my own case it is a sense of myself as a center of existence, caught up in a world of experience bounded by my body, and yet, somehow, not coextensive with it, a world so private that I forever despair of communicating its richness and bewildering variety to another, while longing to do so; a sense of being a center of control, of being able to set into motion from within myself the power to shape my own response to the forces that impinge upon me from without; and a growing sense, as life proceeds, that there are depths within myself outside of my awareness which have influenced my decisions in the past and which I must somehow seize and gradually bring to consciousness if I am ever to be free.

The Berkeley student, in my half-remembered, half-reconstructed image, is smiling. That has special significance for me. I was struck, I recall, by her self-assurance, her sense of confidence: that she stood at the center of her own existence, gazing serenely at the camera and through it to the thousands who would observe her through this technological miracle. "I am here," she seemed to be saying, "and I will be dealt with. I refuse to be numbered and profiled and pigeonholed and objectified. I am a person, and you must deal with me, and you cannot do so by attempting to distill the richness and uniqueness of my existence into a few holes on a computer card."

I must confess that I liked her self-assurance: the reaffirmation of human dignity that she represents to me. It somehow affirms me in my own personhood and self-respect, and in the values that I assign to those concepts as they apply to me and to other men and women.

It is also heartening to me, as a professional psychologist, to know that many of my colleagues are seriously engaged in the effort to revalidate the study of human consciousness as a central focus of concern in the discipline of psychology. Somehow this focus had become lost in the shuffle. Etymologically, the term *psychology* means science of the soul or mind, but someone has already observed that psychology lost its soul at the hands of Freudian determinists and lost its mind as a result of the behaviorists' insistence on objectivity and measurement.

## IN THE BEGINNING

Ironically, the study of consciousness was indeed a central issue in the very first psychological laboratories established in Europe and America. These first investigations, which led to the ultimate separation of psychology from philosophy in the 1870s and 1880s, were strongly influenced by the philosophical doctrines of psychophysical parallelism and identism advocated by the German physiologist Gustav Fechner. His position was a direct outgrowth of Cartesian dualism: the belief that mind and body are two distinct substances with entirely different properties accidentally joined together in the human person.

Fechner's interpretation was much simpler. Psychic events (the on-going experience we have in the stream of consciousness of thoughts, feelings, emotions, impulses, fantasies, sensations, and perceptions) run perfectly parallel to physiological events occurring within our bodily organisms (*psychophysical parallelism*). Though we experience and describe these events as different, they are in reality two sides of the same coin. They are essentially identical (*identism*). The Weber-Fechner laws of psychophysics were the result of these early attempts to establish mathematical links between these two seemingly different sets of events. Subjects in these early laboratories, for example, would report that two weights were just noticeably different to them. These "j.n.d.'s" would, in turn, be linked to actual weight differences and an equation formulated to *predict* from externally measurable stimulus differences to perceptual experience in a lawful manner.

These early experiments were primarily concerned with sensation and perception, though some interesting data were unearthed on topics of broader scope (e.g., the existence of imageless thought, and some of the subjective parameters of decision making). The hope that inspired them was basically an elementaristic one, borrowed from associationist philosophy: that the basic building blocks of consciousness would prove to be simple sensations, and that, understanding these, one could then analyze the more complex structures of perception, thought, and will, and reduce them to their simpler elements: sensations and feel-ings. If these, in turn, could be linked by psychophysical equations to external physical events (stimulus intensity, duration, and the like), the reduction would be complete, and psychophysical laws and theories might eventually be reduced to biochemical and physical terms. Psy-chology would then become a natural science indeed, on a par with physics, chemistry, and biology.

It was an ambitious project, but it failed. The attempt to calibrate introspective judgments in precise quantitative ways proved to be abortive and ultimately unsatisfactory. A few psychophysical equa-tions were established for the simpler dimensions of sensory experi-ence and were incorporated into general psychology; but the more complex dimensions of human consciousness remained elusive and invulnerable to such precise treatment. As we shall see, they simply cannot be accomodated by a natural science, "mental chemistry" model of explanation.

The Gestalt psychologists questioned the very principle of elemen-tarism and successfully challenged the proposition that the psychic experience of perception is merely the additive sum of simple sensations. Or, to use Gestalt terminology, "the whole is greater than the sum of its parts," a conclusion they were able to establish quite emphatically in their own laboratory demonstrations.

## THE RISE OF BEHAVIORISM

The most serious blow to the introspectionism of Wundt and Titchener and to the subsequent study of consciousness by scientific psychologists, however, was the discovery of the conditioned reflex by Ivan Pavlov in the early 1900s. Objectively induced under rigid laboratory controls, quantifiable, publicly observable in terms of related stimuli and responses, the conditioned reflex was seized upon as the new building block for empirical psychology. Led in America by the redoubtable John Watson, psychologists swiftly redefined their discipline as the science of behavior. Behaviorism, termed by Maslow the First Force in contemporary psychology, was born.

### Philosophical roots

This shift from the study of human consciousness to the more objective realm of animal and human behavior was strongly reinforced by important concurrent philosophical trends. Physics, chemistry, and the other natural sciences had already developed powerful methodologies and strategies for scientific investigation with the help of logical positivism, and its offshoot, operationism. Direct historical descendants of the British empiricists Locke, Berkeley, and Hume, and the positivists James and John Stuart Mill, the logical positivists allied themselves very closely with the scientific enterprise.

The love affair between science and positivism was a natural from the first. With their sensistic and antimetaphysical biases, the logical positivists devoted almost complete attention to the development of the philosophy of science and a rigorous scientific logic. Truth-bearing sentences are those which have observable referents. Sentences whose terms cannot be linked to sensible referents are neither true nor false, but simply meaningless.

Obviously, then, scientific statements, derived from carefully controlled observations of public, objective, quantifiable data, best fulfill the criteria of truth-bearing sentences, and are most deserving of credence. Obviously, too, philosophers should aid scientists in developing a foolproof logical system for the construction of theories, from which hypotheses can be deduced for empirical testing, leading eventually to the discovery and establishment of new scientific laws. And since, from the time of Galileo, scientific results have been wherever possible reported in mathematical equations, the development of mathematical logic should most concern the philosopher. By sharpening the tools which scientists use to an ever finer edge, philosophy could best accomplish its own purpose: the never-ending search for truth.

## Operationism

The strategic application of the logical principles so developed came to be known in 20th-century scientific circles as *operationism*. Variables subjected to scientific scrutiny were to be "operationally defined," that is, defined in terms of the techniques employed in observing them. Only in this way, it was felt, could rigorous objectivity be assured. This strategy could be rather easily applied in the physical sciences, where highly accurate measuring instruments had long been developed and employed. But its appeal was strongly felt by the adherents of behaviorism in psychology, also. Influenced by the writings of the physicist P. W. Bridgman (1927), many behaviorists adopted the operational approach, with such success that it soon became the model for all psychological research that aspired to the term *scientific*.

Because of the prestige enjoyed, until recently at least, by the scientific community, prestige not unjustly earned by the startling achievements gained through application of the mathematico-deductive method in the physical sciences, it is certainly understandable that psychologists would be tempted to follow suit.

## Neobehaviorism

The lifework of the neobehaviorist Clark Hull (1952) represents the most outstanding (and influential) instance of this trend in contemporary empirical psychology. Hull deliberately adopted the systematic strategy proposed by the logical positivists and applied himself to the construction of a mathematico-deductive theory of learning, which came to be known as drive-reduction theory. Taking Thorndike's earlier, more loosely defined law of effect, Hull proceeded to construct a rigorous theoretical system, complete with mathematical equations from which further hypotheses and relationships could be logically deduced and empirically tested. White rats were his preferred experimental subjects. All variables were carefully defined according to strict operational criteria (e.g., "drive" by hours of food-deprivation; "response-strength" by number of unreinforced trials to extinction, or latency of reaction time).

Learning is usually defined by most psychologists as a change in the behavior of an organism brought about by interaction with the environment (thus excluding strictly maturational effects). For Hull, learning was always to be understood as a conditioning process in which the organism gradually connects certain responses in its behavioral repertoire with discriminable cues or stimuli from the environment that have proved to be reinforcing in the past. Reinforcement always implies the reduction of unpleasant states of tension called *drives*, which are ultimately linked to tissue-needs, such as hunger or thirst. The learned tendency of an organism to respond in certain specific ways was, for Hull, a multiplicative function of previous habit strength or conditioning, amount of drive, stimulus intensity, and amount of incentive.

It is not my intention to enter into a deeper exploration of the Hullian system, but merely to point out the operational flavor of his terminology and the intricately systematic approach he chose to adopt toward his subject matter. Many, even of his followers, have modified his postulates and conclusions. The most influential of all current behaviorists, B. F. Skinner, has roundly criticized this type of theory construction in psychology, in the belief that much data must yet be gathered before any such elaborate systematization can be attempted, though he adheres strictly to the aims of operationism himself.

For a further critique of Hull's work, I would refer the reader to Hilgard and Bower (1966) or other authors. Certainly it can be documented that the present generation of graduate students in academic psychology has been brought up to revere the laboratory experiment and the operational definition as the ideal form of psychological research. Few departments of psychology would allow a doctoral dissertation to be presented which did not somehow reflect and incorporate this methodological approach.

## Limits of objectivity

This quest for scientific objectivity and quantification is what characterizes the predominant trend in modern academic psychology. I do not question the value of such an aim, nor of its productivity in the past. But, along with others, I do question its pervasiveness, rigidity, and arrogant dogmatism. Much valuable knowledge, applicable even to human behavior, has been gained, particularly in the areas of learning, sensation, and perception, through this strict adherence to positivistic canons of research. Undoubtedly, further gains will accrue from research of this kind.

Ironically, however, as the systematic psychologist Sigmund Koch (1964) has pointed out, the philosophical descendants of logical positivism have moved well beyond the original rigor of the system in their attempts to grapple with the elusive dimension of meaning, and phenomenological philosophy has, for years past, been making significant contributions to Western thought. The latter philosophical system takes as its starting point the experience and raw phenomenon of human consciousness. Koch, consequently, does not hesitate to predict the death of behaviorism as a viable strategy for research on human behavior. My own feeling is that behaviorism, specifically in the anti-theoretical form espoused by Skinner and other experimental analysts of behavior, will continue to function as an important strategy and source of information about certain aspects of human functioning. But precisely because of its systematically necessary exclusion of the subjective data of consciousness, behaviorism will be increasingly relegated to a complementary role as psychologists continue to turn their attention to the complexities of human personality.

This is already happening, as I shall show when, later in this chapter, I trace the rise of the humanistic-existential movement in modern psychology, and its growing reliance on phenomenological methods of research. Interestingly, strict operationists had long been critical of some psychologists' efforts to bend the rules of the operational definition in their attempt to operationalize human experiences, such as anxiety, empathy, or vocational choice. Such criticism is undoubtedly justified. And yet, the very fact that these questionable practices continue to arise points up the painful dilemma which faces the serious student of human behavior. If I am continually forced to modify a tool in order to get the job done, it would seem logical to assume that, in its original form, the tool was inadequate to begin with. It may have served me well in accomplishing simpler tasks, but I may very well be forced to modify it or discard it altogether when faced with a more complex assignment.

Operationism is, after all, just such a methodological tool. It serves us quite well when our sources of information are, *by the very characteristics of the objects of study,* limited to external observation and quantifiable phenomena. Quite literally, we have no other choice. Such is the case with the physical energy systems of inanimate nature and with the biochemical systems of living organisms lower than man on the scale of evolution. Operationism is by far the best tool for controlled observation available to us in such instances, and scientists have used it marvelously well. But the nature of such phenomena constitutes a *limit,* not an advantage.

Human functioning, on the other hand, need not be limited to this objective category, inaccessible from within. It can be studied objectively, with great profit, but we need not so restrict ourselves. In fact, it seems increasingly evident that we are foolish to do so. The fact remains: persons are not simply objects; they are self-conscious subjects of experience as well. They are perfectly aware of certain aspects of their behavior and perfectly capable of communicating this awareness to other subjects. And ironically, the very existence of philosophical systems—not to mention scientific data, laws, and theories—is a function and product of human *consciousness.* Scientific observation implies a conscious observer. This is, perhaps, the one inescapable self-evident facet of reality available to me, as most epistemologists since Descartes have continued to remind us. To ignore the subjective phenomenon of human consciousness in the investigation of human behavior seems as inane as attempting to use a hairpin to open a vault when the combination is available.

The question remains, of course, whether the study of human consciousness can be conducted on a *scientific* basis, or whether it must remain strictly in the philosophical realm. This is, indeed, a crucial matter. The answer ultimately depends, I suppose, on one's philosophy of science, or, more relevantly, on whose paradigm for scientific investigation gains currency among the scientific fraternity (Kuhn, 1962). Neither psychoanalytic, humanistic, nor transpersonal psychologists, as we shall see, think of themselves as philosophers, though they are not unaware of the philosophical implications of their work and may, at times, venture into philosophical speculation themselves. We shall have occasion to describe some of the methods that humanistic psychologists employ for the controlled investigation of human consciousness and its influence on behavior outcomes. Many are well aware of the challenge leveled against their scientific credentials by purists in the field, and have attempted to meet it head on. Others seem content to carry on their work undisturbed by what they apparently consider to be a semantic problem of no particular importance to them.

## DEPTH PSYCHOLOGY

The second major trend in contemporary psychology stems from Freudian psychoanalysis and its offshoots, the depth psychologies, which include the theories of Adler, Jung, Rank, Sullivan, Horney, Fromm, Erikson, and a host of others. As the very name indicates, depth psychology, while certainly not ignoring human consciousness, focuses principally on that mysterious realm which is believed by these theorists to lie *below* the level of awareness, the *dynamic unconscious*. Behaviorists ignore consciousness because it is private, subjective, and therefore invulnerable to objective observation and measurement. Depth psychologists ignore it because, to them, it is relatively unimportant. Their aim may be to bring to awareness what before lay hidden in the murky unverbalizable depths of the human psyche, and they strongly promote this process as necessary for the integration of the human personality. But their attention is fixed on the levels that exist beneath conscious awareness: their structure, contents, and dynamics.

For them, the drama of human existence is played out principally on a darkened stage. The actors are invisible; their interactions unobservable except to a privileged few who are equipped to follow the action by the use of specialized instruments: the psychoanalytic techniques of free association, projective tests, hypnotism, or the interpretation of dreams.

## The dynamic unconscious

The emphasis on the dynamic unconscious, then, is what characterizes the second predominant trend in modern psychology. Human behavior is principally determined by what occurs in the depths of the unconscious mind. Freud suspected this to be true of even normal individuals, as evidenced in his book *The Psychopathology of Everyday Life* (1966). Conscious experience represents only the top 10 percent of the iceberg of human existence and so is relegated to a very subsidiary role by expositors of this movement, also.

There are, of course, important variations within this school of thought. Adler, Jung, the ego-analysts, and the neoanalysts, for example, have contributed much to the later humanistic movement and are not as reductionistic in their thinking as was Freud. The whole depth psychology movement is basically more humanistic and person-centered than the objectivism of the stricter behaviorists and their human engineering approach to human functioning.

Historically, this overriding interest in the nature and influence of the dynamic unconscious is quite understandable. Depth psychology arose from the need to understand *pathological* forms of human behavior. The subjects of investigation were psychically disturbed individuals, and the principal investigators were primarily medical practitioners and psychiatrists. We tend to call such persons disturbed precisely because their expressions of consciousness do not resemble ours, or those of most people with whom we deal in ordinary society.

I vividly remember, for example, a number of persons referred to me for counseling with whom I felt particularly uneasy and out of touch. One was a little elderly lady who lived alone in a dreary room and was constantly frightened by the host of little blue men who scampered in and out of her apartment from a nearby neon sign. Another was a young man who apparently had run away from a mental hospital and wanted to be put in touch with the Secret Service. He was being pursued by the Communists, he claimed, because he had accidentally been photographed next to a well-known Communist defendant in a federal courthouse and the party was out to get him as a presumed agent of the government.

Where no organic deficits can be established, the theory of the dynamic unconscious has been most helpful for the understanding of such bizarre conscious states, and it is much more humane and hopeful in its application than, for example, the ancient suppositions of possession or witchcraft. Undoubtedly, too, the techniques of depth therapy may well constitute a preferred mode of treatment for such extreme pathological cases. But many psychologists today question the wisdom of basing a theory of healthy personality development and functioning on the phenomena of psychopathology.

It does make some sense to describe the healthy, fully functioning personality as one not primarily determined in its activities by subconscious forces. This is, however, a negative approach at best—a definition of health as an absence of disease symptoms. The medical profession has begun to look for a positive health syndrome among people who seldom or never succumb to physical disease. One of the more promising contributions of humanistic psychologists has already been the search for a similar positive syndrome of psychological health. They have deliberately set out to explore those unique sets of circumstances that seem to have enabled certain fortunate individuals not just to remain immune to severe psychological disturbances but to cope constructively with degrees of stress that would overwhelm most men and women. Sidney Jourard, for one, hypothesized a direct relationship between psychological and physical "wellness" and suggested some possible explanations for why psychologically "inspirited" people seem to maintain an optimum level of physical well-being. His research (Jourard, 1971) on the positive effects of self-disclosure to significant others reflects typical humanistic insistence on the need to investigate the overlooked variable of normal human consciousness of self.

## HUMANISTIC–EXISTENTIAL PSYCHOLOGY

A preeminent concern with the specifically human attribute and experience of self-consciousness is what characterizes, for me, the growth of the humanistic-existential movement in contemporary psychology. Years ago, Kurt Goldstein pointed out that language is the Rubicon that animals never cross. It would seem more accurate to say that reflexive awareness, the consciousness of self as an active center of intentionality and experience, is that Rubicon. Language is the symbolization and communication of human consciousness, and the latter is the very foundation of human personality, the felt uniqueness of the individual. It is the source, we shall see, of self-determination or personal freedom. It leads to the need for and growth of society, and makes possible the development of science itself, as well as art, literature, morality, philosophy, and religion. And it is to the credit of this movement that human consciousness has been returned to center stage in the discipline of psychology.

### Origins

Not a remarkably cohesive group, humanistic-existential psychology is a broad movement which spans many continents and embraces a large number of psychologists and psychiatrists, principally in Europe and America, who might variously be labeled as humanists, personalists, phenomenologists, or existentialists. Its protagonists in Europe are primarily analytic psychiatrists who, for the most part, were influenced by phenomenological and existential movements in philosophy. A very partial list would include Paul Tournier (a Swiss personalist), Viktor Frankl (founder of logotherapy), Ludwig Binswanger and Medard Boss (Daseinsanalysts influenced by Heidegger), R. D. Laing (an English analyst influenced by Sartre), Karl Jaspers, Joseph Nuttin, Igor Caruso, Henri Baruk, and others.

The American side of the movement arose independently and, as might be expected, from a more pragmatic, less philosophical base. Leading representatives include Carl Rogers, James Bugental, Eugene Gendlin, William Schutz, Rollo May, Adrian Van Kaam and his associates at Duquesne University, and the late Abraham Maslow, Frederick Perls, and Sidney Jourard. May and Van Kaam have been primarily responsible for linking the otherwise independent groups by introducing the contributions of European thinkers to American readers, as well as through their own writings. The rapid development of numerous human potential or growth centers and the recent proliferation of humanistic institutes and professional journals has been a direct outgrowth of this movement.

This third movement stands, by implication, in contrast to the two previously reigning forces in modern psychology: behaviorism and psychoanalysis. While by no means rejecting the important insights of the depth therapists, particularly in their studies of the influence of the dynamic unconscious on human behavior, nor the contributions of the behaviorists through the application of a rigorous scientific methodology, humanistic psychology stands united in its attempt to broaden the scope of modern psychology.

It generally rejects the inherent biological reductionism tacitly or explicitly assumed by orthodox analysts and neobehaviorists alike, and is groping toward a broader, open-at-the-top perspective toward the science of human experience and behavior. The revolutionary implications of this approach for the philosophy of social science can be sampled by reading *The Psychology of Science* (Maslow, 1966) and *Man and the Science of Man* (Rogers & Coulson, 1968), or the ambitious programs outlined in *Existential Foundations of Psychology* (Van Kaam, 1966) and *Psychology as a Human Science* (Giorgi, 1970).

It would be a serious mistake to assume that humanistic authors constitute a tightly knit school of thought akin to such earlier movements in psychology as Gestalt, functionalism, or even the behaviorism and orthodox psychoanalysis with which they are contrasted. There exists too great a diversity of interests, methodologies, and background for that to occur. Nevertheless, I have been able to discern some common threads of emphasis in my reading of these various authors, which seem to justify the attempt to categorize them under the one rubric. These seven themes of humanistic psychology will be presented in Chapter 3 of this work and constitute its principal subject matter throughout.

## TRANSPERSONAL PSYCHOLOGY

Finally, the emergence of a fourth trend in contemporary psychological circles needs to be mentioned for purposes of completeness. Most frequently termed *transpersonal psychology* by its adherents, it represents an offshoot from humanistic psychology and its antireductionistic, open-at-the-top stance toward the sources of human experience. In alliance with humanistic psychology, it focuses also on the phenomenology of consciousness, but in its *altered states,* states of consciousness which vary from our ordinary waking state and, at times, apparently transcend the impression there generated of personal isolation, centrality, and self-sufficiency.

The early American psychologist, William James, is often quoted in this context:

> Our normal waking consciousness, rational consciousness as we call it, is but one special type of consciousness, whilst all about it, parted from it by the filmiest of screens, there lie potential forms of consciousness entirely different. We may go through life without suspecting their existence; but apply the requisite stimulus, and at a touch they are there in all their completeness, definite types of mentality which probably somewhere have their field of application and adaptation. No account of the universe in its totality can be final which leaves these other forms of consciousness quite disregarded. How to regard them is the question— for they are so discontinuous with ordinary consciousness. Yet they may determine attitudes though they cannot furnish formulas, and open a region though they fail to give a map. At any rate, they forbid a premature closing of our accounts with reality. (1929, pp. 378–379)

His book, *The Varieties of Religious Experience* (1929), is considered a seminal work in this field by modern transpersonal psychologists.

Transpersonal psychology attempts to treat these phenomena scientifically, and with respect. It has cast a broad net, covering topics as diverse as drug-induced states (marijuana, alcohol, and LSD) to the effects of biofeedback training on the control of alpha rhythms and the conscious states that accompany their presence; from dream states to meditation, hypnotic, and autohypnotic states; from the type of altered states of consciousness that accompany intuitive mathematical thinking to mystical and religious experience.

I personally like the exuberant description given by the late Anthony Sutich, founding editor of both the *Journal of Humanistic Psychology* and the *Journal of Transpersonal Psychology,* strange as it must sound to the ears of most academic psychologists:

> The emerging Transpersonal Psychology ("fourth force") is concerned specifically with the *empirical,* scientific study of, and responsible implementation of the findings relevant to, becoming, individual and species-wide meta-needs, ultimate values, unitive consciousness, peak experiences, B-values, ecstasy, mystical experience, awe, being, self-actualization, essence, bliss, wonder, ultimate meaning, transcendence of the self, spirit, oneness, cosmic awareness, individual and species-wide synergy, maximal interpersonal encounter, sacralization of everyday life, transcendental phenomena, cosmic self-humor and playfulness, maximal sensory awareness, responsiveness and expression, and related concepts, experiences and activities. (1969)

With considerably greater brevity, he elsewhere defined transpersonal psychology as concerning itself with those *ultimate* human capacities and potentialities that have no systematic place in the other three movements of contemporary psychology.

### Precursors

Along with William James, the analytic psychologist Carl G. Jung is considered a precursor of the interests of this group by many of its members. His openness to parapsychological phenomena, and his familiarity with Eastern, African, and American Indian world views, so often antithetical to Western ideas of reality, as well as his own archetypal psychology grounded in his concept of a transpersonal collective unconscious, have influenced many authors in this field. His prodigious, pioneering effort to elucidate the contents of this collective unconscious through dream analysis, active imagination, and the analysis of transcultural themes embodied in myths and symbols continues to be treated with respect and admiration by proponents of the new movement. In particular, the Jungian concept of the archetype of the Self and its gradual incorporation in the process of personal individuation has strong transpersonal overtones and continues to influence current speculation.

Contemporary Jungians continue to contribute, from their own perspective, to topics that engage the interest of transpersonal psychologists. Jungians have sponsored an annual conference on archetypal psychology at the University of Notre Dame in which transpersonal themes tend to predominate, and continue to contribute significantly to meetings on altered states of consciousness held annually at the Menninger Foundation in Topeka, Kansas.

Among humanistic psychologists, Abraham Maslow and Viktor Frankl seem to be the principal forerunners of the transpersonal movement. Maslow's suggestions for the development of an empirical "psychology of Being" (1968), based upon the study of self-actualized individuals, and his further elaboration of the experiences of B- (for Being) cognition and B-values, peak- and nadir-experiences, have been of particular importance. Frankl, an existential analyst, has contributed the concept of a "will to meaning" as the fundamental characteristic of human functioning, and has insisted that self-transcendence is a necessary prerequisite for full self-actualization. With this Maslow agreed (1966), and it constitutes a major theme in the transpersonal literature.

Moving more directly into the field of transpersonal psychology itself, note must first be taken of the contributions of the late Italian analyst, Roberto Assagioli. Conversant with the work of Sigmund Freud (his doctoral dissertation in 1910 represented his own views of the limitations of Freudian psychoanalysis), and much more sympathetic to the ideas of Carl Jung, Assagioli developed his own approach and related psychotherapeutic techniques under the label of *psychosynthesis*. In addition to the previously hypothesized realms of a dynamic personal and collective unconscious, he posited the existence of a *superconscious* sphere and transpersonal Self.

> From this region we receive our higher intuitions and inspirations— artistic, philosophical, or scientific, ethical "imperatives" and urges to humanitarian and heroic action. It is the source of the higher feelings, such as altruistic love; of genius and of the states of contemplation, illumination, and ecstasy. In this realm are latent the higher psychic functions and spiritual energies. (1965, pp. 17–18)

In this region also exists the higher, transpersonal Self, of which little is known, but with which contact must be established and maintained for true self-actualization to occur. Repression can and usually does operate against the contents of this region also in the life of the normal person. The aim of psychosynthesis, then, is to harmonize and integrate all these areas of psychic life for full individuation and personal development.

Space does not permit a further elaboration of Assagioli's views, but institutes of psychosynthesis have been established in several different countries to carry on his work.

## Altered states

A more specifically empirical focus and definition of transpersonal psychology has been provided through the efforts of Charles Tart (1969, 1975), Robert Ornstein (1972, 1973), and Kenneth Pelletier and Charles Garfield (1976). Tart, for example, defines an altered state of consciousness phenomenologically as "one in which he [the individual experiencing the state] clearly feels a *qualitative* shift in his pattern or mental functioning, that is, he feels not just a quantitative shift (more or less alert, more or less visual imagery, sharper or duller, etc.), but also that some quality or qualities of his mental process are *different*" (1969, pp. 1–2). Pelletier and Garfield (1976) have used the taxonomy of 20 different altered states (including normal consciousness) provided by Krippner (1972) as a starting point for their own work, and refer to paradigms of the social and psychological processes involved in inducing altered states of consciousness proposed by Zimbardo (1969), Silverman (1968), and Sarbin and Adler (1967).

Both Tart and Ornstein ascribe the growing academic interest in altered states of consciousness (ASCs) to the pursuit of experiences of this kind by many members of the counter-cultural movement of the 1960s. (In this context I recall, also, the enormous popularity of the works of Carlos Castaneda and Carl Jung among student members of this group.) They cite the need for greater scientific objectivity in the study of ASCs, but reiterate the call of many previous humanistic authors for the development of new scientific paradigms for the investigation of consciousness in its varied states. New paradigms are called for, says Tart, because the majority of ASCs are spiritual phenomena with no known physical manifestations. Because they are purely internal (but not necessarily purely subjective) experiences, the older, physicalistic paradigms of Western science are forced to dismiss them.

Tart himself (1972) proposes the intriguing possibility of developing *state-specific sciences*, sciences of particular ASCs elaborated by trained observers able consistently to attain them, and of their relationship, where possible, with ordinary physical reality and its accompanying state of ordinary consciousness (SOC). He admits these have not yet been established—that no scientific data base yet exists for their development, and openly confronts the difficulties inherent in such a task. But he points hopefully to the wealth of data that does exist in the many state-specific technologies for inducing ASCs that have been developed over many centuries in almost every culture known to man.

Tart's recent volume of readings, *Transpersonal Psychologies* (1975), contains not only his own thoughts on current scientific paradigms, state-specific sciences, and parapsychology, but also contributions by modern practitioners of several of these technologies, all written from a psychological perspective. Though admittedly incomplete, the topics covered range from the practice of Western magic to Asian, Indian, Middle Eastern, and Western Christian mysticism and ways of personal liberation.

Carl Jung was one of the first to suggest this application of a psychological perspective to other cultural accounts of personal individuation, in his preface to a book introducing the I Ching to Western readers (Wilhelm, 1967). Hubert Benoit took up the challenge in his work *The Supreme Doctrine: Psychological Studies in Zen Thought* (1955), as did, among others, Alan Watts in his *Psychotherapy East and West* (1961), and Gardner and Lois Murphy in their edited volume, *Asian*

*Psychology* (1968). Tart's contribution has been to provide a sharper focus to this growing body of literature, and an attempt to formulate from it clearer paradigms for further scientific investigation.

Transpersonal psychology, then, represents a promising new approach to topics previously abandoned by scientific psychologists as too metaphysical or mystical. As mentioned previously, it is treated here to give closure to my account of current trends in psychology. I will take note later of its confirmatory criticism of the present exclusiveness of physicalistic paradigms in psychological science, and of its implicit correction of the overly egocentric or ego-isolated view of self-realization presented by some humanistic authors (see Chapter 9).

The borderlines between these four trends in contemporary psychology are less well fortified and patrolled than I may have implied in my presentation of them. I have already indicated some of the crossovers between analytic, humanistic, and transpersonal contributions (many authors assigned to the latter two categories would be especially surprised to find themselves listed in different camps), and later on I will detail some convergences taking place with behaviorism, particularly in its therapeutic applications.

These distinctions are meaningful for content and practice, however, and my focus in the present work will be on humanistic psychology: its starting point in the conscious experience of a personal self, its methodologies, the major unifying themes found within it, its implications for the philosophy of science in the study of human experience and behavior, and its application to various areas of human endeavor (psychotherapy, human relations and management, education, medicine, law, and other related areas).

# 2 Prologue: The Levels of Conscious Experience

In his widely read work, *Beyond Freedom and Dignity*, B. F. Skinner (1971) voices an impassioned plea for the application of behavioral technology to the problems that plague society and, eventually, to the design of an entire culture. The reluctance of the human race to take up the challenge implicitly offered in his earlier utopian novel, *Walden Two* (Skinner, 1948), he ascribes to the "literatures of freedom and dignity" which have molded and sustained the growth of the Western democracies. These literatures, he maintains, have long since attained their noble purposes: the overthrow of aversive systems of control and the safeguarding of society from the threat of their resurgence.

Now, Skinner proposes, these literatures, and the image of autonomous man that they have presented and defended, stand in the way of further progress. In their attack against aversive forms of control (punitive and even tyrannical forms), they have lulled men and women into believing that they are somehow free, self-regulating, self-governing. They have conditioned their adherents to react against *any* form of control, including the benign, positive reinforcement mode of conditioning upon which Skinner's behavior technology is based.

The belief in autonomous man obscures the real situation, Skinner believes, and may lead to ultimate disaster. It renders social control inconspicuous to the very people who have the power to do something constructive about it. As a result, the countermeasures they take are not well designed, and invariably turn out to be weak and ineffectual. He warns:

> This could be a lethal cultural mutation. Our culture has produced the science and technology it needs to save itself. It has the wealth it needs for effective action. It has, to a considerable extent, a concern for its own future. But if it continues to take freedom or dignity, rather than its own survival, as its principal value, then it is possible that some other culture will make a greater contribution to the future. (1971, p. 181)

What Skinner seems to be proposing here is somewhat akin to the Marxist notion of freedom (though he is no Marxist): that person alone is free who understands the inexorable laws of dialectic necessity, and who swims with that particular tide. One cannot change the course of history, but, by learning to ride the wave of the future, he or she can, like the surfer, experience a sense of fierce exhilaration and victory over the very forces that sweep one along.

## The role of understanding

*Understanding* is a key word here. It implies, in this case, a conscious awareness of the laws that underlie and determine the course of natural events. Such coming to awareness through the achievements of scientific methodology gives us the power to see and grasp the forces that previously shaped human destiny in a blind, inevitable way.

Geneticists tell us the day is at hand when we shall have the power, through understanding, to determine the future course of evolution. Marxists deliberately foster the dialectic of antithesis inherent in class struggles to hasten the process of revolution and the synthesis of the classless society that must, from Marxist theory, inevitably follow. And Skinner, understanding the basic principles of reinforcement that shape all human behavior, urges us to get on with the task of deliberately designing the future course of cultural evolution.

This is indeed a heady challenge. And yet Skinner is right. I do find myself resisting it, but my reason for doing so is not the one he presumably would ascribe to me. There is another, truly primal datum of experience, deeper than my belief in personal autonomy, that leads me to resist a description of human experience in purely objective, impersonal terms: the experience of reflexive self-awareness. Without this, the experience of self-determination, or the illusion of it, would be simply impossible. This is the aspect of human existence that has most meaning for me and other humanistic psychologists, the richness of which really cannot be exhausted in objective, positivistic terminology.

Skinner's approach is admittedly an extreme example of current positivism in the human sciences. There are other, more moderate, views. The sociological literature, for example, often uses the term *actor* to refer to the human person. This is closer to the mark from a humanistic perspective, but we are still left with the distinct impression that this actor is completely at the mercy of environmental forces which are ultimately responsible for his or her actions. Attention is therefore quickly focused away from the actor's *subjectivity* to these supposedly more explanatory, external, objective variables. It is this overall positivistic neglect of subjectivity, found even in contemporary cognitive psychology, which is the main issue at stake in the humanistic critique.

## A HUMANISTIC APPROACH

Several approaches have been formulated by humanistic authors for the inclusion of human subjectivity in psychological discourse. Some lean heavily on recent advances in theoretical physics and on the role of the observer in relationship to physical phenomena. Others are derived directly from phenomenological philosophy. The approach I favor, since it depends on neither scientific nor philosophical antecedents, was first suggested by Joseph Nuttin of the University of Louvain (Louven) in Belgium.

Oddly, his work has had more influence on contemporary psychiatry, though he is an experimental and clinical psychologist who has published in both fields. Some of his work has been translated into English, notably his *Psychoanalysis and Personality* (1962). In this volume, Nuttin is refreshingly clear in presenting a rationale for humanistic convictions that are rather vaguely advanced and defended by other authors. I wish here to acknowledge my own considerable intellectual debt to his pioneer efforts. They provide the basis for much that will be proposed in the following sections.

This particular critique involves a prescientific, descriptive analysis of human consciousness which, in turn, results in the elaboration of three distinctive levels of conscious experience. While these levels appear to exist simultaneously, they give evidence of being irreducible one to the other.

## DESCRIPTIVE ANALYSIS OF CONSCIOUS EXPERIENCE

In what follows, I intend to borrow a technique employed, among others, by the European epistemologist, Fernand van Steenberghen (1970), also of the University of Louvain. (Nuttin used a similar approach, though only implicitly—a flaw which I wish to correct here. He may well have been influenced by the earlier writings of his philosophical colleague.)

Before embarking on his *philosophical* analysis of consciousness and "knowing," van Steenberghen literally begins at the beginning, with a carefully detailed *descriptive* analysis of what the experience of consciousness immediately presents to him: the data or phenomena surrendered up by the stream of consciousness as it flows by. These are the givens of experience, from which all further analysis, scientific or philosophical, must proceed. Subsequent analysis of one kind or the other may lead me to conclusions I would never have arrived at by clinging to these first impressions, but I cannot deny or contravene their immediacy.

My consciousness, for example, opens out upon a world which contains many solid objects. The desk before me looks solid, feels solid, and "acts" as though it were basically impenetrable. The impression of solidity is inescapable. And yet, a further scientific analysis assures me that this is not so in any absolute sense. My desk, physicists tell me, is a whirring mass of molecules more densely packed together than the surrounding molecules that make up the air I am breathing but still not the continuous piece of material my senses of sight and touch seem to be revealing to me. And yet my original experience remains.

I would have no alternative but to cling to it stubbornly against all further evidence, unless the scientist can also show me how her facts correspond with mine in some meaningful way. She does, of course. The physicist explains to me that the molecular structure of my body is less densely packed than the field of the desk before me, and so my impression of solidity is a relative one. The physiologist adds his explanation of how visual patterns are reproduced in the occipital cortex of the brain. The scientific description now makes sense to me. What is more, I can go on, in this case at least, trusting my initial conscious experience. I can, for example, lean my elbows on the desk without fear of falling through!

The point I wish to make, however, is that we necessarily begin with these givens of consciousness. Any further analysis we make must eventually make sense in terms of these immediate phenomena, or we have absolutely no basis for accepting it—our *further* analysis becomes truly meaningless in the most radical sense. Conscious experience, then, is the root and the source of all that follows in the acquisition of human knowledge. It may seem tautological to say so, but I cannot "know" that something "is" unless it breaks through to my consciousness.

The assumption, for example, of a dynamic unconscious, collective unconscious, or superconscious realm of being can only make sense in these terms. If such realities exist, we can only know about them through certain phenomena that appear in *conscious* experience, a statement with which, I am sure, neither Freud, Jung, nor Assagioli would disagree.

Besides being the primal root of all further analysis and subsequent knowledge, immediately given conscious phenomena, as we have seen, also necessarily serve as their guarantor and ultimate criterion. I can only accept explanations and conclusions about reality that do no violence to my immediate experience. If they appear to do so (as in the case, for example, of well-known perceptual illusions), then I must be shown that there is no real contradiction between the two.

It is on this immediate basis, and not on a subsequent philosophical analysis, that I would prefer to structure the levels of conscious experience first described by Nuttin. What are the data that are revealed to me by such a purely *descriptive* analysis? To engage in such a task, I must obviously rely on a description of my own immediate experience. If the reader's experience corresponds with mine, we will have a kind of consensual validation. If it does not or if my description is somehow incomplete, the reader must necessarily disagree with me or correct for himself or herself what is missing in my account. Such consensual validation is admittedly all I can hope for, but it will be quite enough for our purposes.

## LEVELS OF CONSCIOUSNESS

**1. *Psychophysiological level.*** Among the contents that exist in my stream of consciousness, I recognize a class of data that obviously refers to my own bodily states. At times I am almost totally unaware of them, as when I am engrossed in a stimulating conversation or watching a gripping movie. Sometimes they force themselves to my attention, as when I feel a nagging pain in the back of my neck or a pounding headache. More often, I become aware of them by simply focusing my attention upon them. At such times I discover, for example, that my foot is falling asleep or that I am in an uncomfortable position—or a bit too warm, or slightly hungry, or somewhat tense. I could go on and on listing such experiences as I monitor my whole body from head to toe, from inside out, but it does seem meaningful to classify all such data of consciousness under the one rubric: *psychophysiological.*

Obviously, some current physiological states can be brought to awareness only indirectly and with the help of special instrumental extensions of our senses (e.g., blood pressure, metabolic activity, and other primarily autonomic functions). We can probably assume there are certain physiological states that are not yet accessible to us in even this indirect fashion.

**2. *Psychosocial level.*** The experience of consciousness also reveals to me that I am a center of awareness, separate from the objects in my environment that come and go (such as the pen I am holding or the table at which I write), as well as from other centers ("persons," I call them) with whom I am somehow able to communicate. I assume, at least, that they are centers like me, though I do not immediately *experience* them as such. The pain another describes to me makes much more sense to me when I have experienced something similar, but I do not feel *his* pain.

My centered awareness is therefore truly unique. It radically isolates me from the environment in which I move. Though always in it, I am somehow different, alone. There are times when I enjoy this experience, but there are other times when I do not.

Loneliness is a very real experience to me; and at such times I long to bridge the gap between myself, the world of objects around me, and, particularly, the world of other persons whom I sense to be like me. Although I never quite succeed in sharing *all* my experiences with others, the extent to which I am able to do so is at times most gratifying (or most frustrating if I fail). If I were not aware of myself, I doubt I should have this need, at least not in the way that I now experience it. It seems meaningful, then, to classify such experiences as a *psychosocial* or concrete, interpersonal dimension of awareness.

**3. Transpersonal level.** Everywhere I go (or stay) I am constantly surrounded by other singular objects, and, usually, by individual embodied persons. Consciousness makes me aware of them, but it also enables me to transcend the here-and-now, the spatiotemporal characteristics in which all these contents are constantly enfolded. I can and do, as Nuttin observes, relate my ephemeral self (ephemeral, because I am quite aware that my consciousness had a beginning) to the world at large, the entire universe. At times I do wonder about this and about my place in it. I lump all these things together and ask questions about the whole of it. I am aware of the passage of time, and yet can project myself into a past which I never personally experienced, or forward into a future that does not yet exist for me but toward which I experience myself hurtling.

Ruminating about my own past, I may feel guilt or satisfaction. Contemplating the future fills me with anxiety or hope. At times I wonder about life, its meaning, and its mystery. I may even wonder about the objectivity, the reality of the very concrete objects and persons my consciousness reveals to me. Not that they are really "there," in my consciousness, but about the kind of reality that they possess apart from me. This more abstract dimension of consciousness, upon reflection, is also inescapable. The term *transpersonal* seems an appropriate label when applied to it.

## Irreducibility

All that has been said so far must seem rather obvious and, perhaps for that reason, a bit pointless. But this categorization into three levels of conscious experience becomes of crucial importance if we can agree to the following: these different experiences move me to do different things *for quite different reasons*. These levels, dictated by the nature of consciousness in me and derived from immediate experience, are, in other words, basically *irreducible*.

I seek out a medical doctor not because I am lonely and eager for human companionship but simply because I am in pain and hope for physical relief. I propose marriage to a particular woman not just to enjoy sexual release with her but because I long to share my life with someone who seems to understand, accept, and love me, and with whom I can be in fairly constant communication. I buy a book by Tillich not merely to while away a lonely hour but chiefly to seek some answers to the ultimate questions of existence.

My physiological needs (for food, water, air, shelter, comfort, relief of sexual tension) may be well met, but I may be almost literally suffocated by loneliness. Or I may be in good physical health and satisfyingly engaged with the world about me and be constantly haunted by the fear of death, an ever-present possibility that could snatch all this away from me.

Each of these levels that consciousness reveals to me seems, therefore, to be supplied with its own singular and irreducible set of needs. And who is to say which is the more basic? Some men and women die of physical starvation; some, as Frankl observes, from a malevolent social environment or for love of a friend; and some people die for abstract causes or languish for want of a meaningful existence.

## Culture and human needs

Nuttin, in this same context, points to an interesting phenomenon in the history of analytic psychology, from Freud through the social analysts to the existentialists. He states:

> It seems quite likely, however, that certain kinds of cultural environment tend to create a critical situation for some human needs, so that these find themselves more frequently exposed to frustration or to states of extreme tension. In such conditions they form a sort of vulnerable zone in psychic life and tend increasingly to attract attention. (1962, p. 181)

The point he seems to be making is that problems which are brought to the analyst in any given generation are reflective of cultural trends and deficiencies. One way of conceptualizing culture, after all, is to view it as a streamlined way of meeting basic human needs on a vast scale. Unmet needs create the problems that find their way to the analyst's couch.

Freud stressed the havoc wrought by repressed sexuality, a problem which seems to have been endemic in the Victorian era in which he grew and lived. His contemporary, Alfred Adler, was struck by the need for power exhibited by many of his patients—victims, perhaps, of the concurrent industrial revolution and its more depersonalizing effects. At the same time, family and social institutions remained relatively stable. With the ensuing breakdown of these cultural constants, problems of social and interpersonal living came to the fore and became predominant in the reflections and theories of the so-called social analysts, such as Erich Fromm, Karen Horney, and Harry Stack Sullivan. And finally, with the breakdown of Western civilization's traditional answers to existential problems (mirrored by the philosophical confusion and the criticism of religious institutions that followed upon World War II), existential needs rose to the surface, and a new school of psychiatry was born.

The history of psychiatry provides us, therefore, with a catalogue of basic human needs, any one of which may result in severe personality disturbance if not gratified by the arrangements of the prevailing cultural or social milieu. It is tempting to compare the results of this brief historical overview with the three irreducible levels of human existence previously noted in our descriptive analysis of conscious experience. Freudian analysis, social analysis, and existential analysis do seem to reflect, respectively, the levels described earlier in this chapter:

1. Awareness of the body and its physiological states.
2. Awareness of self and others.
3. Awareness of Being or existence as such.

### The interpenetration of conscious levels

In spite of these important distinctions, however, Nuttin rightly insists on a holistic view of human existence and experience. Men and women function as total organisms, on all three levels simultaneously. Though logically irreducible, all three levels of awareness exist at one and the same time in any psychic experience.

The most physiological aspects of our experience bear a uniquely human stamp. We share the experience of hunger, for example, with the rest of the animal kingdom. But the process of eating becomes more for us than mere gratification of a physiological need: we attach great social significance to it, as in the institution of the family meal. And in the case of the Christian eucharistic banquet, we even elevate eating to the status of a religious ceremony (communion with God, as well as with one's fellows). One level, of course, may predominate at a given time in a kind of figure-ground relationship, but even sexuality can and does exist for us on all three levels at once, becoming, in the Hindu Kama Sutra for example, an avenue to transpersonal experience.

We say a person acts "like an animal" in attempting to live primarily for the gratification of physiological impulses. And we consider a person foolhardy who attempts to live like an angel, neglecting the physiological and social aspects of existence in an attempt to lead a purely spiritual life.

Internal conflict is obviously, then, an inevitable corollary of this rich diversity in human experience—this complex trilevel nature of human existence. The various desires arising from differing layers of consciousness constantly vie with each other for expression and gratification. From a psychological standpoint, the continuous formation and reformation of human cultures and societies represent our attempts to cope with this problem on a mass scale. Every culture formulates and transmits to its members its own answers to the perennial existential questions posed by consciousness, and develops social institutions to facilitate the satisfaction of all the basic needs in a more or less efficient manner. Culture itself is a uniquely human phenomenon, of course, arising out of the collective consciousness of its members (and perhaps, as Jung would insist, the collective unconscious of the race as well).

As long as a smug ethnocentrism was possible, the culture's answers to life's questions and the cultural forms and guidelines for gratification of individual desires found ready acceptance. Geographical isolation and lack of communication between various cultures, in some instances, helped immeasurably to safeguard and preserve the coping strategies so evolved.

But in this age of instant, worldwide communication and cross-cultural exchange, ethnocentrism and cultural isolation are fast becoming impossible to maintain. In addition to the inherent weakness and subsequent breakdown of obsolete social institutions within a given culture itself, men and women are becoming more and more aware of the very laws of cultural evolution and how culture has influenced their behavior, formed their belief systems, and guided their development from the cradle to the grave.

## Knowledge as power

There is an obvious paradox in the making here. As individuals become more and more conscious of the laws and power of cultural conditioning, they become less and less subject to its effects. Knowledge *is* power. The children who were socialized within our own cultural system are now questioning, in larger and larger numbers, the basic premises on which our culture has been sustained, partly because they now know they *were* socialized. B. F. Skinner's proposal for the deliberate design of a culture by behavioral technologists is doomed to failure as long as enough people are aware of the laws of reinforcement. Freedom is not given. It is gained, in large measure, as a function of increasing *awareness* of the processes that have heretofore conditioned our behavior. The belief in autonomous man is not a mere myth. Autonomy and self-determination become increasingly possible as consciousness grows. And it would appear very difficult to reverse the process in an age when information is so readily available to every man and woman.

This state of affairs creates its own problems, of course. Those of us who have become aware of the effects of cultural conditioning on our own development are thrown back upon ourselves to discover the answers to the questions forced upon us by conscious existence. At least as far as our existential questions are concerned—our search for meaning in our lives—we are free as we never were before to question the answers proposed by our culture, to examine them in the light of other cultural attempts at a solution. Confused by all the relativity that confronts us in our quest, we must take a stand for ourselves, create or discover our own meaning, or give up the search in despair. And as the institutions devised for the satisfaction of our social needs also begin to crumble around us, we are further thrown back on our own resources.

This perhaps explains the insistence of so many humanistic and existential psychologists on the need for an examined life, an authentic existence, a deliberately chosen or created life project. In the same vein, Nuttin calls for a *constructive ideal of personality* to be worked out by each individual in the conscious attempt to integrate the various levels of his or her existence in a harmonious and realistic way.

As he himself has pointed out, we are aided in this project by a dual characteristic of all living systems. Borrowing some notions from biology, we will assert that all living organisms possess an *actualizing tendency,* a pervasive impulse toward their own survival and growth within the possibilities and limitations provided by their environments. In the more complex human organism, this primary tendency operates on all three levels of conscious experience simultaneously and is transformed by the activity of consciousness itself.

Second, living systems are *open* systems, a characteristic that implies a *constant exchange* with the environment at all levels of functioning. No living system is sufficient unto itself. But these additions to our present discussion, together with their far-reaching implications, already involve a further analysis of immediately given experience and will be discussed at a later point (see Chapter 6, with accompanying diagram). For our present purposes, it suffices to note that humanistic authors are almost unanimous in their insistence that true self-realization can only come about from the ongoing conscious attempt to resolve and harmonize the constructive tensions that inevitably arise among the rich variety of qualitatively different human aims that we simultaneously seek to realize.

## THE DIALECTICAL NATURE OF CONSCIOUSNESS

Up to this point, I have endeavored to show that a prescientific, purely descriptive analysis of human consciousness yields at least three qualitatively different, apparently irreducible (though interpenetrating) levels of conscious experience. I have labeled these *psychophysiological, psychosocial,* and *transpersonal,* closely paralleling the terminology employed by Joseph Nuttin. (Other humanistic authors, notably Maslow (1970), Bugental (1965), and the Gestalt theorist Walter Kempler (1973) have proposed strikingly similar terms to describe the same phenomena.) This by no means exhausts the possibilities of such a preliminary analysis. Joseph Rychlak, proceeding in like fashion, has stressed one other important feature: the *dialectical* nature of human consciousness, or, more specifically, of human thought processes, certainly a salient aspect of our conscious experience on what I have called the transpersonal level. Since this additional feature will play a prominent role in our further analysis of the humanistic theme of self-determination or personal freedom (see Chapter 7), a brief description of it will be presented here.

What is at stake here is very important indeed. It is Rychlak's contention that, in overlooking this dialectical feature of human consciousness, modern academic psychologists (including the more recent social learning theorists and cognitive psychologists) are advocating a seriously flawed model of human nature and functioning.

The problem boils down to this: is the human mind, developmentally, a tabula rasa (blank slate) on which sensory experience (and *only* sensory experience) writes? This is the assumption (prephilosophical and prescientific) on which empiricist and positivistic thinkers (and the majority of modern psychologists) base their *further* analysis of cognitive functioning. According to this viewpoint, mind is primarily passive. Impressions are stored, retrieved, and ultimately related by laws of association (proximity, frequency, contiguity of impressions, and so on) extrinsic to the mind itself. Its only activity is a demonstratively logical one, to use Rychlak's term, inexorably and necessarily driven by the logic of experience itself. Mind contributes little, if anything, of its own to the entire process. Induction (the storage of impressions and concomitant regularities and patterns that more automatically than not emerge from "out there") necessarily precedes, limits, and efficiently determines the consequent deductions that are the products of human thinking.

This linear, *demonstrative* model of cognitive functioning, with the addition of corrective feedback loops from subsequent actions that serve to provide additional information, is the prevalent one in current cognitive psychology. The analogy most often made is to the modern computer, that awesome product of human ingenuity. (The programmer's axiom, garbage in, garbage out, is also applied to explain the obvious flaws in human thinking.) We process information, and the accuracy of our conclusions is a direct function of the efficiency and accuracy with which we store experience in the form of impressions, initially, and as further actions provide us with corrective feedback.

## Rychlak's dual model

Rychlak's objection to this model of cognitive functioning (and to the computer analogy which often accompanies it) is not that it is incorrect. Its effectiveness is well established by the outpouring of instructive and successful research that it has generated. What he does object to is the "nothing-but" fallacy (i.e., human cognition is *only* demonstrative in character). We all experience this process much of the time. But we also, immediately and directly, experience another process at work in our cognitive functioning: a process intrinsic to mind itself and independent of all prior external and sensory inputs, though admittedly occasioned by them. This process Rychlak, borrowing the term from Immanuel Kant, calls the *transcendental dialectic* function of mind.

> In the realms of free thought, where the person is not constrained by the demands of what he perceived phenomenally, a kind of speculative reasoning can be carried on which permits us to *transcend* even our categories of understanding. We are not constrained to think rationally [demonstratively]. We can deny our senses. We can challenge space and time as proper coordinates for the ordering of sensation. We can mentally fly above reality to concoct worlds of four dimensions. (Rychlak, 1979, p. 67)

Rychlak goes on, in the same passage, to compare his conclusions, approvingly, with those of Kant: such conscious phenomena reveal a natively *dialectical* component of thinking, a component that needs to be tempered with *demonstrative* strategies for arriving at truth precisely because of its inherent arbitrariness and free play. An equivalent notion is that of self-reflexivity, the capacity of mind "to rise above itself and turn back critically on what it normally does without examination or question." Further, the inherent dialectical capacity of thinking enables us to consider or generate alternatives in direct opposition to previous or present experiencing (as in the examples given above). Therefore, we are *not* simply constrained by previous inputs (as in the computer analogy). Rather, we are constrained to take a position —to make a radically free choice, among the alternatives so generated, about which one should be pursued. It is at this point (the protopoint, Rychlak calls it) that demonstrative reasoning comes into play.

Kant was not, of course, the first philosopher to identify and make use of the dialectical feature of human consciousness in his further analysis of mental functioning, as Rychlak ably and exhaustively documents (1977). Socrates relied on it almost exclusively in the development of the dialogue method of investigation that bears his name. It was recognized by his pupil Plato and the latter's student, Aristotle, who tempered its application with an insistence on demonstrative methods of proof. It was well known to the neo-Platonic thinkers Augustine and Bonaventure and to the neo-Aristotelian philosophers Thomas Aquinas and John Duns Scotus. Ignored by the British empiricists, the dialectic function was resurrected, as we have seen, by Kant, and later extensively analyzed even further by the idealist Georg Hegel, who proposed that mind innately leaps from any proposition (thesis) to its opposite (antithesis), often resolving the apparent contradiction by a new proposition, which incorporates elements of both (synthesis), and so on indefinitely.

The point of all this is that such thinkers universally ascribe to human consciousness a type of process or activity that issues from the mind itself, innately, independent of inputs from prior experience. We have, as the ancients taught us, an *active* intellect as well as a passive one. We do not just respond to reality in a passive, recipient mode. We actively confront it, construe it in different ways, play with alternative possibilities, analogize, and, in the extreme case, even entertain completely opposite premises from those that sensory experience seems to force upon us.

As Thomas Kuhn (1962) has reminded us, this is how science itself proceeds and develops. Copernicus revolutionized astronomy by premising something that goes directly contrary to sensory experience (which tells us that the sun moves around the earth) and the accumulated wisdom of preceding generations. Freud applied physical analogies (borrowed mainly from hydraulics) in his attempt to understand the workings of the unconscious. His success or failure is not the issue here but rather the active effort to order certain phenomena according to a pattern borrowed from another field of experience. Others, as we shall see, have changed *his* premises (and analogies) to their own greater satisfaction.

In all such instances, as in countless less dramatic ones—that the reader can provide from his or her own daily experience—consciousness transcends the mere givens of prior or current experience. What this means regarding the stuff of which mind is composed we leave to the further debate and analyses of philosophers. For the psychologist, however, it represents an aspect of experience that carries widespread implications for our understanding of almost every facet of human behavior.

But this is only one of the threads that are woven through the tapestry of current humanistic thought in psychology. In the following chapter, I will attempt to show how this and the other themes can be related to the descriptive analysis of the levels of consciousness here presented. No pretensions are held on the exhaustiveness of this analysis, but I am comfortable in asserting that it is complete enough to provide a solid rationale and foundation for the effort by humanistic psychologists to move the empirical study of consciousness back to center stage in contemporary psychology.

# 3 The Major Themes of Humanistic Psychology

In the preceding chapter, I referred briefly to an article by Carl Rogers (1964) in which he presents a phenomenological analysis of three ways of knowing: subjective, objective, and interpersonal. "All knowing," he suggests, "consists essentially of hypotheses, which we check in different ways." Differences between the ways of knowing are distinguishable "primarily in the manner in which we check our hypotheses."

Subjective knowing is the most basic of the three and is checked against the inner flow of experiencing as we confront internal and external events. The scientist, for example, confronting a large body of data in which he or she has been immersed, asks in Roger's words, "What is the unity, the central principle, which I sense in all these varied and seemingly disparate events?" The scientist turns to his or her experiencing to try to determine what it is that gives this sense of a commonality. This type of knowing is not infallible in and of itself, and requires further validation against the experiencing of others; but it is this sensing of *pattern*, in inner or outer events, from which all further knowing proceeds in science or in everyday life.

This precisely describes the process I have used in confronting the bewildering array of ideas and data presented by the humanistic and existential psychologists in whose writings I have immersed myself for the past several years. Gradually, some patterns emerged. Finally, it occurred to me that the connecting link between these patterns seems to be a shared emphasis on the species-specific attribute of human consciousness. Applying this template of hypotheses to their work has provided a good fit for me in producing order out of the initial chaos.

The patterns that emerged I will here classify into seven major themes of humanistic-existential psychology. In subsequent chapters, each theme will be discussed in greater detail. Their number and order of presentation, in accordance with the previous discussion, remain somewhat arbitrary and subjective.

## 1. PHENOMENOLOGICAL APPROACH

Because of the universal tendency among humanistic authors to refocus our attention on the specifically human attribute of self-consciousness, all tend to favor a phenomenological approach to the study of human behavior. The European existential analysts generally favor a very conscious empirical adaptation of the phenomenological and existential philosophies (Husserl, Heidegger, Jaspers, Buber, Sartre, Merleau-Ponty, Marcel, and others) developed on the Continent. Each has his own predilection. Thus Binswanger defines his existential analysis as "the empirical-phenomenological, scientific analysis of actual ways and Gestalten of human existence," based on Heidegger's "philosophical phenomenological clarification of the a priori or transcendental structure of human existence as being-in-the-world" (1962, p. 204).

Most American authors, on the other hand, are far less philosophically sophisticated. They tend to begin from a much more pragmatic, less esoteric base, and to develop their own terminology and approach, which, in turn, is heavily laced with methods of controlled observation borrowed, where possible, from operationism. Many, I gather, are even surprised to find themselves designated as phenomenologists.

Rogers, for example, speaks of the individual's "internal frame of reference," a "private world of experience" uniquely built up by highly personal interactions with others in the past. In order to understand and help a client, for example, the therapist must enter into and share the client's private world through a process of "dynamic listening." Empathy is then generated (through a climate of nonjudgmental acceptance or "positive regard"), enabling the client to free the hitherto blocked drive for self-realization and self-determination. Borrowing the notion of self-concept from the sociologists Mead and Cooley, Rogers, in his early work, attempted to operationalize his investigations of the parameters of these and other self-constructs through the application of Stephenson's Q-technique (1953). Jourard's empirical research on the effects of self-disclosure (1971) has already been mentioned. Maslow (1954) conducted interview research on peak-experiences, experiences of heightened consciousness which significantly influenced the lives of his self-actualized subjects.

Whatever terminology is preferred, all seem agreed on the inescapable uniqueness of individual human consciousness and on the importance of understanding *this* person's perception of reality if we are ever completely to understand his or her behavior. Just as important, all these authors also seem to agree that the self, as a "center of intentionality," functions as an *active* agent within its environment and is therefore more than the *reactive* product of the forces that impinge upon it from within and without.

I am reminded, in this context, of Gordon Allport's earlier distinction between a nomothetic and idiographic science of personality (1955), and his own belief that only the latter is possible. I tend also to agree with Rollo May (1969) when he cautions against the danger of tying psychology (and I would include humanistic psychology) too closely to any philosophical system, be it logical positivism, phenomenology, existentialism, or Zen Buddhism. Though a realist myself, I find no personal difficulty in adopting an empirically phenomenological stance toward the understanding of human personality and behavior, while disagreeing with the basic relativism and idealism that seem implicit in the philosophical tradition of phenomenology. However objective the real world may be apart from my perception of it, it *is* my perception of it that motivates and determines my reactions to the people and the objects within it. That seems to be a psychological fact not a philosophical conviction, though philosophers may want to make more of it.

The role of unconscious influences on behavior in all of this is a complex matter, which will be discussed at a later time. Humanistic psychologists differ among themselves in their treatment of the phenomena ascribed to the unconscious by depth psychologists. Nuttin, for example, speaks of a sphere of psychic intimacy (1962, p. 206), which gives an entirely different nuance to data previously described as unconscious (see Chapter 5).

## 2. HOLISM

Many intimations have already appeared in this work of the next major theme in humanistic psychology: its holistic approach to the study of the human person. The meaning of this term, borrowed from Gestalt psychology, which in turn apparently appropriated it from the organismic approach in biology, can be summed up in the Gestalt saying: "the whole is greater than the sum of its parts." The word *Gestalt* itself means *dynamic whole*, and aptly represents the efforts by this early psychological school to counteract the atomistic, elementaristic agenda of both the early introspectionists and the later behaviorists in the discipline of experimental psychology. Their classic work in the psychology of perception, demonstrating that perception is a phenomenon distinct from the mere additive sum of sensations, has long since been incorporated into texts on general psychology and is familiar to every student of this subject, as, to a lesser extent, is Kurt Lewin's field-theory of personality, an early attempt to apply Gestalt principles to this topic (Lewin, 1936).

## Goldstein's influence

The holistic emphasis in humanistic psychology, however, is more directly traceable to the work of the German neurophysiologist, Kurt Goldstein. In his classic research on the behavior of brain-injured patients (1939) and their persistent efforts to reintegrate their entire personalities around the gross neurological deficits with which they were afflicted, Goldstein formulated a holistic approach to organismic functioning that was to have a major impact on humanistic authors. Maslow frequently cites Goldstein's research in support of his own holistic emphasis and the connected assumption of a self-actualizing tendency as the major drive of all living organisms. Nuttin also acknowledges his indebtedness and that of other humanistic writers to this author in his own postulation of a basic drive towards self-realization. Hall and Lindzey, in the first edition of their popular text *Theories of Personality* (1957), present the then-developing humanistic movement under the title "organismic approach" and credit Goldstein's influence as providing the intellectual foundation and inspiration for its contributions to that point.

In a series of experimental studies on patients with severe frontal lobe lesions, Goldstein described how their capacity for abstract thought was seriously impaired. They remained still capable of accomplishing tasks that required a more concrete type of thinking, perceiving, and remembering, but they failed miserably when more general principles had to be applied toward the solution of problems set before them. This finding was straightforward enough and not unknown to other investigators.

But Goldstein was particularly struck by how his patients attempted to reintegrate their entire lives around their deficit so that they could function, as well as possible, within its limitations *as though it did not even exist.* They would become emotionally disturbed when confronted with tasks demanding capacities they no longer possessed for their solution, and they strove mightily to organize their lives into routines where such problems could be avoided. Further, they seemed totally unaware of the purpose of their efforts and of the deficit itself and were quite content with their existence as long as they were successful in their attempts to avoid the unmanageable.

The opposite of holism, as Maslow indicates in this passage, is reductionism: the attempt to reduce complex human functioning to simpler elements, building blocks, or "atoms," which can then be studied and understood more thoroughly and from which one can then predict more accurately, by adding up the properties of these elements, the characteristics of all structures which use them as a base.

We have already seen how the early introspectionists engaged in a kind of mental chemistry in their attempt to reduce all conscious phenomena to simple sensations and perceptions, building up from these to more complex images and thoughts. This effort failed rather quickly, even after feelings and determining-tendencies (will-acts) were added to the list of irreducible elements. Behaviorists then turned to the conditioned reflex in a renewed search for the elusive fundamental elements of human functioning, while Freudians sought to find them in the primitive biological impulses of sexuality (libido) and aggression (a later addition).

This is a "nothing-but" approach to human experience and behavior: consciousness is nothing-but an elaboration of elementary sensations through processes of association; behavior is nothing-but a concatenation of conditioned reflexes, or the outcome of sublimated libidinal impulses. Humanistic psychologists universally reject such an approach, and favor instead the holistic stance advocated by Goldstein and the Gestalt psychologists.

Goldstein concluded from his behavioral observations that the neurological deficits suffered by his patients could not simply be treated as isolated events. They represented instead a loss of potential, and the human organism in such instances reacts *as a whole* to this loss by actively fashioning for itself an entirely new existential Gestalt. This reorganization process, he maintained, was always in the direction of realizing the organism's potentialities to the fullest degree possible; in these cases, of course, to a degree considerably less than had existed prior to their losses. The living organism, in effect, will always do the best it can to actualize its potentialities, whatever these may be, and it will do so as a *unit* along all dimensions of its functioning: cognitive, conative, and affective.

This is exactly how Maslow defines his own holistic approach to the study of personality:

> I don't wish to hazard any large generalizations here, but this I have learned also (as a therapist and as a personologist). If I want to learn something more about you as an individual person, then I must approach you as a unit, as a one, as a whole. The customary scientific technique of dissection and reductive analysis that has worked so well in the inorganic world and not too badly even in the infrahuman world of living organisms, is just a nuisance when I seek knowledge of a person, and it has real deficiencies even for studying people in general. (1966, p. 11)

**The experience of consciousness**

Aside from the behavioral observations from which Goldstein and others have drawn their conclusions, we have also the experience of consciousness itself to justify this insistence on a holistic approach to human functioning. In the descriptive analysis of that experience presented in the previous chapter, I have already indicated that, while it is possible to distinguish three irreducible levels within conscious experience, consciousness itself must be treated as a seamless garment. One or another level may predominate at any given moment, emerging, as it were, from ground to figure; but closer scrutiny reveals that these levels exist simultaneously and constantly interpenetrate one another.

This is not surprising when we recall what the phenomenologists are so fond of reminding us: that consciousness, at least in its normal state, is always an *embodied* consciousness. That it is more than this is seen in as physical an act as eating. The family meal is prepared to gratify our felt physiological need for nourishment; but at its best it is also a social event, momentarily satisfying our hunger for affiliation with others, and even a transpersonal experience, plunging us once again into the family matrix from which we emerged as individuals. But it is always this too in its ordinary state. The mystics, in describing their most transpersonal experiences of union with the divine and upon returning to a normal state of consciousness, inevitably find themselves using physiological and, not uncommonly, sexual terms to recapture the essence of their experience. In doing so, of course, they by no means intend to imply that what they sensed was "nothing-but" a physiological event. Such is the unity of consciousness, however, that even physiological experiences can be effectively used to describe other, quite different, levels of conscious functioning.

This holistic emphasis in humanistic psychology, the refusal to adhere to a rigid reductionistic position, is what gives it an open-at-the-top stance when confronting the phenomena of human experiencing, an openness to the empirical exploration of topics in human psychology that remain anathema to other investigators. At the very least, it bears the promise of retaining some of the qualitative richness and diversity of human experience that other approaches have been accused of omitting from their descriptions.

## 3. THE ACTUALIZING TENDENCY

The next major theme in humanistic psychology is the universal assumption of an actualizing tendency or drive endemic to all living organisms. Applied to the human organism, this becomes translated by many authors into a drive or tendency towards self-realization or self-actualization. In accordance with the holistic approach outlined in the previous section, this has become for many humanists the *only* drive characteristic of all living systems—all others are derived from it or are particularized expressions of it. (Nuttin [1962] does add an important corollary, based upon the fact that living organisms are *open* systems— the correlative need and drive for *contact* with the environment on all three levels of functioning. He derives some interesting consequences from this additional observation, as we shall see later.) We have already seen how the work of Kurt Goldstein particularly influenced the humanists in this respect. Other sources of this construct will be considered in Chapter 6.

For my present purposes, it is important to emphasize that this is the most significant and controversial concept for the study of personality development advanced by the humanists. It reintroduces a *teleological* principle or, at the very least, a growth orientation to that study previously lacking in the descriptions provided by Freudian depth psychology and behaviorism alike. It implies, in effect, that each human individual reacts, in his or her development, to a call and a criterion that exists *within* the organism itself, rather than to blind, chaotic biological impulses on the one hand or solely to the dictates of environmental forces on the other.

It is an antihomeostatic concept in that it pictures the organism as constantly striving to actualize new potentialities as they develop during the course of life, rather than merely seeking to maintain or restore a tension-free state of equilibrium. It is a *process* concept, involving notions of continual change and readjustment in the face of shifting environmental contingencies but always in the direction of a goal or end-point preset within the organism itself. It says, reminiscent of Goldstein's observations, that the organism does the best it can at all stages of its development to actualize the potentialities inherent within it at that particular point in time.

This is a far cry from the notion that human beings merely *react* to external pressures and are simply the product of the vectors impinging upon them from the environment. The latter is still seen in this approach as having enormous importance for the individual but from a different angle. It is here seen as either stifling or facilitating his or her further development according to possibilities that arise, moment by moment, from within the organism itself.

Rogers provides a homely analogy that will best serve to illustrate this point:

> The actualizing tendency can of course be thwarted, but it cannot be destroyed without destroying the organism. I remember that in my boyhood the potato bin in which we stored our winter supply of potatoes was in the basement, several feet below a small basement window. The conditions were unfavorable, but the potatoes would begin to sprout—

pale white sprouts, so unlike the healthy green shoots they sent up when planted in the soil in the spring. But these sad, spindly sprouts would grow two or three feet in length as they reached toward the distant light of the window. They were, in their bizarre, futile growth, a sort of desperate expression of the directional tendency I have been describing. They would never become a plant, never mature, never fulfill their real potentiality. But under the most adverse circumstances they were striving to become. Life would not give up, even if it could not flourish. In dealing with clients whose lives have been terribly warped, in working with men and women on the back wards of state hospitals, I often think of those potato sprouts. So unfavorable have been the conditions in which these people have developed that their lives often seem abnormal, twisted, scarcely human. Yet the directional tendency in them is to be trusted. The clue to understanding their behavior is that they are striving, in the only ways available to them, to move toward growth, toward becoming. To us the results may seem bizarre and futile, but they are life's desperate attempt to become itself. (1977, p. 8)

Humanistic psychologists are therefore by no means blind to the overwhelming influence of environmental factors, in spite of their advocacy of the actualizing tendency. Much of their recent efforts, as I shall show, have been directed toward criticizing and rehumanizing the social institutions that, in modern society, have so effectively operated to stunt and prevent the full development of individual human potential.

### Trusting the organism

An important corollary of this postulate of a directional or actualizing tendency is a basic trust in the human organism, a basic optimism in one's capacity to transcend the binding narcissism and necessary egocentrism of early childhood. Again, there is an element of innatism here, a belief that the very process of self-actualization, when not obstructed, leads inexorably to a kind of self-transcendence, a "moral gift of self," to use Nuttin's term, which embraces and prizes others in an atmosphere of caring and love. Nowhere is this more clear than in the writings of Rogers, whose exuberance in this respect has led critics of his theory to label him everything from Pollyannish to Pelagian.

Undaunted by such criticism, he continues to insist that this has been one of the most surprising and unexpected outcomes of his years of experience in individual and group counseling. My own feeling is that Rogers has laid a sufficient theoretical foundation for an understanding of the problem of evil in man, the recurrent unleashing of destructive forces in the history of human existence, in his subtle analysis of the usual course of human development: the distortion of the more basic, inherent drive toward self-realization of the human organism (which would of itself theoretically lead to a truly positive socialization with others) by a faulty socialization process, which tends progressively to alienate the self from its deepest organismic strivings and experiences.

This aspect of Rogerian theory is often overlooked by his critics and does not seem to have been further explored by Rogers himself. He does seem to base his optimism on a belief in the seemingly instinctive strength of the actualizing tendency, likening it to an almost biological urgency which, though overlaid by layers of social convention, can always be counted upon and tapped by the therapist.

Maslow (1968) shares this faith in the intrinsic positive thrust of the drive for self-actualization, as he prefers to call it, but questions its instinctual strength. Rollo May (1969) addresses himself at length to the "daimonic" forces in man, and sees them as basically neutral in themselves. They are simply "there." Their potential destructiveness, to self or others, stems from their not being admitted to awareness.

Here again we are faced with the preeminent importance of self-awareness. All these authors clearly imply that, to the extent that *all* my personal data are available to my awareness, can be openly "owned" by me and to significant others, to that extent I will be a genuinely caring person who will safeguard the best interests of humanity in general. And in the pursuit of those variables which are functionally related to such openness-to-self, another major contribution to the understanding and betterment of the human condition may be in the making.

Such a faith and optimism in the basic altruistic direction of human existence, however tempered it might be by individual humanistic authors, is obviously in marked contrast to the Freudian view of man. Freud's pessimism is certainly not shared by all depth psychologists (Jung, for one, is a notable exception and has contributed much to the changed perspective of many humanists who are familiar with his work). But few would deny that this is the message Freud conveys, particularly in his dramatic depiction of the struggle within the individual of Eros (the life instincts) and Thanatos (the death instincts) and the inevitable triumph of the latter.

Behaviorists are also, of course, optimistic about the potential of mankind for positive socialization and peaceful coexistence. *Walden Two* (Skinner, 1948), after all, belongs to the genre of utopian literature. But the source of their optimism lies in the power of behavioral conditioning and social engineering. Behavioristic philosophy at least is radically mechanistic in its view of man. Love, for example, is merely a conditioned response in such a system and presumably has no meaning beyond that. Consciousness is a nuisance, and human existence itself has no more dignity than any other reactive outcome of physicochemical forces. Some humanists may indeed share this radical pessimism concerning the ephemeral nature of human life but, through their stress on the unique phenomenon of human consciousness, manage to salvage some shred of value and meaning for human existence.

## The role of consciousness

The actualizing tendency as so far described is primarily, however, a *biological* construct. For full understanding of its functioning in the human organism we must be true to our model and investigate its influence from the perspective of consciousness, or we may fall again into the reductionistic trap of treating the human being as just another if more complicated animal. While in this instance we may not be able to *derive* the existence of such a biological tendency from the phenomenon of consciousness alone, we can certainly hope to learn a great deal about its unique manifestations in the species *Homo sapiens*.

It is my conviction that the attribute of consciousness *transforms* the actualizing tendency in the human organism into a directional tendency that has more to do with the notion of the self as a center of *intentionality* in a more or less constant search for meaning. Retaining its roots in our biological nature and some of the biological urgency and drive-characteristics that such an origin implies, the actualizing tendency, once informed by consciousness, emerges as a "will to meaning," to borrow Frankl's term. I submit that his penetrating analysis of this construct provides a needed corrective to the overbiologism that adheres to the concept of a self-actualizing *drive* presented by Maslow and others.

For Frankl, it should be noted, the will to meaning (the actualizing tendency as transformed by consciousness) no longer functions as a drive. Referring to an empirical corroboration of his will to meaning concept (Crumbaugh & Maholick, 1964), in which the authors speak of this "hypothetical drive in man," Frankl (1969) objected to the application of this term. He disliked its homeostatic connotations (disruption and restoration of physiological equilibrium). We are pushed by drives, but pulled by meanings. Meanings are conscious phenomena: they await discovery by conscious minds, and we remain free to actualize them or not.

There are, of course, so many potentialities within a given individual that emerge in the course of his or her development (including, perhaps, potentialities to evil and destructiveness) that it would be foolish to assume the possibility of actualizing *all* of them in the course of one lifetime. It makes sense therefore to suggest that the blind impulsiveness of the biological drive toward actualization in man and woman is further moderated and directed by the conscious awareness of the options open to the person. *Choices* must be made. The fundamental intentionality or search for meaning characteristic of human consciousness, Frankl would say, is what gives direction and unity to the process of choice. Or, as Nuttin implies when discussing this problem, it is the total *person* who must be satisfied, not the individual need.

## 4.  SELF–DETERMINATION

The subject of choice, as we have seen, flows directly from the theme of actualization just presented. This brings up another striking and important theme in humanistic psychology: the reintroduction of the concepts of will and freedom in their analyses of human behavior and personality. On the one hand, this development might be viewed as an unwelcome resurrection of the tired old freedom versus determinism controversy in philosophy and psychology. It could then be easily dismissed as an unprofitable excursion into a barren wasteland of dead issues.

But I am convinced that more than this is involved. Anyone who focuses on the study of human consciousness, as the humanists have done, must at some time come up against what Freud termed the universal illusion of human freedom. Normal individuals, at least, are convinced that in many instances they possess the capacity to determine their own choices freely. It is my belief that, in tackling this almost universal conviction—its sources and relationships to other variables—humanistic psychologists have provided us with some important new insights into the meaning of will and free self-determination.

Some, like Rogers, did so reluctantly at first, as if walking on eggs. In comments following the delivery of his paper at the Rice symposium on behaviorism and phenomenology (Wann, 1964), he characterized the freedom-determinism issue as a paradox with which he was willing to live: assuming some very real degree of freedom in the clients with whom he worked in therapy; assuming strict determinism when conducting scientific research. In later remarks he drew a potentially helpful analogy to the wave-particle theories of light in modern physics, apparently overlooking the fact that physicists do not hesitate to use *both* seemingly incompatible theories for the generation of scientific research.

Others, like Frankl and May, have plunged into this hitherto forbidden territory with refreshing gusto and enthusiasm. (Psychologists always seem more defensive than existential analysts when addressing the problem of freedom, perhaps because their scientific credentials are more at stake.) Frankl writes: "The freedom of decision, so-called freedom of the will, is for the unbiased person a matter of course; *he has a direct experience of himself as free*" (1965, p. 77).

In a later work Frankl objected more to the "pan-determinism" of orthodox psychoanalysis than to its so-called pan-sexualism. The individual, for him, remains radically free; capable at least of taking a stand toward past conditioning; able to change in an instant and, therefore, basically unpredictable.

> Therefore, we can predict his future only within the large frame of a statistical survey referring to a whole group; the individual personality, however, remains essentially unpredictable. The basis for any predictions would be represented by biological, psychological, or sociological conditions. Yet one of the main features of human existence is the capacity to rise above such conditions and transcend them. In the same manner, man ultimately transcends himself; a human being is self-transcending being. (1963, p. 207)

**The developmental view**

I will have more to say about this problem later on (see Chapter 7), but what seems to be emerging from these investigations is that the subjective experience of self-determination is very much a function of one's self-consciousness and is a *developmental* phenomenon quite closely related to the extent and depth of self-knowledge throughout one's life and to affective components that bear upon psychological health.

Will is not seen as a separate faculty, nor is freedom seen as an absolute given, present from birth. The person, not the will, is seen as more or less free, depending upon many circumstances. There is always, in the writings of the humanists, a relativism and conditionism pertaining to the experience of self-determination, reflecting the fact that more than lip service is being paid to the well-established findings of the biological and social or cultural determinists.

Humanistic psychologists tend to see the capacity for self-determination, then, as an integral part of the whole process of becoming, as an achievement rather than a given, as almost an end-state or goal of the whole developing process of self-actualization, and the accompanying painful, lifelong process of the growth of self-consciousness. But the mere notion that, beginning from a state of rigid conditionism, the human organism—through its species-specific attribute of self-consciousness—is potentially capable of transcending these initial limits is one of the clearest illustrations of how this approach differs from its predecessors without denying their contributions. And the ongoing analysis of the variables that facilitate or retard such a transcendental development promises to become one of the major, and perhaps most enduring, contributions of the humanists to modern psychology.

## 5. THE IDEAL OF AUTHENTICITY

Each of the four movements in contemporary psychology appears to have a distinctive goal in view. For depth psychology, the major emphasis has always been placed on the understanding of the intrapsychic and social determinants of *personality disturbance*. Historically, depth psychology grew out of this abiding interest in the pathological states of neurosis and psychosis. Whatever contributions have been made to general personality theory, and they are many, have issued from this perspective. Behaviorists set for themselves the task of explicating the phenomena of *learning*, the changes that occur in all living organisms as they interact with their physical and social environment. Theirs, as we have seen, is a stimulus-response psychology, dependent for its findings on what is directly observable and measurable in both the physical organism and its internal and external surroundings. To the extent that personality functioning, whether pathological or normal, can be understood as learned behavior in this restricted sense, behavioral psychology has much to say of importance to the personality theorist.

Humanistic psychology seems to have set its sights squarely on the understanding of the parameters of *healthy psychological functioning*. Personality theory is its predominant concern. Health is seen as a positive syndrome. Inescapably, therefore, humanists are forced to make value judgments (as, to a lesser extent, are the depth psychologists and others in their depiction of abnormal behavior). The positing of such value judgments concerning the desirable outcomes of individual human existence is what gives such a philosophical tone to the writings of many humanistic psychologists.

Some (such as James Bugental and Viktor Frankl, or R. D. Laing) borrow heavily and explicitly from current existential philosophy in setting goals for what they would prefer to call authentic human living. Others favor an approach that appeals to an inherent purposiveness discoverable within the basic drive towards self-realization, which lies, they assume, at the core of every living organism. Upon close examination, Rogers's "fully functioning person" and Maslow's "self-actualized person" appear principally to be the natural outcomes of the *unobstructed* development of the process of self-realization. Under ideal conditions of growth, Perls has often stated, the human organism can be trusted to regulate itself towards an optimal integration and interaction with its physical and social environment. These ideal conditions again imply a considerable amount of self-awareness and acceptance within the individual person of all facets of his or her unique experience: emotional, sensory, motivational, and cognitive.

## The inner locus of evaluation

Most humanistic authors presumably agree with Rogers that, for truly authentic self-development to occur, there must take place a progressive shift in the locus of evaluation. Throughout infancy and childhood, the individual takes on, through conditioning or introjection, the values of his or her parents, which in turn are generally reflective of the subculture to which they belong. Theoretically, it is possible that such introjected norms do no violence to the child's own organismic experience, but such an outcome is highly improbable, given the strength of the dependency relationship in which one finds oneself and the relatively weak development of self-awareness during these formative years of life. Whatever happens, a valuing process is imposed on the developing personality from sources outside of itself. That procedure, necessary and inevitable though it may be in the early years of life, must be corrected if the individual is ever to become responsible for his or her own existence. As self-awareness increases, so also does the capacity for creating an authentic existence for oneself, based upon all the data of personal experiencing.

For the fully functioning person, Rogers states, the locus of evaluation comes from within (1961, p. 189). Nuttin speaks of the necessity for developing a constructive ideal of personality based upon an explicit choice of values, which are personally meaningful to the individual, which reflect a harmonious integration of *all* levels of his or her existence, and to which, therefore, one can wholly commit oneself (1962, p. 191).

The process by which this is to be accomplished, though it will be touched upon throughout this work, deserves a more complete treatment in a separate book. For our purposes now, it is sufficient to note that this ideal of authenticity is shared by nearly all humanistic psychologists. It is toward this goal that their combined efforts point.

This is, incidentally, a far cry from earlier emphases on mere *adjustment*, understood as the ability to function comfortably within existing sets of group norms and expectations. Older notions of personality adjustment had a conformist ring to them. The ideal of authentic existence does imply an adjustment of sorts, but it is an adjustment *within* the individual person, a process of internal integration and individuation, which might conceivably lead an individual to reject some of the standards that society attempts to impose upon him or her and to oppose them. Many humanists are quite critical of certain societal norms and institutions, especially when they judge these to be dehumanizing in their influence on individual members.

It should be noted in passing that neither behaviorism nor orthodox Freudian psychoanalysis can even conceive of the problem of authentic human existence in the terms here outlined. Both imprison human existence and behavior in a rigid determinism that allows for no major alteration. Adjustments can be made within the intrapsychic or social determinants of human behavior, but transcendence of this basic determinism from within is simply inconceivable within the systematic framework of both these schools of thought.

## 6.  SELF–TRANSCENDENCE

In the opening chapter of this book, I referred to the "magical moments of self-awareness" that so struck my adolescent client, the awakening she was experiencing from the dreamlike state of childhood, and how this filled her with a sense of excitement but also of anxiety. I was able to share with her similar feelings of my own, for the experience of self-awareness has always been a mystery to me, a great wonder, but also a problem. For it is essentially an experience of apartness, of being somehow separate from all the objects and persons that come and go within it. I, the subject, seem to be the only constant in this ever-flowing stream, at times deeply engaged in it, at other times an aloof and isolated observer. Further, I am quite aware that this experience had a beginning for me, and that, while it has a definite connectedness and continuity to it, sometimes it disappears, as in periods of sleep or unconsciousness. And somehow I have become aware of the inevitability of death, my death, and I dread what this might mean for my present, ongoing experience of consciousness.

The uniquely human experience of self-awareness is therefore, as the existentialists from Kierkegaard to Sartre have reminded us, an occasional source of distress and anxiety to its bearers and of a sometimes suffocating sense of loneliness. We do seek to escape the sense of isolation that it imposes, to forget it, or to transcend it.

It is not surprising, therefore, to discover that humanistic psychologists, in their concentration on the phenomenon of self-consciousness, also deeply concern themselves with the issue of self-transcendence. This too is a constant and major theme in their work, though individual authors approach it quite differently.

The prescientific descriptive analysis of consciousness has revealed to us that the experiencing of it always contains the other, as well as the self. The subject, or the self, is never experienced in a vacuum. This constant polarity of self and other, as the phenomenologists have pointed out, seems necessary for the very existence of consciousness itself. It always "in-tends" or tends toward the other, its objects.

### The transpersonal level

Nuttin (1962) uses this fact, as we have seen, to identify a transpersonal level of human existence where consciousness asks questions about the entire universe of experience to which it opens out, the world of being itself which is disclosed by it. He sees in this the primary source of mankind's scientific, philosophical, moral, and religious strivings and concerns. The basic drive toward self-realization operates on this level also, impelling us to satisfy our need to know, to make sense out of the jumble of impressions that force themselves upon us.

And since life is an open system, depending for its survival and growth on a constant exchange with its environment—incapable of maintaining itself on its own resources—we seek more than knowledge on this transpersonal level. We seek *contact* as well. We long for a sense of connectedness with all that is, an Absolute to which we can commit ourselves, something or Someone larger than our own ephemeral existences to give meaning to our lives, a meaningful place to be within the entire world of Being itself.

As a psychologist, Nuttin does not attempt to provide answers to these compelling existential questions posed by our conscious experience but rightly insists on their presence in our lives and their importance for understanding large segments of our behavior. They constitute a set of uniquely human needs that long just as much for satisfaction as do our needs for companionship, or recognition, or love, or physical nourishment. A human psychology that ignores them is therefore woefully incomplete.

**Emphasis on encounter**

For Rogers, the experience of self-transcendence seems to come principally through true interpersonal encounter, and much of his work has been devoted to the exploration of what makes this possible. Unlike the existentialist philosopher Jean-Paul Sartre, who despairs of the possibility of meaningful encounter or communication with others (as vividly depicted in his play *No Exit* [1947]), Rogers has defined the conditions that facilitate it and the results that follow: a caring and prizing of the other that leads, momentarily at least, to a forgetfulness of one's own self except for the satisfaction that follows from assisting the growth and enhancement of the other. In this, his work is reminiscent of the description given by the existentialist philosophers Martin Buber (1970) and Gabriel Marcel (1951), in distinguishing the I-Thou relationship, where the other is encountered as person, from the I-It relationship, where he or she is treated as mere object. More recently, Rogers has turned his attention to other possibilities for self-transcendence (see Chapter 9).

Perls and his associates in the Gestalt therapy movement also seem to emphasize open encounter with the other, interpersonal or "objective," as the principal means of self-transcendence or connectedness with something larger than self, though they are often accused of an almost irresponsible do-your-own-thing philosophy of life. The authors of *Gestalt Therapy* (Perls, Hefferline & Goodman, 1951) defined the self as the boundary between the individual and the environment. Since this boundary is constantly shifting and changing, they stress the necessity of striving to keep it open—riding, as it were, the flow of experiencing through constant encounter and, in this process, preventing the encapsulation and isolation of the ego.

## Other viewpoints

Maslow's peak-experiences are in reality momentary experiences of self-transcendence. At one point he defines them as "basic cognitive happenings in the B-love experience, the parental experience, the mystic, or oceanic, or nature experience, the aesthetic perception, the creative moment, the therapeutic or intellectual insight, the orgasmic experience, certain forms of athletic fulfillment, etc. These and other moments of highest happiness and fulfillment I shall call the peak-experiences" (1968, p. 73).

On the basis of such experiences, Maslow proposed the possibility of a "psychology of Being," an empirical analysis of the so-called higher states of Being or "farther reaches of human nature" toward which the human race aspires, including a realm of ultimate values that transcend the values corresponding to the ordinary deficiency-needs of the individual self. Primary devotion to the fulfillment of these B-values (wholeness, justice, beauty, truth, goodness, and the like) is what characterizes self-actualized individuals and, in each case, implies self-transcendence through the sense of a personal mission or calling centered around the pursuit of one or another of these ultimate values.

For the existential analyst Viktor Frankl, as we have seen, the very attribute of reflexive consciousness constitutes the individual as a self-transcending creature. A will to meaning is the chief characteristic of human consciousness for him, and a responsible dedication to the discovery and fulfillment of my personal meaning, my unique task and vocation in life, is obviously a self-transcending venture. For Frankl at least, such meaning is not invented but *discovered* in the unique tasks that life sets before us at various times and stages. Life *calls* us to the actualization of individualized meaning, and self-actualization is a by-product of the responsible answer to this call, not an end in itself.

For behaviorists and Freudian depth psychologists, self-transcendence is not a major issue. Skinner does propose an ultimate value—the survival of the species—in *Beyond Freedom and Dignity* (1971), but somehow the individual seems to lack importance in his system except as the individual's illusions of autonomy threaten the future survival of the race and require the attention of social engineers to prevent that from happening. There is, I suppose, a kind of self-transcendence involved in such a process, but it appears more like a negation of self than a positive fulfillment for both the individual and society. Freud, toward the end of his life, toyed with the Greco-Christian concept of *agape*, the possibility of a self-transcending love of the other, but he found it impossible to justify within a system where the ego remains always the servant of the narcissistic, pleasure-bent id.

Jung and Assagioli, on the other hand, postulated the existence of an archetypal or superconscious Self that transcends the boundaries of the personal ego. Self-transcendence is therefore a central issue in their work and an ideal toward which the individual must aspire for complete personal growth and integration. Their influence, along with that of Alan Watts and other psychologists who have introduced Western specialists to Eastern psychological systems, have led, as I have shown, to the development of transpersonal psychology. And one way of defining this movement, as the very title indicates, is to state that its principal concern is the empirical study of those altered states of consciousness in which the experience of self-transcendence is predominant.

## 7. PERSON–CENTEREDNESS

One of the most appealing general characteristics of the humanistic movement, at least to me, is its person-centered approach to individuals and their behavior. For this, more than for any other feature of their work, they deserve to be called *humanistic* psychologists. Atheists, agnostics, or believers, they share an obvious concern and respect for the subjects of their study, for their uniqueness and dignity as fellow members of the human race. I submit that this respect is a direct outgrowth of the central importance given to the study of human *consciousness* in all its dimensions. This focus inevitably exposes the psychologist to the infinite richness and complexity of individual human experience and to an appreciation of its wonders and unique variety akin to that of the poet, dramatist, or novelist.

Treating the subjects of my investigations as co-equal centers of conscious existence is a far cry from looking upon them as specimens or nonconscious robots. The respect which this mental set usually generates tends to preclude, for one thing, the relatively cold manipulation characteristic of the more objective approaches. To be allowed entrance into the private world of another person's experience requires a delicacy and caring of a different sort than is practiced in the more typical scientific laboratory: a caring for the *other* not merely for the objective aims of my research. When I am successful, my own consciousness is expanded in ways not accessible to me through instruments of objective research, such as a microscope or a one-way mirror.

### Purpose versus method

I certainly do not mean to imply that the findings of either behavioral or depth psychology cannot be used for humanistic *purposes*. The type

of programmed instruction developed through the application of behavioristic learning theory may well be the best tool available for
providing a child with the skills needed to develop talents which might
otherwise lie dormant, as Rogers (1969) has pointed out. Removal of
distressing or pathological symptoms through behavior modification
techniques or through the abreactive uncovering of their unconscious
sources in depth therapy may conceivably be the best means for helping an individual actualize himself or herself along certain dimensions
of existence.

But the *methods* of these respective disciplines are not inherently
humanistic or person-centered. The strategy necessarily employed in
behaviorism insists upon treating persons as objects and prescribes a
rigid sort of detachment on the part of the investigator. The same holds
true for depth psychology, which has more or less remained constricted
by the medical model out of which, historically, it grew. By definition it
concerns itself primarily with those aspects of human existence that lie
outside awareness and concerning which the investigator alone is presumably expert. The use of such terms as *diagnosis, treatment, syndrome, neurosis,* and *psychosis* clearly indicates a process of categorization and objectification that is highly antipersonalistic in tone.

Humanistic psychology, at its best, attempts to transcend this subject-object dichotomy and the objectivistic bias characteristic of previous research on human personality. Far from ignoring the subjective
experience of human consciousness, the humanist deliberately engages
himself or herself with it and explores its dimensions in active collaboration with the subject in the hope of helping that subject, and indeed
all people, understand it more fully and utilize it more freely for the
purposes of further growth and development.

The distinction I wish to make is between characteristic methodologies not persons. Paradoxically, findings of the phenomenological, person-centered approach can be used in antipersonalistic ways, as when
a self-styled humanist attempts to *force* people in an encounter group
to "free themselves up." Respect for human persons is basically a
subjective phenomenon, neither automatically generated nor hindered
by any given methodology. But it seems meaningful to distinguish
basic investigative procedures as either object-centered or person-centered. And it is the latter designation that seems to characterize one of
the most distinctive contributions of humanistic psychology.

## A radical approach

While all humanists advocate a person-centered approach in their
empirical research on personal functioning (see, for example, Giorgi,
1970), Carl Rogers stands out as the most radical proponent of this
stance in the sphere of practical application to therapy and to human

relations in fields as broad as education, management, marriage and family living, and the reduction of political and intercultural tensions. First applied in the field of psychotherapy, what he there termed *client-centered* therapy was based on his unswerving belief in a constructive actualizing tendency that lies at the core of human personality.

The full meaning of this construct will be discussed in a later chapter; but basically it includes the belief that, in the climate of certain precisely defined facilitative conditions, change will occur in the direction of more satisfying and constructive personal and social behavior. Such change, he believes, is not caused by the therapist or helper. The latter merely serves as a catalyst or facilitator of tendencies in that direction which are *inherent in the organism itself* but which, for one reason or another, have been stifled or prevented from operating.

> A facilitative person can aid in releasing these capacities when relating as a real person to the other, owning and expressing her own feelings; when experiencing a nonpossessive caring and love for the other; and when acceptantly understanding the inner world of the other. When this approach is made to an individual or a group, it is discovered that, over time, the choices made, the directions pursued, the actions taken are increasingly constructive personally and tend toward a more realistic social harmony with others. (Rogers, 1977, p. 15)

A considerable body of research exists in the field of psychotherapy in support of his views, and Rogers has expanded their application, through the vehicle of the basic encounter group, to the broader areas of human encounter mentioned above. Years of experience, his own and that of his associates, with variations of this approach have strengthened his convictions concerning its efficacy and near-universal applicability. Rogers himself has only recently come to the realization, so often experienced by others, of the revolutionary impact of his thought and in particular of his unwavering person-centered stance (Rogers, 1977—see Chapter 11).

## CONCLUSION

These, then, are the characteristics which, in my estimation, link together the otherwise diverse contributions of humanistic-existential psychologists: a scientific phenomenological approach to the study of human personality, a holistic and antireductionistic emphasis, the assumption of a teleological principle of self-actualization, a belief in the potentiality for a limited form of self-determination or personal freedom, a more-or-less explicit ideal of authentic human existence, a preoccupation with the problem of self-transcendence, and, finally, a valuing of the individual human person. No claims are made for the exhaustiveness of this list. To be frank, these unifying characteristics were chosen to illustrate the major theme of this present work: among all living organisms, humankind alone is meaningfully aware of its own existence. Our capacity for self-consciousness is what distinguishes us from all other beings on the planet. It is the source of our personhood, our dignity, and our freedom, our unique ability to understand and to adjust to our environment, and, potentially at least, to fashion for ourselves or to discover within our own reality the goals and meaning of our own existence.

# 4 Phenomenology and the Science of Person

Abraham Maslow once wrote: "I suppose it is tempting, if the only tool you have is a hammer, to treat everything as if it were a nail" (1966, p. 15). He was referring in this statement to what he termed the *methodolatry* of much of modern psychological science: the persistent attempt to mold all psychological investigations to the Procrustean bed of a model borrowed from the natural sciences, in which the events to be studied must be *publicly* observable, measureable, and replicable. This is the model which currently guides the efforts of most academic psychologists, and it has been, and continues to be, enormously productive.

It also has tended to preclude, as a matter of necessity, the investigation of certain problems in the study of human personality: specifically, the phenomenon of human consciousness and the phenomena of conscious experience. Such events fail particularly to meet the criterion of availability to public observation, in that they appear to be too subjective and private to merit scientific attention. Humanistic psychologists disagree with the rigid application of this model to the study of human experience and behavior and have sought to supplement it (or even, in a few instances, replace it entirely) by the development and application of new models or paradigms of scientific research which would allow them to focus on these neglected issues.

## SCIENTIFIC PARADIGMS

The term *paradigm* is here borrowed from the noted historian of science Thomas Kuhn. In his penetrating analysis of the structure of scientific revolution, Kuhn (1962) reminds us that different paradigms, or models of investigation that guide the thinking and activities of a specific scientific community, have been adopted, modified, and even discarded in the historical evolution of the discipline we call science. Individual paradigms gain acceptance and status because they are more successful than their competitors in solving a specific set of problems that the group of practitioners has come to recognize as acute. The more successful the paradigm becomes in generating productive research on the problems under investigation, the more adherents it draws to its fold, and a process of conservation sets in. The paradigm then becomes, in the view of its practitioners, the only proper way to conduct scientific research, and any attempt drastically to alter it is met with considerable resistance.

According to Kuhn, however, science is a dialectical process between *powers of conservation* and *powers of progress*. Anomalies inevitably occur within any given paradigm, simply because of the restricted focus that characterizes its beginnings. We are reminded once again that science is a further analysis of *experience*. Choices, often quite arbitrary in nature, must be made about which data of experience, and which problems and issues presented by it, will be subjected to such analysis. To choose is therefore also to leave out, to omit. But experience has a way of reasserting itself to the curious investigator. When it can no longer be ignored, and when the existing paradigm can no longer be modified to accommodate it, new paradigms emerge, and a scientific revolution takes place.

"Normal" science, then, concerns itself with investigating phenomena according to established paradigms. "Progressive" science concerns itself with the major anomalies that challenge existing paradigms and seeks to invent new ones that will better accommodate data and problems that can no longer be overlooked. It is easy to see how Kuhn's analysis fits the historical events that led, for example, to the replacement of the Ptolemaic theory in astronomy with the Copernican, or the Newtonian paradigm in physics with the drastic alterations of Einstein's relativity theory. But does Kuhn's analysis also apply to the field of psychological science and, more specifically, to the advent of humanistic psychology, its criticism of behavioral and psychoanalytic paradigms, and its attempts to come to grips in an empirical way with the phenomena of human consciousness?

## Paradigms in psychology

Kuhn himself considers the social sciences to be operating in a preparadigmatic stage, where no one paradigm has yet been adopted by all practitioners. It must be remembered, however, that he uses the term *paradigm* somewhat equivocally—at times very broadly, at other times in the narrower sense of a model used by a few specialists within a particular discipline to cover a very restricted range of phenomena. It seems clear to me that, in the broadest sense at least, the vast majority of social scientists today operate within a paradigm for "doing science" borrowed from the physical or natural sciences. Even Freud viewed himself as a scientist from this perspective, however much his modern critics now question his procedures.

In his book *Psychology as a Human Science* (1970), Amedeo Giorgi traces the historical adoption of the natural science paradigm in psychology to the enormous influence exercised by Wilhelm Wundt, founder of the first experimental psychology laboratory in 1876 at the University of Leipzig. Wundt simply borrowed the experimental observational model already elaborated for scientific investigation in the areas of physics and chemistry in order to establish psychology as a scientific discipline and to separate it from the realm of purely philosophical speculation about the human person. The strategy worked, and its success was further reinforced by the subsequent failure of introspectionism as an investigative tool, the rise of behaviorism, and the concurrent contributions of logical positivism to the philosophy of science.

But Giorgi also points out the arbitrary nature of this choice of paradigm, and the existence throughout the history of psychology of alternative proposals, offered from the very beginning, which by historical accident were relegated to a minority position. The reader is referred to his account of the efforts made by Dilthey, Brentano, Stern, and others in the late 19th century to ground the "human sciences," including psychology, on an entirely different investigative model, anticipating the more current phenomenological approaches now in vogue. These early efforts failed primarily, it seems, because the protagonists of this point of view were unable to create the methodological tools that would have enabled them and others to carry out their program. They tried. Brentano, for example, attempted to shift the focus of early introspectionism away from the *contents* of consciousness, and its elementaristic "mental chemistry" approach, toward a more holistic study of the *process* of consciousness itself, an effort which came to be known as *Act Psychology*. But the tool of introspectionism, as used by these 19th-century investigators, proved to be too imprecise to provide the sort of reliable information that can qualify as scientific in anyone's definition of that term. And, perhaps more important, the mental chemistry model from which it proceeded was still caught in a mechanistic, natural science paradigm that modern humanistic commentators consider totally inadequate to capture the essence of human consciousness.

Giorgi succeeds admirably in documenting not only the reasons for the success of the borrowed natural science model in psychology but also the existence, throughout its history, of a vocal minority who have always decried its shortcomings in providing us with a satisfactory account of human experience and behavior. Simply put, it seems to have been easier to use borrowed tools than to construct new ones. Psychology did become a separate and scientific discipline in the process, and an enormous amount of dependable information was generated as a result. But the nagging questions persist. The anomalies remain and grow more obvious as the historical evolution of psychology continues on its chosen path.

The philosopher of science, Alfred North Whitehead, affirms the position I have taken in the second chapter of this book on the *priority of conscious experience* as the criterion for judging the validity of any further analysis, scientific or philosophical. (Many other philosophers of science have made a similar point. See, for example, Michael Polanyi [1958].)

In his work *Science and the Modern World* (1948), Whitehead reminds us, in effect, that the aim of science is to produce a theory which agrees with experience by explaining the concepts constructed by commonsense observation through the mental constructs or concepts derived from the more controlled observations of science. It is Giorgi's point (and mine) that traditional psychology, while it has enjoyed considerable success in the application of the natural science paradigm, has failed to give us a satisfactory account of important commonsense constructs, such as freedom, choice, intentions, goals, purposive behavior, and most important, the self as conscious initiator and agent of activity.

The whole humanistic movement can be seen, in one sense, as a response to the pressure, grown tremendously over the past three decades, toward the development of a new paradigm in psychology, one that will return again to the starting point of these "lived experiences." The aim of such a new model would be to remove the naivete of common sense, already a prescientific construction, and replace it with a scientific analysis of the phenomena of conscious experience, their relationships to each other, and to the phenomena described by behaviorism and depth psychology, as well as by neurology and physiology.

For example, "common sense" that is derived from my "lived experience" tells me I am somehow a stable center of existence, a "self," persisting through all the changes and stages of my life. I have this inescapable sense of subjective continuity amid all the flow of experiencing. Could not a more scientific analysis shed some light on this experience? How does it develop, and when? Does it differ in different cultural settings? What role does the development of language play in its formation? What precisely are its components (e.g., self-concept, self-ideal, self-esteem) and how do they relate to my ongoing observable behavior, to the physiological changes that occur within me, to my social interactions with others? And how do all these variables in turn affect my sense of self?

Such a scientific analysis (already begun) is obviously a very ambitious undertaking, and it will undoubtedly be left to future historians of psychology to document its success or failure. Its popular appeal, however, is undeniable, as witnessed by the mushrooming proliferation of human potential centers, consciousness-raising groups, and the more academically oriented research institutes, journals, and professional organizations. That most of this has taken place outside the recognized establishment in psychology is evidence of the validity of Kuhn's prediction that new paradigms in science always meet with considerable resistance from the more conservative members of that particular scientific community. Traditional psychology already has a successful paradigm. Its protagonists are quite aware of the anomalies that have been pointed out but remain convinced that they will soon be accommodated within the existing model (Kruglanski, 1976).

Time alone will tell. The most meaningful test for any new paradigm, however, lies in its ability to demonstrate that the methods of investigation it develops to tackle problems previously overlooked meet the criteria of *scientific* validity and reliability, and, further, succeed in doing a better job than the methods it seeks to supplant.

This observation immediately suggests a number of problems.

1. Is it any more possible today to conduct a scientific analysis of conscious phenomena than it was in the 19th century when, by most accounts, the introspectionists failed to do so?
2. If so, does this mean that our present-day view of what constitutes orthodox science, our very definition of science itself as a human endeavor, will be forced to undergo some rather drastic alterations?
3. Finally, should the natural science paradigm be abandoned altogether, at least as it is applied to human subjects, in favor of a new one based upon a thoroughgoing phenomenological stance?

In the present state of flux and controversy within the field of psychology, it is impossible to provide definitive answers to these questions. I would like to present some current opinions advanced by various humanists and suggest some of my own conclusions—but before doing so, another brief historical excursion seems necessary.

## PHILOSOPHICAL CONTRIBUTIONS TO PSYCHOLOGY

I would like to begin with what appears to be an undeniable assumption. Psychology, as we understand it today, is definitely a scientific discipline. It has succeeded in separating itself from its philosophical parentage and is recognized as having done so by the scientific community, particularly in its more experimental, laboratory-based endeavors. This does not mean, however, that psychology now remains uninfluenced by the contributions of various philosophical movements. No branch of scientific endeavor can legitimately claim such immunity.

I have already taken note of the contributions of logical positivism to the development of the natural science paradigm, within and outside the province of psychological science. But there is another major current of philosophical speculation, which developed in opposition to a number of positivistic assumptions concerning the nature of reality and the means of arriving at ultimate truth, whose influence is currently being felt among philosophers of science: *phenomenological and existential philosophy*. This is a very broad current, fed by many authors. In presenting a brief outline of their thoughts, I hope to provide some further understanding of what is meant by a phenomenological approach in psychology, and why many humanistic authors feel more confident that their efforts to develop a scientific approach to conscious phenomena will meet with better success than did their predecessors.

Phenomenological philosophy begins and ends with the phenomena or experiences immediately presented to consciousness. Believing, with the 18th-century philosophers Hume and Kant, that these experiences are all we can know with certainty, the authors who represent this approach begin with the life-world as experienced by conscious subjects, bracket or isolate one or another of the experiences found within it (such as the perception of color, of causality, the experience of consciousness itself, and of human existence), and analyze it exhaustively, while remaining as close to the original experience as possible. In doing so, they hope to discover or unveil the essence of conscious phenomena: those aspects of the given experience that must be present for the phenomenon to exist at all *in consciousness*. Theirs is a metaphysics of *phenomena*; not, as previous philosophers had proposed, a metaphysics of *reality* apart from conscious experience. Their method is reductive, not deductive, and their constant aim is to remain true to the lived experience.

This ambitious program was set in motion at the beginning of this century by the German philosopher Edmund Husserl, the father of modern phenomenological philosophy. His methods were vigorously applied to the analysis of human existence itself by one of his students, Martin Heidegger. Since human existence is what is bracketed by Heidegger (and others) as the phenomenon to be investigated, his approach has been termed *existential phenomenology*, or, more simply, existentialism.

(To be sure, the themes of existentialism had already been addressed a century earlier by Soren Kierkegaard and Friedrich Nietzsche. Heidegger's contribution was to explore such themes using Husserl's newly developed philosophical techniques.)

Heidegger and other contemporary existentialists have exercised considerable influence in the fields of psychology and psychiatry, particularly in that branch of the humanistic movement that has come to be called *existential analysis.* Existential analysts, like their Freudian and neo-Freudian counterparts, are clinicians, mostly psychiatrists, who analyze their patients from this newer existential perspective.

For an understanding of this *empirical* adaptation of modern phenomenological philosophy to psychology, I will turn first to the work of these analysts, who are mostly European. The essence of the phenomenological method, as developed by Husserl and Heidegger, can be boiled down to three consecutive operations.

1.  A careful *descriptive analysis* of some state of consciousness, remaining as close as possible to the immediate "givens" of that experience. (See Chapter 2 for such a descriptive analysis of certain conscious states.)
2.  A *reductive analysis,* based upon this description, to the essential structure of that experience, or to the discovery of those elements without which the experience could not exist. (In Chapter 2, certain states were reductively termed *psychophysiological.* Their essential "structure" is the subjective awareness of some physiological state or event.)
3.  A *categorical analysis,* which involves the further description of connected categories of such structures: broader unities that characterize a range of such experiences (like the relationship between the three apparently irreducible levels of conscious experience described in Chapter 2).

Ellenberger (May, Angel, & Ellenberger, 1958) has aptly described for us the application of these basic elements of the phenomenological method by the existential analysts. Their aim was and remains to explicate the inner phenomenological experience of psychopathological states of consciousness, such as schizophrenia, depression, and obsessive-compulsive disorders. Their method is primarily the time-honored, empirical, case-history approach based upon the experienced analyst's empathic observation and description of these states as experienced by actual patients or, in some instances, on the analysis of written records provided by subjects who have undergone such experiences in the past.

Karl Jaspers, a noted psychiatrist and an existential philosopher in his own right, was one of the first to develop a *descriptive* phenomenology of various psychopathological states and to publish his findings in a textbook on general psychopathology (Jaspers, 1913). *Genetic-structural* analysis in this field was pioneered by Eugene Minkowski, who attempted to define the basic disturbance from which one could deduce the whole content of consciousness and the symptoms of the patient in the disorders of schizophrenia and depression (Minkowski, 1927, 1933). Viktor Von Gebsattel and Erwin Straus are also 'cited by Ellenberger in this context. Finally, *categorical* phenomenology, the reconstruction of the inner world of actual patients through an analysis of their manner of experiencing time, space, causality, materiality, and other philosophical categories, has been applied by a number of analysts including, besides those already mentioned, Ludwig Binswanger, Medard Boss, Roland Kuhn, and others. Rollo May's analysis of the more normal experience of human love, based upon categories borrowed from Platonic philosophy, is a recent example of this approach that is perhaps more familiar to American readers (May, 1969).

## STRUCTURAL PHENOMENOLOGY

These various empirical adaptations of the phenomenological method first devised by philosophers I propose to call *structural phenomenology* for purposes of comparison with the more *functional* phenomenological approach developed by several American investigators. In the latter instance, an effort is made to establish replicable mathematical (or functional) relationships between phenomenological variables or between such variables and their more externally observable counterparts. Structural phenomenology, in my definition of the term, concerns itself with a more *qualitative* description or re-creation of the inner world of the human subjects it chooses for investigation. It seeks to make that inner world more understandable, in all its richness and variety, to other members of the scientific community who are interested in the problems and issues under investigation. It provides a good current example of the sort of *Geisteswissenschaft* first proposed by Dilthey, a specifically human science leading primarily to wisdom, or a reliable understanding (Verstehen) of human experience from within that experience itself. Such a science is obviously less concerned about prediction or about manipulation and control of its subject matter.

Structural phenomenology, in the sense here described, is scientific rather than philosophical, because it is founded on the clinical method, involving observers engaged with actual clients or patients in a clinical setting. Such observations can, it is hoped, be verified and replicated by other trained observers in comparable situations. Certain unique skills are required of such investigators (which will be detailed in a later chapter), just as certain skills are demanded of scientists in other fields, such as botany, for the proper description and classification (e.g., of botanical specimens). The first stages of scientific investigation in any area most frequently involve such a structural, or descriptive-classificatory approach to its subject matter. The point I wish to make is that this effort, though preliminary and rudimentary, is no less scientific or empirical than the later development of more sophisticated, mathematically based models of investigation and is often the necessary prelude to that later stage.

Some examples provided by Ellenberger may help to clarify this issue:

> In their investigations of melancholic patients, both Minkowski and Von Gebsattel found the same basic symptom: time is no more experienced as a propulsive energy. The consequence is a flowing back of the stream of time, comparable to what happens to a river when a barrier is constructed. Therefore, the future is perceived as blocked and the patient's attention directed toward the past, while the present is experienced as stagnating. Many other symptoms may be deduced from this basic disturbance in the experiencing of time. (May, Angel, & Ellenberger, 1958, p. 100)

Ellenberger later describes how Von Gebsattel and Straus arrived at fairly similar conclusions in their genetic-structural analysis of subjects afflicted with obsessive-compulsive neurosis. A good case can also be made, I believe, for the similarity of accounts given by Minkowski and R. D. Laing of the basic disturbance, a loss of vital contact with reality, underlying the disorder known as schizophrenia. We see here the generation of reliable, replicable information by independent investigators, based upon observation, which is the very essence of scientific methodology.

## FUNCTIONAL PHENOMENOLOGY

But scientists also attempt, where possible, to quantify their observations. The establishment of functional mathematically expressed relationships between the phenomena under investigation has many advantages. It gives us not only a greater understanding of *what* it is we are studying but of *how* these events are lawfully related to other data of experience, and leads to better prediction or control, or both.

This method has been called the *hypothetico-deductive* approach to scientific investigation. Certain theoretical assumptions are usually formed in advance on how the data might be related. From these theoretical hunches, produced in the creative or intuitive stages of scientific thinking, specific testable hypotheses are logically deduced and expressed in mathematical form. Controlled observation follows during which the hypotheses are tested and the results of observation tabulated. Verification of the hypotheses leads to further validation of the theory from which they were derived. If unsuccessful, the scientist returns to the drawing board.

Western science has followed this model of investigation since the time of Galileo, and it continues to inspire the work of many humanistic pyschologists. The only real innovation they have introduced is in modifying this research paradigm to include the investigation of *phenomenological* variables, variables that arise from the inner, private experiences and conscious reflections of their human subjects. Direct access to such experiences remains, of course, impossible to obtain, but methods have been devised to enable subjects to communicate such data to investigators in ways that lend themselves to some form of statistical or mathematical treatment.

This is a most desirable procedure, in most instances, but it should not be confused with the essence of scientific investigation. Geologists, for example, have generated a great deal of reliable information concerning the nature and causes of earthquakes. Few would deny the scientific character of such information. Because further advances in this field have led to the establishment of certain lawful, quantifiable relationships between the events that lead to the production of earthquakes, the day seems to be at hand when their occurrence can be predicted with considerable accuracy. And some geologists have gone so far as to suggest methods of preventing (and therefore, in some sense, of controlling) their occurrence at all. Geology is therefore advancing to a more sophisticated stage of development, but it was no less scientific when it was based primarily on descriptive, reliable accounts of its subject matter. Structural phenomenology seems to qualify as a science in much the same sense.

The application of phenomenological methods in psychology, however, should not be construed as ending at this point. From the very beginning of the modern humanistic movement, a *functional* phenomenology was developed, primarily by a number of American psychologists who had been previously trained in the application of positivistic models of research (unlike the European analysts who had been schooled in the methods of psychoanalysis). These involve, as we have seen, the searching out of *measurable* relationships between the variables under investigation in the hope of discovering lawful patterns among them.

## Rogers's self-theory

Carl Rogers and his associates appear to have been among the first to attempt the development of such a functional phenomenology, along with their contemporaries Henry Murray (1938) and Gordon Allport (1955). Rogers initially engaged himself in the elaboration of a new approach to psychotherapy, later to be labeled *client-centered therapy*. In the process of doing so, he began almost immediately to speculate on certain theoretical assumptions that seemed intuitively to be guiding his practical efforts or that arose from the responses he was evoking from his clients in his attempts to encounter them in their own inner world of experience. From these observations, a phenomenological *self-theory* emerged that has come to be associated with his name. It is not my purpose to present an in-depth account of self-theory (see Combs & Snygg, 1959) but merely to point out that it was framed in the traditional positivistic paradigm and modified to fit phenomenological variables. I will choose two of his constructs to illustrate my point: self-concept, self-ideal, and the relationship between them.

Self-concept was defined by Rogers as the conscious awareness of "the patterned perceptions of the individual's characteristics and relationships, together with the values associated with these" (1951, p. 515). It is, in effect, the individual's conceptualized awareness of the sort of person he or she is. It can be ascertained by having the individual respond to statements put in the form: "I am the kind of person who . . ." Self-ideal represents the concept the individual has of the sort of person he or she aspires to become, and can be determined by a person's response to statements of the form: "I would like to be the kind of person who . . ."

In their early investigations of self-theory and its usefulness in describing and measuring therapeutic outcomes, Rogers and his associates used a statistical methodology suggested by William Stephenson (1936, 1953), called Q-technique. This is a correlational procedure which allows the investigator to measure the strength of the relationship among precisely the sort of variables Rogers was proposing to investigate.

The process is begun by asking subjects to sort a number of self-statements (e.g., "I am satisfied with myself") into a forced normal distribution of nine piles ranging from "least like me" to "most like me," a scaling technique called a Q-sort. The same statements are then sorted by subjects into an identical number of categories based upon the kind of person they would like to become. The two sets of categories are then mathematically correlated to determine the strength of relationship between the self-concept and self-ideal (a correlation of +1.00 would indicate a perfect correspondence between the individual's self-concept and self-ideal; 0.00, no significant correspondence at all; and −1.00, a perfect negative correspondence between these two self-constructs).

The investigators had assumed that there would be a linear or direct relationship between congruence of self-concept and self-ideal and personality adjustment as measured by independent tests. The thinking behind this assumption was that, where there is a large discrepancy between an individual's concept of what he or she is like and would like to become, a greater degree of dissatisfaction with oneself will be experienced, resulting in poorer scores on tests of personal adjustment. Conversely, where there is little discrepancy, greater personal satisfaction will be felt, resulting in higher adjustment scores. This seems straightforward enough and almost obvious in terms of common sense.

The results, however, were quite surprising to the investigators. The mathematical function that appeared was more U-shaped than linear.

This means that poorer adjustment scores were characteristic not only of subjects whose self-concept and self-ideal sorts were very discrepant, as had been predicted, but also of some subjects whose sorts were *least* discrepant. Better adjustment scores were usually found where there was *some* discrepancy between these sorts but not to a notable degree. This would seem to indicate personality adjustment may be related to a kind of constructive tension that exists between these self-constructs in an individual's phenomenal world, where the discrepancy is not so large as to be a constant source of discouragement but large enough to motivate further efforts to growth.

On the other hand, as Butler and Haigh point out in the same volume: "It is quite certain that a correlation of unity between self and ideal would not indicate perfect adjustment. Indeed, the only self-ideal correlation above .90 was achieved by an individual (in another study) who was clearly paranoid. Tentatively the speculation would seem warranted that extremely high self-ideal correlations are likely to be products of defensive sortings" (Rogers & Dymond, 1954, p. 73). However that may be, the illustration just given serves to demonstrate how phenomenological variables can be subjected to the type of empirical investigation that is here termed *functional* and how such investigations can lead to the development of a more sophisticated scientific theory involving testable hypotheses and the discovery of lawful, mathematically expressed relationships between such inner variables.

These early methods were admittedly crude and tentative, at least compared with those already long developed for more objective research, but they marked a beginning. The present author was the first to apply Q-sort methodology to Donald Super's self-concept theory in vocational psychology, with modest success (Tageson, 1960), but this line of research has since been abandoned in favor of more sophisticated methods, such as the use of Osgood's "semantic differential" (Osgood, Suci, & Tannenbaum, 1957) for the testing of self-theory. (See Maddi [1980] for further information on this point.)

Rogers himself later turned to other projects having more to do with therapists' attitudes involved in successful therapeutic interventions, and with the construction of a process scale to measure constructive personality change within or outside the area of psychotherapy. Both these efforts, as we will later see, have led to some notable advances in our understanding of these important issues from a modified phenomenological stance.

## CURRENT EXAMPLES OF FUNCTIONAL PHENOMENOLOGY

Self-theory has undergone considerable alteration since its beginnings in the work of Rogers and his associates and the formulations of Combs and Snygg (1959). While its current methodologies have been recently criticized by Ruth Wylie (1974), its viability and further use-fulness continue to be defended by M. Brewster Smith (1978) and others. This debate need not detain us here, since there are other examples of functional phenomenological approaches to an under-standing of human behavior which are equally current and continue to stimulate a body of highly instructive research. I will present a brief summary of two such current avenues of experimental investigation.

## Kelly's personal construct theory

From the 1930s on, George Kelly (1955), a clinical psychologist and personality theorist at Ohio State University, formulated what came to be called *personal construct theory*. Kelly was a true phenomenologist (and humanist), arguing that psychological reality is the product of our active and continual search for and creation of meaning in an otherwise unstructured phenomenal world. In a review of recent research derived from Kelly's theory, Greg Neimeyer provides the following helpful summary:

> The individual's primary vehicle for structuring experience is the con-struct. A construct may be regarded as a perceived basis of discrimina-tion among three or more things. As such it reflects an awareness of the way in which some things are alike and different from others (Bannister & Mair, 1968). In construing a set of colleagues, for example, one might perceive some of them as selfish, others as selfless; some as outgoing, others as shy; some as competent and others not, and so on. Each of these dimensions of discrimination is termed a construct and each serves as a bipolar template along which the entire set of colleagues may be ordered. Taken collectively, myriad such dimensions form a construct system; a systematic conceptual template for interpreting and anticipating experi-ence. (Neimeyer, 1980, p. 18)

In his original formulation, Kelly (1955) articulated his theory by way of this fundamental postulate and 11 corollaries. His corollaries encompass various features of such construct systems: their range, individual uniqueness, the similarity of certain constructs to those of other subjects, their hierarchical organization, effects on interpersonal development and understanding, and the rules that govern how they change over time in response to new experiences.

In order to tap into an individual's repertoire of personal constructs, Kelly devised an ingenious instrument called the *Role Construct Reper-tory Test* (RepTest). For example, a subject may be asked to name a number of significant people in his or her life, group these into triads according to role titles (father, mother, best friend, employer, and so on) provided by the investigator, and indicate one important way in which two in each triad are alike and different from the third. For example, a subject might indicate that mother and best friend are alike in being "warm," whereas his or her employer is "cold." Results of all such comparisons are laid out on a grid and analyzed to identify the bipolar (dialectical) constructs used by the subject to interpret other people (role constructs).

Numerous variations have been introduced into this methodology to generate information of interest to various researchers. Subjects, for example, can be asked to *predict* what constructs other people might use to evaluate mutual acquaintances, and these in turn are compared with their own (or with the other people's evaluations) to identify areas of similarity and disagreement. Subjects may be asked to *rank* their own constructs and those of others according to their relative importance in evaluation of behavior (thus providing information about their hierarchical ordering). The *number* and *variability* of constructs generated can be used as measures of constriction or openness in the individual's construct system.

All these and other variations have been used by Kelly himself and subsequent researchers to investigate topics as different as psychopathological construct systems (Kelly, 1955), changes in self-constructs as a function of successful psychotherapy (Meador & Rogers, 1973), and, most recently, interpersonal attraction (Neimeyer, Banikiotes, & Ianni, 1979; Banikiotes & Neimeyer, 1980), the development of interpersonal relationships (Salmon, 1970; Perry, 1977; Duck, 1973, 1977, 1979); and their deterioration (Neimeyer, 1980). In this latest research, the authors derived their hypotheses directly from Kelly's Sociality and Commonality Corollaries, arguing that interpersonal understanding and construct similarity are positively associated with relationship satisfaction. Empirical results bear out this contention. Conversely, where expectancies for such understanding and similarity are high but not confirmed by subsequent experience, it is expected that relationship deterioration will occur. Neimeyer is currently testing this hypothesis.

The RepTest methodology used in these studies lends itself quite readily to conventional statistical analysis, a feature which places them squarely in the category of functional phenomenology as defined in the present volume.

### Rychlak's logical learning theory

Another current example of this category of research is to be found in the work of Joseph Rychlak and his students, presently at Purdue University. Rychlak, a clinical and experimental psychologist, studied under George Kelly at Ohio State in the 1950s. He subsequently developed his own theoretical and methodological approach, which he calls *logical learning theory,* and has long been an advocate of a "rigorous humanism" (1977) in the belief that it is quite possible to subject humanistic theory to strict scientific test and verification. Indeed, it is his belief that this must be done if humanistic psychology is to remain viable as a force within modern psychology as a whole.

Logical learning theory began to take shape about 20 years ago as a result of Rychlak's conviction that the previously neglected dialectical aspects of human consciousness needed to be reintroduced into the study of human learning, along with the exclusively demonstrative features then in vogue (see Chapter 2 for his definition of this important distinction). Kelly, as we have seen, had already introduced such dialectical features to the study of human personality in his personal construct theory and the methods (bipolar constructs) chosen for its exploration.

Human logic, in Rychlak's understanding, is both dialectical and demonstrative. His basic contention is that there are a number of *subject-contributed variables, independent of environmental inputs or antecedents,* that affect the course of human learning. A particularly important theoretical construct, from which one such variable can be determined, is *affective assessment.* This is the dialectical judgment of like-dislike, which we innately apply to the stimuli, environmental events, and even our own previous responses to these, that impinge upon our consciousness from within and without.

> We begin from the Kantian assumption that humans *at birth* have the capacity to judge, evaluate or assess environmental circumstances (inputs, stimuli, etc.). Judgment is an *active* process of bringing mentality to bear. This notion of assessing one's environmental circumstances is my "Kantian (a priori) category," we might say. (Rychlak, 1976, p. 138)

It is important to realize from the outset that Rychlak is here referring to an innate *process* of dialectical judgment (remarkably similar to Carl Rogers's concept of an organismic valuing process [1951]). He is not claiming that we are born with certain innate *preferences,* though this may be possible. Some people (e.g., masochists) learn to *like* certain forms of pain. Others cringe from pain in all its varieties. The point here is that no one remains neutral in the presence of such stimuli. An individual will always *evaluate* them in some dialectical or bipolar fashion.

Rychlak draws a theoretical distinction also between *affective assessment* and *emotion.* Affective assessment always implies a judgment or appraisal of a situation as it *affects* me. This can be arbitrary, based, for example, on previous premises that I have adopted but that are subject to change. Emotion he refers to the physiological accompaniments that occur automatically (demonstratively, or in efficient-causal fashion) in response to the situation. More often than not, as rational-emotive and cognitive therapists have recently reminded us, emotional responses are linked directly to our cognitive assessments. A student who is operating under the premise "I must receive all As" may become devastated and experience a deep emotional depression over receiving a B. If he or she can change that premise to read "I hope to receive some decent grades" (and assesses a B as decent), the emotional reaction will be considerably different and more positive. His or her grades will, however, be evaluated along a like-dislike polarity. It is the latter process or activity that the subject contributes to the further elaboration of learning. As Rychlak puts it:

> I believe that, in addition to "responding" to environmental factors, human beings are also continually assessing their life circumstances. One of the clearest definitions of final causation is precisely this ability to judge (evaluate, assess, etc.). When we judge something we assess its status *in terms of* or *for the sake of* something else. (1976, p. 120)

It is these meanings, premises, or assessments that we carry forward in further learning. Rychlak's theoretical analysis thus clearly preserves and specifies the humanistic contention that we are telic (goal-oriented) organisms engaged in purposeful behavior.

Rychlak then proceeded, in the manner of doing science that can only be called classic, to develop a technical measure (methodological variable) from his theoretical analysis. This functional measure of affective assessment he calls *reinforcement value* (RV). It is defined as:

> The operationalized measure (metric) of affective assessment achieved by asking subjects to prerate for likeability materials (verbal, pictorial, etc.) which they may be asked to learn or otherwise deal with in an experimental context. It is assumed that a rating of liking reflects positive affective assessment and a rating of disliking reflects a subject's negative affective assessment. Considered from its background theory, reinforcement value is a nonfrequency measure of meaningfulness. (1977, p. 506)

In some of the initial experiments conducted by Rychlak and his associates, for example, subjects were simply asked to rate CVC trigrams (consonant-vowel-consonant nonsense syllables, such as HIB, LAT, SUL, and the like) on a four-point scale of like much, like slightly, dislike slightly, dislike much. The use of such a four-point rating scale with no intermediate zero, borrowed from Berg (1957), was chosen because of its dialectical implications, along with an effort "to dimensionalize [i.e., slightly, much] the direction of this either-or decision" (1977, p. 370).

It should be emphasized that *reinforcement value* so defined has always been treated by these researchers as a subject-contributed (idiographic) variable, not as one tied to the particular stimuli themselves (nomothetic variable), though this can also be computed. Proceeding along traditional verbal-learning methodology, they quickly discovered that trigrams with positive RV values for the subjects (determined in advance) were more readily learned than those which had been negatively evaluated. So was launched a whole program of research, covering the past 20 years, which has proved to be highly instructive. Designs were carefully crafted to insure that reinforcement value, as a measure, is independent of association value (familiarity) or frequency considerations, issues raised by various critics from their more demonstrative perspective (the possibility that RV might be directly caused by such external features). Thus Rychlak can confidently state:

> We argue that reinforcements are not *only* in the environment, or in the tissue needs of the body, as modern learning theories imply. Reinforcements are positive or negative thanks *also* to a contribution made by the affectively assessing human organism who must come at life each day. (1976, pp. 138–139)

The full range of this research program and its outcomes have been made available to the interested reader in Rychlak's book *The Psychology of Rigorous Humanism* (1977). A much briefer summary is presented in Rychlak's contribution to the edited volume *Humanism and Behaviorism: Dialogue and Growth* (Wandersman, Poppen, & Ricks, 1976, pp. 141–143). Following are some of the more interesting findings reported there.

1. Positive reinforcement-value effects have been found not only in the learning of CVC trigrams (Rychlak, 1966), but also in the learning of words (Andrews, 1972), abstract designs (McFarland, 1969), and names-to-faces (Galster, 1972).
2. Schizophrenics or normals with negative self-concepts diminish this RV effect or reverse it entirely by furthering negative meanings more readily than positive ones (Rychlak, McKee, Schneider, & Abramson, 1971; Rychlak, Carlson, & Dunning, 1974).
3. Underachievers learn what they like dramatically better than what they dislike; overachievers seem to rise above this factor (Rychlak & Tobin, 1971).
4. Learning disliked materials prior to liked materials led to a significant improvement in the learning of the latter, in comparison to other conditions. Reversing the procedure (learning liked materials first) at times resulted in a decrease in performance on the second task (learning disliked materials). This finding leads Rychlak to speculate about the phenomena underlying discounted formal discipline theories in education (e.g., that learning Greek or Latin would facilitate the learning of other unrelated subjects, such as mathematics) (Rychlak & Tobin, 1971; Rychlak et al., 1974).
5. Black females learn more along RV lines than do white females in trigram-learning tasks, again leading Rychlak to speculate:

> Could it be that much of the so-called black inferiority to whites on academic tasks and tests of intelligence is due to some such affective

factor? What if we were to find that blacks are predominantly "inferior" on their *disliked* tasks and IQ items? How could this finding be dealt with *vis-à-vis* the typical genetic explanations proffered to account for such racial differentials? (1976, p. 142)

Interestingly, these results are reported in the context of a contribution entitled: "Is a Concept of 'Self' Necessary in Psychological Theory?" Rychlak concludes that indeed it is, and provides a clear-cut illustration of a functional phenomenological approach at work. Some further examples of this approach will be given throughout this work. Enough has already been presented, however, to indicate its basic thrust, the fact that its origins were independent of European phenomenological philosophy, and its ability to apply a more advanced technology to phenomenological data.

## RADICAL VERSUS MODERATE APPROACHES

I have proposed this distinction between a *structural* phenomenology, seen as based upon an empirical adaptation of a method borrowed from modern phenomenological philosophy, and a *functional* phenomenology, derived from a modification of the more traditional scientific paradigm based upon positivistic philosophy, in order to highlight a controversy that has developed within the humanistic movement. The central issue in this growing argument revolves, I believe, around *the role of measurement* in scientific psychology.

Structural phenomenologists tend to see the goal of measurement as being applied to the human sciences, including psychology, as a peripheral concern. They would opt instead, as we have seen, for a more thoroughgoing empirical but *qualitative* description of conscious phenomena as the principal aim of the psychology of the future. They distrust the preoccupation with measurement concerns as a distracting holdover from the natural science paradigm, with which psychology unfortunately and arbitrarily saddled itself in its historical beginnings. Quantification, they claim, is just another form of the reductionism that has plagued psychological science from the start, in that it attempts to reduce the phenomena of human experience to spatiotemporal categories in ways that violate their integrity and strip them of their vital meaning and importance.

This purist and radical phenomenological approach is ably defended in this country by Adrian Van Kaam (1966), Amedeo Giorgi (1970, and Ernest Keen (1975). As of this date, it represents a minority position in humanistic psychology, as it has historically in the field of academic psychology as a whole, but it is beginning to gain the attention it deserves. Departments of phenomenological psychology, representing this radical approach, have already been founded at the universities of Duquesne and Dallas, though it remains much more firmly established in European settings.

Most American humanists, however, maintain a more moderate position and continue to espouse the functional form of phenomenology previously outlined as a supplement to existing traditional approaches. Rychlak (1968) ably documents the contributions which have been made by both paradigms (dialectical versus demonstrative traditions) in the area of personality theory. Rogers (Coulson & Rogers, 1968) has often argued for this complementary approach and has consistently advocated the goal of measurement, where possible, for phenomenological investigations. Maslow (1966) has rightly pointed out that scientific knowledge is a matter of degree and that any increment of knowledge or of reliability is better than nothing. His statements were made in the context of justifying the early rather crude and tentative efforts of humanistic psychologists, including his own, to subject phenomenological variables to scientific measurement. Neatness and precision, he remarked, are the end-stages of scientific knowledge, but he never seems to have lost sight of such an outcome as a desirable goal for the newer, modified paradigm.

More recently, the noted developmental psychologist Irvin Child, in his book *Humanistic Psychology and the Research Tradition* (1973), has taken both traditional and humanistic psychology to task for their respective defects, after outlining the virtues of both approaches. The virtues of traditional psychology, he insists, lie in the pursuit of verifiability, objectivity, and precision. In doing so, however, traditional psychology has fallen into the trap of allowing the availability of methods to determine the subject matter studied, an argument reminiscent of Maslow's accusation of methodolatry. The most serious defect of the traditional approach has been the exclusion of experience or awareness from its investigations. "But it is reasonable to expect," he concludes, "that scientific study of a subject matter will involve improvement of inference rather than the elimination of the subject matter" (1973, p. 9).

Humanistic psychology is criticized by Child for its frequent vagueness and lack of precision, and for what he terms its "marked tendency toward lack of verifiability" (1973, p. 20). Its principal virtue, he maintains, lies in the reintroduction of the topics of experience and awareness to general psychology. That he feels this can be done through a more precise functional methodology is evident from his brief review of the work of Abraham Maslow, whom he admires for theoretical contributions but criticizes for slipshod methodological approach. Child credits Maslow for developing two novel techniques for studying topics of great interest to humanistic psychologists: a device for measuring an individual's sensitivity to artistic styles and the interview methods by which he gathered information concerning peak-experiences and their occurrence in the lives of self-actualized subjects and others. Both techniques, Child feels, are potentially valuable, but Maslow, though well-trained in experimental psychology, applied them and reported his results in an extremely informal fashion, often overlooking even the most elementary principles of scientific control. Child makes his point gently, but it is well taken:

> Perhaps he was simply making a wise decision about what activity of his could contribute most effectively at the time to the movement of which he was so important a part. If his examples were to set the general pattern for humanistic psychologists, however, the theoretical work he and others have done would remain sterile; pertinent factual study is equally essential to the breeding of new generations of scientific knowledge. (1973, p. 21)

The purpose of Child's book is to further the rapprochement between humanistic and traditional psychology in the direction of what I have termed functional phenomenology, and he points to the significant contributions of Jean Piaget and Lawrence Kohlberg in his own field of developmental psychology as models of what he has in mind. His criticism of the existing state of affairs reiterates the earlier comments of Sigmund Koch (1964), who boldly forecast the death of rigid behaviorism, but has been equally vehement in castigating humanistic psychologists for their lack of precision in defining and quantifying the variables they have proposed for study.

What Koch and Child are proposing is precisely the aim I see embodied in the continuing efforts of the functional phenomenologists. I am in basic agreement with the position that furthers the maintenance of *both* paradigms in psychology and that sees them as supplementary in nature. In the next chapter, I will present arguments in favor of the goal of measurement for phenomenological investigation and for my belief that the type of reductionism here involved is not as pernicious as other forms that have characterized psychology in the past, and may indeed even be necessary for the further development of a truly scientific phenomenology.

This more moderate position is well represented in a statement by Gardner Murphy:

> The year 2000 can come, and the 21st century can offer less terror and more joy, but only if psychologists have learned both how to look inside and how to look outside, how to recognize the reciprocities of inner and outer, through methods that are as far-ranging and as deeply human as is the human stuff that is being studied. (In Misiak & Sexton, 1973, p. 135.)

## SCIENCE AND PHENOMENOLOGY

The distinction just made between radical and moderate phenomenological programs and their suggested application to the science of psychology underlines my contention that humanistic-existential psychology is by no means a monolithic movement. The controversy, involving as it does basic methodological approaches, is a serious one. Both sides will undoubtedly continue to press their claims, and as far as I am concerned, this is all to the good. Psychology stands to benefit in the process, however the controversy is resolved. The discovery of new methods and new techniques of investigation always injects new life into the very bloodstream of scientific endeavor. The efforts now going forward bear much promise in that they encompass topics of supreme importance for psychology: the mysterious phenomena of consciousness itself and their relationships to human behavior.

History will again be the arbiter in deciding which view, radical or moderate, will prevail. The outcome will also determine some answers to the questions proposed earlier in this chapter. The discussion that followed their presentation suggests these further observations.

1. It does now seem possible to conduct a scientific analysis of conscious phenomena with greater success than was feasible for the 19th-century introspectionists. Structural phenomenologists have already begun to apply an empirical version of the newer phenomenological methods developed in philosophical circles with which the early introspectionists were unacquainted. (For some recent examples, see Giorgi, Fischer, & Eckartsberg [1971–]; van den Berg [1972; 1974]; and Valle & King [1978].) This approach has already proved to be fruitful and suggestive, as we have seen, for a descriptive science of psychopathological states of consciousness. And there is no reason why it cannot also be applied with equal success to other altered states as well.

Functional phenomenologists point to the fact that the introspectionism of the 19th century was not all that unsuccessful. Where careful scaling techniques were evolved, introspectionism contributed much to the general psychology of sensation and perception. The fault with introspectionism lay primarily in its naturalistic assumptions, its focus on the *contents* of consciousness, and the attempt to reduce these to simpler elements. The focus should rather be shifted again to functional relationships between conscious and other phenomena through the development of newer, more sophisticated scaling techniques similar to those already developed for perceptual psychology but applicable to other areas of investigation, such as self-constructs, cognitive strategies, or a number of other purely experiential variables. In fact, this is currently being done. A recent article surveys research of this type and suggests guidelines for its further development (Price & Barrell, 1980, pp. 75–95).

2.   Radical phenomenologists do propose some very drastic alterations in the definition of science as it is usually presented by its present-day orthodox adherents, at least where the human sciences are concerned. Their own adherence to phenomenological philosophy is total. The philosophy of science, in their view, should be derived exclusively from this philosophical position, which they believe has rendered logical positivism, the previous base, obsolete and passé. Current scientific goals of strict objectivity and precise measurement would be altered in the process. As Giorgi points out, quoting Strasser, "objectivity" does not mean "no subject" in phenomenological philosophy. It can and does often mean "interpersonal" or "intersubjective" knowledge, not purely personal knowledge. He therefore suggests the use of the term *accuracy* in place of objectivity as a goal for scientific knowledge (Giorgi, 1970, p. 122).

Measurement would be, as we have seen, a peripheral concern in the new psychology as in other human sciences, since measurement reduces the qualitative richness of human experience to mere numbers resulting in a severe loss of vital information.

The moderate approach would not drastically alter our present-day view of what constitutes orthodox science but would simply modify or stretch it to include phenomenological variables. The aims of strict objectivity and public observation would be abandoned or at least supplemented by inclusion of inner experience as a valid topic of investigation, and intersubjective validation substituted where necessary, as suggested by Carl Rogers (Coulson & Rogers, 1968), and by Charles Tart (1972) in his proposal for state-specific sciences. But this is done rather in the spirit of accommodating new data than in proposing a totally new paradigm for all psychological investigation. Measurement, where possible, remains for these authors an important criterion for scientific sophistication.

3.   Radical phenomenologists do indeed favor the abandonment of the natural science paradigm in favor of a new one based upon a thoroughgoing phenomenological stance. Giorgi, for example, is quite aware of the changes that have occurred within the more traditional model since it was first adopted in the 19th century, but he leaves no doubt in the reader's mind that for him at least this is not sufficient. He rejects the view that the problem for psychology is simply one of cultural lag. Psychology, in his view, needs to do much more than keep abreast of current developments, philosophical or otherwise, in the natural sciences, such as physics, or even the life sciences, such as biology.

> In the latter cases psychology would still be *imitating* other approaches rather than defining its field for itself; it would still be merely *accepting* a

world view rather than constituting its own world view based upon its intrinsic questions and its own data. (Giorgi, 1970, p. 124)

## Coexistence: The moderate approach

Moderates, as we have seen, opt for coexistence, and are much less likely to peg their own endeavors to any one philosophical position. If a philosophically derived paradigm, such as the natural science model proposed by logical positivism, gets in their way, they do not hesitate to abandon it in order to justify their own concern for the inclusion of conscious experience and phenomena as legitimate topics of inquiry. The behavioristic program, for some of the moderates at least, is seen as a valuable complement to their own work, and they do not hesitate to derive inspiration and ideas from the various psychoanalytic schools of thought while remaining critical of the exclusivity and priority claimed by these respective approaches for our understanding of human experience and behavior.

Finally, while most moderates would presumably agree with Giorgi's statement, "To assume that objectivity necessitates measurement is to confuse degree of determinateness with objectivity" (1970, p. 118), they still aspire to as high a degree of determinateness or precision as possible in their own work and continue to pioneer new techniques for the expression of functional relationships between conscious and other phenomena.

Their own answer to the question, Can we have a *science* of conscious phenomena? is a resounding yes. The ultimate answer, of course, depends on how the scientific community continues to define science. If it can accept the definition of science as the establishment of stable patterns of relationships among *any* phenomena from which we can get reliable and, where possible, measurable information, then the moderate approach as outlined here can be rather easily accommodated and recognized under currently prevailing scientific norms. Radical phenomenologists, as we have seen, represent a more serious threat to the scientific establishment and are less likely to be welcomed with open arms.

My own bias is toward the moderate approach. I prefer not to peg psychology to phenomenological philosophy any more than to logical positivism or to any other philosophical position. I have my own presuppositions and convictions, because, as a human being, I philosophize, too. But I do agree with the more radical humanists that, for a complete science of human behavior, we need to tackle head-on the species-specific attribute of self-reflective consciousness. This, in my view, is *the* human phenomenon par excellence, not self-determination or autonomy as presented by B. F. Skinner in his attack on humanistic proposals for psychology. Self-determination is properly a *derivative* of the attribute peculiar to a self-reflective organism. Philosophers will undoubtedly continue to speculate on the implications of this all-important human phenomenon through their own methods of inquiry. New philosophical movements may well develop as a consequence, as they have repeatedly in the past.

Sigmund Koch has alerted psychologists to the promising contributions, for example, of modern linguistic analysis, an approach to the philosophy of meaning which is both critical of logical positivism and its influence on the philosophy of science and supportive of a more subjective and experiential approach:

> But even more directly relevant to the issue at hand, certain former positivists (e.g., Carnap, Feigl) have decreed—if only guardedly—a relegitimization of *introspection*. Thus Carnap, in 1956, rather grudgingly points out:
> "Although many of the alleged results of introspection were indeed questionable, a person's awareness of his own state of imagining, feeling, etc., must be recognized as a kind of observation, in principle not different from external observation, and therefore as a legitimate source of knowledge, though limited by its subjective character." (1964, p. 22)

Later works quoted by Koch have gone far beyond these first timid breaks with the positivism of the past and have already influenced the so-called hard sciences far more than most psychologists realize. More recently, the "critical realism" of Fernand van Steenberghen (1970) and other neo-Scholastics and the "transcendental realism" of the British neo-Marxist philosopher Roy Bhaskar (1979) provide new perspectives, both critical of logical positivism and pure phenomenalism, on the philosophy of social science.

It would seem, therefore, that psychologists need to keep abreast of current philosophical movements, particularly as they affect the philosophy of science that underpins their own continuing efforts. Koch even argues that psychology as a science should be contributing more to this ongoing dialogue than it has in the past. But in my view, it would be just as big a mistake to put all our eggs in one philosophical basket as it is to neglect what philosophers of various schools have to say about the nature of human knowledge and the role of conscious experience.

If the subject of our investgations is human functioning, we are in a privileged position. We have seen that there is sufficient justification from current philosophies of science not to limit ourselves to the investigation of so-called objective phenomena, as we are forced to do in respect to inanimate, nonconscious objects. The effort to do so may continue to be highly instructive, but the application of scientific methods and discipline to the study of conscious phenomena is a needed and promising corrective to the limited programs of the past.

## PREDICTION AND CONTROL

A final brief word needs to be said concerning prediction and control as significant aims in science. It is certainly true that, as scientific understanding of a subject matter progresses, the ability to predict and control outcomes in respect to that subject matter increases enormously. This is generally seen as a highly desirable consequence of continuing scientific investigation, though not an essential ingredient in the definition of science as such. An example has already been given from the field of geology. Paleontology and astronomy might also be cited as instances of recognized scientific fields where control of the events studied is, to say the least, a highly remote possibility.

What of psychology? Are prediction and control of human behavior possible and legitimate aims for psychological science? My answer would be yes and no. Even in physics, considered popularly to be the most precise of the sciences, accurate prediction is not always possible. We need only be reminded of the Heisenberg principle in subatomic physics to substantiate that statement. The problem for psychology is magnified by the possibility of a limited degree of personal freedom in the conduct of human affairs, but more will be said of this in the chapter on self-determination. There it will be argued that predictability is still possible to some extent, not only in a broad statistical sense for larger groups of subjects but even where individual subjects are concerned, provided we accept the possibility that the self may be considered another teleological agent of change in the causal sequence of events. This implies a deeper understanding of the individuals involved in such sequences, a difficult but not impossible task.

Where control is concerned, the issue is more complex. At first blush, humanistic psychologists would not agree that control of human behavior is a legitimate aim for psychological science. Maslow states that the aim of humanistic science is to *release* the individual from external controls; to make him or her freer, more creative, more inner-determined, less predictable to the observer, though perhaps more predictable to self (1966, p. 40). Sidney Jourard reaffirms that goal:

> A humanistic psychologist, like his less humanistic colleagues, is concerned to identify factors that affect man's experience and action, but his aim is not to render man predictable to, and controllable by, somebody else. Rather, his aim is to understand how determining variables function, in order that man might be liberated from their impact as he pursues his own free projects. (1967, p. 109)

I am sure that other humanists would agree that personal liberation, not control, is a principal aim of their endeavors. Carl Rogers's person-centered approach (1977) is another striking example of this view, as is the stance toward the science of sociology advocated by Peter Berger

(1963). All humanists vehemently object to B. F. Skinner's proposals for a society completely engineered by an elite corps of behavioral specialists, as well as to the pessimistic, unyielding determinism of the Freudian view of human nature.

What they seem to be objecting to, however, is the employment of psychological understanding for the control of individuals *by others*. Most humanists, I feel, would agree with the statement that the fruits of psychological understanding ought to be made available to all individuals so they might exercise greater control over their own personal destinies. Behaviorism and depth psychology can be of significant aid in such a project by helping the individual understand how he or she has been conditioned in the past by contingencies of reinforcement or unconscious influences beyond personal control or awareness, how these influences continue to operate, and how they can be incorporated and managed for greater self-control in the future. In this sense, knowledge of psychological principles is like knowledge of nuclear energy. Both can be used for good or ill. Control of human functioning is not only a possible aim for psychological science, but a legitimate one if returned to its human subjects.

# 5 Holism versus Reductionism

Many images have been etched on the consciousness of modern men and women by the powerful media of communication at our disposal. One of the most vivid of these must surely be the moon rocket. The thunderous sound of the blast-off rings in all our ears. The majestic, incredible sight of that metallic skyscraper poised above its launching pad, slowly gathering momentum and flaming off into the heavens is one we can all recall at will. The eerie vision of the astronauts hopping across the barren surface of the moon seems so unreal that it boggles our imagination.

What also boggles the imagination, of course, is the enormous amount of money, technological skills, and organization that has been poured into our space exploration program. Many dispute the assignment of so many of our national resources to this particular program when other domestic problems remain unsolved and grow steadily worse. But the question remains: why this prodigious expenditure of effort and money to explore the moon and eventually the outermost reaches of space? What is it that motivates us and captures our imagination, perhaps even in spite of ourselves?

I suppose a Freudian analyst would have a field day with this phenomenon. The rocket: a phallic symbol reaching out to penetrate the virgin moon. Aggressive male sexuality seeking to capture the trembling heavens in its passionate embrace and subdue them to its will. After all, space exploration is predominantly a male enterprise. A virile, young president set the program into motion. There were no female astronauts at first, and who remembers the few female technicians at Mission Control?

I am not just being facetious in presenting this amateur analysis. Sigmund Freud, in his *Civilization and Its Discontents* (1961), proposed the thesis that all human endeavors, including science and technology as well as art, literature, philosophy, and religion, can be traced back to one of two basic biological instincts: sex and aggression. The rise and progress of human civilization, he believed, are to be explained by virtue of the fact that society, in order to survive, must curb the natural expression of these instincts. Human sexuality and aggressiveness must therefore find other creative outlets through the process of sublimation. But since biological drives require biological objects and activities for their full gratification, sublimated activities provide only partial satisfaction. Surplus energy continues to accumulate, and so civilization continues to expand and grow, restlessly seeking new worlds to conquer—new socially acceptable safety valves to serve as outlets for the biological forces that drive us on.

I do not wish to deny the insightfulness of the Freudian explanation of human endeavor. Aside from its drama and daring, it contains, I suspect, more than a grain of truth. What I object to, along with other humanistic psychologists, is its unquestioning assumption of reductionism, an assumption which is also explicitly or implicitly accepted by contemporary behaviorism and which is therefore so characteristic of modern psychology. I propose to examine that assumption in some detail, to expose the damaging effects it has had on the scientific investigation of human behavior, and to suggest what I consider to be some promising alternatives.

## VARIETIES OF REDUCTIONISM

There are, in reality, two forms of reductionism prevalent in the contemporary sciences of man.

1.  The belief that all sentences describing social and psychological events in a lawful way (so-called sociological and psychological laws) will eventually be reducible to sentences describing physiological (neural) events. These, in turn, will someday be reducible to sentences describing the physical and chemical events which underlie all reality in the universe at large. Because of the complexity of social and psychological events, dependent as they are on such highly evolved neural structures, this step-by-step reduction to the simpler, more parsimonious laws of physics and chemistry will obviously not occur overnight. Sociology, psychology, and the other sciences of human behavior are therefore justified in developing their own language of discourse, separate from the other, more basic sciences of matter, for strategic purposes. They must maintain their own autonomy until enough data has been collected and unified to make the reductive

procedure possible. The ultimate goal, however, must always be kept in mind: the unification of all science through the basic mathematical language of physics and chemistry and the concurrent reduction of all interactions to their physicochemical components.

This is indeed an ambitious prospectus for science. That it is no mere pipe dream is illustrated by the publication of the *International Encyclopedia of Unified Science* (1970), an overt attempt to begin implementation of just such a project.

Because of the first step involved in this process, I shall call this approach *biological reductionism* and attempt to demonstrate how it pervades both modern behaviorism and Freudian psychoanalysis and with what consequences. It seems impossible to escape the conviction that an unblushingly materialistic philosophy underlies this particular stance toward science, a materialistic monism as crude in its own way as the assertions of the 17th-century British empiricist Thomas Hobbes.

2. A second, quite different variety of reductionism is found in the persistent attempt to reduce the qualitative aspects of human behavior, including conscious behavior, to quantifiable phenomena. A simple illustration would be the measurable components of the experience of light, color, and sound, such as wavelength, intensity, and threshold values. This is a less crude form of reductionism, motivated more by a concern for scientific rigor than by any necessary philosophical presuppositions. It can be, and often is, simply a methodological strategy which need not involve a denial of its limits in representing the data of reality as best it can, while retaining an awareness that much of reality's inherent richness is left aside in the process.

The following fragment of dialogue between Carl Rogers and Gordon Hall clearly reflects this awareness and the dilemma it poses for those who wish to construct a more complete science of man:

**Hall:** I have a feeling that you get your sense of reductionism from your experience of trying to study therapy after having been in the experience of therapy; and that somehow taking measures of self-concept and getting ratings of segments of tape, etc., really loses sight of what it was like.

**Rogers:** I guess that probably is part of my frustration: wondering how the hell you can have a non-reductionistic approach to such an experience and yet still—because I do have some liking for the term—still have it scientific. (Coulson & Rogers, 1968, pp. 162–163)

The point I will try to make is that we probably cannot have a purely nonreductionistic science in this sense of reductionism but that we can and should repudiate the biological form. For clarity's sake, I shall term this second form *mathematical reductionism*—the reduction of qualitative aspects of human experience, wherever possible, to quantitative terms. While not the essence of the scientific approach, it certainly represents its most sophisticated and stable expression. As long as scientists realize its intrinsic limitations (its inability to encompass the full richness of reality and human experience), it can serve a most useful and valuable purpose.

## BIOLOGICAL REDUCTIONISM

It should be clear by now that I regard the viewpoint of biological reductionism as intrinsically damaging to the science of psychology. It presents a nothing-but view of man by simply assuming a crudely mechanistic philosophy of reality. By refusing to accept any sort of qualitative distinctions between inorganic matter, organic systems, and conscious life, it must necessarily consider human consciousness a nuisance, a mere epiphenomenon (an "oozing of the brain," one author, whose name I have repressed, called it) accompanying the much more important interaction of complex, highly evolved neural structures which are ultimately reducible to their physicochemical components. Matter, in this system, is not unlike the nonconscious "dead" matter of the 17th-century mechanists. Its evolution into ever more complex structures is rigidly determined by its basic properties. Some make explicit the implication that the appearance of what we term *life* is a fortuitous event, a highly improbable accident arising from the chance juxtaposition of certain molecular arrangements with certain unusual environmental conditions.

My purpose here is not to enter into this age-old philosophical dispute but merely to point out that it *is* a philosophical dispute and that both previous forces in contemporary psychology simply opted, because of the prevailing zeitgeist, for the mechanistic view.

### The behavioral position

In behaviorism, biological reductionism is clearly seen in the assumption that all so-called higher human drives are eventually reducible to tissue-needs. Such an assumption is quite explicit in the works of Clark Hull and implicit in the writings of B. F. Skinner. In Hull's drive-reduction theory (1952), the only innate, given drives in the human organism are physiological ones: hunger, thirst, sex, pain avoidance, and other drives required for biological survival. These are the so-called primary drives, arising from tissue-needs generally involving an uncomfortable tension-state as the organism seeks to enhance and reproduce itself. All other drives that motivate human behavior, the so-called social drives (for recognition, belongingness, love, power, self-esteem, and knowledge itself), for example, are ultimately reducible to these primary physiological drives, and are therefore termed *secondary, acquired,* or *learned.* The principle by which this is accomplished is the process of *secondary reinforcement*, the conditioning process by which, pyramidlike, new drives can be built up on natural drives through association with their satisfaction.

The drive for affiliation with others in society, then, presumably arises because such affiliation proves successful in maintaining a set of circumstances in which the primary drives are well assured of gratification. Gordon Allport (1961), impressed as was Hull by the fact that such secondary drives normally become predominant in adult human life, granted them "functional autonomy." By this he meant that in ordinary human behavior they come to function *as if* independent of their physiological origins, so much so, in certain cases at least, that an individual might pursue satisfaction of a social need to the detriment of his or her physiological survival. He did not seem to have realized that by merely labeling this strange phenomenon, he by no means explained it but clung instead to the basic assumption of reductionism. He did manage, however, to soften its impact. Psychologists could at least begin to study these so-called derived states of the organism in their own right, without bending over backward to elaborate their presumed link to physiological sources.

## The Freudian position

The Freudian analytic position is remarkably similar to that of the behaviorists, though derived quite independently. Many neobehaviorists, in fact, were quick to note the resemblance and attempted to translate Freudian concepts into their own more operational terms (Dollard & Miller, 1950). During his later years, Freud (1955) divided all human drives into two major categories: those derived from the life instincts (Eros) and those stemming from the death instinct (Thanatos). He even attempted to link his life and death instincts to the basic physiological process of anabolism and catabolism as described by the German physiologist Gustav Fechner, whose work Freud so admired.

Most of the needs arising from the life instincts (e.g., hunger, thirst, the need for oxygen, and the like) are adequately met by the arrangements of modern civilization for most men and women. Only when human beings by some unusual circumstances are seriously deprived of the physical sustenance they need do these drives assume major importance in motivating their behavior. Freud therefore concentrated most of his attention on the sexual drive, or libido, for it is in response to this drive that society takes strong, restrictive measures in order to prevent its exercise from interfering with the broader welfare of the species. Aggression, Freud felt at this point in his life, stems from the death instinct, which has an equally biological origin. Freud often vacillated in his discussion of the origin and role of aggression in human life, but in no case did he neglect to ascribe it to biological sources.

Freud, like Allport, was keenly aware that many facets of human behavior, such as social, religious, and scientific pursuits, at first blush bear little resemblance to their supposed biological sources. Later, ego-analysts were to ascribe considerable autonomy to ego-functions (such as perception and cognition) in a manner reminiscent of Allport's functional autonomy. Freud, however, stoutly maintained in his brief, later work *The Ego and the Id* (1961) that the ego remains always the servant of the id (the innate biological reservoir of all human driving forces).

In order to explain this apparent anomaly (behavior motivated by apparently nonbiological needs), Freud put forth his concept of *sublimation*. He apparently borrowed the term from chemistry, where it refers to a substance passing from the gaseous to the solid state without passing through the intermediate liquid stage. The properties of the substance in the gaseous state certainly do not resemble its properties and activity in the solid state, and yet they remain the same substance with identical molecular components. The application of this analogy to human behavior is too obvious and too well known to require further elaboration. It served admirably to preserve the basic assumption of biological reductionism.

Freud's explanation of the origin of moral behavior is another case in point: the process whereby the external restrictions imposed by society become incorporated into the individual's superego can be readily translated into the behavioristic principles of reinforcement and from these reduced to the satisfaction of primary, physiological needs.

## The humanistic position

Humanistic psychologists do vary in their explanations of the ultimate origin of human needs. Generally, however, they prefer to adopt a stance that is philosophically open at the top. In keeping with their phenomenological approach to human experience, they tend to look at the data of human behavior as "lived." Many deliberately avoid the temptation to reduce needs and drives to simpler sources, while recognizing that they do indeed exist and operate at several levels simultaneously. Theirs is a more holistic approach, which attempts to keep in focus the rich complexity of human motivation at all levels of functioning. To return to my earlier example of the motivation behind our current efforts to explore and conquer space, the humanistic psychologist might well include in his or her account elements of unconsciously sublimated sexuality and aggression but would also accept the consciously experienced need to explore the unknown, "to unravel the mysteries of space," as even more determinative of our behavior, along with a competitive desire to get there first, which is motivated by psychosocial needs for national prestige and recognition.

Some, such as Viktor Frankl (1965) and James Bugental (1965), are openly antireductionistic in their approach. They clearly imply that certain drives, such as the need to love and the need to know, are species-specific to man, once transformed by consciousness, and therefore deserve study and respect in themselves. Joseph Nuttin (1962), whose position I have presented more thoroughly in a previous chapter as most closely paralleling my own, simply claims, on avowedly philosophical grounds, that higher human needs are irreducible to lower biological ones. I think he is right, probably because I hold similar philosophical views. But to avoid such philosophizing as much as possible, I have proposed a rationale for antireductionism that does not lean for its efficacy on philosophical argumentation but simply substitutes the observation that the phenomenon of self-awareness is the species-specific characteristic of humanity par excellence, and that the mere existence of human consciousness generates its own set of needs and drives irreducible to the biological characteristics shared with other animal organisms. This is as far as I care to go. I am willing to relinquish to philosophers the arguments concerning the source and essential nature of human consciousness. Whether it implies a spiritual principle opposed to the crude materialism of the mechanists or the Chardinian view that sees "matter" and "spirit" differently than did the mechanists and dualists of the 19th century (Pierre Teilhard de Chardin, 1965) does not really concern me as a psychologist.

It should be repeated in passing that the existence of human consciousness is here considered a self-evident phenomenon of experience. It is not a philosophical statement, nor is the establishment of the existence of consciousness in any way a philosophical conclusion. Consciousness is a primal experience without which neither philosophical speculation nor scientific investigation can proceed or be understood. As an experience, it is obviously quite different from the biological phenomena that support it in human beings and that exist without it in lower organisms. My awareness of breathing, for example, is in a class by itself. Respiration can continue without my being aware of it, as when I am in a deep sleep or a coma. Being aware creates its own problems, its own needs and drives, different from basic tissue-needs. And as Maslow indicates, the needs and drives which arise from the existence and functioning of consciousness may be just as "instinctoid" as those which are simply biological.

Many humanists are quite willing to accept the insights of the behaviorists by admitting the possibility that the same laws (e.g., of reinforcement, extinction, generalization, and discrimination) may very well apply to this new set of needs and drives as well. They may also be inclined to accept the Freudian process of sublimation to explain certain apparently higher forms of human behavior, in whole or in part (such as, perhaps, fanatic and almost paranoid devotion to a cause). What they do reject is the nothing-but implications of behavioral and Freudian explanations: "higher" human activities are "nothing-but" the outcomes of secondary reinforcement of primary drives or of the process of sublimation. Humanists and transpersonal psychologists as well feel that we should remain open to the possibility that, where human behavior is concerned, something more than biological forces may be at work, something grounded in the mysterious phenomenon of consciousness itself.

## HOLISM

In contrast to biological or even mathematical reductionism, the holistic approach to the study of personality, so characteristic of humanistic psychology, is difficult to define and even more difficult to implement. By implication, it means studying the individual as a whole, without dissection into part-processes or, where this is unavoidable, without losing sight of the unity which characterizes human experiencing and consciousness. In practice, as one would suspect, holism has many facets, as authors successively attack and seek to strike down the many dichotomies which continually crop up in the psychological literature: mind-body, conscious-unconscious, subject-object, or self and other. I will content myself with presenting a few of the more significant of these facets of the holistic approach and attempt to demonstrate once again the unifying power of the concept of self-awareness as the common thread that unites them all.

Nuttin (1962), as we have seen, proposes three irreducible levels of conscious experience: psychophysiological, psychosocial, and transpersonal. The drive for self-realization and the correlative need for contact with the environment suffuse all three of these levels, resulting in a bewildering array of personal and sometimes conflicting needs and goals. For full growth and personal realization, he warns us, all three levels must be taken into account. No one of them can be substantially neglected without serious detriment to personal functioning as a whole. Obviously, if my physiological needs are not met, I will cease to exist as a biological organism. Unmet psychosocial needs (e.g., for companionship, love, and recognition) will result in a suffocating sense of loneliness or debilitating loss of self-esteem. And if I lose a sense of the meaningfulness of my personal existence in the larger scheme of things, I may well fall prey to one of the existential or noogenic neuroses so graphically described by Frankl and other existential analysts. *All* the data potentially available to my conscious awareness must therefore be appropriated, squarely faced, and somehow harmoniously balanced by me in the ongoing quest for complete personal development. Repressions or distortions at *any* level can interfere with that process and cripple or stunt my growth as a fully human being.

But Nuttin is quick to remind us of his own holistic convictions concerning human personality. Individual needs can be left ungratified, without serious damage, if the person as a whole gains basic satisfaction from his or her existence or life project. And so it is ultimately to the transpersonal level that he or she turns for the possibility of resolving the conflicts that normally arise in the clash of varied personal needs. It is at this level, it appears, that the constructive ideal of personality must be consciously fashioned by the individual and continually checked against the data of his or her ongoing experience.

Nuttin's prescriptions for the development of such a constructive ideal do sound somewhat vague and idealistic, even in the case histories which he presents, but other humanistic authors serve to fill the gaps. Maslow (1970), for example, warns us of the *prepotency* of physiological and social safety-needs in his hierarchical theory of human motivation. These deficiency-needs, or d-needs, *must* be met rather early in the developing organism before the Being-needs (B- or meta-needs) can be expected to emerge. Only then will the individual experience the leisure, so to speak, and the freedom to seek full self-actualization. Maslow would agree, however, that once this has occurred, self-realization results from the self-transcending life projects to which his chosen subjects universally and enthusiastically devoted themselves. Rogers and Perls, in turn, give us a more convincing account of how individuals can come in contact with previously denied or distorted aspects of their experiencing and reclaim them toward a more integral and balanced lifestyle. Their contributions will be presented in greater detail in Chapter 8 but are mentioned here to corroborate Nuttin's view of the process of self-realization.

## THE LIFE–CYCLE APPROACH

Charlotte Bühler, one of the recognized founders of humanistic psychology, adds a further dimension to the concept of holism in the study of human personality:

> As far as the theoretical frame is concerned, wholeness of the personality has to be considered not only horizontally but also longitudinally. We must have concepts and methods to encompass the whole of the life cycle as well as the whole of personality. (1967, p. 86)

Beginning in the 1930s, she devoted her long and distinguished career to the scientific study of such individual life cycles. Working at first with diaries of infant and adolescent development and experience and relating these to the individual's history, she later found methodological support for her efforts in Gordon Allport's monograph, *The Use of Personal Documents in Psychological Science* (1942), his longer systematic exposition of idiographic methods in *Pattern and Growth in Personality* (1961), and in Michael Polanyi's approach to the philosophy of science (1958).

Her conclusions are quintessentially humanistic. Human lives are purposeful, intentional. She agrees with other humanists that we attempt to actualize our individual potentialities, to find personal fulfillment through accomplishing certain things in the world, through self-transcendent goals. When we are fortunate enough to be successful in this venture, our deepest personal needs are satisfied.

Actualization, for Bühler, is a developmental process. The self-image we seek to realize is vague at first but, for some at least, becomes increasingly clear as they become more aware of their own existence, past, present, and future. Something that is seen as meaningful becomes a constituent part of their lives as a whole.

*Intentionality* toward one's life therefore becomes an essential component of the life cycle, consciously or unconsciously; a unifying concept for the understanding of human development.

> Intentionality in these theories (May, 1965; Bugental, 1965) is seen as relating the individual to the whole of his being and of the world. In my own theory, it relates the individual also to the whole of his life and is more concretely involved with his development and with the buildup of his experiences. In all these theories, the meaningfulness of the individual's experience is considered of the essence. (Bühler 1967, p. 87)

Bühler was quite aware of other research programs devoted to the study of life cycles, such as those proposed by Havighurst (1952) for the investigation of developmental tasks and Erikson (1959) for the exploration of psychosocial phases of development, but viewed them as deficient in respect to this unifying concept. While they have provided a good deal of interesting and important data on the human life cycle, they lack this overarching component of intentionality that alone conveys the lived experience of human development. The humanistic psychologist must therefore supplement such studies, important as they are, with idiographic data derived from phenomenological studies of individual lives. For this she prescribed two methods of research:

The use of individual interview and biographical techniques, and their validation along the lines suggested by Gordon Allport (1942).

A number of different techniques, best illustrated in modern humanistic and existential psychotherapy research (Bühler was a noted psychotherapist herself), which involve the idea of *participating experience* (the therapist acting as a participant observer).

These two techniques complement one another. Biographical techniques and interview methods (already a form of participating experience) provide a more comprehensive account of the human life cycle, but psychotherapy often opens up a depth of penetration unavailable to the other methods and can lead to a more comprehensive understanding of the structure of the client's life cycle.

> Psychotherapy, therefore, appears to be the most appropriate technique for this modern research which, through participating experience, tries to understand in depth an individual's self-direction within the total frame of his life cycle. (1967, p. 89)

An excellent illustration of this approach, which met with Gordon Allport's whole-hearted approval, can be found in an early work of Charles Curran (1945), a psychotherapist and educator trained by Carl Rogers at Ohio State.

## THE MIND–BODY DICHOTOMY

Still another facet of the holistic approach to be found in current humanistic psychology is the attempt to overcome the dichotomy or dualism of mind and body that has characterized Western scientific notions since the time of Descartes. Simplistically, this dichotomy proposes that human beings are dualistic creatures, composed of a bodily organism which functions much like a machine inhabited, somewhat uncomfortably, by a spirit or mind that is immaterial in nature and follows its own laws and destiny. Body and mind may interact at times, but their mode of being is basically separate and ultimately incommunicable one to the other.

The literature on this topic is quite extensive, and no attempt will be made here to exhaust it. (This is the "ghost in the machine" view of human nature so ably attacked by B. F. Skinner in his previously quoted discussion of the autonomous man.) I will focus instead on some current concerns as they apply, first of all, to the field of medicine and our concepts of physical and mental disease. The mind-body dichotomy as applied to this field tended to see physical disease as a breakdown of the bodily machine caused by simple deterioration, accident, or injury, or by the invasion of alien bacterial or viral substances. Mental disease, such as schizophrenia, is seen as the product of disordered thought processes probably beginning in early childhood, though a large group of investigators still holds the conviction that such disturbances also have a physiological origin, as yet not completely understood.

The holistic approach attempts to transcend this dichotomy by simply pointing out that conscious experience is always an embodied experience (even in so-called paranormal out-of-the-body reports) and that the entire body is itself the seat of consciousness. It refuses, on the one hand, to reduce the human organism to a machine and, on the other, to idealize the purely rational or cognitive components of consciousness. A typical illustration of how this approach is applied toward a more unitary concept of disease in all its manifestations is provided by the thought of the late humanistic psychologist, Sidney Jourard, in his book *The Transparent Self* (1971).

He begins his provocative discussion of this topic by stating: "There is growing reason to suspect that hope, purpose, meaning, and direction in life produce and maintain wellness, even in the face of stress, whereas demoralization by the events and conditions of daily existence help people become ill" (Jourard, 1971, p. 75). Citing evidence for this position (Schmale, 1958), he then suggests an hypothesis to guide further research: "The hypothesis is that dispiriting events render an organism vulnerable to the always present forces of illness, . . . while inspiriting events mobilize the forces of wellness latent in all organisms" (1971, p. 76).

Sickness is seen by Jourard as both a response and a signal: a response to dispiriting events in an individual's life frame and a signal to him or her of the need for change in the direction of a more meaningful mode of existence. The healthy individual, he hypothesizes, is the one who finds life replete with meaningful relationships and transactions and is flexible enough to accept the challenge of needed change as soon as he or she begins to feel dispirited by the way things are.

Sickness, he concludes, must be treated holistically. There must first of all be faith in the effectiveness of healing rituals—in the transaction with physician or therapist. He suggests the need to study these healing rituals in depth, to identify the psychophysiological mechanisms, the "healing reflexes" within the patient's own organism that are brought into play by such rituals, found in various forms in all societies including our own.

> If we had a program devoted to identification of the factors in the so-called placebo effect, to understanding of the relation of faith to healing, just as we did in the case of the development of polio vaccine, we might learn much that is new about illness and recovery therefrom. (1971, p. 79)

Ultimately, there must be a restructuring of the patient's entire lifestyle so that, following a medical cure, the patient does not return to a way of life that promises to "do him in" all over again. Some of Jourard's suggestions foreshadow the recent development, in humanistic circles, of centers for holistic medicine and of alternative approaches to the treatment of the mentally ill (which will be presented in a later chapter on practical applications); one other is: "In fact, we need a new specialist—one who helps people find new projects when their old ones, the ones which made life livable, have lost meaning" (1971, p. 98).

Jourard's thinking is not unique. Carl Jung had advanced similar notions decades before, and the burgeoning field of psychosomatic medicine (Alexander, 1950) is based on similar propositions, at least where this type of disease is concerned. Jerome Frank's influential study of healing rituals, in his *Persuasion and Healing* (1961), antedates Jourard's own suggestions in this vein. He himself cites another, more contemporary work by David Bakan, *Pain, Disease and Sacrifice* (1968), and, in particular, Bakan's concept of *telic decentralization*, as paralleling his own theory of "dispiritation" or disease as "dis-ease." Bakan's term "refers to a relinquishment of the purposes (telos) that give direction and meaning to a person's life (at the phenomenological level) and isomorphically permit the organization and form of subordinate processes to operate unchecked by the higher centers. He sees such 'decentralization' as a factor in cancer and other physical diseases" (Jourard, 1971, p. 99). Like Jourard, Bakan posits telic decentralization as both a condition for self-destruction and an invitation to growth or further differentiation of an organism or a person.

Here again we see the interpenetration of the levels of conscious experience, together with the basic unity of human personality posited by Nuttin. Frankl and the existential analysts have identified a specific type of neurosis rooted in a loss of meaning on the transpersonal level. Jourard and Bakan suggest that the virulent effects of losses or deficiencies on either the transpersonal or psychosocial level may well extend to the physiological level, also affecting the body's immune system and lowering its resistance or alertness to the agents of physical disease or to the dangers that exist in the environment. (Frankl [1963] also hinted at this possibility, hypothesizing that loss of self-esteem and meaning led to the death of many of his fellow prisoners in the Nazi concentration camps who might otherwise have survived.)

None of these authors would suggest that *all* physical disease or injury should be ascribed to events of a higher psychological order (in fact, the opposite may well hold true in cases where the onset of unavoidable disease or injury may affect an individual's functioning on these other levels as well). However, their hypothesis remains an intriguing one, deserving of further scientific investigation.

## THE CONSCIOUS–UNCONSCIOUS DICHOTOMY

Precisely because of their holistic assumptions concerning the functioning of human personality, humanistic psychologists are generally quite uncomfortable with the rather strict demarcation of conscious and unconscious spheres of activity postulated by the psychoanalytic schools. They are especially critical of the view that the dynamic unconscious represents a personality of its own, often functioning in almost complete opposition to the intentions and goals of its conscious counterpart and therefore of much greater importance than the latter for the explanation and understanding of human behavior. Nor are they happy with the contention of depth psychologists that the contents of the unconscious are so deeply hidden, even in the so-called normal individual, as to be practically inaccessible to him or her without the expert assistance of an analyst versed in highly specialized, esoteric methods of investigation, such as narcoanalysis, hypnoanalysis, dream analysis, or free association.

Many humanistic psychologists with whom I am acquainted attempt to solve the problem by simply dismissing it (as do, of course, most behaviorists), focusing exclusively on conscious functioning and denying or ridiculing the concept of the unconscious. Others, and I would include myself in their number, take very seriously the phenomena uncovered by thousands of analytic investigators and attempt to fashion a new schema or set of constructs and methods to encompass them from a more holistic viewpoint.

Rollo May (1958) puts the issue very nicely. Pointing out that most existential analysts deny the concept of the unconscious because it tends to split the being of the person into parts (being, they hold, is at its core indivisible), he agrees that this cellar view of the concept has indeed led to pernicious results. It allows modern men and women to rationalize their behavior ("my unconscious did it"), to refuse to take responsibility for their own actions.

But Freud, May insists, made a great discovery symbolized in his notion of the unconscious depths of personality. Freud enlarged the sphere of human personality by challenging the Victorian preoccupation with rationalism and voluntarism and pointed to the forgotten, irrational aspects of experience: the hostile and sexual impulses that lie in the depths of personality structure, which we find unacceptable and refuse to admit into the full light of consciousness.

This enlargement of the concept of human personality must not be lost in efforts to restore a more holistic view: the current humanistic-existential emphasis on the basic unity of the human personality.

> Binswanger [a leading existential analyst] remarks that, for the time being, the existential therapists will not be able to dispense with the concept of the unconscious. I would propose, rather, to agree that being is at some point indivisible, that unconsciousness is part of any given being, that the cellar theory of the unconscious is logically wrong and practically unconstructive; but that the meaning of the discovery, namely, the radical enlargement of being, is one of the great contributions of our day and must be retained. (May et al., 1958, p. 91)

### The body as repository

What do humanistic authors, who take the data of unconscious functioning very seriously, offer in place of the traditional analytic perspective? Two somewhat different viewpoints will be mentioned. The first is most clearly represented by Alexander Lowen (1958, 1965, 1967, 1970, 1971, 1972), a student of Wilhelm Reich and founder of a method called *bioenergetics,* which has in turn influenced many Gestalt therapists. Lowen's contention is simply that the body is the repository of the unconscious or, more accurately, those aspects of body functioning, such as posture, breathing, or muscular tension, of which we are ordinarily not aware. We can become aware of them by the use of certain exercises that will force them into consciousness and subsequently allow us to integrate them more completely into our total functioning.

Lowen insists, as do other humanists, that "the individual is a unity and his psychic and somatic functioning are simply different aspects of his unitary being" (1974, p. 266). He is less reductionistic than was Reich (for whom the body *is* the unconscious) but agrees with the latter that the psychic resistances and repressions of classical psychoanalysis, one's "character armor," show up as "bodily armor" in the form of muscular tensions and rigidities. He notes, for example, "Emotions are bodily events; they are, literally, motions or movements within the body that normally result in some outward action" (1974, p. 26).

Unconscious efforts to suppress emotions that, for some reason, are deemed unacceptable to consciousness (such emotions as anger or sexual excitement, for example) are revealed in a chronic spasticity or tension of the muscles normally used to express them. Lowen's own therapeutic approach, called bioenergetics, is twofold:

1.  Through various bodily exercises, to put the subject in touch with these chronic tensions and to release them. This in turn invariably releases the strong emotions or feelings previously bound by the muscular spasticities.
2.  To relate these released feelings to the early conflict situations with which they were associated and subsequently repressed.

This is straightforward analytic therapy and must also be done, according to Lowen, in order to effect enduring personality change.

> But bioenergetics is also an analytic therapy which promotes a patient's understanding of how his difficulties developed and why they remain in force. It differs from other analytic therapies in that the analysis includes the body and its manifestations, as well as the psyche and its productions. (1974, p. 267)

This last statement expresses Lowen's convictions that psychological insight into repression and resistance may not of itself be sufficient. The body is the repository of the unconscious, and direct body-work is often needed to unlock the physical tensions and holding patterns that have become so ingrained in the individual's characteristic stance toward his or her private world of experience. These continue to function, through force of habit, even though the reasons for their existence *are no longer valid*—a point which has been seized upon·by many Gestalt therapists in their insistence on working upon the here-and-now problems of their clients and upon the residual effects of an outmoded past on their present bodily and psychic functioning.

Similar notions and methods have been proposed by Ida Rolf (1972) and Moshe Feldenkrais (1949; 1972) who, along with Lowen, have influenced many humanistic psychologists through workshop presentations at the Esalen Institute in California. William Schutz (1967, 1971) gives a brief account of these and sensory awareness exercises that have been popularized at this noted humanistic center. By all accounts, these techniques are very powerful and effective, though there has been considerable criticism of the outdated 19th-century neurophysiological theories upon which they were originally based. For that reason and because of a lack of extensive supportive research and follow-up studies, such practices remain somewhat controversial, even in humanistic circles. The proliferation and presentation of a wide variety of such techniques at meetings of the Association for Humanistic Psychology alienated several of the more conservative founders of this organization, though many subsequently renewed their memberships.

## The intimate conscious

The second approach to be considered toward the resolution of the conscious-unconscious dichotomy is taken by a group of humanistic authors represented, among others, by Nuttin, Rogers, and Jourard. Less analytic in its origins than "the body is the repository of the unconscious" position just outlined, it relies instead on the typical humanistic-existential starting point of conscious awareness and proceeds from that focus. This position rephrases the analytic question: "Why are certain data of experience so deeply unconscious and practically inaccessible to awareness, while others are so easily admitted into consciousness?" into "Why are such data *not more fully conscious*, and how can we make them so?"

Nuttin is an interesting case in point. Trained in both clinical and experimental psychology, he retained an abiding respect for the contributions of Freud and his successors; but, like Maslow, he remained critical of the attempt to fashion a theory of normal personality on the basis of data provided by the prevailing analytic preoccupation with pathological behavior (or equally by the preoccupation with simpler animal organisms so characteristic of the experimental laboratory).

For an understanding of normal personality development, he suggests, it would be better to replace the analytic view of the unconscious with his own notion of "psychic intimacy," or an "intimate conscious" zone of experience. This more intimate sphere of personality remains accessible to conscious awareness, as evidenced by the fact that we may choose to disclose it to a small circle of family members or close friends, but remains hidden from view in the larger social context within which we generally operate.

> It is a fact that in our culture, at least, one can divide the psychic contents into several layers, belonging either to the "intimate" or to the "public" part of personality. As lived at the most intimate level of personal consciousness, personality is not absolutely identical with the personality which lives and unfolds in the realm of public and social life. (Nuttin, 1962, p. 207)

It is, Nuttin believes, the socialization process which is responsible for creating this division at the core of personal functioning. Taking a developmental perspective, he traces the process whereby a child, experiencing impulses that come into conflict with the image of ideal functioning imposed by its family (reflecting cultural norms), quickly learns to suppress certain forms of behavior from *public* expression. Such impulses and forms of behavior are then relegated to a more or less *private* sphere of consciousness.

The tensions thus generated between the private and public or social aspects of personal functioning, between the "intimate conscious" and the "persona" or public mask developed by the individual, must somehow later be integrated for a balanced and authentic mode of existence. Both are real, and both represent valid and essential aspects of full human functioning. To neglect one at the expense of the other would be equally disastrous.

Nuttin suggests three phases for the potential integration of these differing psychic contents.

1. Self-acceptance. This involves remaining in touch with the intimate sphere of personality and positively accepting it as an integral part of oneself.
2. Identification of those social roles and forms of expression which are most in accord with the data of the intimate conscious.
3. Reduction of antagonism between the two:

> In the course of this stage or aspect of integration, the two spheres succeed in growing together into the unity of a *social ego*, in which the *intimate* part is no longer a frustrated ego and the *social* part no longer a "mask" but a form of expression—always, it is true, incomplete—of the integrated realistic ideal of the personality. (Nuttin, 1962, p. 209)

We must constantly bear in mind that Nuttin is here discussing *normal* personality development. The implication is that under normal circumstances, the data of the private ego remain accessible to consciousness, though they exist on the fringe of awareness, so to speak, while the person is functioning in his or her adopted social roles. The right setting can and will elicit such information and bring it into focus without too much difficulty. Pathology is seen here as the exception not the rule. The psychopathological case would arise only under those conditions where the more immediate social environment has been so punitive or inconsistent in response to the contents of the intimate sphere of consciousness—the forbidden impulses and feelings of the child—that it is forced to distort or deny them entirely. (These incidentally may be of a higher order of experience as well as the lower order described by Freud.) In such cases, they may eventually become truly inaccessible to the individual, or unconscious, though retaining a malignant dynamism in one's life resulting in neurotic or psychotic behavior.

This is a neat compromise, justifying as it does the centering of attention on conscious processes in normal functioning so characteristic of the humanistic approach, while accommodating the analytic view of the unconscious in descriptions of abnormal behavior.

## The Rogerian approach

A remarkably similar approach to the conscious-unconscious dichotomy, though quite independent in its origins, is taken by Carl Rogers and his associates. Seldom if ever does Rogers use the term *unconscious* as a noun, though he often speaks of basic experiences of the organism as being unconscious, denied to awareness, or reaching consciousness in forms that are greatly distorted. (Here, of course, he is speaking of experiences that are potentially admissible to consciousness—certain biological states of the organism are never directly so, though we may gain indirect knowledge of them in other ways.)

Rogers posits a somewhat similar division in the core of personality to explain this phenomenon, again relying on a developmental perspective. The division here is between the inherent actualizing tendency of the organism, defined as "the inherent tendency of the organism to develop all its capacities in ways which serve to maintain or enhance the organism" (Rogers, 1959, p. 196), and the developing self-concept of the child. An "organismic valuing process" accompanies the basic actualizing tendency, enabling the infant "to value positively experiences which he perceives are enhancing his or her organism and to value negatively those experiences which appear contrary to his actualizing tendency" (Meador & Rogers, 1973, p. 130). But this soon begins to work at cross-purposes with other experiences which the child encounters in its phenomenal world and which soon come to be an integral part of its growing self-concept.

These other experiences come from the social or interpersonal sector of the child's phenomenal field and interact with its *need for personal regard*. Rogers postulates, again from clinical data, that this is a particularly potent and universal human need. It can only be satisfied by others and, in the child's case, by those powerful agents of society—its own parents.

Parents do not, of course, value equally all aspects of their children's behavior. In socializing the child to their and society's norms, they will often interdict certain forms of unacceptable behavior and, by implication, the very impulses that are the sources of such behavior. A child raids the cookie jar before dinner. Mother (or father) says: "Put it back—you'll spoil your appetite." The child, frustrated, blurts out: "I hate you! I wish you were dead!" Mother (or father) replies, in an angry, threatening tone: "Don't you *ever* say that again!" The message to the child is loud and clear: such impulses are not acceptable: you are bad, worthless, unacceptable to me when you feel and say such things.

This sort of experience repeated over time leads, Rogers claims, to the introjection of *conditions of worth,* which are frequently at odds with what the child is actually experiencing and therefore with its basic actualizing tendency. They become an integral part of the child's self-concept and come largely to determine its feelings of self-worth. (In our example, this could be prevented by the parent saying to the child, in effect: "I know you're angry with me, and that's understandable and OK, but you can't have the cookie now!") The child's experience of anger is thereby legitimized; behavior alone is interdicted.

At this point in the development of the individual, a divisive bifurcation (Rogers & Wood, 1974, p. 219) occurs in the basic actualizing tendency. The total organism (I would call this *the real self*) continues to seek actualization, to maintain and enhance itself, and to value those experiences that lead in that direction but *so does the self-structure or self-concept.* The vulnerability of the child to the conditions of worth, his or her need for acceptance from parents and other significant individuals, determines the ultimate outcome. The latter process is clung to at the expense of the former. And where the incongruence between the two is particularly large, the seeds of maladjustment are sown.

Rogers, like Nuttin, points to the necessity of overcoming this division at the core of personality for healthy and balanced personality development (both processes, for him, make up the total personality of the individual [1959, p. 526]), and suggests a way out of the impasse.

Rogers in effect, puts flesh on the bones of Nuttin's description of the integration process. What he proposes is that the interpersonal process by which the actualizing tendency originally came to be split into two divergent directions needs to be corrected by another, equally powerful interpersonal process in which the divisive conditions of worth are now absent. In the safe, unthreatening, caring, nonpossessive, empathetic, but genuine relationship of the client-centered approach (or its equivalent in other, more natural relationships), previously denied or distorted experiences will once again emerge into awareness, become accurately symbolized and integrated into the self-concept, and allow the actualizing tendency to operate in a unitary, more holistic way. Harmony will be restored, where before there was division, and the ideal of the fully functioning person (Rogers, 1961) will be approached.

The holistic nature of this account is evident in Rogers's insistence that the actualizing tendency, and the vicissitudes to which it is subject, remains the principal explanatory concept for the understanding of personality development. Unconscious defense mechanisms do develop as a result of the socialization process, but the unconscious does not exist as a separate entity or personality, following its own laws and separate destiny. Further, these unconscious processes can be made available to the individual in an encounter where the therapist or agent of change first enters the conscious, phenomenal world of his or her companion and proceeds, at the companion's pace and by engendering a climate of interpersonal safety, to the enlargement of that person's experience of being.

Noteworthy too is the absence of dependence on the more esoteric methods of the analytic schools for entering the realm of the unconscious. Rogers freely admits that certain conditions must be met for this type of interpersonal communication to occur. But in a project with schizophrenics, whenever they did occur, even if primarily on a nonverbal level, progress was achieved in the predicted direction as measured by various indicators of improvement (Rogers, Gendlin, Kiesler, & Truax, 1967).

### The role of self-disclosure

It is in this context of intimate versus public spheres of consciousness, of lost dimensions of personal existence resulting from the process of socialization, that I would like to fit the research of Sidney Jourard and his associates on the topic of self-disclosure (1958, 1968, 1971). Following a lead suggested by other investigators (Lewin, 1935; Block, 1952; Block & Bennett, 1955), Jourard (1958) hypothesized that "accurate portrayal of the self to others is an identifying criterion of healthy personality, while neurosis is related to inability to know one's 'real self' and to make it known to others." Much of his early work was devoted to the development of reliable self-disclosure questionnaires, rating the amount of disclosure by his subjects on topics of varying personal significance (e.g., attitudes and opinions, tastes and interests, work or studies, money, personality, and body) to different target persons (e.g., mother, father, male friend, female friend, and spouse). Once this had been accomplished, he and his students began to apply this interview schedule to the investigation of certain simpler correlates of reported self-disclosure behavior.

Some interesting results were obtained by this methodological approach, which are reviewed in his book *Self-disclosure: An Experimental Analysis of the Transparent Self* (Jourard, 1971). Unfortunately, his work on this project was cut short by his untimely death, and it cannot be said that he was able completely to confirm his original hypothesis, though the results he did obtain are, at the very least, provocative.

I will content myself with a presentation of two of his research findings and their implications for our present discussion of the effects of the socialization process on the development of an intimate sphere of consciousness and the means by which such private contents can be integrated into total personal functioning.

The first of these is included by Jourard in his discussion of some lethal aspects of the male role in his book *The Transparent Self* (1971). Commenting on the actuarial statistics that indicate an earlier death age for men over women in our society, Jourard analyzes the male role as requiring men to be tough, achieving, objective, and emotionally unexpressive (Parsons & Bales, 1955). And yet, he insists, men are just as capable as women of experiencing the full range of human emotions and feelings. The role, however, demands that the man hide his real self, ultimately from himself as well as from others. Jourard's own research on self-disclosure has shown that men typically reveal less personal information about themselves than women.

> If self-disclosure is an empirical index of openness and if openness is a factor in health and wellness, then research in self-disclosure seems to point to one of the potentially lethal aspects of the male role. Men keep their selves to themselves and impose thereby an added burden of stress beyond that imposed by the exigencies of everyday life. (Jourard, 1971, p. 350)

The parallels here to the ideas advanced by Rogers and Nuttin concerning processes previously labeled *unconscious* seem quite obvious. Another research finding sheds further light on the recovery process, in support of Rogers's views on the effect of therapeutic interpersonal encounter. It has to do with the facilitating effect of *mutual* self-disclosure in such a relationship. Jourard calls this the *dyadic effect* (i.e., disclosure output to a specific target-person is highly correlated to the amount of disclosure input by that same person) (1971, p. 232).

He applies this finding to psychotherapy, urging therapists, following his own practice, to disclose themselves where appropriate to patients. This should in turn encourage authentic self-disclosure from the patient to get in touch with previously denied feelings and impulses that must somehow be integrated into the process of healthy personality development. (Rogers would presumably agree. Personal genuineness is one of the conditions which therapists must provide to facilitate constructive personality change in their clients and, in his view, may well be the most important [Rogers & Wood, 1974].)

## THE SELF–OTHER DICHOTOMY

Fascination with the self as the center of consciousness leads to a dichotomy to which some humanistic psychologists themselves are prone: the self-other dichotomy. The rather narcissistic emphasis on self-realization or actualization, on doing your own thing presumably even at the expense of others (found more in practice than in the writings of humanistic authors) is illustrative of this point. Abraham Maslow, toward the end of his life, reacted strongly to the attempts of others to pervert his own thinking about peak-experiences in that direction (1971, p. 344).

Since this problem will be treated in much greater detail in the chapter on self-transcendence, I will simply summarize here some of the more holistic approaches toward resolving the self-other dichotomy found in a representative sample of humanistic authors.

The existential analysts find a ready solution to the solipsism and narcissism to which an overemphasis on self-consciousness might lead by simply pointing to the philosophical premise upon which their thought is based. Man is "Being-in-the-world" (Binswanger, 1963). Human consciousness necessarily in-tends toward the other and in-cludes it as a given of existence. It essentially contains not only the *Eigenwelt* (own-world or world of the self), but the *Umwelt* (the physi-cal and biological ground of my existence), and the *Mitwelt* (the inter-personal world) with which the self is in constant transaction and without which consciousness itself could not exist.

Rogers (1959), on his own terms, seems to be in complete accord with this position. His account of the development of the self-structure and self-concept necessarily entails an ongoing interaction with significant others, and it is the caring encounter with the other that facilitates personal growth. Nuttin (1962) and Jourard (1971), as we have seen, certainly agree.

Some humanists have turned to Eastern philosophies in their at-tempts to overcome the self-other dichotomy. Eastern thought is rich in notions concerning the illusory nature of the "skin-encapsulated ego" (Watts, 1961). The various Eastern ways of liberation seem united in their attempts to so free the individual of such illusions that he or she may attain the transcendental state of cosmic consciousness (Murphy & Murphy, 1968; Tart, 1975). Jung (1959) and Assagioli (1965), from a more Western perspective, speak of an archetypal or superconscious

Self, transcending the personal ego, with which we must integrate our personal identities in order, paradoxically, to reach full individuation.

The common thread in all these efforts to transcend the dichotomy of self and other seems to be, to paraphrase the biblical adage: we must lose ourselves in order to find true self-fulfillment. This can be done unconsciously, of course, as well as consciously. The immersion of self in a transcendent cause (found, for example, in totalitarian societies), can bring with it a sense of personal fulfillment in working toward "the new society." But where this occurs as a result of social conditioning, humanists would insist, the results are never as satisfying to the individual or to society in general as when self-transcendence proceeds from a conscious, examined choice based on all the data of personal experiencing.

## COMMON THREAD

This leads us to another common thread that unites all the various facets of the humanistic holistic approach concerning the levels of conscious experience, the life cycle itself, the body-mind, conscious-unconscious, and self-other dichotomies I have been describing. The common emphasis throughout all these efforts is on the necessity of including *all* aspects of existence or experience in conscious awareness, trusting that in so doing, the individual will move toward full personal development and integration in ways that will benefit not only oneself but society as a whole.

In particular, where the theoretical attempts to resolve the conscious-unconscious dichotomy are concerned, I personally remain somewhat dissatisfied. I suspect, from personal exposure to Jungian methods and ideas, that there is more to the unconscious, even under normal circumstances, than psychic contents relegated to an intimate, private sphere by the mere process of socialization. The "other" may be more mysterious than the "significant others" referred to in this account, and I prefer to keep an open mind on this possibility. But if such experiences are there, it remains true to say that the aim of the humanistic approach applies here, also: to include them among the data that require integration toward full human development.

## MATHEMATICAL REDUCTIONISM

If we grant that human needs and drives exist at levels that may be, in fact, irreducible to other, lower levels of functioning, and if these higher needs and drives are generated in the basically private domain of individual human consciousness, inaccessible to direct observation of others, we are brought right back to the problem discussed in the previous chapter: can such phenomena be studied scientifically? It would be easy to dismiss this problem by appealing to the old adage of logic: "*ab esse ad posse valet illatio*" (one can infer the possibility of something from its existence). In this case: people are doing it, therefore it can be done. A further examination of the issues, however, may prove instructive.

Earlier in this chapter, I proposed a distinction between biological and mathematical reductionism. If biological reductionism (and the further reduction to physicochemical laws) is held to be essential to the scientific enterprise, then the study of consciousness as a phenomenon in itself is ultimately unscientific and even meaningless. (Proximately, it might be considered a legitimate scientific venture for an intermediate stage of knowledge, if the proponents of this view did not also insist that all scientific data must be public, or directly observable.)

Mathematical reductionism, on the other hand, is simply the attempt to reduce all aspects of experience, where possible, to quantifiable terms. (The scientist who maintains that *only* the quantifiable aspects of reality can be said to exist is philosophizing: such a philosophical position has been called scientism and need not concern us here.) This is a strategic approach to knowledge of reality which can properly be called scientific as opposed to philosophical, theological, or aesthetic.

The scientist, for example, is confronted by the phenomenon of sound. The scope of his or her inquiry is restricted to relating this phenomenon to other natural phenomena. Vibrating objects, the scientist discovers, affect the surrounding medium in wavelike form. These waves in turn strike the structures of the ear to set off neural impulses to a certain area of the brain. Throughout the process, he or she attempts to establish *functional* relationships expressed as accurately as possible in mathematical form, between the phenomena involved. Number of cycles per second is related to pitch; harmonic relations are expressed in mathematical terms. If the scientist cannot somehow explain the aesthetic experience of harmony in some form of mathematical relationship, he or she simply leaves it alone. The nonmeasurable (strictly qualitative) aspects of reality are considered beyond the scope of the investigations.

In this view, science consists in the discovery of reliable functional relationships between phenomena (the term *functional* is borrowed directly from mathematics, as in $y$ is a function of $x$, and implies the aim of measurement.) What cannot somehow be quantified, therefore, is considered outside the scope of science.

Certainly an experience, any experience, is reduced by this process. But as a behaviorist colleague once pointed out to me, a purely phenomenological description of an experience also "reduces" it—to words. If the phenomenologist wishes to place ultimate value on the experience itself, he or she should say nothing about it. I think my colleague was right. Any "word" about an experience (scientific, philosophical, theological, or purely descriptive) impoverishes the full experience *as lived*. Possibly, it can never be exhausted. It can only be approached by talking or thinking about it. (Gendlin [1973] describes a type of verbal interaction that succeeds in "carrying forward" for the subject the meaning implicit in the raw, felt experience, but this does not obviate the fact that the experience itself is not exhausted in such a process.)

The scientific "word," in one sense, impoverishes the experience even more than other approaches by focusing on only the quantifiable aspects of it. And yet it may lead to valid discovery of certain aspects of the experience as given (i.e., the *ordered, patterned* aspects of relationships *uncovered* by letting the phenomena reveal themselves).

That we can propose a science of human behavior in this sense has been demonstrated quite clearly by the behaviorists. The problem remains: can we include in this project the data of human consciousness, data that are not *directly* observable? As pointed out in the previous chapter, I see no difficulty in doing so if we define science simply as the attempt to establish reliable functional relationships between the phenomena of experience. Our measurements of conscious phenomena, as they relate to each other and to other natural phenomena, may necessarily be more crude and unreliable, less precise and exact. But if it can be done at all, the payoff may be enormous in terms of relevance, increased understanding of human behavior, and improved ability to make meaningful statements about problems of universal human concern.

To obtain the data reported in the preceding chapter on the relationship between self-concept, self-ideal, and personal adjustment, Rogers and his colleagues (Rogers & Dymond, 1954) had to depend for the most part on reports from their subjects of their own conscious appraisal of themselves in response to items such as "I am the kind of person who . . . ." or "I would like to be the kind of person who. . . ." Such data, when correlated, proved quite reliable in predicting, in somewhat surprising ways, to an external criterion of adjustment. Clearly, we know more about an important human concern than we did before, or if we knew of this relationship before the experiment was performed, we now know it more reliably. It is hard to see how such data could ever have been gathered through purely external observational techniques.

Behaviorists criticize such experiments on the grounds that they merely establish an R-R relationship (one set of responses is related to another set) instead of an S-R approach (where stimuli, deliberately manipulated in a controlled way by the experimenter, are related to responses). Granted that this approach does not exemplify the ideal form of scientific investigation, the strictly controlled laboratory experiment (and aside from the fact that behaviorists in their own research often use the terms *stimulus* and *response* in highly questionable ways [Breger & McGaugh, 1973]), it does often succeed in establishing empirical relationships that are often quite enlightening and useful.

More recently, researchers have been studying the relationship between certain states of consciousness produced, for example, by Zen meditation exercises and the output of alpha brain waves (Kasamatsu & Hirai, 1966). This has led to further investigation exploring the possibility, through immediate feedback processes, of teaching human subjects to produce alpha waves at will and even to control certain other autonomic functions of the body. Here, in particular, we find a close correspondence between certain conscious states of mind, as produced and reported by experimental subjects, and other natural phenomena, in this case of a physiological nature. A more refined type of measurement is already possible, and the relationships being established are of a truly functional and empirical variety.

In Chapter 1 during the discussion of transpersonal psychology, I mentioned that Charles Tart (1969, 1975) has even proposed the notion that we might eventually find ourselves establishing state-dependent sciences. Under such a proposal, subjects who experience states of consciousness other than what is usually characterized as normal, whether through biofeedback training, meditation, drugs, or hypnotic trances, would be especially trained in the art of scientific observation to report on the phenomena they encounter and to test hypothesized relationships that occur in such altered states. Normal consciousness, it was there suggested, needs to be thoroughly explored by such means also.

This procedure should not be construed as a return to the instrospectionist approach that captured so much attention in the early history of empirical psychology. The introspectionists of the Würzburg school were primarily interested, as we have seen, in identifying the basic *structures* and *contents* of consciousness, such as the differences between sensation, perception, imagery, and thought (imageless or otherwise), determining tendencies, and whatever other elements of consciousness might be discoverable. The results of their efforts are of more use to epistemologists and phenomenological philosophers than to scientists. Because they paid so little attention to a search for functional relationships between the phenomena of consciousness and to the problem of quantification, except for their psychophysical experiments, their methodology proved to be a poor basis for scientific psychology and was subsequently dropped. Depth psychology often limits its scientific viability by a similar attempt to delineate the underlying structure of the unconscious, as in Freud's constructs of id, ego, and superego. Such structuralizing may have definite heuristic value for psychotherapists and philosophers, but it resists incorporation into the necessary mathematical reductionism that characterizes the scientific strategy.

Humanistic psychologists, particularly in the American camp of the movement, tend to avoid this kind of structural phenomenology in favor of a more functional one. Some of the qualitative richness of conscious experience may be lost in the process, as Rogers complains, but at least the phenomenon of human consciousness is becoming a respectable topic in scientific circles after having been relegated to the outer reaches of metaphysics and mysticism for so many decades. The prospects for developing a true science of human consciousness are bright. If this project has any success, a wealth of reliable and highly relevant data concerning human behavior, previously lacking because of our methodological shortsightedness, will be made available to us. This could be a quantum leap in the behavioral and social sciences of enormous importance.

# 6 The Actualizing Tendency

Life is a wondrous thing, a thing of mystery and beauty; tenacious, hardy, greedy for survival and growth. The myriad means it has developed to adapt itself and subsist in a hostile environment are the delight of biologists, the wonder of poets. Its bewildering, infinitely various forms stagger the imagination; its fantastic profusion and complexity are the despair of the mind that tries to comprehend.

What distinguishes life from the nonliving, the "dead" matter of the rest of creation? Scientists tell us that, in contrast to inanimate compounds, life is an open system, balanced in a precarious equilibrium with the environment in which it is immersed, deriving from it the energy and the materials it needs to fashion the complicated stuff of its existence.

Inanimate matter, from molecules to mountains, forms a closed system, jealously hoarding the energy with which it was initially endowed. It seals itself off from its environment, exchanging nothing with it, dumb and passive, until the merciless onslaught of external forces tears down its structure, unlocks its energy, and scatters it to the winds.

Plant a stick in the ground. If the wood cells are dead, the stick stands, mute and impotent. Wind and sun leach the moisture from it, erode its surface, leave it dry and cracked and brittle. Living things entwine themselves around it or burrow into it and suck from it what they need. Slowly but inexorably what remains will crumble into dust and mingle with the soil or be blown away by a vagrant breeze.

But if a spark of life lingers within it, an astounding thing will happen. Tiny tendrils will sprout from its base and drink the moisture from the soil. The few living cells will absorb carbon dioxide and sunlight from the surrounding atmosphere, and the mysterious chemistry of life will be renewed. New cells will form and combine, and burst into stronger roots, shoots, and branches and leaves. And from this slim rod a sturdy tree may grow and subsist for years.

Truly life is a remarkable thing. And human life is the most remarkable of all. The attribute of self-consciousness alone is enough to stamp us as unique among all other living creatures, enriching our lives and, at the same time, complicating them enormously. We have already discussed the distinct planes of conscious experience on which we function: the psychophysiological, psychosocial, and transpersonal. But these are relatively static descriptors. We need now to consider the dynamic force that urges us on to activity at all three levels of experience, the basic driving force that energizes the complex apparatus of our particular form of life.

## NEEDS AND DRIVES

I speak of this dynamic force as singular. This accords with the practice of most humanistic authors in their commitment to a holistic approach to the description of human experience and behavior. In particular, it emphasizes the belief that a single organizing principle can be found to account for the complex domain of human motivation. Such a principle has been called by various names: the "actualizing tendency" (Rogers), the "drive toward self-realization" (Goldstein, Nuttin), the "drive toward self-actualization" (Maslow), but the basic concept is the same. All these terms imply an intrinsic principle of growth, an unfolding toward some as yet unrealized state of completion, a self-regulating process that leads to an ever more complex integration of developing functions. The biological analogies are clear and often explicitly made: the acorn and the oak, the embryo and the adult organism. In each case we are given the sense of a set of potentialities genetically given at birth (or fertilization) which simply require the provision of proper environmental conditions for their actualization.

At first glance, this account seems to be a reversal of prevailing psychological notions of motivation. Here a *drive* always corresponds to a *need* and results from it. The organism's need for nutrients produces specific hunger-drives, tendencies to action, impulses to acquire what is needed. The need for liquid nourishment creates a thirst-drive; the need to reproduce, a sex-drive, and so on.

Such, for example, was the position adopted by the influential American neobehaviorist, Clark Hull (1943). Tissue-needs create deficit states within the organism that in turn bring about or cause the resultant drive. So-called higher human needs (and their corresponding drives) are built up, pyramid-fashion, through a conditioning process by association with the arousal and gratification of these primary physiological states.

Because of the complex structure of the human organism, an infinite list of such needs and drives can be constructed. Even the humanistically inclined personality theorist Henry Murray (1938) listed 28 such human needs: for acquisition, achievement, recognition, dominance, autonomy, aggression, abasement, affiliation, play, cognizance, to name but a few. But nowadays the tendency, at least among current humanistic authors, is to reduce this list to a few broad categories, such as those already proposed in this work, while subordinating all of them to the functioning of a basic actualizing tendency in constant interaction with the environment.

The shift in thinking here is a subtle one. It is not a simple reversal of the Hullian position (needs acting as efficient causes for resultant drives). Rather, a new note is added. The actualizing tendency, in the humanistic account, does not act as an efficient cause. What is being introduced here is a teleological principle, a *final cause*, a directional goal intrinsic to the organism by virtue of which it is pulled by what lies ahead rather than merely being pushed from behind. The existence of needs and drives in the traditional sense is maintained in this account, but their overall functioning is subordinated to the operation of this overarching directional thrust in ways that will presently be explored.

## SCIENCE AND TELEOLOGY

Before proceeding to that, however, we must take note of a serious difficulty that is posed by postulating a teleological principle. Traditional science is made uncomfortable by the notion that something which lies in the future, something therefore not yet in existence, can in any way affect some present state of affairs. More important, such an assumption appears to be, *in principle*, untestable according to accepted canons of scientific procedure. I may, on the basis of present observations and measurements, attempt to predict the future while waiting to see what occurs. But I cannot, by definition, observe, or manipulate, or measure some state of affairs which does not yet exist. Wherever possible, therefore, science attempts to avoid teleological explanations and to stick to directly observable phenomena.

Part of the reason for this may well be the fear that some invisible hand operating outside the laws of nature would have to be postulated as accounting for the supposed directionality of events, a literal *deus ex machina*. Earlier scientists did not hesitate to embrace such notions. As a result they were often tempted to abandon further exploration in the belief that they had already explained a phenomenon by appealing to a teleological principle. Aristotle, for example, taught that bodies fall because it is their destiny to seek the center of the earth. Modern scientists are understandably suspicious of such assumptions.

The program of depending upon what can be observed and measured directly has worked quite well in the physical sciences. It does not work well in the life sciences and for good reason. Some notion of directionality seems inescapable here as a necessary inference from observations repeatedly made ex post facto (after the event). Given the right conditions, an acorn always becomes an oak and *only* an oak. The embryo regularly matures into an adult specimen of its species in predictable, invariant, observable stages marked by successive differentiation and integration. Observations, after the fact, of countless instances of this sort have led biologists to *infer* the existence of a teleological principle to account for this phenomenon.

Such observations are possible simply because what was once in the future has now occurred and is in the accessible past. The conclusion is inescapable: living organisms are somehow programmed to reach certain end-states, given the proper environmental conditions. Many earlier biologists simply stopped at this point, attributing such phenomena to the operation of a mysterious vital principle or life force different in kind from the purely mechanical energies studied in physics and chemistry, incapable of being analyzed scientifically. Modern biology has broken through this cul-de-sac and has pushed the boundaries of scientific exploration outward by identifying, in the intricate intracellular DNA code, the precise mechanism through which the inferred directional tendency of living organisms operates. There *is* a program, we are told, and this is how and where it operates.

Mysteries remain, of course. Where and how did it originate? Under what combination of circumstances in the universe as we know it can such an effect be expected to occur? And what capabilities are we to attribute to the "stuff" of which such a universe is composed, capabilities that include the evolution of mind and reflexive consciousness itself? The search continues.

## HOMEOSTASIS AND GROWTH

While biologists have achieved a certain level of comfort with teleological principles, in some sense, as necessary for the scientific exploration of the development of living organisms, most psychologists have not. Traditional accounts of the interaction of the human organism with its environment depend instead solely on the principle of *homeostasis*. We have already discussed the Hullian behavioristic theory:

tissue-needs arise periodically within the organism in the form of deficits. These in turn are experienced as internal noxious stimuli which *drive* the organism to search the environment for what it needs. Once the appropriate objects are identified and consumed, equilibrium is restored until the sequence begins anew. Learning (defined as a change of behavior through experience) occurs as a direct consequence or effect of this quest for homeostatic balance. The probability of certain responses is increased through their success in restoring equilibrium (reinforcement). Unsuccessful responses are simply dropped from the behavioral repertoire (extinction).

Traditional Freudian explanations of behavior, though more florid, are strikingly similar. Here the emphasis is on the cyclical emergence of instinctual impulses (notably sex and aggression) which create tension (noxious internal stimulation, again) within the organism. The ego searches the environment, matches what it finds to the needs of the organism (the original meaning of identification in the Freudian lexicon), and engages in tension-reduction activities. Ideally (for good mental health) it will choose socially approved activities. Failure to do so will result in punishment, which can lead to symptom formation or to socially deviant behavior. In either case, a precarious balance will be restored until the next round of impulses inevitably appears.

Both schools of thought pay lip service to maturational events while dodging their teleological implications. The heaviest emphasis is consistently placed on changes of behavior through success-learning in the interests of maintaining homeostatic balance or, in the Freudian theory, the operation of a "will to pleasure" where pleasure is understood as the experience of tension reduction in very similar fashion.

It is difficult to understand why psychologists do not, generally speaking, follow the example of their biological colleagues by incorporating teleological premises into their theories. Freud was undoubtedly constrained by the mechanistic version of materialism prevalent in his historical context; Hull by a strong antimentalistic bias shared by the radical behaviorists who preceded and followed him. (There was one exception: Edward Tolman [1932] proposed a "purposive behaviorism" in contrast to Hull's drive-reduction theory, but his "cognitive maps" mechanism [Tolman, 1948], applicable even to lower organisms, was swept aside by the antimentalistic fervor of the period. Currently, Albert Bandura [1969] and other social learning theorists have resurrected this controversy by including some mentalistic concepts, such as observational learning, in their largely behavioral accounts.)

The neglect of teleology is especially difficult to understand when we take everyday conscious experience into account. The proposition that future goals exert an influence on present behavior certainly comes as no surprise to any conscious subject. Even if we accept the Freudian assumption that the choice of particular goals is determined unconsciously by past events, they still represent a not-yet-existing end-state to which I aspire and toward the attainment of which I shape my present behavior. (If I want to buy a house, I begin saving my money and contact a realtor. If I want to write a book, I find myself curtailing other activities that were quite reinforcing in the past.) This that-for-the-sake-of-which I act is, technically speaking, the final cause (telos) of my behavior not its efficient, mechanical cause. But it is a cause, it influences my course of action as a directional principle, and knowledge of it would appear to be required for an adequate explanation (and prediction) of my behavior.

It is a central theme of humanistic psychology that such teleological premises must be woven into the science of human behavior. We have already seen, in the preceding chapter, how Charlotte Bühler insisted on the necessity of inserting a knowledge of conscious (or unconscious) life goals into the understanding of life-span development. It will be my purpose now to develop this theme further and indicate how humanistic authors interweave the biological and phenomenological aspects of it into a unified picture of the tendency toward self-realization.

## HISTORICAL ORIGINS

Teleological notions have a venerable history in Western thought, dating back to the very origins of philosophy and science in our culture.

### The Aristotelian legacy

Aristotle was perhaps the first to give them clear articulation in his famous doctrine of the *four causes*. These he understood as principles logically (and ontologically) required to explain the existence and changes of any substantial entity. We can exemplify his notions by applying them to the creation of one of those remarkable Grecian statues. The *material* cause is the block of marble with which the sculptor begins. It already has certain properties which made it admirably suited for his purposes. The *formal* cause is the blueprint or idea of the finished form, the structure of the figure to be produced. The *efficient* cause is the force or motion he applies through hammer and chisel to the marble block before him. And the *final* cause is the purpose which motivates his activity: to give expression to some creative urge within him, to immortalize his patron, or, perhaps more crassly, simply to earn a commission.

The existence of the statue, Aristotle believed, can be adequately comprehended if and only if we take all four of these causes into account. In this particular example, of course, both the formal and final causes require intervention by an external intelligent agent. In the case of living organisms, he taught that the form and the telos are embedded within the organism itself as part of its nature. Ultimately, an intelligent agent was presumed to be responsible for that state of affairs (a Prime Mover or supreme intelligence), as well as for the natural motions or changes of inanimate substances.

These notions were reintroduced to Western thought in the Middle Ages by way of Islamic sources and became an integral part of the Scholastic tradition, which still perdures. The notion of an intrinsic telos for physical and chemical substances was largely abandoned after the Renaissance but remains a part of our biological understanding. The debate here is over the necessity of postulating a supreme intelligence to account for its presence versus the blind operation of processes like natural selection in the course of evolution. That ongoing debate need not concern us here, though it obviously has important implications for disciplines like theology and philosophy. Of more immediate concern for my present purposes are two propositions that can be derived from the Aristotelian legacy.

1.  Living organisms do appear to follow an intrinsic telos or directional thrust, however this may have originated.
2.  Intelligent (conscious) activity does often transcend the here and now by proposing goals or purposes to be attained in the future, and such goals do affect behavior in present time as final causes in the Aristotelian sense.

We will see how humanistic authors attempt to take into account and reconcile both propositions. This last statement should not be construed as meaning that most humanistic theorists have read Aristotle or his Scholastic or neo-Scholastic followers. The tradition is pervasive enough in the background of Western thought, but the progenitors of current humanistic thinking are more immediate. They include a very wide assortment of recent thinkers whom Joseph Rychlak (1968) would include in the *dialectical* (versus *demonstrative*) tradition of personality theorists. It is not my intention at this point to burden the reader with a long list of such names and influences. Some of them, however, will be mentioned in the following account of how various humanistic psychologists incorporate this central theme into their work.

## Carl Rogers's actualizing tendency

Over 30 years ago, Carl Rogers (1951) framed the following proposition and gave it a central place in his theory of personality:

The organism has one basic tendency and striving—to actualize, maintain, and enhance the experiencing organism. Rather than many needs and motives, it seems entirely possible that all organic and psychological needs may be described as partial aspects of this one fundamental need. (Rogers, 1951, p. 487)

How then do we define it operationally? As was suggested above, ex post facto:

. . . by comparing the undeveloped with the developed organism, the simple organism with the complex, the organism early or low on the evolutionary scale with the organism which has developed later and is regarded as higher. Whatever generalized differences are found constitute the direction of the basic tendency we are postulating. (Rogers, 1951, p. 489)

Rogers's postulation of this "actualizing tendency," as he prefers to call it, grew first and foremost out of his own experience and that of his associates in the conduct of psychotherapy.

It is our experience in therapy which has brought us to the point of giving this proposition a central place. The therapist becomes very much aware that the forward-moving tendency of the human organism is the basis upon which he relies most deeply and fundamentally. (Rogers, 1951, p. 489)

It was only then, by his own account, that Rogers sought support for this growing conviction in the experience and writings of others. He quickly found it. Besides the phenomenological theorists Donald Snygg and Arthur Combs already mentioned, he quotes Prescott Lecky (1945), Abraham Maslow (1943), O. Hobart Mowrer and Clyde Kluckhohn (1944), Andras Angyal (1941), and a host of others. And in the arena of clinical experience, he finds confirmation in the work of Kurt Goldstein with brain-injured soldiers (1940, see Chapter 3), Harry Stack Sullivan with psychotics (1945), and the neo-Freudian analysts Karen Horney (1942) and Otto Rank (1945) with neurotics. (Rogers had attended workshops and compared notes with some of Rank's American followers early in his own career.)

Rogers has never wavered in assigning this actualizing tendency a central role in both theory and practice. His *person-centered approach*, as it is now called, is squarely based on the belief that the helper's or consultant's role is primarily to provide the relationship conditions that will facilitate its functioning, and enable it to emerge from the encrusted layers of dependency that have all but smothered it. Over and over again, he insists that the organism and its basic tendencies can be trusted, provided—and here he adds the link between the two propositions previously derived from the Aristotelian legacy—all the data of experiencing are allowed entry into consciousness and become accurately symbolized. "When all the elements are *clearly perceived*, the balance seems invariably in the direction of the painful but ultimately rewarding path of self-actualization or growth" (1948, p. 218)(emphasis added).

The difficulties encountered in the course of self-actualization are clearly stated and examined in the Rogerian account, along with the conditions which must be provided for its attainment. They will be recounted in Chapter 8 of this volume under the heading of authentic human functioning. And later in this chapter, we will explore further the link between consciousness and this biological, organismically based tendency. That it remains a central, unifying theme in Rogers's own thinking is abundantly clear from the following passage in his most recent work. Indeed, it has become broadened, somewhat tentatively to be sure, to include the nonbiological world as well. After reviewing some recent theoretical work in physics, chemistry, and the philosophy of science, Rogers states:

> I hypothesize that there is a formative directional tendency in the universe, which can be traced and observed in stellar space, in crystals, in microorganisms, in more complex organic life, and in human beings. This is an evolutionary tendency toward greater order, greater complexity, greater interrelatedness. In humankind, this tendency exhibits itself as the individual moves from a single-cell origin to complex organic functioning, to knowing and sensing below the level of consciousness, to a conscious awareness of the organism and the external world, to a transcendent awareness of the harmony and unity of the cosmic system, including humankind. It seems to me just possible that this hypothesis could be a base upon which we could begin to build a theory for humanistic psychology. It definitely forms a base for the person-entered approach. (Rogers, 1980, p. 133)

## Maslow's self-actualization drive

Abraham Maslow, another of the founders of humanistic psychology, was quite familiar with Rogers's work and thinking. (At one point, he served a visiting fellowship at one of the institutes in California with which Rogers was associated.) In an earlier period, he also knew and admired Kurt Goldstein, whose researches and subsequent convictions concerning a unifying tendency toward self-realization we have already reviewed (see Chapter 3). Though favorably impressed by these thinkers, Maslow remained somewhat unconvinced, apparently because of the flavor of instinctive urgency that his colleagues seemed to be applying from the biological analogies to which they constantly referred. As a result, his own thinking about this topic is both more subtle and more ambivalent.

On the one hand, for example, his "drive toward self-actualization" is most often depicted as one of *many* tendencies of the human organism. It is placed at the apex of a hierarchical pyramid of human needs and drives (physiological needs, safety needs, needs for recognition and esteem, and the like), all of which are more powerful (prepotent) driving forces. Consequently, such lower needs (d-needs or deficiency-motivated needs) must somehow be basically and consistently satisfied before the self-actualization needs (personal-growth needs) can even emerge and become salient as motivators of human behavior. The latter, therefore, are instinctoid rather than instinctive, weaker, more easily overridden by daily concerns, defective learning, or cultural pressures (Maslow, 1968; 1970).

In the context of our previous distinction between efficient and final causes of behavior, it would appear that Maslow, in such passages, is conceptualizing the drive for self-actualization in the more traditional sense. It is simply viewed as one of many such *efficient* causes of behavior. Perhaps without realizing it, in such descriptions he is still laboring under the influence of the behavioral learning theories to which he was initially exposed. This would explain his hierarchical principle: physiological needs are stronger because directly linked with the tissue needs of the biological organism. Social needs derive their potency by association with physiological gratification, but because the link is more indirect, they are presumably less powerful motivators of human behavior. (Early theorists were puzzled by the evidence that this might not be so—for example, in the case of a political prisoner who embarks on a hunger strike to defend his cause even to the point of death. Gordon Allport [1961] attempted to salvage the situation by bestowing "functional autonomy" on such higher drives while upholding their derivation from biological sources.)

The highest of these drives, according to Maslow, is for self-actualization. Its links with biological necessities are even more indirect, if not totally nonexistent. (Maslow vaguely refers, at times, to an instinctlike need for completion or for integration.) It is, therefore, the weakest of all as an effective (efficiently causal) motivator. At one point Maslow (1968) claims that it may not even necessarily emerge when the other, lower needs are sufficiently gratified.

The confusion here is obvious and understandable. Maslow is simply caught in the older, traditional model in which he was trained, a model which still, in his defense, dominates current psychological thinking. He is closer to the mark, it seems to me, when he describes his "drive" for self-actualization as antihomeostatic, involving growth-needs, needs for fuller being, rather than the kind of need or impulse to action which arises from mere disturbance of equilibrium.

On the other hand, Maslow's ambivalence is shown in his frequent description of what he terms our *inner nature*, the "essential core" of personality. He describes it as biologically based and therefore, in part, universal, composed of our natural capacities, morally neutral, a guide to our life. He states: "Even though weak, it rarely disappears in the normal person—perhaps not even in the sick person. Even though denied, it persists underground *forever pressing for actualization*" (1968, p. 4) (emphasis added).

Its weakness he again ascribes to the fact that we are not as instinct-driven as lower organisms. We are instead more dependent on our cognitive capacities, more flexible, more free to develop in ways of our own choosing, and, by the same token, more susceptible to sociocultural influences and pressures.

In spite of his ambivalences, therefore, he is definitely on the side of a growth model rather than a homeostatic one in describing human development. He is openly critical of the latter. It cannot, he states, account for "growth of the personality, increases in wisdom, self-actualization, strengthening of the character, and the planning of one's life. . . . Some long-time vector, or directional tendency, must be invoked to make any sense of development through the lifetime" (1968, p. 30).

Maslow reiterates what seems to be the only scientific means for validating such a concept: inference from observations made after the fact. In his case, this involved a study of the lives of people whom he felt everyone would agree were not merely healthy but exceptional specimens of humankind: "self-actualizers."

> Such people become far more self-sufficient and self-contained. The determinants which govern them are now primarily inner ones, rather than social or environmental. . . . They are the laws of their own inner nature, their potentialities and capacities, their talents, their latent resources, their creative impulses, their needs to know themselves and to become more and more integrated and unified, more and more aware of what they really are, of what they really want, of what their call or vocation or fate is to be. (1968, p. 35)

This inner nature is, in turn, the source of an *intrinsic conscience*, an "unconscious or preconscious perception of our own nature" (1968, p. 7), potentially accessible to awareness and therefore potentially available as an inner gyroscope for fashioning my own authentic existence (see Chapter 8).

When writing in this vein, Maslow clearly shares the Rogerian understanding of an actualizing tendency in this teleological (final causal) sense, as well as the Rogerian optimism concerning the end-states toward which it points. After reviewing his own findings and a body of other evidence derived from clinical, personological, and test data, he concludes:

> We can certainly now assert that at least a reasonable, theoretical, and empirical case has been made for the presence within the human being of

a tendency toward, or need for growing in a direction that can be summarized in general as self-actualization. . . . That is, the human being is so constructed that he presses toward fuller and fuller being and this means pressing toward what most people would call good values, toward serenity, kindness, courage, honesty, love, unselfishness, and goodness. (1968, p. 155)

Maslow has given us some hints, in his references to awareness, as to how his own ambivalence can be resolved. The next author to be presented develops the picture more clearly.

## Nuttin's "drive" for self-realization

Of all the humanistic authors surveyed in this volume, only Joseph Nuttin seems to have been directly familiar with and influenced by Aristotelian teleological notions concerning both the biological and cognitive features of human behavior. (Another writer, Joseph Rychlak, whose experimental research has been summarized in Chapter 4, also borrows directly from Aristotle's doctrine of the four causes. But his application of teleological principles is focused rather exclusively on the cognitive and volitional aspects of human behavior, with adaptations inspired by the thought of Immanuel Kant. The biological overtones of an actualizing tendency are relatively absent in his chosen focus on the cognitive realm.)

While maintaining a keen appreciation of Freudian contributions, Nuttin remains critical of the exclusively homeostatic model embedded in Freudian theory. His immediate mentor is Alfred Adler, to whose individual psychology Nuttin devotes a lengthy appendix to his own treatise on a dynamic theory of normal personality. Adler was clearly a proponent of finalism in his own explanation of human behavior, though Nuttin is quick to point out the rather unscientific, Lamarckian twists that Adler gave to this doctrine. Others who prominently influenced Nuttin's own formulation include Otto Rank, Kurt Goldstein, again, and Carl Rogers, whom he met on visits to the United States.

Nuttin's basic approach has already been presented in Chapter 2 and will be briefly recapitulated here with the addition of further necessary details.

1. The human organism is differentiated from all lower organisms by the capacity for reflexive consciousness.
2. A descriptive analysis of reflexive consciousness reveals at least three irreducible levels of conscious experience: the psychophysiological, the psychosocial, and the spiritual (relabeled transpersonal).
3. All living organisms are open systems in constant need of contact and exchange with their environments.
4. Where lower organisms are concerned, the biological mechanism

of homeostasis is of paramount importance. It remains predominant as the mechanism for self-realization at the psychophysiological level of human functioning, but even here it is at times significantly transformed by the specifically human capacity for self awareness. (E.g., homeostatic mechanisms alone are insufficient to account for human eating behavior or for the elaborate social and economic systems we develop to assure ourselves of a constant and varied supply of food.)

5. Self-consciousness becomes an increasingly important factor in determining our needs and corresponding drives at the psychosocial and transpersonal levels of experience.

6. Overall, however, our behavior is motivated by the effort to realize ourselves—to actualize our varied potentialities at all levels of our experience. This is the unitary *"drive" for self-realization*. The potentialities are there from the beginning—they "press for actualization," to use Maslow's phrase. To actualize them requires constant exchange with the environment on all levels of experience.

7. Conflict is inevitable, given this rich complexity of the human organism and the wide variety of needs that emerge at the different levels of experience. It is impossible to develop all our capacities equally or to gratify all needs simultaneously. Conflict produces tension.

8. Since, unlike lower organisms, we are not guided by instinct, choices must be made. The end-states of personality development are therefore not carved in stone (unlike, e.g., embryological development). In early life such choices are, by and large, unconsciously made, guided by cultural and familial ideals of personality. In some instances, this can lead to the unconscious *repression* of certain needs that are incompatible with cultural demands. Such repressed needs retain their dynamic force, at times with destructive consequences. The Freudian formula fits well here.

9. It therefore becomes necessary, as life proceeds and self-awareness develops, for the individual to develop a constructive ideal of personality, taking into account all the data of experiencing and making *conscious* choices about which capacities and needs should be actualized or acted upon, which ignored. It is therefore the person who must be satisfied not the individual need. Such decisions will presumably be guided by meanings (values, ideals, and so on) derived from the transpersonal level of experience fitted to the individual's unique life situation. If such ideals can be realistically approached and remain personally satisfying, incompatible needs can be safely ignored (consciously *suppressed*) without fear of unconscious reprisals.

Perhaps an illustration would help at this point. A medical student may have to postpone the gratification of certain social needs—and perhaps less pressing physiological ones—in order successfully to pursue his or her studies. This need not be damaging to personality development as long as the pursuit of such a goal is personally gratifying (for example, not dictated primarily by the expectations of others) and based on very real personal capacities and interests. Of course in the long run, some gratification and integration of these social needs will have to occur for well-rounded personality development.

Nuttin's views can now be diagrammed as in Figure 6–1. The horizontal lines indicate the irreducibility of the three levels of conscious experience. The wavy line connecting them depicts the notion that they do, however, exist simultaneously (see Chapter 2). Specific needs issue from each level, but there is a superordinate *"drive" for self-realization* (arrow on left side) acting on all levels and serving as the unifying teleological thrust of the human organism. I have added a more modern, less reductionistic term: *actualizing tendency.* Since all life is an open system, the arrow on the right indicates the correlative

**FIGURE 6–1**
**Diagram of Nuttin's theory of personality**

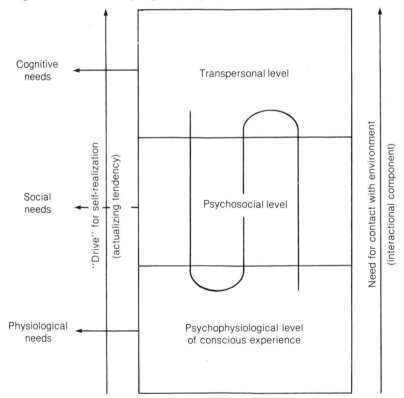

"*need" for contact* (exchange) with the environment on all levels of experiencing (modern term: *interactional component*). No level is self-sufficient, nor is the organism as a whole.

While the actualizing tendency is rooted in the very biology of the organism, it is also deeply affected by the human capacity for reflexive consciousness. Consciousness in general has shaped the cultural goals, ideals, and values that become normative for our lives. Self-consciousness gives us the potential at least to personalize these, to fashion an individual fit in accordance with our own unique talents and capacities (and powers of critical evaluation), and, even in some instances, to transcend them.

As Nuttin himself puts it:

> The general tendency towards self-realization which runs through the whole of man's psycho-physiological organism is undoubtedly a biological reality. . . . We must first of all realize, however, that on the human level, this universal "drive" involves new and irreducible forms, because it is at work in a kind of psychic life which can know and desire realities that transcend the limits of the material universe. The fact that the human psyche "opens out" by means of consciousness to a world beyond that of organic impressions, and is thus not simply "affected" by, or "absorbed" into, biological realities, gives to the dynamism of human self-realization an entirely new form of existence. (1962, p. 188)

We will see later how Nuttin carries these notions forward to depict the conditions for fashioning an authentic human existence (see Chapter 8). Already we can note how his description preserves the experience we all have of intentional or purposeful activity, how the latter transforms (gives new, specifically human forms to) the general teleological or directional tendencies of all living organisms. The two aspects of the Aristotelian legacy mentioned earlier in this chapter are preserved and combined in this account. And we are now in a position to understand the enormous variability to be found among human individual and cultural forms of self-realization. The contrast with lower organisms is obvious, and human reflexive consciousness is again the key.

## Other viewpoints

The image of a key is apt enough as long as we understand it as a master key. Consciousness presents us with many alternatives, many doorways to the future. We unlock one (usually, to stretch the metaphor, one on which opportunity knocks) and pass through to find ourselves in a room where other choices must be made. There is an inner press to go on, though we may elect to stay put (not without guilt) for fear of the unknown in the passageways that lie ahead. The choice, within certain limits, is ours; the goals not rigidly predetermined. We will choose a better course and a more satisfying outcome if we listen to our own inner guide as it evaluates the ongoing experiences we encounter and as we begin to set a destination for ourselves in accordance with its voice.

For the existential analyst Viktor Frankl, this inner guide is the pervasive *will to meaning*, yet another term for the basic component of intentionality so characteristic of human consciousness. To live satisfying lives, authentic lives, we must discover a purpose for our existence. And that purpose or meaning needs to be uniquely our own, discovered in the arena of our own capabilities, talents, interests, limits, and opportunities. Thrown into life, unguided by instinct, we must find the "courage to be," to use Paul Tillich's phrase (1952)—the courage to take responsibility for the task of fashioning from this raw material a meaningful existence.

As we saw in the introduction to this theme in Chapter 3, Frankl's position is explicitly antihomeostatic. The will to meaning is not a drive in the traditional sense. It issues from the highest, transpersonal level of conscious experience, the level that transcends the here and now biological framework of our lives by encompassing the past and the future in its gaze and asking the tormenting questions "Why?" "What is the purpose of my existence?" Lacking an answer, our lives are a void.

Drives, Frankl (1966) points out, merely push us from behind. Meaning pulls us from ahead—a task to be accomplished, a goal to be fulfilled. We need purpose more than we need food, or shelter, or sex, or friendship, or recognition. But if meaning is there, it exists *for its own sake*, apart from us, and we are left free to fulfill it or not, as we choose. I think what Frankl is saying is that *all* of existence has meaning or it does not. If it does, I must discover and *participate* in it to realize my own existence. I cannot merely create it *ex nihilo*, out of myself. No organism is self-sufficient. Psychology, as Ernest Becker (1973) has stated, can take us this far but no farther. We see once again that the need for meaning is not a tissue-need, a physicochemical deficit or imbalance. We are here in the realm of *final* causes.

Both Carl Rogers, and Fritz Perls, the founder of Gestalt therapy, would concur that there is no predetermined end-state or set goal for human self-realization. For these theorists, self-realization is a continuing *process* marked by free or by full functioning. The latter involves openness to all our experiencing accurately symbolized in sharp awareness. We must learn to trust the organism's own valuing process and follow where it leads. Meaning is implicit in experience, states Eugene Gendlin (1979), an associate of Rogers for many years. The organism is self-regulating when allowed to function freely, claimed Perls. His own description of how this process works sounds suspiciously homeostatic, but his colleague Joel Latner (1974) assures us that full functioning leads to ever-greater complexity and integration, to the creation of larger and more encompassing Gestalten, culminating in a kind of cosmic consciousness in which we find revealed the meaning of existence itself.

However this may be, it is clear that these theorists see the process as open-ended, one of continuous "becoming" (Allport, 1955). It is a process in which self-awareness again plays a pivotal role in facilitating movement toward a goal whose outlines can be foreseen only dimly if at all. As a process, it involves *change*—as new experiencing is assimilated in the course of development. And because we are conscious, choices must be made and these continually checked against the wisdom of the organism and its internal valuing process.

While what is here being described implies a constant state of flux, there is also in the writing of these particular authors an explicit faith in the forward-moving, positive directions that will result from such a conscious, responsible commitment to the process of becoming. It is this faith in positive outcomes that most disturbs many critics of humanistic psychology. Do not our destructive tendencies and potentialities also press for actualization? And if so, how can we be sure that they will not win the battle for attention among our many needs?

This objection will have to be fully faced in the final chapter of this book, but the answer can be briefly sketched here: humanistic psychologists challenge their critics to prove that destructive tendencies, which obviously exist, are somehow inherent in the human organism as a kind of death instinct in the Freudian sense or as a residue from the instinctive biograms inherited from our animal ancestors, which the sociobiologists claim (Tiger & Fox, 1974). Such tendencies, according to most humanists, *arise only in reaction to dehumanizing environments.* Unfortunately, such dehumanizing conditions abound, from the early family life of many individuals to the later institutional settings in which human development commonly takes place. When such conditions are eased, as in a good therapeutic setting, destructive responses are no longer required and will fade away. Following the logic of these convictions, humanistic psychologists first concentrated on developing the many popular growth centers of the human potential movement, which do focus on the self-actualization of the individual. But more recently, the new leadership among them has become more socially conscious and is beginning to pay greater attention to preventive measures—through their efforts to rehumanize the more powerful social institutions (see Chapter 11).

Still another founder of modern humanistic psychology, the American existential analyst Rollo May, also underlines the transforming effects of consciousness on the actualizing tendency inherent in all living organisms. After pointing out that the term *being* in the phrase "human being" is originally a participle not a noun depicting a static entity, he adds his own preference for the term *becoming*. He then goes on to state:

> Thus, being in the human sense is not given once and for all. It does not unfold automatically as the oak tree does from the acorn. For an intrinsic and inseparable element in being human is self-consciousness. Man (or *Dasein*) is the particular being who has to be aware of himself, be responsible for himself, if he is to become himself. (May et al., 1958, pp. 41–42)

We are therefore neither merely homeostatic beings, as traditional psychology implies, nor driven by purely biological finality. We are, to coin a term, *homeokinetic* (Tageson, Koval, & Bartlett, 1974). We either change, or we die, psychologically. And constructive change can only occur if we lead an examined life, consciously fashioning from the data of full experiencing the unique meaning of our existence.

Such consciousness, however, always involves *choice*. Rollo May, in concert with other authors here surveyed, points out that we can, at any given moment, choose also *not to be* (i.e., not to continue the process of becoming what we are capable of being). Anxiety, in his analysis, is at least partially the experience we have when faced with the challenge of growth.

> Anxiety occurs at the point where some emerging potentiality or possibility faces the individual, some possibility of fulfilling his existence; but this very possibility involves the destroying of present security, which thereupon gives rise to the tendency to deny the new potentiality. (May et al., 1958, p. 52)

And guilt is the feeling we have when we refuse the challenge. It arises from the sin against the self, so vividly described by the neoanalyst, Karen Horney (1937). We are responsible beings, beings who not only must respond but are somehow accountable for our responses. This, of course, implies freedom and leads directly into the theme of self-determination, a difficult topic which we must now explore. This will in turn prepare the way for a more complete discussion of how humanistic psychologists describe the characteristics of a truly authentic human existence and the conditions required for attaining that elusive goal.

# 7 Self-determination

> One difficulty of the freedom-determinism issue is that it suggests an absolute choice: man is either free or not. The choice is not that simple. There are surely areas in which human behavior is determined very largely by the interaction of physiological processes and environmental factors (such as food, water, air), by prior learning, by socialization in childhood. Psychology seeks to find lawfulness in behavior wherever it can be found; such lawfulness implies some measure of determinism, but not necessarily an absolute determinism. Science does not require such absolutes.
>
> Hilgard, 1962, p. 148

This statement, enunciated by an eminent experimental psychologist in the third edition of his widely used college textbook, represents a striking departure from a viewpoint previously prevalent in scientific psychology. (Earlier editions of this text contained no mention of the topic of volition or human freedom.)

Why this shift away from the prevailing paradigm of hard determinism, a shift already perceptible in the early 1960s, and rapidly gathering momentum since? I would contend that it reflects the influence on Hilgard and some of his more open-minded colleagues of the developing humanistic-existential critique of existing paradigms. It is this critique which is responsible for the resurgence of interest in the age-old freedom versus determinism controversy. Its history among psychological circles in Europe and America has been ably chronicled, from the beginning of psychology as a scientific discipline to the mid-1950s, by Roberto Zavalloni, an Italian social psychologist. His book was made available to English-speaking readers in 1962 by the present writer and a colleague under the title: *Self-determination: The Psychology of Personal Freedom* (Zavalloni, 1962).

In this work, Zavalloni accurately predicted that the problem of personal freedom, long considered a dead issue in most contemporary psychological circles, would once more become a respectable topic in academic and clinical psychology. My purpose in this present chapter is briefly to review the more current developments on this subject over the last two decades and to demonstrate its logical connection with the other themes characteristic of the humanistic-existential movement.

Zavalloni attributed the renewed interest among certain psychologists in the freedom-determinism controversy to then-current developments in the field of psychotherapy stemming from the influence of European phenomenological and existential philosophers on a group of European analysts. This is a somewhat narrow interpretation, though correct as far as it goes. I would rather ascribe it to the emergence of a broader movement, spanning both continents, and dubbed by Abraham Maslow as the evolution of a Third Force in contemporary psychology (Tageson, 1971). The origins of this broader humanistic-existential movement I have already traced in the first chapters of this volume.

I hope to show that the humanistic-existential perspective represents a radically new approach to this very old problem. Earlier philosophers and some psychologists reified our cognitive functions by speaking of entities or faculties called *intellect* and *memory*. Volitional functions were ascribed to a faculty called *will*, whose task it was to choose among the alternatives for action proposed by the intellect. The question was then posed: is the will *free* in carrying out its decision-making task? Can it rather arbitrarily choose among the alternatives presented by the intellect, or are its choices determined by the weights attached to each of these alternatives by previous experience, the varying strengths of competing motives, and other preexisting conditions? Freedom, according to its protagonists, was seen as an innate property of the faculty of will.

Only in the presence of the Absolute Good, argued the medieval philosopher Thomas Aquinas, does the will lose its freedom. Since it tends toward the good, it *must* choose the Absolute. But since we never have a direct vision of God *in via* (during our mortal life on earth), the will remains free to choose among the lesser, more imperfect goods or values presented to its perusal. His antagonist, John Duns Scotus, balked at even this limitation on the freedom of the will and advocated an even more radical indeterminism.

The terms used in these ancient debates and the "faculty psychology" from which they are derived are no longer, of course, in vogue, at least in psychological circles. Current humanistic advocates of psychological freedom use a different language derived predictably from their more holistic approach to personal functioning. The issues addressed in this newer, more phenomenological language are, however, quite similar. It remains to be seen whether this fresh approach will carry the day in intellectual circles. So far at least, it has succeeded in reopening the debate on what had until recently been assumed to be a closed topic. And since the humanistic-existential movement in psychology has been primarily responsible for authenticating the newfound respectability which the discussion of personal freedom presently enjoys, I feel I am justified in presenting the theme of self-determination as one of its most distinguishing characteristics.

This is not to say that an emphasis on self-determination or personal freedom is now the major coin of the realm. Hard determinism is still very much with us, Hilgard and others notwithstanding, in both academic and clinical psychology. I will therefore briefly review this position from its two major intellectual sources before presenting the humanistic critique.

## HARD DETERMINISM: THE NATURAL SCIENCE PARADIGM

American academic psychology is still for the most part highly positivistic in its outlook and strategy. Most experimental psychologists in particular adhere to the methodology of operationism, requiring that the definition of psychological variables for scientific study be derived from externally observable and quantifiable data. With the rapid and almost universal adoption of this natural scientific paradigm, the mentalism and introspective methodology of the founders of scientific psychology were abandoned in favor of more objective methods of verification.

Some psychologists with a particular interest in the study of personality development or social behavior remained willing to accept the verbal report of experimental subjects as admissible evidence and even to infer from such reports the existence of such intervening variables as "attitudes," or "motives," or, more recently, "cognitive strategies." But they remain committed to the task of anchoring such variables to more observable stimulus inputs and response characteristics. (*Anchoring*, in most such cases, implicitly follows the assumption of a straight-line causal sequence: previous stimulus inputs are held to be entirely responsible for the contents and patterning of such mediators, which in turn immediately cause the ensuing response. This, according to Rychlak (1977, 1979), represents an inadmissible confounding of a theoretical assumption with an otherwise sensible methodological strategy). Radical behaviorists remain suspicious of all such mediating organismic variables and opt for a stricter S-R analysis of human as well as animal behavior.

Despite this argument over acceptable methodology, both camps in academic psychology, in adopting the paradigm of natural science, also accepted its assumption of strict or hard determinism. As applied to the discipline of psychology, the assumption is that all behavior is strictly determined by previous stimulus inputs (including, of course, the stimuli that result from the previous behavior of the organism). Given the ability to pinpoint these antecedent conditions, behavior can be accurately and lawfully predicted in every instance.

Understood as a set of paradigmatic assumptions adopted for the conduct of scientific investigation, this is a defensible position. Operating within it, academic psychologists, to their credit, have produced an enormous volume of instructive research in the areas of sensory processes, perception, learning (conditioning), memory, social processes, and related topics. In other instances, as, for example, in the writings of the radical behaviorist B. F. Skinner, this particular paradigm for scientific study is extrapolated into what amounts to a philosophical dogma concerning all human behavior.

I have two comments to make at this point. To a modern philosopher of science, this sort of extrapolation from a useful scientific paradigm to a general philosophical statement is simply illegitimate. Second, the adoption of a naturalistic paradigm in psychological science appears to have been rather arbitrary, a historical accident (Giorgi, 1970). Such paradigms flourish and prevail as long as they are useful and constructive in guiding research. The limits of this particular paradigm, including the assumption of strict determinism in human behavior, may now have been reached. Joseph Rychlak (1977) points this out in his humanistic critique of social learning theory and the newer emphases in cognitive psychology, which, he feels at least, still labor under the restrictions of the older paradigm. As we saw in Chapter 4, he has proposed and carried out a rigorous program of experimental research based on alternative assumptions. And Sigmund Koch, another leading systematic psychologist, is of the opinion that by clinging to a paradigm that is no longer prevalent even in the natural sciences, behaviorism itself is a dying cause (1964, p. 21).

However that may be, the Skinnerian perspective is still very current, and I propose now to examine it in further detail as representative of a still prevalent hard determinism in modern psychological science.

## Hard determinism: The behavioral view

For Skinner and other radical behaviorists, all animal and human behavior is derived from two sources.

*1. The genetic constitution of the organism.* This source developed over eons of evolutionary process—dominated by the principle of natural selection and leading to the survival of some species and the disappearance of others. As a result of this process, every living organism is born into the world with a distinctive set of biological givens, which determine both the limits and characteristic potentialities of that organism's behavior. These can be thought of as a set of reflexes and, in some instances, instinctual patterns of behavior more or less modifiable by learning.

Where the human species is concerned, Skinner feels, we know very little about these biological givens and tend to assume too much. For this reason he remains opposed to any emphasis on the hereditary determination of human behavior, including the Freudian instinct theory and presumably the newer sociobiological approaches (Wilson, 1975), believing them to be poorly grounded on hard scientific evidence. Historically, he is convinced, psychologists have been prone to explain too much by reference to unvalidated instinctual patterns, imprinting, and the like that have been simply extrapolated from studies of lower organisms, thus cutting off further investigation of the more accessible influence of the second source of human behavior: learning through reinforcement. He therefore has consistently preferred to follow this more accessible route to its ultimate limits, while waiting for the human biologists and geneticists to fill in the gaps in our present knowledge of the hereditary components of behavior.

Interestingly, one of his students and colleagues, Richard Herrnstein, has recently argued that those limits may now have been reached: "We now know enough about the quantitative laws of conditioning to see that we are lacking the parameters that could make behaviorism truly practical" (1977, p. 602).

These parameters have to do with a set of *inborn motivational dynamics* that vary within and across individuals in a given species and presumably between the various species themselves. Certain classes of stimuli and response are now known to vary in their susceptibility to conditioning. Insufficient attention has been paid to classifying drives that sensitize organisms differentially to reinforcement, and so on. Therefore, he argues, the assumptions on which current behavioral engineering rests are too simplistic, and its attempts to predict and control behavior are bound to fail until these variables are more completely understood and factored into the quantitative laws which behaviorists seek to derive.

Skinner, of course, did not take this criticism lying down (1977, pp. 1006–1012), but Herrnstein has held his ground (1977, pp. 1013–1016). If his analysis is correct, it will not only affect the future course of behaviorism but may provide the basis for a rapprochement with the humanistic movement. The latter assumes innate tendencies toward self-realization, or a will to meaning, or, as Rychlak (1979) would insist, an inborn capacity for a type of dialectical reasoning that transcends the immediate facts of experience. This point will be explored in greater detail after considering the Skinnerian position on the second major source of human behavior.

**2.  *Learning through reinforcement.*** As has just been pointed out, Skinner and most other radical behaviorists prefer to operate under the assumption that most human behavior is learned behavior. And most such learning, they maintain, occurs under the model of operant or instrumental conditioning. Every organism, including the human, by virtue of its genetic endowment spontaneously emits a range of responses called *operants*, or responses for which no immediately preceding external stimuli can be observed. Given this operant base, all subsequent responding or behavior depends on the consequences which follow these initial endeavors (Thorndike's law of effect).

Responses which lead to favorable consequences for the organism are said to be positively reinforced—the probability of their occurring again under similar circumstances is increased. Punishing or aversive consequences generally lead to inhibition of response and to the further negative reinforcement of any operants that result in escape for or avoidance of the aversive consequences (the probability of the occurrence of such escape or avoidance responses in the future is likewise increased). Operants that lead to neither favorable nor unfavorable consequences are extinguished over time (the probability of their reoccurrence is progressively lessened); they are simply dropped from the repertoire of spontaneous behavior.

An example, which has some bearing on our future discussion of this approach, may help to illustrate this position. Infants universally and spontaneously begin to emit a wide range of vocalizations. They babble. Some of these vocalizations, not unsurprisingly, resemble recognizable words in a given language. When an infant emits, among a host of other sounds, ma-ma or da-da in the presence of its parents, certain consequences highly favorable to it immediately follow! Other vocalizations similar to the language content prevalent in the environment are likewise reinforced. And as time goes on, vocalizations that meet with little or no response from the environment are dropped; others, spontaneously emitted or imitated, are inhibited from occurring because of unfavorable consequences, and new ones are learned that serve the same purposes of expression without such aversive effect (e.g., "tinkle" for "pee," or vice versa). The particular language repertoire of the infant is thus gradually shaped from these initially spontaneous vocalizations and eventually added to through the operation of the same principles of association and reinforcement.

It should be noted in passing that modern specialists in linguistics and psycholinguistics are quite aware of the behavioral account but tend to dismiss it as trivial and peripheral to an adequate understanding of the development of linguistic competence (Chomsky, 1972, pp. 1–23). My purpose in including it here is simply to illustrate the principles of operant conditioning and to introduce the important concept of the *verbal community* as it relates to the further conditioning of human consciousness, behavior, and the "illusion" of self-determination or personal autonomy that seems inevitably to result according to the behavioral perspective.

Skinner and his associates readily admit that the human organism is the most complex of all living systems. Human behavior is accordingly shaped in many subtle ways, including the complex reinforcement contingencies provided by the verbal community in which it occurs. Nor is human consciousness itself denied. Rather, its essence is seen as closely linked with the development and use of symbolic language. It is basically a talking to oneself, a phenomenon produced by the interaction of the individual with the verbal community.

In this respect, the language labels that we learn concerning events external to the organism have a distinct advantage. Such events can be equally shared and observed by others in the verbal community. Consensual agreement and a high degree of accuracy in labeling them are therefore possible.

States Skinner: "Parents teach a child to name colors by reinforcing correct responses. If the child says 'blue' and the object before him is blue, the parent says 'Good!' or 'Right!' If the object is red, the parent says 'Wrong!' " (1971, p. 106).

But this advantage does not accrue to internal, private events, such as feeling-states and emotional responses. Since these are unobservable by the verbal community, it cannot help us much here and the labels we learn are often imprecisely applied. As Skinner puts it:

> In general the verbal community cannot arrange the subtle contingencies necessary to teach fine distinctions among stimuli which are inaccessible to it. . . . As a result the language of emotion is not precise. We tend to describe our emotions with terms which have been learned in connection with other kinds of things; almost all the words we use were originally metaphors. (Skinner, 1971, p. 106)

For the behaviorist, it would then appear that the so-called unconscious of the depth psychologists is simply a congeries of inner events that have either never been labeled or have been imprecisely labeled in our interaction with the particular verbal community with which we have been engaged. This is an intriguing perspective, and its consequences will be discussed shortly. For my present purposes, it is enough to state that consciousness of these inner emotional states is, for Skinner and his associates, simply irrelevant anyway, since feeling-states and emotions are the by-products of behavior, never causes in their own right. While consciousness of them does exist, it can therefore safely be ignored and should be in any scientific analysis. Behavior alone—and its twofold origins in the evolutionary history of the individual and the contingencies of reinforcement to which he or she have been subjected—are the only proper topics of concern.

We are now in a better position to understand the radical behavioristic stance on the issue of self-determination. The conscious feeling of autonomy which we all share, the sense we have of a measure of self-control over our respective destinies, the conscious conviction that the self can function as a causal agent in determining a future course of behavior, are all illusions. We are simply unaware, at the time of responding, of the vast array of previous contingencies and schedules of reinforcement that impinge on the present moment and, in actual fact, completely determine whatever choices we make. The notion of autonomous man is an unfortunate myth, an imprecise label which we and the rest of the verbal community have learned to apply to this state of ignorance. Skinner seems somewhat inconsistent here. By his own analysis, such conscious illusions and the fervid emotions that accompany them apparently cause a great deal of behavior of the sort that greatly concerns him, leading, he fears, to the potential extinction of our culture unless they can be eradicated once and for all (1971, pp. 181–83).

In no way does Skinner deny the uniqueness of the self, as I have pointed out before. Each conscious self is different and distinguishable from all others by virtue of its hereditary endowment and peculiar history of reinforcement. However, he categorically denies that the self can function as an active, much less free, agent of behavior, an independent cause among other internal and external determinants. Instead, it should be seen as the sum total of all such influences, a passive product, the shifting point at which all these vectors meet.

The Cartesian analogy is inappropriate. The self is not a homunculus pulling the levers of a machine. There is no homunculus, and we are not machines. We are living, biological organisms, as such more complex than any machine but subject only to the laws of heredity and reinforcement. Consciousness itself is a special product of the interaction between human organism and environment, an interesting phenomenon but of limited scientific significance.

Skinner clearly rejects both halves of the Cartesian dualistic explanation of the nature of man: the use of a machine metaphor to account for biological properties and the assumption of a qualitatively different spiritual substance to account for mind and its cognitive operations.

The genius and durability of the Skinnerian form of behaviorism lie especially in its atheoretical stance: its refusal to speculate about why reinforcers reinforce. Other neobehaviorists were not so reticent. Clark Hull and his associates theorized that reinforcers served to reduce the noxious internal stimulation that arises from recurring biological tension states (drive-stimulus reduction theory). So-called social reinforcers (approval, recognition, attention, and the like) gain strong reinforcement properties from their association with these primary, physiological-need-reduction operations according to well-established conditioning principles. The Hullian formula reads somewhat as follows: all learning is a function of reinforcement, and all reinforcement is ultimately ascribable to the reduction of noxious physiological (and therefore internal) drive-stimuli. This formula quickly proved inadequate in the face of many learning phenomena (latent learning, learning in the absence of identifiable noxious stimulation, and so on).

Skinner therefore abandoned such theorizing as unnecessary. In his experimental analysis, which has as its classical scientific aim the prediction and control of behavior, one need only identify the reinforcers that particularly affect a given organism. If the probability of eliciting a certain response is increased by giving a child a pat on the head when he or she emits that response, then the pat on the head is a reinforcer. If the corresponding probability is less when he or she is given M&M's under similar circumstances, then the pat on the head is a more cogent reinforcer. One need not ask why. Different organisms will respond differently to different reinforcers; and different schedules in the application of reinforcement will also produce differential effects. With the identification of these conditions, we have enough knowledge to proceed toward shaping the behavior of a given organism in any direction we wish within the biological limits of its repertoire.

Some commentators (Breger & McGaugh, 1965; Estes, 1969; Brown & Herrnstein, 1975) remain convinced that both operant and respondent conditioning control *performance* (the elicitation of already learned responses) and not learning itself, as both Hull and Skinner propose. If this distinction holds up, it has important consequences that may even suggest a possible rapprochement between humanistic and behavioral approaches. If, for example, meaning-fulfillment is a basic human need, as some humanists maintain, then the provision of meaning may well serve as a cogent reinforcer. And if the Skinnerian principles of reinforcement are indeed laws of performance, they may powerfully aid the humanistic investigator in his or her study of this aspect of human experience and behavior. It is my contention that the Skinnerian atheoretical sword can be used to cut both ways!

One further point before I turn to the psychoanalytic version of hard determinism. Skinner openly implies that *knowledge* of reinforcement principles will enable its possessors to reshape the environment in certain desirable ways, by, for example, deliberately removing the need for aversive control and substituting in its stead situations leading only to positive reinforcements. Is there an implication of transcendence here, even of a limited form of freedom? At the very least, this contention appears to imply some priority of conscious knowledge or awareness over behavior. Albert Bandura (1969), Skinner (1974) and other behaviorists who favor the operant model of conditioning, tend to explain away this apparent concession to intentionality on the basis of a prior conditioning of awareness, thus holding fast to their assumption of rigid determinism. Other commentators (Carpenter, 1974; Rychlak, 1977) remain critical of such efforts. Their criticisms will be presented toward the end of this chapter.

### Hard determinism: The Freudian view

There seems to be little doubt that Sigmund Freud (and his more orthodox followers to the present day) adopted, in theory if not always in practice, a strictly reductionistic and therefore deterministic view of human behavior. Influenced by the prevailing philosophical scientism of the Victorian era and his own understandable excitement at having discovered and explored the far-ranging effects of what he called the *dynamic unconscious,* Freud readily admitted the universal illusion of free choice but felt he also had neatly explained it away. The *du sollst* (*thou shalt*) of Immanuel Kant's categorical imperative, and the subsequent implications for human freedom and responsibility which that philosopher had drawn from this universally shared conscious experience in his influential *Critique of Practical Reason,* were brilliantly reduced to the unconscious formation of the superego through the blind, uncritical, and unfree identification with parental standards in early childhood.

In his *Critique of Pure Reason,* Kant had instituted what has come to be called a Copernican revolution in philosophy. The so-called categories of reality (space, time, substance, accident, quality, quantity, causality, existence itself, and so on) which Aristotle and the realists who followed him had confidently attributed to the objects of our knowledge, Kant attributed to sense and intellect themselves. They are, in effect, a priori forms of sense and mind, the spectacles through which we must of necessity view all reality. The *noumenon,* or thing-in-itself, can therefore never be known in its pristine reality. Phenomena alone are the true objects of knowledge. Noumena must be presumed to exist—they are the raw material fed into the hopper of knowledge—but by the time we become consciously aware of them, the innate a priori forms of sense and cognition have already done their work of sorting. As a result of this devastating critique, Kant and many philosophers after him believed they had effectively undercut the philosophical discipline of metaphysics, the attempt to establish the ultimate and objective principles of reality. Included in this, of course, was the effort to establish a rational, objective, universally valid philosophy of morality, based ultimately upon a metaphysical proof of the existence of God.

Kant, a good Lutheran, was understandably disturbed by his own conclusions. He therefore attempted, in his *Critique of Practical Reason,* to rebuild the edifice of moral philosophy on an irrational base, the overwhelming sense or *feeling* of moral responsibility which pervades human experience. In arguments too detailed and delicately articulated to reproduce here, he set out to demonstrate that this universal human experience of the categorical imperative inevitably leads to the concept of a transcendent God and therefore to a well-founded belief in human freedom, moral responsibility, and accountability, and even to the necessity of postulating an afterlife in which ultimate justice would prevail.

It is this construction that Freud set out to demolish through his own doctrine of the unconscious formation of the superego. In an analysis remarkably akin to more current models of conditioning, Freud attempted to show how the archaic superego is already formed in infancy, before the dawn of full consciousness, through parental reward and punishment. Desperately in need of parental approval, the infant, under normal circumstances, attunes his or her behavior to parental restrictions and approbations. Eventually, around the fourth or fifth year (the so-called oedipal period of development), through a process (again unconscious) of identification, the child internalizes these moral sanctions. They now become an integral part of its own personality, the third system (along with id and ego) that will henceforth characterize the individual.

Conscience, for Freud, is simply this superego at work, rewarding the individual with self-approbation for living up to the standards of conduct thus internalized, haunting him or her with guilt if they are violated. Morals therefore equal mores in the Freudian system. The *du sollst* of Kant has exogenous social origins, unconsciously and uncritically assimilated during the vulnerable period of infancy and early childhood. The categorical imperative has no intrinsic merit upon which to build the Kantian edifice of objective morality, and its corollaries of human freedom and responsibility.

Predictably, therefore, Freud took an equally uncompromising stance toward the concept of human freedom and for much the same reasons: "You have an illusion of a psychic freedom within you which you do not want to give up. I regret to say that on this point I find myself in sharpest opposition to your views" (1921, p. 38). And elsewhere Freud speaks of "our suppressed acts of violition which nourish in us the illusion of Free Will" (1950, p. 388).

(At least so speaks Freud the theorist. As a practitioner, he finds himself occasionally guilty of a [Freudian?] slip: "After all, analysis does not set out to abolish the possibility of morbid reactions, but to give the patient's ego *freedom* to choose one way or the other" [1927, p. 72, emphasis added]).

How does Freud, the theorist, justify his claim that personal freedom is illusion? As we have seen, Skinner was to claim that we believe ourselves to be free simply because, at the moment of decision, we are unaware of the myriad preceding contingencies of reinforcement that in fact predetermine the outcome. Freud's explanation is similar: we are by definition unaware of the unconscious determinants that enter into the production of even normal behavior. In his *Psychopathology of Everyday Life* (1966), Freud analyzed, from his own experiences and those of friends and patients, innumerable instances of mental errors or slips—forgetting of names, numbers, and words and other seemingly insignificant lapses in daily life—demonstrating how these apparently trivial accidents can be accounted for by unconscious mechanisms of defense. He then extrapolates this line of argumentation to establish that there is nothing accidental or spontaneous in psychic life.

In this respect, Freud makes a rather curious distinction. As far as he can observe, the conviction of freedom does not reveal itself in serious and important decisions; in these we have rather an impression of psychic compulsion. He states: "It is in trivial and indifferent decisions that one feels sure that he could just as easily have acted differently, that he acted of his own free will and without any motives" (1938, p. 162).

Zavalloni gives us a perspective on this position, which would certainly be shared by those who have developed a thoroughgoing phenomenological analysis of the experience of freedom:

> It is difficult to understand how Freud can deny a universal experience which testifies precisely the opposite of what he says, namely, that freedom actually would appear only in serious and important decisions, while trivial and indifferent decisions become almost automatic. The reason for this fallacy can be found perhaps in the erroneous presupposition that freedom implies the exclusion of all motivation (as appears in the passage just quoted). In the last analysis, when the Freudian school rejects freedom, it bases itself entirely upon the success of psychoanalysis, which attempted to establish the existence and nature of determinism in many cases until then inexplicable. There is no doubt that psychoanalysis can claim real successes. But wherein do these successes lead us to modify the essential position of the problem of free will? What psychoanalysis has contrived to explain are such phenomena as the lapsus [lapsus linguae], dreams, mental disturbances, and neurotic symptoms. But what sensible person has ever dreamed of denying that the facts in question were determined? It is astonishing, Dalbiez points out, that Freud imagines that his opponents could regard the lapsus as a free act (Freud, 1921, pp. 37 ff.; Dalbiez, 1941, p. 296). Let us say once and for all that the problem of free will need not be discussed in a field where it does not arise. (Zavalloni, 1962, p. 50)

Some attempts were indeed made on the part of a few orthodox analysts to move psychoanalysis toward a softer position on the issue of determinism. Maryse Choisy, for example, carefully distinguished between the censorship and ego-ideal dimensions of the superego, ascribing the possible later achievement of a measure of true liberty to the ego-ideal. When we pass from the anachronistic superego to the ego-ideal, she wrote, "we pass from commandments to norms, from determination by others to auto-determination" (1951, p. 83).

Gregory Zilboorg, the noted analyst and historian of medical psychology, more authentically adopted the position that, notwithstanding

Freud's explicit denials, orthodox psychoanalysis leaves the door open to free human activity. He wrote:

> To dismiss psychoanalysis despite the fact that so many objections to it which have been raised can be met with comparative ease, to dismiss it without further examination because it seems to be in conflict with the postulate of free will, means to disregard the fact which has been repeatedly stated and demonstrated in these pages, that psychoanalysis is not a philosophy, nor has it ever discussed seriously the question of free will. (Zilboorg, 1943, p. 330)

Nevertheless, few strictly Freudian analysts, in this author's estimation, would be likely to take up the challenge that Zilboorg proposed.

With the notable exception of Alfred Adler, Carl G. Jung, and Otto Rank, who early broke from the orthodox Freudian camp, most older members of the analytic tradition can undoubtedly be counted among the staunch advocates of the unconscious determination of human behavior. Thus A. A. Brill, one of Freud's first American followers and translators, was to write:

> It was not, however, until I read Freud's "Psychopathology of Everyday Life" and after analysing my own faulty acts and dreams, that psychic determinism became clear to me. For Freud demonstrates clinically what Spinoza formulated in his system of thought. (Brill, 1938, p. 600)

And, according to Eric G. Howe, Freud ended the interminable controversy between liberty and determinism, declaring conclusively that "freedom is an illusion" and that our behavior is determined by forces and experiences of which we are for the most part unconscious. Much of what we consider free seems, after psychoanalytic investigation, merely the last link of a chain whose origin must be sought in the unconscious sources of human action. We are the victims, Howe claimed, not of an eternal fate but of an eternal compulsion, whose origin lies outside our own experience and probably even outside our consciousness (1931, pp. 59ff.).

Among the early dissenters from this position, Alfred Adler, Otto Rank, and Carl Jung, in particular, deserve special study but lie beyond the scope of this presentation. Another interesting group, comprising the so-called ego-analysts, also merit special mention, particularly within the parameters of this present treatment. Heinz Hartmann, Ernst Kris, and to some extent Erik Erikson in his studies on ego-identity, tend to stress the autonomy of the ego in the dynamic structure of personality. Breaking with Freud on the notion that the ego is and always remains the servant of the id, drawing its energy solely from that primordial and blindly instinctual source, these authors attempted to lay a more independent foundation for the ego's functioning (Roazen, 1971). In so doing, they seem to open up the possibility that the ego may be endowed with a noninstinctual source of energy proper to itself and may therefore be free of the unconscious, biological determinism attributed to it by Freud. While Erikson, for one, seemingly succumbs to an environmental determinism instead, the suggestion is a provocative one and is taken up much more strongly by the humanistic-existential authors whose position I will now detail.

## SOFT DETERMINISM: THE HUMANISTIC–EXISTENTIAL VIEW

The viewpoint adopted by humanistic psychologists on the freedom-determinism issue is quite clear, unambiguous, and universal. Taking into account the data established by both behaviorism and psychoanalysis, the human organism is seen as still retaining the potentiality for a limited degree of self-determination or personal freedom. Whence this agreement? As already intimated when mention was made of the earlier ego-analysts, those psychological schools are most sympathetic to the concept of personal freedom which give central importance to the notion of an autonomous ego or self, or active center of intentionality. Representatives of the humanistic-existential movement, as we have seen time and time again, seem universally struck by the undeniable phenomenon of self-reflective awareness or self-consciousness. They hold up this facet of human experience, along with language and culture, as being species-specific, belonging exclusively to the human organism. They tend to see this self-aware ego as an active core of behavior and not merely the passive product of environmental and unconscious forces.

Beginning with the immediate prescientific *experience* (not assumption) of the self as an *active* agent vis-à-vis the internal and external environment, they remain unimpressed by any scientific analysis which attempts to classify this experience as illusory, as in the Skinnerian attempt to define the self as merely an individual repertoire of behaviors. How, they simply ask, can the undoubted impression of activity provided by direct experience arise from pure passivity? The flaw in such analyses, they claim, lies in the innate restrictions of the borrowed natural scientific paradigm in which they are framed. This Lockean paradigm, as Rychlak (1977) prefers to call it, allows of no other outcome, given its assumption of purely mechanical causality.

Small wonder then that humanistic and transpersonal psychologists have universally embarked on a search for new paradigms in order intellectually to justify the essence of this primordial prescientific experience. Rychlak favors the Aristotelian concept of telos, final causality, or purposiveness as reframed in Kantian philosophy. Many others find themselves in essential agreement with the "being-in-the-world" concept of Heidegger and other existential phenomenologists. The ego or self, for all humanists, is the center wherein perceptions, feelings, emotions, thoughts, needs, and drives (conscious or unconscious) are *actively* integrated, harmonized, and expressed in outward behavior. And they tend to focus their investigations on this active center of intentionality rather than on the peripheral stimuli and responses.

Writers representative of this approach may differ widely in their more-or-less naive philosophical assumptions concerning this self-conscious center. Rogers, for example, was initially much influenced by the instrumentalism of John Dewey and the "looking-glass self" notion of the sociologist Charles Cooley. However, all assign to it a definite note of agency or activity proper to itself, some active subjectivity as opposed to other selves and to objects, however these latter are defined.

## May's concept of intentionality

A good current example of this trend is provided by Rollo May in his popular and accessible book *Love and Will* (1969). In formulating the distinction, heretofore a rather elusive one to most academic psychologists, between animal awareness and human consciousness, May seizes upon the concept of *intentionality*. "By intentionality," he says, "I mean the structure which gives meaning to experience" (1969, p. 223). Philosophers will, of course, find themselves on familiar ground as May traces the development of this venerable concept from the ancient Greeks through Aquinas to Kant, Brentano, Husserl, Heidegger, and Merleau-Ponty. May himself confesses to a Midwestern predisposition toward realism, but without digressing farther into a discussion of his own philosophical position, I merely wish to indicate how strongly certain members of this new psychological approach feel about their convictions and how much they rely on the experience, in human consciousness, of an active center of intentionality.

Man, for May, Frankl, and other representatives of this movement, is the being who actively searches for *meaning* in the stimuli that bombard him from within or without and who is constantly engaged in constructing (or perhaps discovering) ever new meanings for himself and others in and through his experiences or actions. It is within this framework that most of these authors see the possibility of a relative but true personal freedom, or better, self-determination.

In brief, to the self experienced as separate from others and from the myriad objects available to it for the gratification of its needs (and even, indeed, experienced as separate from or transcendent over the varied components that are part of its own processes), a choice is possible. And to the extent that one is consciously aware of and can consciously *own* one's deepest needs, feelings, and values, one will be enabled to choose freely, without compulsive necessity, among the various alternatives which promise, to a more or less equal degree, some measure of self-enhancement, self-realization, or self-fulfillment. (Those familiar with the writings of authors like May, Rogers, and Maslow will certainly be aware that such self-fulfilling choices are often, at their best, highly altruistic.) Thus May can write:

> I am proposing a description of human beings given motivation by the new possibilities, the goals and ideals, which attract and pull them toward the future. This does not omit the fact that we are all partially pushed from behind and determined by the past, but it unites this force with its other half. Eros gives us a causality in which "reason why" and "purpose" are united. The former is part of all human experience since we all participate in the finite, natural world; in this respect, each of us, in making any important decisions, needs to find out as much as he can about the objective facts of the situation. This realm is particularly relevant in problems of neurosis in which past events *do* exercise a compulsive, repetitive, chainlike, predictable effect upon the person's actions. Freud was right in the respect that rigid, deterministic causality does work in neurosis and sickness. But he was wrong in trying to apply this to all human experience. Purpose, which comes into the process when the individual becomes conscious of what he is doing, opens him to new and different possibilities in the future and introduces the elements of personal responsibility and freedom. (May, 1969, p. 93)

Zavalloni employs very similar terminology in constructing the link between self-consciousness and voluntary activity:

> We have seen in the introduction to this present study that human behavior presents two phases, one internal and the other external. The internal phase reveals a "center of intentionality," which is the unifying principle of man's various operations and has its origins in a "subject" who is also a center of cognition, or of consciousness (Miller, 1942; Abramson, 1954). Consciousness is the activity of a knowledge which is essentially reflexive—the activity of a subject who returns upon himself. In some of our actions we are "actors" and "spectators" at the same time; we think and we know we are thinking. At this point consciousness becomes self-consciousness. Consciousness does not exist to the same degree in all human activities. The highest degree of consciousness is reached in voluntary activity, which implies a discussion and a value-judgment on the various possibilities of action and the active intervention of the conscious subject to give or refuse his assent. Consciousness is the *conditio sine qua non* of voluntary choice. (Zavalloni, 1962, pp. 264–65)

Both authors in their various ways are here expressing the essential transcendence of reflexive consciousness (i.e., its ability to transcend the spatiotemporal boundaries of immediate experience, to reflect on the past and rehearse the future while generating alternative possibilities, to detach itself from the immediate moment and the forces impinging on it *while still immersed in the process of experiencing them*). It is this phenomenon, above all, which makes the concept of self-determination intelligible.

## Rychlak's concept of telosponsivity

Joseph Rychlak, the experimental psychologist who has long been advocating a new, scientifically rigorous humanistic paradigm for the investigation of human behavior, has provided a more recent, very penetrating analysis of this phenomenon. In basic agreement with authors previously cited, he insists that the capacity for self-determination, or free will, is rooted in the very nature of human consciousness. ("Nature" here is to be understood in the structural phenomenological sense based upon a thorough analysis of what the *experience* of consciousness immediately reveals.)

It is difficult to do justice to Rychlak's rich and detailed account of the phenomenon of human awareness and cognition (1977, 1979, 1980). Briefly, as we have already seen in Chapter 2, he questions the assumptions, derived from Lockean philosophy and characteristic of much of modern psychological theorizing, that the human mind is merely a tabula rasa (blank slate) registering stimulus inputs from the environment and arriving at conclusions (and responses) in strictly unilinear, *demonstrative* fashion. This, he maintains, is only partially true. While we do often reason and act in such computerlike fashion from the facts (inputs) of experience, there is another feature of human consciousness that must not be overlooked. To describe this unique facility he borrows the Kantian term *dialectical transcendence*. I have elsewhere referred to this phenomenon as the self-reflective capacity of consciousness. Here it implies the ability to stand apart from the demonstrative process, be aware that it is occurring, and *entertain the possibility that things could be different.* (Alfred Adler was reputedly fond of reminding his students, whenever he generalized or ventured a prediction, "Everything could also be quite different" [Mosak, 1979, p. 57], a good illustration of the dialectical mind at work.)

Rychlak, along with other investigators, views this dialectical capacity as an *innate* facet of human consciousness. Briefly, it is the capacity to transcend present and even past inputs of experience, to generate and consider alternative possibilities (even some that are impossible to realize and therefore can never actually exist). Given a certain set of premises, the human mind, much like a computer, often does operate in demonstrative, unilinear fashion. But it is also uniquely capable of *changing the premises at any time.* It appears on close inspection to be *free* to do so in a very radical sense.

A vivid example of this capacity at work can be found in the development of non-Euclidean geometry. One of the axioms of Euclidean geometry is that parallel lines can never meet. Challenging that premise (which appears from normal experience to be so self-evident) was one of the imaginative leaps that led to the development of a radically different geometry, which Einstein was to find so useful in formulating his general theory of relativity.

Rychlak, in an analysis that need not detain us here, points to the structure of language itself as embodying both unipolar, demonstrative *signs* and other bipolar terms that necessarily imply their opposite in conveying their meaning. Left, for example, cannot be understood without its intrinsic relationship to right. The analysis of language, particularly *symbolic* language, reveals, he argues, the structure of consciousness itself as intrinsically dialectical as well as demonstrative.

If consciousness indeed operates in this fashion, two conclusions immediately follow by necessity.

1.  The mind is capable of standing apart from both immediate and past experiences. In so doing, it is capable of considering or generating alternative possibilities (some of which have *never* been reinforced in the past). This is the transcendent or reflexive capability of human consciousness and involves an agency or activity intrinsic to it, having nothing to do with previous inputs.

2.  Operating in this fashion, we must then necessarily *choose* to affirm a set of premises on which to base our future actions. Not to do so would result in paralysis, an inability to act at all. (This is not mere speculation. The obsessive-compulsive neurotic, driven by unconscious needs for perfection, suffers from just such a paralysis of will. Unable to discern the *perfect* choice among the alternatives generated by conscious imagination, he or she hesitates to act at all, puts off making any decision, procrastinates. Therapy for such a person involves the process of uncovering and challenging the unconscious need for perfection, changing the *hidden* premise which leads to such debilitating indecisiveness.)

This antecedent choice (conscious or unconscious) of a set of premises which will serve to guide future activity, Rychlak terms a *telosponse*. And since the affirmation process involves some premises generated by the dialectic itself and not therefore based on previous or present experience alone, the outcome cannot be simply predicted in linear, efficient-causal fashion on the basis of such experience (or its concomitant reinforcing properties). In other words, *telosponding*, a unique feature of *human* consciousness, is qualitatively different from mere *responding*, as defined by the behavioristic paradigm in which the response is pictured as being totally determined by the antecedent stimulus input.

*Telos* in Greek means end, goal, purpose, reason why. A telosponse is therefore an adopted or chosen meaningful premise for the sake of which subsequent behavior is engaged in. There is a causality at work here but only in the ancient Greek philosophical sense of *final causality*—that for the sake of which subsequent events occur.

With this analysis we return once more to the humanistic view that men and women are telic organisms whose behavior is, under normal circumstances, guided by conscious purposes or goals. According to Rychlak:

> . . . *free will*, or psychological freedom becomes the *capacity which an individual has to transcend and thereby alter the grounds (meaningful premise, affirmation etc.) for the sake of which he or she is determined.* If human beings reason dialectically, *then* they will never be totally under the control of unidirectional (demonstrative) inputs from the environment. They will be capable of transcending the meanings of such inputs, in self-reflexive fashion—. (Rychlak, 1980, p. 29)

Freedom therefore enters the picture at the point where the telosponse or affirmation of premises is made (given, I would add, certain conditions of awareness to be described in the next section). Once this has occurred, behavior follows *sequaciously*, to use Rychlak's term. It becomes telically determined (and highly predictable). Freedom and determinism are therefore not incompatible but work hand in hand where human behavior is concerned.

Certain consequences follow from this description. In order fully to understand (and predict) human behavior, we cannot rely on behavioral observations alone. We must also use a phenomenological approach to gain information on the conscious premises (purposes, goals) by which our subjects attempt to guide their behavior. Knowing this, our predictions will gain in accuracy and precision, always bearing in mind that our subjects remain free to change such premises in the future.

Second, freedom remains somewhat conditioned by the subject's state of awareness. For the exercise of authentic freedom, the subject must be aware of all the *relevant* data of experiencing, including the *hidden* (unconscious) premises that have guided behavior in the past. Freedom remains always a part of the human *potential*, given the very nature of human consciousness. The actualization of this potential requires that certain conditions be met (to be explored in the next section and in Chapter 8 on the ideal of authenticity). This is what is meant by the term *soft* determinism, used here to characterize the position of most humanistic-existential theorists.


## Consciousness, health, and freedom

It is important at this juncture to realize and point out the links between self-consciousness, self-determination, and psychological health and maturity that have been forged by these and other humanistic authors. To the extent that an individual has been victimized by unconscious compulsions, which by definition are not available to awareness, or to the extent that his or her self-consciousness is impaired by altered states of consciousness (sleep, hypnosis, certain drug-induced states, and the like), to that extent he or she is not capable of true self-determination. Will is not seen by these authors as an autonomous faculty, separate in its functioning from other current aspects of personality. Theirs is a much more holistic approach and avoids the danger of excessive rationalism to which Aristotelianism and Cartesianism led, and which remains a potential source of faulty emphasis in any extrapolation of the ego-analytic theories. As May puts it:

> Later ego analysts have developed the concept of the "autonomy of the ego." The ego is assigned the function of freedom and choice. But the ego can only exist as part of a totality. And it is in this totality that will and freedom must have their base. I am convinced that the compartmentalization of the personality into ego, superego and id is one reason that the problem of will has remained insoluble within the orthodox psychoanalytic tradition. (May, 1969, p. 199)

The humanistic approach therefore implies that psychological freedom or the power of self-determination is inextricably bound up with the degree and extent of self-awareness and is thereby closely correlated with psychological health or authenticity. A person is victimized and unfree to the extent that his or her motivations and action-tendencies lie outside the sphere of conscious awareness and control. Even here, Tournier (1957) and Frankl (1978) would maintain, a significant vestige of freedom may exist in that the person remains free to search for personal meaning in his or her "illness" and to adopt an attitudinal stance or posture toward it:

> Attitudinal values, however, are actualized wherever the individual is faced with something unalterable, something imposed by destiny. From the manner in which a person takes these things upon himself, assimilates these difficulties into his own psyche, there flows an incalculable multitude of value-potentialities. This means that *human life can be fulfilled not only in creating and enjoying, but also in suffering!* (Frankl, 1965, pp. 105–106)

## The developmental dimension

Another clear implication arising from the humanistic analysis is that psychological freedom is not a given existentially. It is instead progressively and painfully *won*. The process is seen as a developmental one, a becoming, which, like Jung's similar process of individuation, progresses through a person's life. (This is not meant to deny that the *potential* for such development lies rooted in the very nature of human consciousness and is therefore constantly present.)

My own understanding of the humanistic account is best articulated by the concept of a *zone of personal freedom.* This concept should be understood as having highly dynamic and relative implications: the zone of personal freedom varies widely among individuals and within each individual according to the specific situations with which he or she is faced. It expands or shrinks accordingly but, under ideal developmental circumstances, can be expected to enlarge progressively over time.

As can be seen from Figure 7–1, I visualize the zone of freedom as tridimensional, developing along three relatively independent axes. (Conversely, the various restrictions or limitations to human freedom can be plotted correspondingly, as we shall see.)

**FIGURE 7–1**
**Developmental dimensions of personal freedom**

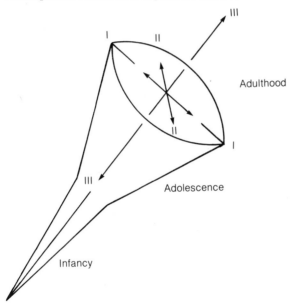

Axis I, roughly reflecting Carpenter's helpful distinctions (1974, pp. 121ff.) refers to the essential *cognitive* basis of freedom in its developmental aspects. Primarily, it involves the normal progression toward full cognitive development described by Jean Piaget and his associates, including the capacity for reflexive awareness. The implication here, of course, is that children (and the severely retarded) are relatively unfree (though hardly unspontaneous) in their behavior.

Axis II reflects the *environmental* (Carpenter's term: *physical*) aspects of free human activity. Freedom of choice implies the existence of options, on the one hand, and my cognitive awareness of such options on the other. If my environment is so restrictive in any given situation as to provide no opportunities for choice (or I remain unaware of the opportunities that are indeed present), the scope of personal freedom is accordingly diminished. Imprisonment of any kind, physical or metaphorical, is an obvious example. Both the convict and the housewife and mother, who *feels* herself entrapped by her family responsibilties, certainly experience a dimunition of their psychological freedom. (This is not meant to discount Frankl's observation, noted above, that a vestige of *attitudinal* freedom can still remain under severe environmental restrictions. This axis therefore represents the merely *extrinsic* limitations to the exercise of personal freedom. It deserves inclusion [consider the value we place on our political freedom] but is less central for our understanding of psychological liberty.)

Axis III reflects the influence of unconscious determinants or restrictions of behavior, however these are conceptualized (repression, or prior conditioning of which I remain unaware. Carpenter's corresponding term: *emotional* freedom). The implication here is that as I incorporate more and more of the unconscious depths of my personality into conscious awareness (or the heights, as I become progressively more aware of previously hidden or unrealized potentialities), I thereby grow in psychological freedom.

The well-known story, perhaps apocryphal, of the professor who was conditioned by the students in his class to write only on the left side of the blackboard will serve as a simple illustration of this point. As the story goes, the students in a class on operant conditioning decided to shape the professor's own behavior. They did so by reinforcing him, through signs of avid attention, every time he wrote on the left side of the board. Whenever he moved past the center to the right, his efforts were met with bored inattention. Soon their goal was achieved. My point is: as soon as the professor became *aware* of what was going on, he would from that moment become free to do what he pleased (and presumably to find ways to change his students' behavior in the future!).

Thus, one who in Rogers's terms becomes more *fully functioning* (i.e., more open to one's entire organismic experiencing, one's unconscious, and to the undistorted surrounding realities, interpersonal and objective), thereby becomes also more free and truly self-determining. Rogers's concept of the locus of evaluation progressively shifting to oneself, in the case of the psychologically healthy person, has special significance in this context (1969, pp. 249ff.).

The opposite, of course, is also true. The person who remains closed to large areas of his or her experience and whose perception of the other remains contaminated by projection, distortion, or denial, remains to that extent unfree.

The importance of this third, more vertical axis in the development of consciousness toward the progressive attainment of true self-determination is easily overlooked. Most adult human beings, it can be assumed, have reached a level of normal reflexive awareness and have some options available to them. But this can be, and I suspect often is, a minimal achievement. I can, for example, consciously choose the practice of psychotherapy as my career goal and find the opportunity to enter a training program for that avowed purpose. I have certain conscious intentions and objectives in mind which are quite clear to me and even a wealth of information concerning my own intellectual aptitudes and the requirements posed by that particular profession. In addition, I have the necessary financial support and am accepted into the program. But a shrewd supervisor, if I am fortunate, will see to it that I become aware of my *unconscious* needs also and will at least begin the process of alerting me to the deeper sources of my motivation to be of help to others in order that my choice and subsequent functioning may become more free and truly more effective. The possible applications of this model are, of course, legion.

## Contributions of the humanistic approach

To repeat a point made previously, humanistic-existential psychology presents a more dynamic, personalistic concept of human freedom than is found, for example, in the Aristotelian-Scholastic or other more rationalistic viewpoints, while maintaining the traditional wedding between intentionality, or cognition, and self-determination, or volition. Zavalloni states this newer, more personalistic viewpoint well:

> Freedom, as a property of a rational being, comprises in its actual functioning both reason and will simultaneously. The free act develops from the basis of complex human motivation as the result of these two psychic functions intimately joined in a vital union. The concomitant presence of these two factors in every act of voluntary decision is undeniable. Man acts as the entire subject of the various dimensions of his personality. For this reason we must say that the *capacity of self-determination, of acting freely, belongs properly to man and not to his volitive function alone.* Human freedom is not the mere expression of a voluntary act; it is essentially the property of a person who determines himself in favor of a preferred value. Rudolf Allers is right: "The question of freedom of the will is somewhat one-sided. It is not the will as a psychological function but the whole human person that is free" (1931, p. 43). The free act is the expression most typical of man, and it involves his entire personality. (Zavalloni, 1962, pp. 269–70)

# 8 The Ideal of Authenticity

Drink from your own wells. Sup at your table. Speak from your own heart. Go where your legs take you. Know your own mind. See through your soul's eye. Follow none but your own self. For each man has his own pathway, and whoever would be your guide cannot help but lead you astray.

Tiro

Authenticity implies being true to a norm discoverable from *within* the individual person. This next theme, common to most humanistic and existential psychologists, arises quite naturally from the preceding ones. The human capacity for reflexive awareness is again the absolute prerequisite: the ability to treat self as an object of experience and knowledge, to evoke the past and anticipate the future, to become aware of one's own intrinsic impulses, talents, limitations, and past conditioning. Holism, as we have seen, implies the necessity for integration of all the levels of human experiencing, and the actualizing tendency provides the trend and direction for individual growth. The capacity for at least a limited degree of self-determination in the face of the many alternative possibilities revealed by conscious examination implies choice and responsibility to self (along with the inevitable, specifically human accompaniments of anxiety and guilt). And as we shall see, authenticity, as defined and explained by the humanists, requires self-transcendence and is essentially a person-centered concept with strongly idiographic components.

As the chapter title indicates, in discussing the theme of authenticity we are dealing with an *ideal* form of personality development. This

necessarily involves making *value judgments* concerning optimal human functioning and the ultimate goals of human living. Such value
judgments are undoubtedly implicit in all personality theories. (Surely
we would all agree that psychopathology is *bad* and mental health is
*good*, however we are inclined to define these conditions. But in so
defining them, we must rely on some norm, or value, against which to
measure optimal or disturbed human functioning.) Most humanists
openly discard the possibilty of a value-free science of personality, and
are quite explicit in proposing norms of optimal functioning, with the
added note that these can best be ascertained by the empirical examination of the healthiest human individuals we can discover, those whose
lives would presumably inspire universal admiration and acclaim. The
concept of authenticity seems best able to describe the outcome of
current humanistic investigations.

In order to establish a context for the theme of authenticity as
expounded by humanistic-existential authors, I will first present some
notions of optimal human functioning favored by representatives of the
behavioral and depth psychological approaches, postponing until the
next chapter a discussion of the contributions of transpersonal psychologists.

## BEHAVIORISM

For a number of reasons, the ideal of authenticity as implying an
intrinsic, consciously discoverable, somewhat idiosyncratic norm for
individual development is not looked upon with favor by most behaviorists. B. F. Skinner, the foremost contemporary proponent of the
rigorous experimental analysis of behavior, remains openly critical of
any attempt to include elements of consciousness as either independent or dependent variables in a scientific account of human behavior
(1971, 1974). Skinner's position is, self-admittedly, not value-free. As
we have seen, he does propose an ultimate value: the survival of the
human race. However, he feels this can only be achieved if we disabuse
ourselves of the notions of human freedom and dignity espoused by
humanists of all stripes. Within certain given parameters that are biologically and/or genetically based, human behavior is strictly conditioned by environmental contingencies (with a heavy emphasis on the
latter).

Skinner is a hard determinist who is personally and for theoretical
reasons opposed to the use of aversive controls in the shaping of human
behavior. (Their use is not only painful and unpleasant for the subjects
involved but often leads to unpredictable or disadvantageous outcomes.) He favors an engineered society based upon the positive reinforcement of desirable behaviors and culminating in an utopian exis-

tence for all concerned marked by the absence of violence, war, crime, avoidable disease, injustice, and the other social ills that presently bedevil us. Positively, the characteristics of such a society would include cooperativeness, the fair distribution of goods and services, equal dissemination of culture and education fitted to the talents of individuals, the encouragement of creativity (genetically based differential talents), and other qualities of the good life envisioned by many of his humanistic colleagues. For Skinner, however, reliance on consciousness-raising techniques and an inner directional tendency of the individual organism to pursue what is best for itself and society as a whole is too unreliable and theoretically inadmissible. In his elegant and parsimonious system, consciousness is a product, or better, a byproduct of little scientific significance, not an agent transcending environmental determinants.

Much the same can be said for *social learning theory*, a contemporary variant of behaviorism, which does allow for such cognitive factors as attitudes or "attributions" as intervening or "mediating" variables between environmental stimuli and human response. Despite the inclusion of such cognitive and therefore conscious variables, the similarity to humanistic or truly phenomenological paradigms is more apparent than real. Rychlak (1977), for one, has ably exposed the cause-effect, "hard" deterministic thinking behind the theoretical perspective in which Skinner's black box is simply filled with inputs *previously* conditioned by environmental stimuli.

It should be reiterated here that behaviorism, in all its variant contemporary and historical forms, is more a learning than a personality theory. As extended to human functioning, it stresses the developmental acquisition of adequate or maladaptive behaviors as defined by the group and society into which the individual is being socialized. As such it has provided a great deal of valuable, empirically based information on the socialization process as it affects all human individuals during a particularly vulnerable period of their lives. Infants and children *are* vulnerable during these initial stages of development, humanists maintain, precisely because reflexive consciousness itself is a developmental phenomenon, a mere potentiality at birth which is not fully actualized until well into adolescence, if then. Included in this developmental sequence is the capacity to recognize what is happening to us, the ability critically to evaluate what is going on, and the consequent ability to assume a stance toward all that, contemplate alternatives, and perhaps choose a different course of action. Until that developmental process (roughly parallel to the stages of cognitive development described by Jean Piaget) has reached its apex, it can be assumed that the human organism is as much subject to the behavioral laws of conditioning as are the lower organisms from which these laws were generated. It is at this point, however, that humanists and behaviorists part company.

With this perspective in mind, it is easy to see why behavior therapists adopt a basically pragmatic, operational view toward the definition of adaptive or maladaptive behavior. For the behaviorists, then, *society* sets the norm not the individual. Subjective distress remains an important clue for the individual that something has gone awry and ought to be corrected but only because such distress is a function of some aversive consequence of my behavior vis-à-vis important controllers of the reinforcement I need. Maladaptive behavior can thus be defined as whatever violates significant cultural norms.

This will vary, to be sure, between cultural groups and even among the various subcultures within a given society. (Behaviorists, like their humanistic counterparts, do not subscribe to a medical disease model of personality disturbance, except in the relatively rare number of cases where such physical causes can be clearly demonstrated to exist.) Adaptive and even optimal human functioning can be defined as those behaviors which assure the individual of satisfactory or optimal access to the sources of reinforcement that a given society controls. Under most circumstances, these are good, practical criteria for determining the need for therapeutic intervention, though they do not answer an important question posed by some commentators: How does one determine whether a given society or important subgroup is itself sick or disturbed in respect to the kinds of norms it establishes for individual behaviors?

## DEPTH PSYCHOLOGY

When pressed to describe what he believed to be the most important characteristics of healthy personality functioning, Sigmund Freud is widely quoted as having replied: "the ability to love and to work." By this he was understood to mean: (a) the ability, during one's years of maturity, to maintain a lasting, intimate relationship with a member of the opposite sex, including the capacity for mutual sexual enjoyment and orgasm through intercourse; and (b) the ability to sublimate or channel instinctual energies into some creative contribution to society according to one's inherent talents. While this too can serve as a pragmatically useful criterion for healthy functioning, humanists again object to its theoretical basis.

### The Freudian model

The Freudian model is derived from an energy transformation, biophysical metaphor. The individual is born with a certain quantum of energy derived from biological sources and tied up predominantly with the biological instincts of sex and aggression. These together comprise the inherited component of the personality system called the *id*. Tension is repeatedly built up within this system, and in its discharge, pleasure is experienced. The so-called pleasure principle is and remains always the basic motivating force of personality functioning. The id remains, however, a more or less self-contained system which can only gratify its instinctual impulses through the human capacity for fantasy (the primary process).

Since this procedure is not realistically gratifying to the individual, those biological components of the organism (or id) that provide access to the external environment (sensory, motor, and, later, cognitive processes) are constellated into another component of personality, the ego. Ego-functions gain strength (energy) from the id for their own further development by establishing and maintaining contact with environmental sources of gratification for id impulses that prove to be realistically satisfying. The ego consequently operates on the reality principle and by means of the secondary process, involving sensation, perception, motor activity, memory, and, eventually, thinking. Freud (1961) stoutly maintained (against some of his followers who came to be known as ego-analysts) that the ego remains always the servant of the id and never becomes truly autonomous in its functioning. (If it should fail in its task, Freud theorized, the id reclaims the energy invested in the ego and returns to primary process or fantasy sources of gratification. This appears to be the first historical attempt to explain the psychodynamics of schizophrenic withdrawal and fragmentation of ego-processes).

The final component of personality functioning begins to develop, Freud maintained, as soon as the questing ego, in its continuing search for realistic sources of gratification, runs headlong into social reality. Society (presumably out of some collective biological instinct which promotes the survival of the species as a whole) places certain restrictions on the indiscriminate satisfaction of sexual and aggressive impulses. The infantile ego, through its reality-testing function, discovers these restrictions during the course of its ongoing interactions with those powerful agents of society, one's parents. And so the socialization process begins and continues as other significant agents of society begin to enter the picture. Given the helplessness and utter dependency on the environment so characteristic of human infancy and early childhood, there are no alternatives. The growing child *must* conform or run the intolerable risk of alienating the most consistent and dependable gratifiers of its ever-recurring needs.

In the beginning, according to Freud, the budding ego learns of these restrictions through its encounter with a system of more or less consistent rewards and punishments for certain specific behaviors. During the oedipal phase of development (sometime between the ages of four and six), through unconscious processes including identification (too complex to describe at this point), these standards become incorporated or introjected into the personality itself. They now become my standards: certain behaviors that were previously rewarded become part of *my ego-ideal;* behaviors that were punished are now part of *my conscience,* and I reward or punish myself (through self-approval or guilt) for conformity or nonconformity to the standards I have learned. Together, these new components of personality comprise a third system, the superego (or *über-Ich,* that which stands *over* the ego in a judgmental or moralistic sense).

In the Freudian schema, therefore, the ego is the executive arm of the personality and the mediator between the impulsive, pleasure-seeking id and the restrictive, moralizing superego. Intrapsychic conflict is inevitable in such a system. Optimally, the ego learns how to gratify the id by channeling its libidinal and aggressive energies into socially acceptable activities (a process which Freud termed *sublimation*). This is obviously a delicate, homeostatic balancing act. If successful, the ego maintains its own position at the helm of personality functioning, continuing to capture energy from the id for the further development of its own processes.

There remains, however, a conformist ring in the Freudian account of optimal human functioning. Ultimate human values become equated with the *mores* of a given society in this system. Conscience has an exogenous origin and is not, as some humanists maintain, an intrinsic, endogenous component of personality. Narcissism (the pleasure principle) remains the most fundamental driving force in human functioning. In his later years, Freud toyed with the notion that it might be possible for human beings to transcend their basic narcissism through truly altruistic behavior (notably, in a discussion of the Pauline concept of agape, or altruistic love), but the threat to his already well-developed theoretical system was probably too great for him to do any more than hint at such an eventuality.

A few of Freud's earliest followers gradually began to disagree with one or another of his basic theoretical assumptions and were eventually expelled from their positions in the newly formed psychoanalytic societies. These neo-Freudians, as they came to be called, established their own version of depth psychology and began to entertain views of optimal human functioning that were to exercise a discernible influence on the thinking of contemporary humanistic and existential psychologists. I will content myself with presenting some ideas formulated by two of these early dissenters, *Alfred Adler* and *Carl Jung,* in the effort to demonstrate how they foreshadow current notions of authenticity. (The contributions of a third neo-analyst, Otto Rank, have already been presented in the discussion of the related theme of self-actualization.)

## The Adlerian model

*Alfred Adler,* whose influence is openly acknowledged in the works of the humanist, Abraham Maslow, and the existential analysts Rollo May and Viktor Frankl, proposed the concept of a *creative self* in his later writings (Adler, 1964). This core idea, which served to unify his entire theory of personality development and functioning (Hall & Lindzey, 1970), is strikingly similar to the notion of the self as an *active* center of intentionality so favored by modern phenomenologists (May, 1969) and central to the thinking of all humanistic psychologists. In brief, Adler, like the humanists, takes quite seriously the universal human experience of the self as an *agent* of behavior and not the mere passive product of forces impinging on the individual. Adler, again like the humanists, consequently depicts men and women as capable of purposive action in pursuit of self-determined life goals once the nonconscious influences which determined the early course of development are brought to awareness. His major concepts of personality functioning are so parallel to those of current humanistic psychologists that Adler should probably be considered among their number (Mosak & Dreikurs, 1973; Ansbacher, 1974) were it not for his understandable lack of acquaintance with contemporary existential phenomenology and scientific methods of validation. He must certainly be considered one of the forerunners of this current trend, and there is renewed interest in his writings for their heuristic value.

Adler's portrayal of optimal human functioning centers around the notion of *social interest:* the self-determined choice of a lifestyle that transcends the egocentrism or narcissism of the Freudian pleasure principle.

> The "psychologically healthy" or "normal" individual may be defined as one who has developed his social interest, who is willing to commit himself to life and the life tasks without evasion, excuse or "sideshows" (Wolfe, 1932). He can then employ his energies in being a fellowman with confidence and optimism in meeting life's challenges. He has his place. He feels a sense of belonging. He is contributive. He has his self-esteem. He has the "courage to be imperfect," and possesses the serene knowledge that he can be acceptable to others, though imperfect. (Mosak & Dreikurs, 1973, p. 50)

Adlerians, as do others, dispute the origins of the capacity for social interest in the human individual. Some consider it a psychological construct, a product of social learning. Others, like Wexberg (1929), saw it as an integral part of the biological purposive pattern, a notion parallel to the Rogerian concept of the direction implicit in the actualizing tendency as it unfolds in the human organism. Be that as it may, the Adlerian goal of completion (Adler, 1958), perfection (Adler, 1964), or mastery (Adler, 1926) closely approximates current ideals of self-realization and authentic human living. All depend for their actualization on the successful strivings of a conscious, creative self to fashion or discover a personally satisfying and meaningful pattern out of the bewildering welter of life experiences in which all of us find ourselves immersed.

## The Jungian model

Another depth psychologist and early dissenter from the Freudian position who went on to develop a more intrinsic criterion for optimal human functioning is *Carl Gustav Jung.* I must take note of an interesting phenomenon here concerning the influence that Jung has exerted on contemporary psychologists. Behaviorists tend to ignore him completely, sensing no doubt his radically different metaphysical assumptions, his unique phenomenological approach to "psychic reality," and his emphasis on the constructs of a "collective unconscious" and "archetypal symbols" that presumably exert an enormous influence on human behavior. He is simply dismissed as being too philosophical, mystical, or esoteric.

Humanistic-existential authors, while better acquainted with the Jungian contributions, remain uncomfortable with his persistent emphasis on the Unconscious (collective as well as personal). His use of this construct as a noun, in agreement with Freud, implies for these authors an inadmissible dichotomy at the root of human functioning which tends to violate their own holistic assumptions. (For this reason, they tend to favor the Adlerian approach, which avoids reification of "nonconscious" processes and simply defines the unconscious as the "nonunderstood" [Mosak & Dreikurs, 1973, p. 39]). It is the transpersonal psychologists, with their more contemporary emphasis on altered (non-"normal") states of consciousness, who are more likely to be at home with the Jungian approach and to look to him for guiding ideas and inspiration.

Nevertheless, it seems to me instructive to present the Jungian concept of authentic human functioning, in the belief that it bears a striking resemblance to current humanistic emphases, though admittedly from a somewhat different vantage point. (It is my further personal conviction that humanistic-existential authors might benefit a great deal in the future development of this approach from a closer scrutiny of the Jungian contributions, a point that will be developed at greater length in the final chapter of this work.)

Two of Jung's principal concepts will be explored to illuminate his position on this topic: the process of individuation and his own version of an actualizing tendency: the transcendent function. Both are required to understand his views on the emergence of the Self, which is given a unique definition in Jungian thought.

*The individuation process.* Simply stated, the individuation process is the lifelong tendency of the human organism to attain a stable unity marked by increasing conscious *differentiation* (and *integration*) from both the collective unconscious, our universal psychic inheritance, and the external collective forces that impinge upon us from society during the early processes of socialization. For Jung, psychic reality transcends individual human consciousness in the same manner that the biological species transcends the individual biological organism. Given such a system, the psychic inheritance of certain potentialities for behavior is just as sensible a construct as the inheritance of certain biological potentialities.

Scientifically, we understand the transmission process through which the latter is accomplished (the genetic code, and so on) much better, Jung would maintain, than we do the former. But just as the individual biological organism represents a unique, nonrepeatable instance of the species, *so also should the psychic component of that organism.* To accomplish this, it must differentiate itself from both the collectives, unconscious and societal, while remaining in contact with and in some degree dependent upon them. The innate tendency to move toward this goal is what Jung seems to mean by his individuation process, a concept obviously akin to the actualizing tendency postulated by humanistic psychologists.

To do so, Jung maintains, we must consciously own, appropriate, integrate, and express what is uniquely our own from this dual inheritance in the face of societal attempts to define our existence purely on the basis of the numerous roles we are called upon to adopt. Such roles are inevitable: child, parent, male, female, husband, wife, student, worker, and so on. To play them stereotypically is to lose our individuality. Therefore, one aspect of the individuation process is creatively to adapt the role of our own individual personality or conversely to express our individuality in and through the various roles we must necessarily fulfill. To do less leads to psychological death. This much seems clear and incontrovertible to most humanists (Maslow, 1968; Jourard, 1971). Much more controversial is the Jungian addition that we must eventually come to terms, again through conscious appropriation in an individual way, with the archetypal themes and symbols that at first unconsciously dominate our psychic life: most notably persona and shadow, anima or animus (for males and females respectively), self, birth, reproduction, death, and a host of others.

The initial developmental task, according to Jung, dominates the first half of life and follows upon the acquisition and maturation of personal consciousness, or ego, during childhood and early adolescence (Jung, 1933, pp. 95–144). It involves the thrusting of the ego onto the stage of life in the period from adolescence to midlife. "The significance of the morning (of life) undoubtedly lies in the development of the individual, our entrenchment in the outer world, the propagation of our kind and the care of our children" (Jung, 1933, p. 109). During this period we are forced to limit ourselves to the attainable and to differentiate particular aptitudes, for in this way the capable individual discovers his or her social being. However, by limiting ourselves to the attainable, we must necessarily renounce, for a time at least, all other potentialities.

The first half of life is therefore governed by the emergence of personal consciousness out of the mists of infantile "unknowing" and the development of the persona, the face we present to the external world in accordance with its demands and expectations. This is an archetypal theme, common to the experience of all men and women in every generation and culture since the dawn of human history and symbolized by the universal myth of the hero who overcomes all obstacles, slays all the dragons, and overpowers all his enemies in his quest for glory. This is an inescapable task and an important, vitally necessary achievement.

This differentiation of individual consciousness and this finding of one's own unique niche in society is an integral part of the individuation process but only the first part. Perhaps for most people, unfortunately, it is taken for the whole.

Jung would presumably have agreed with Joseph Nuttin, the humanistic psychologist whose position on authentic human living I will consider next, concerning the myriad potentialities that, under normal circumstances in our society, open up before the expanding consciousness of each individual. Choices have to be made, and this inevitably implies that the selection of certain avenues of development will lead to the bypassing of others which are perhaps equally promising. For Jung, these neglected potentialities, along with the natural, ever-recurring, more primitive impulses that are deemed shameful or unacceptable by society, these "glowing coals under grey ashes," are relegated to the individual's "shadow" complex. (Jung believes that we tend to project these shadow elements within ourselves onto others. The evil I hate and fear "out there" is a potential also within me; the envy I feel toward you may issue from an unfulfilled potentiality within myself; my attraction toward another may be based on a warmth and sensitivity openly displayed by her that lie dormant within me.)

Jung delighted in exposing the polarities within human personality. The accomplishment of the tasks of the first half of life necessarily results in a certain one-sidedness of development, an inevitable imbalance. The task of the second half, then, is to reduce that imbalance, to develop hitherto neglected aspects of personal functioning and thereby achieve integration or wholeness.

A certain conscious concentration on one's own psychic life should therefore characterize this period. Lost sensitivities need to be resurrected and developed, gaps in previous development filled. The outcome of this final phase of the individuation process is the *emergence of Self* which, for Jung, is obviously more than the ego and much more than the persona. Its symbol is the *mandala,* the quartered circle, one or other version of which is found in all cultures and which additionally often appears in the dreams of those who have embarked on the path of true individuation. It is a symbol of the completion or wholeness for which we all yearn.

**The transcendent function.** Jung's concept of the transcendent function should be of interest to those humanists who ascribe to the notion of an actualizing tendency that pulls us toward self-realization. In terms of the latter, it can be conceived of as that aspect of the actualizing tendency that tends toward the unification of all the several systems of personality toward the goal of perfect wholeness. Its aim, according to Jung, is "the realization, in all of its aspects, of the personality originally hidden away in the embryonic germ plasm; the production and unfolding of the original, potential wholeness" (Jung, 1933, p. 108). The transcendent function operates at first unconsciously. Its quest is universally mirrored in the myths and symbols, religion, and art of humankind. The purpose of this book would not be served by exploring the wealth of data that Jung has amassed from these sources in support of his position. What is of interest is his contention that *conscious* appropriation of these tendencies is ordinarily required for success in this venture, particularly in societies such as ours that overvalue the period of youth and its necessary concentration on a narrowing of consciousness to the tasks that befit that stage of development.

> In primitive tribes we observe that the old people are almost always the guardians of the mysteries and the laws, and it is in these that the cultural heritage of the tribe is expressed. How does the matter stand with us? Where is the wisdom of our old people—where are their precious secrets and their visions? For the most part our old people try to compete with the young. In the United States it is almost an ideal. (Jung, 1933, p. 110)

The answer to this problem would seem to lie in the conscious recognition of the tasks appropriate to the various stages of the individuation process and in the consciously guided effort to fulfill its purposes and goals: survival and achievement for the first half of life, the attainment of wisdom and preservation of culture for the second. It is in this respect that Jung's ideas most closely parallel humanistic thinking on the authentic human life, along with the postulation of *intrinsic* criteria for determining the direction and goal of optimal human functioning.

## HUMANISTIC–EXISTENTIAL VIEWPOINTS

The humanistic-existential approach picks up and elaborates on this notion of intrinsic criteria for the determination of optimal human functioning. This idiographic emphasis on individual differences is firmly based on major foundations: human biology and the phenomenological study of human consciousness. Modern biology continues to amass information on the enormous range of individual differences that exist within the human species, *within even normal limits,* across the subspecialties of anatomy, morphology, physiology, and biochemistry. It is by now an axiom that no two individuals (even monozygotic twins) are exactly alike thanks to differences presumably arising from genetic constitution, or prenatal environment, or both (Williams, 1973). Humanists ascribe to this biological diversity the highly individualized clusters of talents and potentialities, the unique, nonrepeatable endowment bestowed on each member of the species. This is a facet of human functioning often overlooked in our scientific quest for general laws, uniformities, and statistical averages.

Humanists add to this the equally important conclusion that each individual develops, through consciousness, his or her own unique frame of reference or private world of experience. Together, these form the basis of my unique Being-in-the-World, and it is within these parameters that I must fashion my own authentic expression of human existence. The ideal of authenticity implies that it is *my* potential that must be discovered and actualized, and it is in this sense that humanists postulate an *intrinsic* criterion for human growth and development. Each author gives his or her own insights into what this entails or focuses on one or other aspect of the process of self-discovery and actualization. However, as we shall see by examining in some detail the viewpoints of various authors on this theme, there is a remarkable degree of agreement among them.

## STRUCTURAL ORIENTATIONS

### Nuttin's constructive ideal of personality

Presentation of the views of the Belgian humanist, Joseph Nuttin, on optimal or authentic human functioning can best be accomplished by integrating the contributions from his work already outlined in the previous chapters of this volume. The reader will recall (from Chapter 2) his postulation of three irreducible levels of conscious experience: psychophysiological, psychosocial, and transpersonal or spiritual. The basic drive toward self-realization, the fundamental drive of the human organism, attempts to actualize the myriad potentialities that arise from each of these levels, from the growth, development, and reproduction of our biological organisms, through the enhancement of our social and interpersonal relationships, to the development of a personally satisfying and meaningful relationship to the whole universe of Being of which we are a part. Truly basic and irreducible needs are therefore associated with each of these levels. They are many in number, inevitably conflict with each other, and demand concomitant interaction with the environment at all levels for their gratification. Since it is obviously impossible to gratify all such needs or to actualize all such potentialities simultaneously, choices must be continually made. In the long run and fortunately for the individual involved, it is the *person* who must be satisfied (in keeping with Nuttin's holistic emphasis) not the individual need.

Nuttin (1962) draws an important distinction here between the *nonsatisfaction* of a need and its *frustration*. Nonsatisfied needs (or, concurrently, nonactualized potentials) are those which a person deliberately chooses to set aside or neglect in the pursuit of a personally fulfilling life plan or, to use his own term, *constructive ideal of personality*. Such needs and potentials gradually lose their dynamic force and over time cease to influence the individual's behavior. Urgent sexual needs, for example, gradually lose their dynamic force—provided the individual has chosen to bypass their gratification in order to pursue a course of action which is on the whole more gratifying to him or her as a person, as, for example, in a celibate ministry or the avid pursuit of exciting scientific discoveries. (Given their physiological origin, however, such needs could presumably be expected to recur with full dynamic force if alternate pursuits eventually ceased to be as fulfilling as they once were.)

Frustrated needs (and/or potentials), on the other hand, are those which the individual would very much like to satisfy (or develop) if he or she were not restricted from doing so by forces beyond his or her control (social restriction, neurotic guilt, fear of consequences, and the like). Consciously suppressed or unconsciously repressed, such needs or frustrated potentials retain their dynamic force (à la Freud) and continue to influence the individual's behavior, usually through maladaptive outlets. Thus, for example, a young man or woman who has not consciously chosen to bypass sexual gratification in favor of other pursuits that provide basic fulfillment and whose sexual drives are restricted from normal expression for whatever reason may well develop "perverted" outlets of gratification (voyeurism, fetishism, compulsive masturbation, neurotic obsessions, and so on).

Frustrated needs in particular are generally relegated to the intimate sphere of consciousness (see Chapter 5). Whether derived from a higher or lower level of functioning, they continue to exercise an influence, generally maladaptive, on an individual's behavior. Nuttin, therefore, insists that, for optimal human functioning, two courses of action are necessary. First of all the individual must consciously recover, face, and assimilate such data to the public sphere of consciousness and, second, consciously forge for himself or herself a *constructive ideal of personality* realistically in accord with all the facts about himself or herself so uncovered. In this way, the individual may for a time at least bypass the gratification of certain needs without harm in the pursuit of a realistically gratifying life plan or ideal that will prove to be ultimately and deeply fulfilling.

What Nuttin is advocating here is obviously consonant with the existentialist dictum: an *examined life* is required for authentic human functioning. Ideally, all data from all three levels of experiencing must be consciously assimilated and processed, in Nuttin's view, toward the construction of a realistic and attainable ideal for each individual. No level can be entirely bypassed in this search for authenticity. Basic physiological needs must, of course, be consistently met for the organism to survive at all and be enabled to pursue other, higher levels of development. The overt expression of sexual needs, according to Nuttin at least, comprises a special case, involving as it does the survival of the species rather than the survival of the individual organism as such. Such needs do need to be tamed in order for other developments to occur, but this is a far cry from the reductionism implied by the Freudian concept of sublimation. Their expression does need to be harmonized and integrated into the psychosocial and transpersonal forms of existence consciously adopted by the individual. Only thus can sexuality be humanized and transformed from its primitive instinctual base.

***The gift of self.***   At the psychosocial level, Nuttin draws an interesting distinction between the psychic and moral gift of self. The *psychic gift of self* is a necessary but not sufficient condition for ideal functioning at this level of experience. It is simply the "ability to concentrate on some activity to the complete forgetfulness of self" (1962, p. 242).

Nuttin gives the example of the shy person who, overly preoccupied with his own fears, cannot truly benefit from his contact with others. Such psychological preoccupation with self-concerns, however motivated, prevents the effective contact with the impersonal or personal other required for development on this plane. No living organism can feed on itself and hope to grow. The student reading a text will learn nothing if he or she cannot concentrate on the material presented.

Beyond this prerequisite, however, a *moral gift of self* is also occasionally necessary for complete growth and development of the personality. The student who is able to concentrate on the text but only for the purpose of memorizing items of information required for an examination may indeed pass the test yet fail to learn much in the process. In this context it is the *aim* or *intention* of the activity that makes the crucial difference, involving, in this case, a more or less complete openness to and respect for the object apart from any egocentric concerns.

The point that Nuttin is making here is further underscored, as we shall see, by the Rogerian concept of "unconditional positive regard" for the other and Maslow's thoughts on B-cognition and B-valuing to be taken up in the next section.

**The transpersonal level.** Finally, for Nuttin, the examined life or the development of a constructive ideal of personality involves conscious effort on the third level of experiencing: the spiritual or transpersonal. The previous two levels, it will be recalled, concern experiencing of a very concrete sort: the biological givens of our existence or the individual objects or persons that consciousness continually reveals to us. On the transpersonal level, "man is a being who asks himself questions *about his very existence*" (1962, p. 246). It is at this more abstract level, a level made possible by the type of consciousness we possess, that such existential questions arise and demand to be answered. This need to know, this search for contact with some absolute value that can situate us in the universal order of things and thereby give us a sense of personal meaning, is not reducible to tissue-needs or the need for some form of social validation of our existence. It is a requirement posed by the very nature of consciousness itself.

Psychology, as Nuttin rightfully points out, cannot of itself provide the answers. But it should not shy away from underlining the existence of this basic human need, the varied forms of behavior that issue from it, or its effects on normal or abnormal human conduct. Nuttin himself outlines some of the forms in which it manifests itself in religion, philosophy, politics, science itself, esthetics, the quest for salvation or personal immortality (for example, through one's works or offspring), or for some form of integral self-actualization. He does not seem to have been familiar with the works of Viktor Frankl but is in remarkable agreement, as we shall see, with Frankl's very similar observations and conclusions. Both insist that the satisfactory development of this aspect of human potential is necessary for a fully authentic human existence. Its frustration can only lead to existential despair and eventually to dysfunctional behavior. This is not to say, in Nuttin's terms, that it cannot be bypassed for a time without harm to the personality. But it will recur and apparently does so particularly during the normative crises of adolescence (the stage during which abstract cognitive development first matures) and of middle age, in accordance with Jung's previously quoted observations. Suffice it to say that this basic human need and/or potential must at some point be integrated into the individual's constructive ideal in a personally meaningful way.

Presumably it is also at this transpersonal level of conscious functioning that the work of integration will take place. Cultural institutions, for a growing number of moderns, no longer serve the function of providing ready-made answers to the broad existential questions. More and more we are thrown back on our own resources and must rely on our own intrinsic criteria for assessing the validity of the answers we encounter. The ideal of authenticity itself may indeed be a byproduct of present cultural confusion and heterogeneity. The problems loom larger on that account.

## Maslow's self-actualized person

Abraham Maslow reiterated many of the points developed in Nuttin's account of optimal human functioning and added some original features of his own. First of all, he repeated Nuttin's call for the creation of a psychology of normal or healthy personality development to be based not so much on the data of animal experimentation or psychopathology, as has often been the case, but on data gathered from normal or healthy human specimens. Maslow took this a step further, suggesting that psychologists might well concentrate their research efforts on the selection and intensive study of the healthiest, best-functioning human specimens available: "the most creative, or the strongest, or the wisest, or the saintliest" (1971, p. 9). Or, as he himself put it: "I propose for discussion and eventually for research the use of selected good specimens (superior specimens) as biological assays for studying the best capability that the human species has . . ." (1971, p. 5).

Maslow had high hopes for this venture, believing that the exhaustive study of such biological assays would eventually lead to a normative science of human behavior, uncovering not only the "farther reaches of human nature," (the highest potentialities to which men and women can aspire) but even an objective, biologically based system of values by which to guide human aspirations and conduct.

Maslow himself (1954) initiated a research program to identify a number of so-called self-actualized persons and study their distinguishing characteristics and ways of behaving. While his efforts have been justly criticized for their methodological deficiencies (Child, 1973, p. 21; Schultz, 1977, p. 79—Maslow himself served as the nominating committee for his self-actualizing subjects!), the underlying idea is sound enough and amenable to better-controlled methods of observation. The conclusions he drew from his exploratory observations led him to believe in the possibility of establishing an empirical psychology of Being (1968), a scientific description of end-states, states of human perfection or "full-humanness," or, in a word, of highest human authenticity.

Several of his conclusions are provocative and highly interesting. They will be presented here with the caveat that they are not as yet well supported by solid empirical evidence and are solely for the purpose of delineating his views on what constitutes optimal human functioning.

*The need-hierarchy.*    Maslow's theory of motivation postulates a hierarchy of basic human needs similar to Nuttin's description in many respects. At the bottom of the ladder are the physiological needs of the organism, followed by safety-needs (for security, stability, protection, order, and freedom from fear and anxiety), the belonging- and love-needs (social-needs), the esteem-needs (ego-needs), and finally, the need for self-actualization (fulfillment and creativity).

However, Maslow adds a very important note concerning the relationships between these various levels. He hypothesized that lower needs are *prepotent* (i.e., that needs at the lower end of the hierarchical ladder must be satisfied at least partially before higher needs become psychologically salient). Simply put, people who are literally starving to death have little or no energy left to invest in the higher forms of self-fulfillment or even in maintaining their social position or self-esteem. Conversely, as needs lower on the scale are satisfied, at least to some extent, new ones at the next higher level emerge from ground into figure and clamor for gratification.

Maslow's hypothesis also implies that the general actualizing tendency operates more powerfully (prepotently) at the four lower levels of the hierarchy. This in turn leads him to conclude that self-actualization needs (needs for personal growth and integration) are not as strongly instinctive as the lower needs and can rather easily be overshadowed in the presence of pressing demands from the lower levels of functioning. However, they are based on the inner nature of the individual and are presumably never rendered completely inoperative.

Maslow elaborated this position further by drawing a distinction which apparently implies a qualitative difference between needs that arise from the four lower levels of his scale and those that emerge from the highest. The former he lumps under the rubric of *deficiency-needs*, while reserving the term *growth-needs* for those that arise from the level of self-actualization (1968, p. 21ff). Deficiency-needs (D-needs) imply a deficit in the organism, a lack of something required for its survival as a physiological or social being. Growth-needs, while also arising from a lack or deficit (of completion, perfection, integration) do not have mere survival or maintenance of the organism as their aim but rather its enhancement or further development. Maslow prefers to call these B-needs (needs for fuller Being) or meta-needs (needs that arise after the d-needs have been met). D-needs act as noxious or unpleasant internal stimuli, operate more on a homeostatic basis, and, as it were, push us urgently from behind. B-needs pull us from ahead, as from an ideal, yearned-for state of Being that draws us ever onward and upward.

Perhaps the flavor of this distinction will come through by citing the example Maslow gives of happy, secure children who do not have to be pushed to grow but rather seem to enjoy the developmental process as it unfolds:

> In these children we see clearly an eagerness to grow up, to mature, to drop the old adjustment as outworn, like an old pair of shoes. We see in

them with special clarity not only the eagerness for the new skill but also the most obvious delight in repeatedly enjoying it, the so-called Funktions/Lust [function-pleasure] of Karl Bühler. (Maslow, 1968, p. 24)

As this passage implies, however, the route to self-actualization always lies through the gratification of the more basic survival needs. They remain prepotent. Nor does their gratification, according to Maslow, ensure that self-actualization will automatically follow. For this to occur, further environmental facilitation is required. The environment must actively support and encourage the growth tendencies that ensue, and the individual must discover within it "some values which he strives for or gropes for and to which he is loyal" (1971, p. 301). In this Maslow adopts a position quite similar to Nuttin's concept of the "moral gift of self" and Frankl's position on the discovery of meaning through interaction with one's own unique life task.

Be this as it may, it is through the study of self-actualizing persons, Maslow claimed, that we can best hope to define what is meant by optimal or authentic human functioning. He has described many of their characteristics quite extensively in his major publications but offered the following distillation of his findings based on their clinically observed characteristics:

1. Superior perception of reality.
2. Increased acceptance of self, of others, and of nature.
3. Increased spontaneity.
4. Increase in problem-centering [a focus on problems outside themselves].
5. Increased detachment and desire for privacy.
6. Increased autonomy and resistance to enculturation.
7. Greater freshness of appreciation and richness of emotional reaction.
8. Higher frequency of peak experiences.
9. Increased identification with the human species [social interest].
10. Changed (the clinician would say improved) interpersonal relations.
11. More democratic character structure.
12. Greatly increased creativeness.
13. Certain changes in the value system [meta-motivation by the more objective B-values]. (Maslow 1968, pp. 25–26)

In the same passage, Maslow indicates his awareness of the rather static nature of his description of the self-actualized person—that he is depicting an end-state rather than the process of arriving there. Earlier he had introduced some concepts that shed further light on these process dimensions. The first, and perhaps most important, is the notion of an *intrinsic conscience,* which serves as a potential guide to authentic development.

***The intrinsic conscience.***   Freud, as we saw, equated human conscience with superego, the internalization of cultural norms through an unconscious identification with the values of one's parents during childhood. Maslow joins Erich Fromm (1947) in criticizing the nothing-but flavor of this concept. (Superego or conscience is nothing-but the unconscious introjection of cultural mores.) To be sure, superego, or something very like it, does exist and is probably predominant in the early stages of moral development.

> But there is also another element in conscience, or, if you like, another kind of conscience, which we all have either weakly or strongly. And this is the "intrinsic conscience." This is based on the unconscious and preconscious perception of our own nature, of our own destiny or our own capacities, of our own call in life. It insists that we be true to our inner nature and that we do not deny it out of weakness or for advantage or for any other reason. (1968, p. 6)

Here again we see the humanistic-existential emphasis on intrinsic criteria for authentic human development: a kind of psychic gyroscope that can be trusted to keep us on the right path when consciously adverted to. Guilt may be simply neurotic (superego guilt). But, as the existentialists remind us, there is also good guilt, the kind that warns us of stunted development, an opportunity for growth which has been missed for lack of courage. From it we may learn where the true path to authenticity lies, just as the experience of anxiety may serve as a signal of some emerging potentiality which, for any number of reasons, we fear to actualize (May, et al. 1958). An important part of the process of living authentically is to learn how to identify this inner guiding mechanism, read it properly, and act upon its directives. I will return to this point when discussing the contributions of Rogers and Perls. Their work, far more process-oriented than the rather static descriptions provided by Nuttin and Maslow, provides greater specificity on how this can be accomplished.

***The peak-experience.***   A second concept provided by Maslow is that of the peak-experience. Self-actualizers, Maslow believed, have more of these or have them more frequently. However, they also can and do occur on occasion to most men and women. For all of us, Maslow was convinced, they serve as acute identity experiences, transitory moments of self-actualization that point to what is possible. Consequently they can, when properly appreciated and understood, motivate us toward further growth and exploration. He defines them as:

> . . . basic cognitive happenings in the B-love experience [when we are able to love someone or something *for its own sake* and not out of some felt deficiency we are seeking to gratify], the parental experience, the mystic, or oceanic, or nature experience, the aesthetic perception, the creative moment, the therapeutic, or intellectual insight, the orgasmic experience, certain forms of athletic fulfillment, etc. These and other

moments of highest happiness and fulfillment I shall call the peak-experiences. (1968, p. 73)

By responding to the following instructions, which Maslow presented to a large sample of college students, the reader will gain a clearer and more personal glimpse of what he meant by a peak-experience:

I would like you to think of the most wonderful experience or experiences of your life; happiest moments, ecstatic moments, moments of rapture, perhaps from being in love or from listening to music or suddenly "being hit" by a book or painting, or from some great creative moment. First list these. And then try to tell me how you feel in such acute moments, how you feel *differently* from the way you feel at other times, how you are at the moment a different person in some ways. (1968, p. 71)

The examination of hundreds of such protocols is what led Maslow to the conclusion that "any person in any of the peak-experiences takes on temporarily many of the characteristics which I found in self-actualizing individuals . . ." (1968, p. 97).

One of the most characteristic features of peak-experiences is a type of cognition which Maslow termed *B-cognition* (1968, p. 86), a concept strongly reminiscent of Nuttin's "moral gift of self." This is a passive type of knowing which relates to the object *as it is in itself,* in a nonattached, contemplative manner. This is in sharp contrast to our ordinary mode of cognition, d- (for deficiency-motivated) cognition. Here we are much more active. We work on the object, classifying it, arranging it, relating it to our own needs or fears or interests. We seek to know it *for our sake* rather than its own. We go to an art museum, for example, to improve ourselves. We buy a catalog and study the paintings and sculpture carefully, classifying them according to period, memorizing names of artists, comparing styles, all in order to impress our friends at a later date, to show how cultured we are. This is d-cognition. It is often useful and frequently necessary (e.g., in order to pass an art history exam). Occasionally, perhaps even during this process, we are simply overwhelmed by the beauty of a particular work of art. We are caught by it. We sit down enraptured, catalog forgotten. Time seems to stand still as we contemplate it, wholly receptive to its intrinsic harmony, the subtle interplay of light and shadow, color and line. We are moved by it, even to tears, and we rise from the experience refreshed, tranquilized. This is B-cognition, a peak-experience in this instance that contains its own validity.

**B-values.**  These are important experiences. B-cognition alone leads to the comprehension and appreciation of the B-values, the intrinsic values (Hartman, 1959) contained in Being itself. They are out there waiting to be discovered but only through this passive, receptive, contemplative mode of knowing.

Authentic human functioning, Maslow strongly implies, is marked primarily by the pursuit of these B-values. They function as meta-needs in the lives of his deficiency-need-gratified, self-actualized subjects. Less concrete than the lower needs in his hierarchy, they are nevertheless just as basic. They are present in all of us. Gratified, they lead to optimal development and functioning. Ungratified, they result in a group of neuroticlike illnesses that Maslow termed the *metapathologies*, somewhat broader in scope but similar to the concept of existential or noogenic neurosis developed by other authors of this school (Frankl, 1965; Maddi, 1967).

Table 8–1, reproduced from Schultz (1977, p. 67), provides a list of

**TABLE 8–1**
**Maslow's meta-needs and metapathologies**

| *B-values* | *Metapathologies* |
| --- | --- |
| Truth | Mistrust, cynicism, skepticism |
| Goodness | Hatred, repulsion, disgust, reliance only upon self and for self |
| Beauty | Vulgarity, restlessness, loss of taste, bleakness |
| Unity; wholeness | Disintegration |
| Dichotomy-transcendence | Black/white thinking, either/or thinking, simplistic view of life |
| Aliveness; process | Deadness, robotizing, feeling oneself to be totally determined, loss of emotion and zest in life, experiential emptiness |
| Uniqueness | Loss of feeling of self and individuality, feeling oneself to be interchangeable with anyone |
| Perfection | Hopelessness, nothing to work for |
| Necessity | Chaos, unpredictability |
| Completion; finality | Incompleteness, hopelessness, cessation of striving and coping |
| Justice | Anger, cynicism, mistrust, lawlessness, total selfishness |
| Order | Insecurity, wariness, loss of safety and predictability, necessity for being on guard |
| Simplicity | Overcomplexity, confusion, bewilderment, loss of orientation |
| Richness, totality, comprehensiveness | Depression, uneasiness, loss of interest in the world |
| Effortlessness | Fatigue, strain, clumsiness, awkwardness, stiffness |
| Playfulness | Grimness, depression, paranoid humorlessness, loss of zest in life, cheerlessness |
| Self-sufficiency | Responsibility given to others |
| Meaningfulness | Meaninglessness, despair, senselessness of life |

Source: D. Schultz, *Growth Psychology* (New York: D. Van Nostrand, 1977, p. 67). Adapted from A. H. Maslow, *The Farther Reaches of Human Nature* (New York: Viking Press, 1971, pp. 318—19). Reprinted by permission of Brooks/Cole Publishing Co., Monterey, Calif.

such values or meta-needs and the connected metapathologies hypothesized by Maslow.

Since Maslow's B-cognition and B-values involve a form of self-transcendence, they will be further discussed in the next chapter. For my purposes here, it is important to note that they are discoverable in the peak-experiences of all men and women and illustrate a central feature of Maslow's depiction of authentic human functioning.

### Frankl's will to meaning

The last item on Maslow's list of B-values, meaningfulness, leads naturally to a discussion of Viktor Frankl's conception of what is required for authentic human existence. Simply stated, it is the "will to meaning" that must be actualized, uniquely for each person, for authentic human functioning to occur.

In Chapter 6 of the present volume, I have suggested that Frankl's contributions have provided a needed corrective to an overly biological view of the actualizing tendency as it presumably operates in the development of human personality. The evolution of human consciousness, Frankl reminds us, has been accompanied by a lessening of dependence on blind, instinct-driven behavior characteristic of lower organisms. While vestiges of such instinctive behaviors remain (how much is still a matter of considerable controversy), consciousness, according to Frankl and most humanists, continually transforms these tendencies to a higher plane of activity. (Maslow, as we have seen, prefers the term *instinctoid* to describe this state of affairs.)

In particular, the directions taken by the actualizing tendency in humans are largely a matter of choice or, more accurately, a series of choices constantly being made in the course of the human life span. Put another way, consciousness opens out to an array of options that are available to us for the gratification of our basic needs, at whatever level these emerge.

Frankl also maintains (see Chapter 7) that we retain a radical freedom or capacity for self-determination in the face of these many options. We are therefore *responsible* for our choices, and "being-responsible" is a basic attribute of human existence (Frankl, 1965, p. 36). Personal acceptance of responsibility is, therefore, a major prerequisite for authentic human functioning. As Schultz aptly states:

> Healthy persons will bear this responsibility, despite the brief and transitory nature of life, using their time wisely lest their work (their lives) remain undeveloped. If we die before we finish sculpting the form of our lives, what we have done is not negated. The meaningfulness of a life is judged by its quality, not its longevity. It is less important that the work of life be finished than that it be begun and continued on a high level. "Sometimes the 'unfinisheds' are among the most beautiful symphonies" [Frankl, 1965, p. 66]. (Schultz, 1977, p. 110)

Frankl's own experiences in the Nazi concentration camps fortified his earlier growing dissatisfaction with the Freudian and Adlerian versions of psychoanalysis under which he had been trained. To Freud's "will to pleasure" and Adler's "will to power," Frankl contrasted his own notion of a "will to meaning." These former conceptions he viewed as aberrations that occur when the will to meaning remains unfulfilled. This search for meaning, he maintains, is another essential attribute of human consciousness revealed by a rigorous phenomenological analysis of its nature and activity. (The technical phenomenological term *intentionality* has roughly the same sense. Consciousness is said to in-tend its objects, constantly searching to discover and grasp the meanings implicit in our ongoing conscious experiences.)

Using this analysis and his own experiences in the Nazi death camps as a basis, Frankl maintains that meaning is constantly to be discovered by each of us in the daily encounter with our unique, individualized life situation. There is no general meaning to life uniformly imposed on all. Life confronts each of us with different tasks on the basis of our unique abilities, interests, and opportunities.

> In the light of existential analysis there is no such thing as a generally valid and universally binding life task. From this point of view the question of "the" task in life or "the" meaning of life is—meaningless. It reminds us of the question a reporter asked a grand master in chess. "And now tell me, maestro—what is the best move in chess?" Neither question can be answered in a general fashion, *but only in regard to a particular situation and person.* (Frankl, 1965, p. 60, emphasis added)

***Transcendent values.*** Frankl is certainly not to be numbered among those nay-saying existentialists who, like Jean-Paul Sartre, conclude that life is ultimately meaningless and absurd. The values that give my life its ultimate meaning are out there, in a real sense objective and waiting to be discovered. They are not created *ex nihilo* in some purely arbitrary fashion.

> Value is transcendent to the act which intends it. It transcends the value-cognitive act which is directed toward it, analogous to the object of an act of cognition, which likewise is situated outside of this (in the narrower sense of the word cognitive) act. Phenomenology has shown that the transcendent quality of the object in the intentional act is always already present in its content. If I see a lit lamp, the fact that it is there is already given along with my perception of it, even if I close my eyes or turn my back to it. In the perception of an object as something real is already contained the implication that I recognize its reality independently of its perception by myself or anyone else. The same is true of the objects of value perception. As soon as I have comprehended a value, I have comprehended implicitly that this value exists in itself, independently therefore of whether or not I accept it. (Frankl, 1965, pp. 400–401)

But Frankl is equally insistent in his contention that these objective values (obviously similar to Maslow's B-values) are best discovered through the individual's conscious, responsible confrontation with his or her own singular life situation:

> Perhaps the law by which man's responsibilities are revealed only in concrete tasks is more general than we imagine. Objective values become concrete duties, are cast in the form of the demands of each day and in personal tasks. The values lying back of these tasks can apparently be reached for only through the tasks. (1965, pp. 41–42)

Through a process of structural phenomenological analysis (see Chapter 4), Frankl arrives at three distinct classes of values that provide meaning to individual lives: *creative, experiential,* and *attitudinal.*

*Creative values* are those which are realized in creative action. These are discovered in the course of the responsible attempt to actualize one's own potentialities and talents or those of another. Sharing one's insights, developing a musical, artistic, or other talent, aiding a family member or student to discover and develop his or her unique potential, doing a job as well as one can, represent a few examples of this category.

*Experiential values* are realized in receptivity toward the world, in surrender, for example, to the beauty of nature or art. These are the B-values of which Maslow spoke, appreciated in moments of ecstasy (Frankl gives the examples of a music-lover listening to his favorite symphony or a mountain-climber confronted by an alpine sunset after an arduous climb). They are not to be underestimated, Frankl states, in their ability to convey fullness of meaning to human life.

*Attitudinal values* are those which are realized in confronting the limitations of our existence, even inescapable loss and suffering, with acceptance and courage. These instances offer the last and perhaps the best opportunity for the realization of values. They exist in the moral sphere of our existence, and we remain ultimately responsible for their affirmation or denial. They can be realized in a life that is neither rich in creation nor in experience.

It comes as no surprise, given his own personal background, that Frankl has become the most eloquent spokesman among humanistic-existential authors for the role of suffering in the potential development of an authentic human existence. He is no advocate of masochism. He merely points to the inevitability of suffering in the course of human life in view of inescapable personal and environmental limitations. But in the face of such limitations, he insists, we remain free: free to embrace suffering with courage and dignity or to succumb to it in self-pity or despair. His works are filled with examples of individuals who have added new meaning to our concepts of human potential and dignity through the responses they have consciously chosen to make to a wide variety of such predicaments. Maslow had called these "nadir-experiences" in contrast to the peak-experiences on which he concentrated his attention, and he briefly speculated on their possible role in the process of self-actualization (1968, p. 84). Frankl confronts them squarely.

*Self-actualization through meaning-fulfillment.* He is equally insistent that self-actualization can only occur as a byproduct of meaning fulfillment. Consciously sought as an end in itself, it must remain forever elusive. In Frankl's own words:

> Self-actualization is not man's ultimate destination, not even his primary intention. Self-actualization, if made an end in itself, contradicts the self-transcending quality of human existence. Also self-actualization is, and must remain, an effect, namely, the effect of meaning fulfillment. Only to the extent to which man fulfills a meaning out there in the world, does he fulfill himself. Conversely, if he sets out to actualize himself rather than fulfill a meaning, self-actualization would immediately lose its justification. (1969, p. 116)

Here again we see postulated, as in Nuttin's work, a very high correlation between self-realization and a personally satisfying form of self-transcendence, the theme of the next chapter. That Maslow was in basic agreement with this position is verified by his statement:

> My experience agrees with Frankl's that people who seek self-actualization directly, selfishly, personally, dichotomized away from mission in life, i.e., as a form of private and subjective salvation, don't, in fact, achieve it. . . . Or to say it in a more positive and descriptive way, those people in our society selected out as self-actualizing practically always have a mission in life, a task which they love and have identified with and which becomes a defining characteristic of the self. (Maslow, 1969, pp. 128–129)

For Frankl, then, authentic human living requires a personal, idiosyncratic actualization of the will to meaning, the essential characteristic of human consciousness. Remaining consciously open to the varied experiences with which life confronts us, we are constantly challenged to respond by drawing on our own intrinsic potentials and resources through creative, responsible action. Inescapable limitations, personal or imposed from without, are to be borne with dignity and courage. So reacting, we will fashion an authentic existence, and life will reveal its meaning to us, uniquely and differentially. Failure to respond on any of these three dimensions (a loss of nerve, so to speak) will result in frustration of the will to meaning.

The metapathology (to borrow Maslow's term) that may ensue from failing to actualize experiential, creative, and attitudinal values, Frankl calls "noogenic [existential] neurosis." Persons so afflicted live in an "existential vacuum" and may display all the symptoms characteristic of the more familiar guilt neuroses that arise from the interplay of sexual and aggressive impulses with the restraining forces of super-ego or society. In this case, however, the guilt is existential, arising from the failure of nerve, described above, and based on more intrinsic criteria of evaluation. Frankl devised his own version of existential analysis, called *logotherapy*, for the treatment of such conditions and has outlined several intervention strategies for therapeutic application which have been widely used by humanistic psychologists (Frankl, 1955).

The flavor of this approach can perhaps best be appreciated by an admittedly simple case (viewed in this light) from Frankl's own file (1963, pp. 161–162). A high-ranking diplomat came to Frankl's clinic in Vienna to continue psychoanalytic treatment begun five years previously in another city. When asked why he had entered analysis in the first place, the patient stated that he had become dissatisfied with his career, particularly because he found himself in frequent disagreement with his own country's foreign policy. His analyst had interpreted his difficulties as arising from an authority problem stemming from his childhood relationship to his father. His dissatisfaction and rebellious-ness were nothing-but a projection or transference of his childhood conflicts to these new father-figures: his superiors and the authority vested in his own government. After a few interviews, Frankl quickly came to the conclusion that the patient's will to meaning was being frustrated in his current vocation, that he truly longed to give it up and pursue a different kind of work. Since there was no hindrance to his doing so, the decision was made and carried out, with highly gratifying results confirmed in a follow-up report five years later.

The diplomat's case clearly underlines Frankl's contention that noogenic neuroses "do not emerge from conflicts between drives and instincts but rather from conflicts between various values" (1963, p. 160) and that logotherapy "regards its assignment as that of assisting the patient to find meaning in his life" (p. 163). Finally, logotherapy (together with other humanistic approaches) "considers man as a being whose main concern consists in fulfilling a meaning and in actualizing values, rather than in the mere gratification and satisfaction of drives and instincts, the mere reconciliation of the conflicting claims of id, ego and superego, or mere adaptation and adjustment to the society and environment" (1963, p. 164).

## PROCESS ORIENTATIONS

While the positions reviewed so far on the theme of authenticity have definite process implications, they tend to be rather prescriptive and idealistic in tone. The end-states of self-actualization or authenticity are well described; but not much light is shed on the processes by which one gets there or overcomes the resistances or blocks toward progress in that direction which inevitably arise in the course of human development. The final two authors to be considered, both founders of major humanistic psychotherapeutic movements, provide the needed supplement to these more static descriptions.

## Perls's "free-functioning" organism

Nuttin, in his pioneering effort to understand healthy personality functioning, postulated two basic and correlative drives: (a) The *drive toward self-realization* at all three levels of conscious experiencing: psychophysiological, psychosocial, and transpersonal, and (b) since life is an open system, the corresponding *need and drive for contact with the environment* at all three levels for the gratification of basic needs and continuing development of the individual (Nuttin, 1962).

He and the other authors presented in this chapter have described for us the characteristics of the self-actualized or authentic individual, concentrating on the fulfillment of the drive toward self-realization. Frederick (Fritz) Perls and his associates in the Gestalt therapy movement have focused instead on the *contact* feature of this model of human development and have thereby considerably sharpened our understanding of the processes involved in achieving this goal or in frustrating its attainment.

For Perls and his associates, experience itself occurs at the boundary between organism and environment.

> Experience is the function of this boundary, and psychologically what is real are the "whole" configurations [Gestalten] of this functioning, some meaning being achieved, some action completed. . . . We speak of the organism contacting the environment, *but it is the contact that is the simplest and first reality.* (Perls, Hefferline, & Goodman, 1951, p. 227; emphasis added)

These "wholes" do not include everything but are definite, unified structures. No single function of any organism, animal or human, exists in a vacuum: nourishment and sexuality, perceptual or motor functions, feeling or reasoning, all involve this interaction of organism and environment. A truly holistic psychology, these authors insist, must begin here and, where the human organism is concerned, must include the social, cultural, and historical field in which the individual finds himself or herself immersed.

Walter Kempler, an early associate of Perls at the Esalen Institute and one of the first to apply Gestalt principles to family therapy, adds a third type of organism/environment interaction (besides the psychophysical and psychosocial interactions implied above), thus paralleling Nuttin's three levels: "The third stage . . . is often associated with a sense of continuity with the universe at large and derives its title—spiritual—from that pathognomic trait" (Kempler, 1973, p. 262).

*Definition of the self.* The Gestalt definition of the self is strongly pegged to this emphasis on the contact boundary between organism and environment and is required for our further understanding of this approach to authentic human functioning. It is simply the system of contacts at any moment or, better, the contact boundary at work actively forming figures and grounds. Criticizing the Freudians and neo-Freudians, who reduce the self to the organism alone or conversely to the interpersonal society, these authors insist:

> But the self is precisely the integrator; it is the synthetic unity, as Kant said. It is only a small factor in the total organism/environment interaction, but it plays the crucial role of finding and making the meanings that we grow by. (Perls, Hefferline, & Goodman, 1951, p. 235)

Here again we encounter the widespread humanistic emphasis on the self as active center of intentionality. Gestalt theorists conceptualize this activity as a continuous process in which the self successively creates and destroys Gestalten, configurations of organismic needs and the environmental resources available for their satisfaction.

For ideal, authentic functioning, the self must be exquisitely attuned not just to the single need that emerges as figure from ground but to the whole context of organismic needs with which it remains articulated. And on the environmental side of the interaction, the self must be selectively attentive and creatively adaptive in its efforts to fashion a solution to the problems created by emerging needs. Nor is this to be construed as a merely homeostatic process. Lower, physiological needs may indeed be prepotent, in the Maslovian sense, but their consistent gratification leads to the emergence of higher, ever more complex requirements along the lines previously described by Kempler. Joel Latner, another Gestalt theorist, also addresses this issue, pointing to "the last Gestalt":

> The momentum of our development is toward wholes that encompass more and more of the potential of the organism/environment field. In the more advanced stages of this process, we are embracing ourself and the cosmos. The [last] Gestalt is: I and the universe are one. All of me and all of the infinity of activities and energy around me, people and things, all of them all together are one figure. Nothing is excluded. (1973, p. 226)

Gestalt therapy, according to Kempler, intervenes at the psychophysical level with the intent of sharpening and clarifying the immediate experiencing of awareness that occurs at the contact boundary between organism and environment. Kempler calls this *psychophysical awareness,* in contrast to *intellectual awareness,* which is a reflexive act once removed from the here-and-now experiencing that precedes it. (Gestalt therapists tend to sound anti-intellectual in their pronouncements because they do stress the psychological difficulties that result from an excessively cognitive stance toward reality, typified best perhaps by the stereotype of "the academic personality.")

***Free-functioning and neurotic interaction.*** Authentic functioning, from the Gestalt viewpoint, therefore implies the ability to go with the flow. Following a suggestion made by Kempler (1973), it can be diagrammed, somewhat simplistically to be sure, in Figure 8–1.

**FIGURE 8–1**
**Free-functioning**

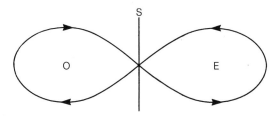

In the figure, $O$ = the organism and its emerging needs, $E$ = the environment with which it interacts, and $S$ = the self functioning at the contact boundary.

For *free-functioning* to be maintained, the following requirements must be met.

1.  Sharp psychophysical awareness, centered in the self. This includes the ability of the self accurately to identify and label the emerging needs of the organism, without defensiveness or denial, as well as the ability to attend to the environmental field and remain open to what it realistically contains. (This in turn explains the present-centered, here-and-now emphasis of Gestalt therapy.)

2.  A clear-cut, accurate sense of where the boundary lies between organism and environment. Failure of the self to recognize where this boundary actually lies or shifting it too far in either direction can lead to many of our psychological difficulties, as will be presently illustrated.

Gestalt theorists have identified four basic styles of neurotic interaction at the contact boundary: introjection, projection, confluence, and retroflection. All are seen as processes which interfere with the free, authentic functioning of the self not as personality types. And all of them involve a serious and disruptive displacement of the contact boundary between organism and environment.

1.  *Introjection.* When we are hungry and take in food, our bodies normally assimilate the nutrients by breaking down the food into small

bits by chewing, thus aiding the digestive process of converting food-stuffs to the chemicals that we need. Where we swallow the food in chunks, we become uncomfortable, and the proper digestive process does not occur. Psychologically, we can swallow various ways of acting and feeling without breaking them down to see if they fit our individual needs and experience. This process of taking in undigested attitudes, values, and the like is called *introjection.*

Introjection can be useful at times. Last-minute cramming may get a student through an examination. But he or she will not have learned very much. The material has not been chewed over long enough for it to be assimilated as true personal learning. Introjection can also be healthy when it is a free process of trying on different roles to get their feeling and decide if they fit one's preferred lifestyle.

Indiscriminate introjection, however, can lead to pathology by pre-venting the individual from developing his or her own unique person-ality. The introjector, as Rogers would say, operates from an "external locus of evaluation" and becomes a puppet whose strings are pulled by others. Indiscriminate introjection implies that even contradictory con-cepts can be absorbed, leading to inevitable conflict and discomfort. "Do unto others as you would have them do unto you" might well be introjected along with its opposite: "Do unto others *before* they do unto you." Such conflicting, unassimilated values can lead to psychological paralysis and confusion.

The introjector has therefore moved the contact boundary too far within the organism (i.e., he or she has mistaken what belongs to the environment as being a part of the organism itself), as shown in Figure 8–2.

**FIGURE 8–2**
**Introjection**

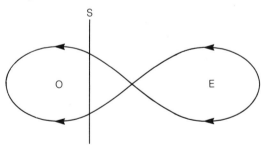

Organismic needs and experiences are overlooked in favor of what "they think"; and the needs and expressions of the group become the determiners of personal attitudes and action.

2. *Projection.* The opposite of introjection is projection. Here the

contact boundary is unconsciously shifted toward the environment in such a way that the latter is not realistically experienced (see Figure 8–3). Here, elements which really arise from the organism are experienced as though belonging to or arising from the environment. "They think," as in "they are all out to get me," should really be "I think" in the sense that "I do not approve of my own impulses or attitudes."

**FIGURE 8–3**
**Projection**

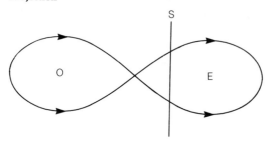

Projection is based on observation, and so, like introjection, it has its positive side. We plan our lives and maneuver the elements in our field by observing and making assumptions. Often with reference to another person, one says, "If I were in your shoes, this is what I would do." Here, one gives advice based upon one's own experience and derived assumptions about the world, but there remains an awareness that what is being said is "owned" by the individual and may or may not be appropriate for the other.

But projection is considered neurotic when it allows us to "disavow and disown those aspects of our personalities which we find difficult or offensive or unattractive" (Perls, 1973, p. 37). We attribute to others what is true about ourselves and thus fail to give the environment its due. The paranoid represents the classic example of extreme pathological projection. The "ego" has become inflated, as in the diagram of Figure 8–3, and the environment is misperceived.

3. *Confluence.* In confluence there is no movement of the contact boundary toward or away from the organism. Confluence is characterized by the *disappearance* of the boundary, as in Figure 8–4.

When we are keenly concentrating on something, sometimes we experience a feeling of being one with the environment. Such experiences, though rare, are normal and may even constitute one of Maslow's peak-experiences. However:

> The person in whom confluence is a pathological state cannot tell what he is and he cannot tell what other people are. He does not know where he leaves off and others begin. As he is unaware of the boundary between himself and others, he cannot make good contact with them. Nor can he

**FIGURE 8–4**
**Confluence**

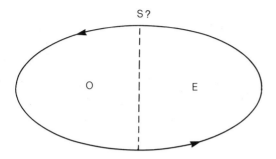

withdraw from them. Indeed, he cannot even make contact with himself. (Perls, 1973, p. 38)

Again, neurosis begins with the failure to act on our high-priority needs. If, for example, a person wants to cry but resists and to aid in that resistance contracts the diaphragm, the capacity to breathe and the urge to cry are both confused. As various activities become confluent, the individual *becomes* that confusion, no longer aware of his or her own needs or how to attain them.

Prejudice is a common example of confluence that takes on the form of "Why aren't you like me?" Because there is no boundary, the confluent individual cannot comprehend differences. "I" and "out there" *must* be the same. Thus, the confluent individual says "we," and it is difficult to tell to whom he or she is referring.

4. *Retroflection.* Individuals engaged in the retroflective process generally maintain a clear idea of the separation between self and environment. Unfortunately, they draw the contact boundary right down the middle of the organismic side of the interaction, which is illustrated in Figure 8–5.

**FIGURE 8–5**
**Retroflection**

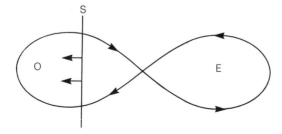

The retroflector does to himself what he would rather do to others, turning against himself.

As in the other three types of neurotic process, some retroflection is healthy and necessary. We simply cannot act out every impulse we have without being physically or psychologically destructive to others. But suppressing these impulses because they are destructive is not the same as turning them against oneself. Depression and self-punitive activities are common examples of a pathological retroflective process. The secretary who experiences anger at her boss for piling on more work at quitting time might well have the impulse to throttle him. She would be just as foolish to resist this idea, in horror at herself for having it, by jumping out the window of her 10th floor office as to carry out its original aim (Lavalle, 1977).

Perls comparatively sums up for us these four neurotic processes: "The introjector does as others would like him to do, the projector does unto others what he accuses them of doing to him, the man in pathological confluence doesn't know who is doing what to whom, and the retroflector does to himself what he would like to do to others" (Perls, 1973, p. 40).

Gestalt therapists have been very innovative in devising techniques to restore the contact boundary to its proper position in order to promote a free-functioning process marked by clear perceptions of both organismic needs and environmental resources. A discussion of these methods is beyond my present purpose, which is simply to emphasize their process description of authentic human functioning. By maintaining free functioning in present-centered awareness, the self can in turn rely on the self-regulating tendencies of the organism/environment interactions to attain the ideal of authenticity and reach the last Gestalt.

### Rogers's fully functioning person

The final position to be presented on the humanistic theme of authenticity also features, in its most recent formulations, a strong process orientation. It has been developed by Carl Rogers and his associates in the client-centered movement in psychotherapy and is epitomized by Rogers's description of the fully functioning person (1961, 1963). His description, as we shall see, closely parallels the Gestalt view of the free-functioning organism. However, the methods used by client-centered therapists to facilitate movement in this direction are quite different from the Gestalt techniques, and there is a much stronger emphasis on research validation, of the functional phenomenological variety, of process movement and outcomes, an emphasis notably lacking in the Gestalt therapy approach.

The developmental stages of Rogerian thought on the topic of constructive personality change form a progression marked by the interaction of expanding clinical experience with feedback obtained through research investigations (see Chapter 10). In the middle, self-theory phase of client-centered thought, authentic human functioning was described as a nearly perfect congruence of the self-concept with ongoing organismic experiencing. Maladjusted functioning could be expected to follow upon considerable discrepancy between the self-concept and the real, ongoing experience of the organism, as in the diagram in Figure 8–6.

**FIGURE 8–6**
**Incongruence**

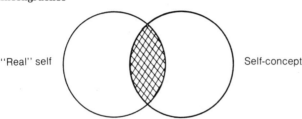

The self-concept was theorized as a relatively closed Gestalt formed during the developmental stages of infancy and childhood under the influence of conditions of worth placed upon the individual by significant others. These definitions of self, frequently at variance with the individual's own experiences of ongoing interactions with the environment, are presumably "bought" and maintained in functioning because of the developing person's pervasive need for positive regard. The inherent actualizing tendency thus becomes split, functioning to preserve and enhance both the real experiencing self and the somewhat discrepant self-concept.

Efforts at this stage were devoted to establishing and validating the type of interpersonal interaction, through therapy or more natural life situations, which could be expected to reduce this discrepancy and foster greater congruence between self-concept and experiencing organism. In the consistently safe climate provided by the helper's unconditional positive regard, empathic understanding, and own genuinity, incongruence in the other is reduced, and he or she learns to trust more in the experiencing self. Rigid self-constructs are relaxed, new experiences previously denied to awareness are assimilated into a new self-Gestalt, a more fluid configuration now, which becomes more and more the basis for self-evaluations.

> The person now functions in many ways similar to the infant except that the fluid processes of experiencing have more scope. The mature individual, like the child, trusts and uses the wisdom of his total organism, but in a knowing way, in an aware way. He uses all his faculties. (Rogers & Wood, 1974, p. 220)

While it is still possible to observe this change occurring in therapy or in any situation where the "necessary and sufficient conditions of therapeutic personality change" are present (Rogers, 1957), Rogers and his associates next turned their attention to a more intricate elaboration and validation of the process elements already implicit in the description given above. They sought to supplement these before-and-after snapshots of changing self-Gestalts with a more detailed and flowing motion picture or "Brownian motion" description of the process of therapeutic change. They developed and validated a *process scale* on which change is seen as occurring along a number of continua, each continuum divided into seven stages. They then hypothesized that in any successful therapy, a client's behavior would move upward on these pathways from whatever point he or she begins (Rogers & Wood, 1974, p. 220).

***The process scale.*** Rogers and his colleagues, in developing their process scale, have differentiated six modes of experiencing and have found it possible, with good interjudge reliability, to delineate seven stages of process for each mode from the lower to the higher end of the continuum. Criteria for distinguishing the various modes and the process stages within them have been developed for rating of client statements from recorded interviews. Operationally, the fully functioning person can therefore be defined as one who operates predominantly in the seventh stage in each of the following modes of experiencing.

1. *Change in relationship to feelings.* On the lower end of the continuum here, the client does not recognize or own personal feelings. For example, he or she may hear voices suggesting dirty or murderous impulses that cannot be admitted as coming from self. Farther on, feelings may be described as past objects in an intellectualized way but, at the upper end of the scale, are sensed, differentiated, and expressed in the living moment.

2. *Change in manner of experiencing.* In this mode, extensively described by Gendlin (1961, 1962, 1963), the client "moves toward living his experiencing, trusting it, and using it as a referent for guiding him in his encounter with life. He is no longer characterized by remoteness from his experiencing nor does he discover its meaning only after it is long past" (Rogers & Wood, 1974, p. 221).

3. *Change in personal constructs.* This mode, previously described and researched by Kelly (1955), has to do with the ways in which the individual construes his or her experience. At the lower end of the continuum, personal constructs are rigid and treated as unchanging facts: "I can't ever do anything right." Farther along, such constructs are recognized as such, and the individual begins to see alternative possibilities. At the upper end, experience is never given more than a tentative construction, and ongoing experience guides its formation and adaptability to new circumstances.

4. *Change in communication of self.* This mode, similar to Jourard's variable of self-disclosure, ranges from a strong unwillingness to communicate self to a loss of inhibiting or inappropriate self-consciousness. At the upper end, clients are able accurately to identify and express the complexity of their feelings, in the moment, to the significant other (therapist, friend, or spouse).

5. *Change in relationship to problems.* Clients at the lower end of the continuum in this mode either do not recognize the existence of personal problems or perceive them as entirely outside themselves. Rogers gives the example of a mental patient who states: "I sleep a little too much. I have a bad tooth problem and a couple of others like that." The upper stages are marked by the acceptance of personal responsibility for one's problems and a willingness to understand and confront them in relationships with others.

6. *Change in interpersonal relationships.* Marked fear and avoidance of close personal contact with others characterize the lower end of the continuum for this mode of functioning. As therapy progresses, the client increasingly moves away from the sterile intellectualizations and superficial disclosures of the beginning stages to a more intimate, genuine engagement with the therapist, a sharing of his or her deepest inner reactions, positive or negative, in the ongoing relationship. Ideally, this increasing freedom in the therapeutic relationship begins to generalize, where appropriate, to other significant encounters.

In a statement which might have been written by a Gestalt theorist, Rogers and Wood conclude: "At the upper end of the scale these strands tend to converge, becoming one. The seventh, or final, stage is more of a trend or goal, than something which is fully achieved. It is a description of the 'fully functioning person' " (Rogers & Wood, 1974, p. 224).

Initial validation studies of the process scale were conducted as part of the University of Wisconsin research project with schizophrenics (Walker, Rablen, & Rogers, 1960; Tomlinson, 1962; Tomlinson & Hart, 1962). Later applications to the study of individual process movement in encounter groups (Clark & Culbert, 1965; Culbert, 1968; Meador, 1971) have further established that "significant behavior variations are discernible over the course of individual or group therapy using the process variables" (Meador & Rogers, 1973, p. 149).

Rogerians continue to emphasize the more general attitudinal characteristics of therapists over the specific techniques designed to increase self-awareness favored by Gestalt practitioners. Rogers and Wood (1974, p. 225) conclude:

> The research on client-centered therapy seems to suggest that personality change—positive movement on the process scale—is initiated by *attitudes* which exist in the therapist rather than primarily by his knowledge, his theories, or his techniques (Rioch, 1960; Truax & Mitchell, 1971).

The research evidence in support of this position, to be summarized in Chapter 10 of this volume, is indeed impressive. In practice, many humanistic therapists have adopted both points of view and freely mix both approaches in their efforts to facilitate movement toward more authentic modes of functioning on the part of their clients.

## CONCLUSION

This last section concludes my account of the humanistic theme of authenticity. In contrast to the more conformist notions of adjustment implicit in the approaches of orthodox psychoanalysis and behaviorism, humanistic authors, following leads provided by Rank, Adler, Jung, and other neoanalysts, have developed their own phenomenological perspectives on authentic human functioning. Nuttin, Maslow, and Frankl represent a more structural approach with their analyses of the value contents, the "meta-motivations," that characterize the lives of authentically functioning individuals. The Gestalt and client-centered theorists focus instead on the functional, process-oriented variables that presumably lead to such desirable outcomes. The wedding of these variant accounts of content and process leads, in turn, to a more coherent description of this important theme. All would agree that authenticity is a highly individualized accomplishment, to be judged on the basis of unique, intrinsic criteria but sharing in common several characteristics: informed individual choice based upon clear awareness and integration of all levels of personal experience, guided by an intrinsic conscience and a basic trust in the wisdom of an organism that has all the data of experiencing at its disposal.

The next chapter will be devoted to a theme implied or expressed in all these accounts of authentic human functioning or self-actualization: the theme of self-transcendence.

# 9 Self-transcendence

We come now to the striking paradox so clearly enunciated by Viktor Frankl. We do not achieve self-actualization by seeking it directly in the sense of an egocentric concentration on our own psychic navels. Narcissus perished by becoming enamored of his own reflection in the pool. So shall we, Frankl would say, if we make the same mistake. And yet that is where we all begin. The experience of self-consciousness is most immediately the experience of myself as a center of intentionality, a constant center around which all else revolves. "I am" is the surest proposition I can enunciate. I stand *here*, and the whole panorama of what is clearly not me unfolds before my gaze. When I move, it moves with me. I watch it all from the centerpost of my own conscious subjectivity. I even watch myself think, and feel, and suffer, and exult, and strain toward what I perceive to be out there.

I apparently don't have much control over the things that are not me—that confounded step I didn't see tripped me up—but for sure it is happening around me. Strangely, I surmise that you are such a center too. I hope, at least, that I'm not writing in a vacuum. I assume, and in fact I am very confident about this, that my words are part of the out there for you and that you experience yourself as the center of *your* world. I intend to communicate with you, to treat you as a fellow subject of consciousness, to share my perceptions with you. To the extent that I succeed, I will somehow break the shell of my own initial isolation. It's lonely in here.

This attempt to communicate, however we do it, is, of course, already a form of self-transcendence. Success brings a quick stab of joy and comfort. But there is yet another fear, beyond the fear of isolation. It is the fear that *we* are alone, in an unheeding universe in which only we are conscious. The quick stabs are perhaps just that—fleeting, transitory, *as are we*. For I am well aware of the fragility of my own existence and yours in the world as I experience it. Other organisms suffer death; we suffer also from the knowledge of death.

I certainly do not wish to underestimate the value for our lives of a satisfying communion with others. Deprived of it, we suffocate from loneliness. What I would stress here is an even greater need—the need to feel grounded in some absolute order of things, to feel that my own wispy existence (and yours) has some stability, some purpose or meaning. This, after all, is the other pole of consciousness, the mystery of *things*, the sometimes wonderful, sometimes terrifying realities that unfold before me. Instinctively, I reach out to them, trying to understand, to discover some order in the chaos that assaults me. I am . . . you are . . . things are. That much is given to me. Very little else is immediately clear.

Perhaps this simple desire to *know* is the most basic and specifically human of all desires. And linked with it is a strong desire or need to *commune* (feel at one) with all that is, to feel a part of something larger, more stable, more enduring than myself. That kind of knowledge alone can tell me who I am, and only by acting on its implications can I realize myself. Just as by communing with others like myself I attempt to escape the isolation with which I begin, so also by participating in a meaningful way with the whole of reality do I anchor my own (and your) admittedly unstable existence.

Surely this is a psychological phenomenon that must count heavily in any attempt to understand and explain human behavior. I can think of no other way to approach it than phenomenologically. It is demonstrably one of the central themes in humanistic-existential psychology, and it will be the burden of this chapter to present some of the variety of ways in which this group of authors addresses the problem of self-transcendence.

## NUTTIN'S TRANSPERSONAL LEVEL OF EXPERIENCE

Joseph Nuttin's theory of personality development, diagrammed in Chapter 6, provides a helpful starting point and framework for this discussion. The needs that issue from his third, transpersonal, level of conscious experience are precisely the cognitive needs mentioned above. They devolve from the capacity of reflexive consciousness, at its highest level of functioning, to jump from the particular objects, persons, and events that confront us at any given moment to a concern about reality as a whole. Why is there anything rather than nothing? How did it all begin—if indeed there was a beginning? How explain the patterns and regularities I discern in many of the phenomena that consciousness reveals to me—the cycle of the seasons, the rising and setting of the sun, the majestic panoply of the stars, the birth, growth, and death of living things around me? By such questions and a host of others that experience forces upon me, I occasionally at least rise above the daily preoccupation with more concrete concerns.

This need to know ranges from a rather calm, dispassionate intellectual curiosity ("Where do babies come from, Mother?") to a fierce desire to grab reality by the throat and shake some meaning out of it ("Why do we have to die? What happens to us then?"). It ebbs and flows, becoming especially poignant during adolescence, often in midlife, again in our declining years. But surely Nuttin is correct in describing it as a vital human need, as vital as the needs for nourishment, air, and shelter, or the need to connect to others, to love and be loved.

This capacity of consciousness to trancend the here and now, to encompass the whole of reality in one sweeping embrace, is what renders this need, in Nuttin's estimation, irreducible to the more concrete, particularized levels of human existence. It operates at a more general, abstract level, concerned with existence itself: truth, beauty, justice, good and evil, suffering in all its forms, right and wrong, ultimate meaning, order and chaos, design and chance. It is the source of some very distinctive forms of human endeavor: science itself, religion and theology, philosophy, exploration, art and literature, myth-making, law, invention, and technology.

Scientists connected with the space exploration program had their curiosity piqued recently by the discovery that one of Saturn's outer rings presents an unusual pattern. It looks like a twisted rope. How come? And how do we explain their excitement over this unexpected phenomenon? Frustrated sexual drives seeking a sublimated outlet? Nothing so physiological. Eros is indeed involved, but it is the Eros of mind: seeking to comprehend, needing to connect the unknown with the known, to bring order out of apparent chaos, to generate knowledge and understanding.

This is what we require to realize ourselves at this level of experience: knowledge of self and knowledge of the world in which we have our existence. Contact with experience of the other in interaction with our peculiar form of consciousness engenders this need in us. The knowledge we gain in this way serves other needs as well, of course. Ungoverned by programmed instincts, we need it in order to survive biologically and to gain the skills we require to satisfy our social needs. But sometimes we enjoy it for its own sake—for the sheer satisfaction of knowing. And, ultimately, Nuttin claims, we seek it in order to connect ourselves with the rest of existence, to unite self and all that is other in some meaningful way and thus transcend our otherwise basic isolation.

> On this spiritual and transcendent level of our human existence the need for *contact* manifests itself in specific forms. Before any biological or bodily interaction, and even before communion of any other kind with his fellow-men, man needs a more universal sort of communication and support and integration; he needs *to be able to know and feel himself* integrated into an absolute order of existence. (Nuttin, 1962, p. 249)

What Nuttin is here describing is a basic thirst for an Absolute, a stable ground to serve as an anchor for our own ephemeral existence, the need to know and feel oneself as a precious stone in some universal mosaic. He goes on to describe the specific forms that this need has taken in human history: religion (which originally meant a bond, link, or connection, in this case to an Absolute understood as God); philosophy, even in its materialistic forms; dedication to a Cause—humanity, communism, the state as a superior entity; a conception of the self as a link in the chain of evolution leading to some unknown but more perfect state of being; the desire for immortality through survival of biological death through one's offspring or one's works.

Historically, culture and the concomitant institutions for acculturating its members served to provide the needed answers. These too were varied—consider the differences between Western Christianity and Eastern religions on this score. But considered again as a streamlined way of meeting basic human needs, culture and the answers it provided did slake the individual's thirst for meaningful explanations of his or her personal existence while providing a set of clear principles by which to guide one's actions. However, Nuttin points out, that resource is quickly becoming unavailable to many modern men and women in this age of enlightenment, of cross-cultural exchange, and convictions of cultural relativity.

> In a time like ours, when the various attachments to past and future, to the earth and the family—when the thousand and one things to which existence attaches itself, and which give existence its meaning and value—have been dissolved, man feels utterly "uprooted." The need to find some absolute meaning in life, i.e., the need to become integrated with existence, makes itself felt more and more imperiously. (1962, p. 249)

This, Nuttin feels, is particularly evident in the growing number of individuals, in Western society at least, who are afflicted by existential despair, a sense of the horror and emptiness of their isolation and the absurdity of existence. There does appear to be ample documentation from clinical and other sources of a new pathological syndrome called *existential* or *noogenic neurosis*. Its existence and the concurrent rise of existential analysis in recent decades, already adverted to in these pages, provide convergent validity to Nuttin's claim that we are here dealing with a basic human need—the need for self-transcendence.

What is psychology's role in meeting this crisis? We will need to keep this question in mind as we turn now to some more recent efforts to explore its ramifications.

## VIKTOR FRANKL'S WILL TO MEANING

Enough has already been said throughout these pages about Viktor Frankl's existential, logotherapeutic approach to indicate his position on the theme of self-transcendence. It is an absolutely pivotal concept in his thinking. Self-actualization is and can only be a byproduct of meaning-fulfillment. A narcissistic preoccupation with the self, the subjective pole of consciousness (in the pursuit of happiness instead of meaning), leads to hyper-reflection and a neurotic blocking of the flow of experience. Frankl provides a vivid, practical example of the effects of hyper-reflection in his analysis of sexual dysfunction: concentration on one's own pleasure and performance instead of attending to one's partner is frequently self-defeating. The method he suggests for overcoming this source of dysfunction (de-reflection) has been widely and successfully adopted by many sex therapists (Kaplan, 1974).

For Frankl, as for Gendlin (1979), the meanings to be fulfilled are implicit in experience and therefore unique to the individual, since no two of us experience reality in exactly the same way. They are to be found in the *objective* pole of consciousness (including the self considered as object: one's unique capacities, gifts, or talents, for example).

Put another way, the meanings to be fulfilled are equivalent to the values to be realized at any given moment in time, whether creative, experiential, or attitudinal (see Chapter 8). Either brought about by my own choices (e.g., my commitment to another person) or presented to me by circumstances beyond my control (e.g., illness or loss), the ongoing events of my life are out there, in the objective pole of conscious experience, pregnant with potential value and meaning. Reflection is required, of course, to perceive that value or meaning, and I am accordingly responsible for actualizing it—once conscious of it, I can choose to fulfill it or not. When the choice to do so is made and carried out, the meaning is fulfilled, the value realized, and I am thereby more content, more actualized.

Frankl reminds us that we need not think of this process as necessarily involving heroic undertakings. It is available to all in the responsible facing of one's daily tasks. We all admire the craftsman who pursues his or her craft, however modest, with diligence, integrity, and responsibility. We do not think highly of a brilliant surgeon who is not "true to her gifts" and does shoddy work. Surely we are implying here the existence of some transcendent value which evokes our spontaneous reactions. There is indeed a universality implied in this, but it can only be come at through the unique, individualized set of circumstances with which my experience confronts me. And the biblical injunction holds: we must lose self to gain it—the paradox of self-actualization through self-transcendence.

Frankl does speak at times of a *super-meaning*, an ultimate, universal meaning. He, unlike Freud, remains open to this possibility, though dubious that psychology alone can establish its validity.

> Pascal long ago remarked that the branch can never grasp the meaning of the whole tree. . . . For all that man may occupy an exceptional position, for all that he may be unusually receptive to the world, and that the world itself may be his environment—still, who can say that beyond this world a super-world does not exist? Just as the animal can scarcely reach out of his environment to understand the superior world of man, so perhaps man can scarcely ever grasp the super-world, though he can reach out toward it through religion—or perhaps encounter it in revelation. (1965, pp. 31–32)

Belief in a super-meaning, on such terms, he states, is definitely therapeutic. Nothing lacks meaning within a framework of genuine faith. Nothing goes unnoticed or unrecorded. All of us, Frankl states, have a conscience and must take it seriously. Logotherapy teaches people to see life as an assignment, a series of tasks to be responsibly fulfilled. The religious person, he points out, goes a step farther:

> They also experience the authority from which the task comes. They experience the taskmaster who has assigned the task to them. In our opinion we have here an essential characteristic of the religious man: he is a man who interprets his existence not only in terms of being responsible *for* fulfilling his life tasks, but also as being responsible *to* the taskmaster. (Frankl, 1965, pp. 58–59)

In addition to the clinical case studies reported by Frankl and his associates (Frankl, 1975, 1978), some empirical evidence has been found that supports some of his views. Most of it is based on correlational studies relating scores on the purpose-in-life test developed by James Crumbaugh (1968) to a number of other variables. As predicted, PIL scores are unrelated to age, sex, IQ, educational level, or personality traits (Crumbaugh, 1968; Yarnell, 1971; Meier, 1973; Ruch, 1973). A significant negative correlation ($r = -.68$, $p < .001$) was found between purpose in life and fear of death (Durlak, 1972). And the ability to recognize the "unconditional meaningfulness of life" apparently cuts across religious affiliation to different denominations (Meier, 1973) and is not dependent on religious beliefs alone (Murphy, 1967; Durlak, 1972).

## MASLOW'S B-DOMAIN

Abraham Maslow, as we have already seen, agreed with Frankl's dictum that self-actualization is a byproduct of self-transcendence. His rather cavalierly chosen sample of self-actualizers was, he stated, clearly differentiated by their devotion to a cause, their sense of a mission, vocation, or transcendent purpose in life. They were characteristically able to lose themselves in their work, in their love for another, their concern for succeeding generations, their appreciation and dedication to the transcendent values of beauty, truth, justice, order, harmony, or goodness. They could do so, he felt, because their own physiological and ego-needs had been basically gratified and they were thus free to contemplate, be open to experience without defensiveness or need, appreciate the world of Being upon which consciousness opens *for its own sake* rather than for their sake by merely perceiving what was in it for them.

Such values exist, Maslow claimed, and are discoverable when we are psychologically free to contemplate the world revealed by experience rather than having to act upon it for our own needy purposes. Self-actualization according to Maslow also requires self-transcendence: the ability to lose self in the values inherent in Being but follows only upon gratification of basic deficiency needs.

For us lesser mortals caught up in the daily routine of satisfying our needs for physiological and psychosocial survival, there are the occasional *peak-experiences* that unexpectedly sweep us off our feet, those precious moments when, almost in spite of ourselves, we are overwhelmed by sudden, transitory glimpses of the B-values: the beauty and grace of a child's unselfconscious movements in play, the glory of a spectacular sunset, a creative inspiration or sudden insight, the spontaneous admiration we feel in the presence of true greatness, daring, or unusual skill, the unimpeded flow of our own powers in those rare instances of seemingly effortless action.

Maslow makes quite clear his optimistic belief that through a careful phenomenological analysis of such experiences and of the lives of healthy, self-actualizing specimens of humanity, it will be possible empirically to discover and elucidate the meanings and values implicit in the domain of Being revealed by conscious experience. This requires an open, contemplative, almost passive type of cognition opposed to the usual instrumental, action- or goal-oriented sort of knowing in which we are more often forced to engage. This *B-cognition*, as he called it, fixes upon the transcendent object of experience as unrelated to the self, existing in its own right. It is in this domain of Being, revealed by the objective pole of conscious experience and possessed of qualities not bestowed by the conscious subject or under his or her control, that Maslow presumes to discover the transcendent values and meanings of human existence.

This is his way of saying that meanings and values are implicit in the reality that we consciously experience. Discovering them and serving them is the requisite for true self-actualization, full humanness. He adds the cautionary note that we must be psychologically free to do so, unencumbered by the prepotent needs for survival and safety; a helpful addendum to the previous accounts.

Maslow does tend to slight the fact that experience also reveals its ugly, disordered, terror-inducing "evil" aspects, though he takes note of their existence. Here is where Frankl is at his best—through his emphasis on attitudinal values, in contributing to a fuller humanistic account of the role of self-transcendence. He seems here to be postulating a second-order type of transcendence whereby we remain free to transcend these suffering-inducing aspects of reality through subjective acts of human courage.

We note for later reference that Maslow did not feel it necessary to postulate the existence of a superworld, the realm of an Absolute transcendent Other who, as in some major religious accounts, has established the reality which confronts human consciousness and gives it, along with ourselves, ultimate meaning and direction. In a preliminary work (Maslow, 1964), he openly discounted the necessity of making such assumptions. Reality, as capable of being known through the process of B-cognition, reveals all we require to live by and give meaning to our lives. B-values can be *empirically* derived and will be found to be transcultural, universal, capable of being validated pragmatically and scientifically. In his last work (Maslow, 1971), he remained staunchly committed to this basic position, a sort of natural, Taoistic religiosity, while backing down somewhat from his earlier sweeping criticisms of religious institutions.

## PROCESS THEORIES AND SELF–TRANSCENDENCE

At first glance, it is difficult to see how the process theories of self-actualization advocated by Carl Rogers and Fritz Perls (see Chapter 8) incorporate the theme of self-transcendence into their accounts of ideal human functioning. And yet, in Roger's description of the fully functioning organism, note how the isolation of the self, the experience with which we all begin, is all but overcome:

> The new self-Gestalt is a fluid changing configuration becoming more and more the basis for self-evaluations. The endpoint of therapy (though not the endpoint of change or growth) sees the perception of self as radically changed. It is more fluid and less rigid and static, *the "I" almost lost in the individual's perceptual field.* (Rogers & Wood, 1974, p. 220; emphasis added)

Ongoing experience, Rogers adds, becomes the referent for evaluation and action: "Each experience determines its own meaning, and is not interpreted as a past construct" (Rogers & Wood, 1974, p. 225). Meaning is again seen to be implicit in experience. Complete openness in reflexive awareness uncovers that meaning and serves as a reliable guide to conduct.

Attempting to live this process in his own life has led Rogers himself, in recent years, to be more open to a range of psychic experiences that have puzzled him and confounded some of his previous views of reality. Some of these happened while he was in Brazil conducting a person-centered workshop (personal communication, July, 1978). Others occurred at the time of his wife's death (following over 50 years of marriage) and have led him to write:

> All these experiences, so briefly suggested rather than described, have made me much more open to the possibility of the continuation of the individual human spirit, something I had never before believed possible. These experiences have left me very much interested in all types of paranormal phenomena. They have quite changed my understanding of the process of dying. I now consider it possible that each of us is a continuing spiritual essence lasting over time, and occasionally incarnated in a human body. (Rogers, 1980, pp. 91–92)

As we have seen, Rogers also confesses to being excited about a hypothesis he finds shared by others: that the universe itself is marked by a transcendent harmony and unity potentially available to human consciousness (1980, p. 133). More frequently, this conviction tends to occur in so-called altered states of consciousness. He himself believes he has experienced it in occasional episodes when he is at his best as a therapist or group facilitator. In such moments:

> Our relationship transcends itself and becomes a part of something larger. Profound growth and healing and energy are present. . . .
>
> Our experiences in therapy and in groups, it is clear, involve the transcendent, the indescribable, the spiritual. I am compelled to believe that I, like many others, have underestimated the importance of this mystical, spiritual dimension. (Rogers, 1980, pp. 129–130).

At a minimum, such experiences involve a loss of the sense of being an isolated self, a variety of self-transcendence that results, momentarily at least, and often more enduringly in subsequent consciousness, in a healing of the initially felt split between self and other on both an individual and more cosmic level.

Such is also the conclusion of the Gestalt therapist Joel Latner (though Perls himself apparently did not arrive at this point). Recall again Latner's statement that "the last Gestalt" arrived at through the process of a free-functioning, sharply aware human organism is: "I and the universe are one. . . . The farther reaches of this process are traditionally matters for philosophy and religion" (1974, p. 225). Again, a boundary is reached in our presentation of the theme of self-transcendence.

## THE ASIAN CONNECTION

Awareness of this recurring boundary has led many humanistic psychologists to an exploration of Eastern thought and so-called ways of liberation. The reason for this is simple: Western psychological science, as Charles Tart has observed, has no categories for the description of spiritual or mystical phenomena. Its assumptions concerning human behavior have been rather uniformly and tiresomely physicalistic and reductionistic. In his estimation, it is therefore completely inadequate for dealing with the spiritual side of human experience, "that vast realm of human potential dealing with ultimate purposes, with higher entities, with God, with love, with compassion, with purpose" (Tart, 1975, p. 4).

There have been exceptions, of course. I would note here the archetypal psychology of Carl Jung and his followers and some of the thought reviewed in this chapter. But these positions are very controversial and not well received in most academic departments of psychology. It is interesting that Jung and most of the humanists reviewed here frequently refer to Chinese Taoism in particular in their attempts to find some philosophical categories and language correlates capable of expressing the burden of their thought.

This attempt to break free of Western physicalistic categories to accommodate the upper reaches of human potential as envisaged by humanistic psychologists has already spawned a vast literature on so-called Eastern psychologies, which I here refer to as the *Asian connection*. We cannot hope to review it all (some of the historical origins of this interest and a few of its seminal works have been charted in Chapter 1) except to note that much of it has to do with the problem of self-transcendence, the theme of the present chapter.

How is this so? The work of Alan Watts, humanistic theologian and prolific author of works on the philosophy and psychology of religion, will serve as a helpful starting point. In his book *Psychotherapy East and West* (1961), Watts called our attention first of all to the fact that Eastern thought tends to be holistic—it does not compartmentalize knowledge into separate disciplines like religion (or theology), philosophy, sociology, psychology, and the like, as we do in the West. Second, he claims that much of what we conceive to be Eastern religious practices are in reality more akin to the aims of Western insight psychotherapy. They are best described as ways of liberation, intended to lead their practitioners to full self-actualization through self-transcendence.

> Buddha saw into the nature of man during his enlightenment. He realized intuitively that his own True-self was intrinsically perfect, that all men are inherently perfect—that is, every man possesses the potentials of perfection waiting to be actualized.

Man's function in the universe, Buddha concluded, is to awaken his Original-mind that has been covered by the dust of intellection and delusions of the relative world, to identify with universal Consciousness through zazen and self-realization, then to live a life of selflessness, wisdom, and compassion and eventually to attain nirvana. (Owens, 1975, p. 165)

The language, from the pen of an American practitioner of Zen Buddhism, sounds esoteric to Western ears, but its correspondence to the humanistic themes presented in this and the preceding chapter seems clear.

Every culture contains implicit religious or metaphysical views concerning the nature of the universe in which we live and the place that humanity occupies within that universe. We drink in such ideas with our mother's milk. They inform the institutions of the societies in which we live; in a word, they construe reality for us and define the social and psychological coordinates of our space. We live in separate realities, to use Castaneda's term (1971), dependent on the cultural matrix in which we were formed. And yet within many of these cultures, and especially within the more enduring ones, schools of wisdom developed disciplines in which a favored few might learn to escape the "social construction of reality" (Berger & Luckmann, 1966) and arrive at both knowledge of ultimate Truth and communion with ultimate Reality.

These are the quiet revolutions, led by sages, gurus, shamans, saints and mystics, spiritual masters and mistresses, who have reached enlightenment and have taught others to question the reality they have learned to take for granted, reaching beyond it to a more cosmic, transcendent vision. And so we find the disciplines of Yoga within Hindu culture; Buddhism in Southeast Asia; Taoism in the midst of Confucian Chinese culture; Stoicism in ancient Greece and Rome; Zen, a mixture of Taoistic and Buddhistic disciplines, in Japanese society; Sufism within Islam; Hasidism in Eastern European Judaism; and closer to home, the disciplines of ascetical and mystical theology within the Christian traditions (not to mention Western magical practices that date back to the pagan, pre-Christian era).

There are some differences, of course, among these traditions, but many common elements are being found. They are all ways of liberation from the ultimately false dualities experienced by the social ego (called *maya* in Yogic philosophy): the dualities of self and other, matter and spirit, pain and pleasure, life and death, suffering and enjoyment, God and devil. "So maya means the world of impermanence and relativity. It has pragmatic validity but not ultimate reality. A person who realizes the ultimate stops craving for ever-changing things of the world of maya" (Chaudhuri, 1975, p. 249).

Often, through ascetical practices, always through contemplation and meditation, the novice-learner, after the necessary grounding in his or her own cultural view of reality, is led step by step to break through the illusion of a "skin-encapsulated," isolated ego to a vision of the absolute order of things and a blissful communion with the very ground of Being.

There are some interesting and often quite different metaphysical and theological assumptions behind these various approaches, but what particularly interests the humanistic psychologist is the process involved in attaining what is obviously an ideal of self-realization. Without belaboring the point, there are some noteworthy parallels here to the aims of traditional, insight-oriented psychotherapies in modern Western society.

As Watts puts it:

> The main resemblance between these Eastern ways of life and Western psychotherapy is in the concern of both with bringing about changes of consciousness, changes in our ways of feeling our own existence and our relation to human society and the natural world. The psychotherapist has, for the most part, been interested in changing the consciousness of peculiarly disturbed individuals. The disciplines of Buddhism and Taoism are, however, concerned with changing the consciousness of normal, socially adjusted people. (1961, pp. 15–16)

The parallels are even clearer with the aims of the human potential movement and the numerous growth centers to which it has given rise (see Chapter 11). Here too programs are universally geared not to the mentally disturbed but to the normal individual who wishes to improve the quality of his or her life. And pertinently many of these offerings are derived from Eastern disciplines.

## Taoism: An example

In what, precisely, do these changes of consciousness consist? It would appear from the accounts given by Watts and others that they involve a gradual shift from the experience of the conscious self as an isolated ego to a state in which the self is experienced as an integral part of the larger whole in which it is embedded. It is important to emphasize that this is a shift in *experience* not merely in conceptualization. The resultant experience is one of unity not separation; of being at one with the One, with Being as a whole. It has been called the *mystic experience*, the experience of cosmic consciousness.

> Wherever the great mysticism has come, it has offered to replace popular or local religion with a new and universal allegiance. Folk beliefs about gods and spirits give place to a metaphysic of the utmost generality for those who can rise to it. The mystic's passion is satisfied only with the

sense of the Ultimate Reality, the God, Godhead or Godness that is back of the world of mind and nature. . . . The mystic report is that: *Reality, however designated, is One; it is an all-embracing unity from which nothing can be separated.* (Blakney, 1955, p. 29)

Examples could be multiplied to show how mystics of all faiths and religious traditions have arrived at this similar point: an appreciation of and sense of communion with the unity of all Being, the reconciliation of all opposites and dichotomies. Occasional peak-experiences apparently give way to a plateau of conscious experience (Maslow, 1971, p. 348) in which the initial sense of isolation and separation is finally and consistently overcome.

These are heady notions, exotic-sounding to most Western ears. As students of consciousness, however, humanistic psychologists are keenly interested in them. Transcultural in extent, ancient in origin, yet found throughout the history of humanity, they cannot be lightly dismissed. Taoism is an example of one such perspective, chosen because so many of the humanists quoted in this volume refer to it.

Taoism represents one of the two main currents of indigenous Chinese religious philosophy. Its founder, Lao-tzu, was a contemporary of Confucius, the originator of the other current. Both lived in the sixth century B.C. (Buddhism, which also became very popular in China, was imported from India in the early centuries of the Christian era.) Where Confucianism was solid and practical, focused on hierarchical social relationships, ethics, and morals, Taoism was intensely personal and mystical, though it also, of course, had practical implications. The expression given it by Lao-tzu was impressionistic and intuitive through his great poem, the *Tao Teh Ching,* often translated as *The Way of Life* (Blakney, 1955; Sih, 1961). It was given a more orderly, philosophical mode of expression by Chuang-tzu two centuries later (Murphy & Murphy, 1968).

Taoism, as we would by now expect, sought to liberate its adherents from the artificial social conventions (so characteristic of Confucianism) that had displaced the inherent harmonies of nature. *Tao* itself can be translated as "The Way of Nature," "action," "process." There are no things in reality, no entities, only a constantly changing series of interrelated processes emanating from an unchanging source. "Tao can be talked about, but not the Eternal Tao. Names can be named, but not the Eternal Name" (Sih, 1961).

According to this doctrine, we really have no choice but to trust the processes of nature, including our own organismic process—to go with the flow, as a current phrase has it.

Human nature could be trusted enough to leave itself alone because it was felt to be embedded in the Tao, and the Tao was in turn felt to be a perfectly self-consistent order of nature, manifesting itself in the polarity of *yang* (the positive) and *yin* (the negative). Their polar relationship made it impossible for one to exist without the other, and thus there was no real reason to be for *yang* and against *yin*. (Watts, 1961, p. 89)

Evil comes from good, good from evil. Each complements the other in the orderly process of nature, just as life follows death and death life. The process is somehow harmonious, and we must submit to it. Chuang-tzu relates the following apocryphal story of a meeting between Confucius and Lao-tzu:

> Confucius visited Lao-tzu, and spoke of charity and duty to one's neighbor.
> Lao-tzu said, "The chaff from winnowing will blind a man's eyes so that he cannot tell the points of a compass. . . . And just in the same way this talk of charity and duty to one's neighbor drives me nearly crazy. Sir! strive to keep the world to its own original simplicity. And as the wind bloweth where it listeth, so let virtue establish itself. Wherefore such undue energy, as though searching for a fugitive with a big drum [who will hear you coming and make his escape]." (Browne, 1961)

Essential to the doctrine of Taoism, therefore, is the principle of *wu-wei* (let be), or noninterference with the Tao. More than distant echoes of this philosophy are clearly to be found in the therapeutic processes advocated by Carl Jung, Carl Rogers, and Fritz Perls (labelled *Taoistic therapies* by Abraham Maslow).

We cannot, of course, avoid living by social conventions. The Taoistic solution (along with other ways of liberation) is to see them as such, to play the game, the social roles, while seeing through their artificiality and the divisions they impose to the reality beyond. All the world is indeed a stage on which is enacted the play of Being. But the play is *not* the thing. To take it too seriously as though it were is to court despair. We must enact the play playfully while remaining detached.

Nonattachment (together with noninterference) is therefore one of the central axioms of Taoism. Desires come and go, rise and fall within us. That is part of Tao. To cling to them, enthrone them as the key to happiness, is to oppose the ebb and flow of Tao. Lao-tzu writes:

> As for holding to fullness,
> Far better were it to stop in time!
>
> Keep on beating and sharpening a sword,
> And the edge cannot be preserved for long.
>
> Fill your house with gold and jade,
> And it can no longer be guarded.
>
> Set store by your riches and honor,
> And you will only reap a crop of calamities.
>
> *Here is the Way of Heaven:*
> *When you have done your work, retire!*" (Sih, 1961)

Process is all. Flow with it and you will be in harmony with nature, the Absolute. As Arthur Deikman, a Western psychiatrist and student of the East advises: "So ask a different question [not 'What should I do?' which implies that others must provide the answer for me, but]: 'Where does my energy want to go?'" (1976, p. 146). My nonstriving energy, the flow of Tao within me. To answer such a question, one must turn inward, meditate, be passive and receptive, let go of the mode of action and striving to discover the direction which Action itself (the Tao) wishes to take. How remarkable here the resemblance to Rogers's "full-functioning" and to Perls's "free-functioning" organism (see Chapter 8).

In this sketchy presentation of Taoistic doctrine, I have obviously not been able to capture its many subtle nuances. But perhaps enough has been said to indicate that it does indeed have to do with the theme of self-transcendence, a method of overcoming the experience of ego-isolation with which we begin. The implication, in other doctrines of liberation as well as in Taoism, is that the isolation experience is generated by the process of socialization to which we are all necessarily subjected, an analysis of the origin of self-consciousness quite similar to that charted by George Herbert Mead (1934), the prominent Western sociologist.

Liberation, therefore, does not involve loss of consciousness but a higher form of consciousness, consciousness in an altered state. Loss is implied here: the loss of the experience of self as *the* center of the universe, of the isolation of self imposed by social learning. But there is apparently great gain also: the experience of being part of something larger, some Absolute which anchors our own existence. As Lao-tzu says of the Sage:

> Is it not because he is selfless
> That his Self is realized? (Sih, 1961)

What has been said about Taoism should not be taken to mean that this is the only possible route to self-transcendence. Taoism, for one thing, implies an immanentist viewpoint concerning the Absolute, a metaphysical position which holds that Nature itself is All: Being and Nature are one. This position is not quite the same as Western materialism, on the one hand (since consciousness is emphasized in Taoism), or Judaism, Islam, and Christianity on the other. These latter are "religions of the Book," which teach that God, the Absolute, transcends Nature itself, which He has created, and that He has revealed Himself to us in the course of history. These also have given rise to "spiritual technologies," as Charles Tart calls them, alternate routes to self-transcendence. What interests the humanistic psychologist, I would point out again, is their very existence, the states of consciousness they engender, and the methods used to achieve such states.

## TRANSPERSONAL PSYCHOLOGY

Such considerations have led a growing number of humanistic psychologists to the empirical study of these and other altered states of consciousness, the offshoot of humanistic psychology which has come to be known as transpersonal psychology. Since the origins and chief concerns of this movement have already been presented in Chapter 1, I will not repeat them here but will only add some observations that will serve to highlight the empirical phenomenological approach, both structural and functional, which is also characteristic of this movement.

An altered state of consciousness has been defined as one in which the individual "clearly feels a *qualitative* shift in his pattern of mental functioning, that is, he feels not just a quantitative shift (more or less alert, more or less visual imagery, sharper or duller, etc.) but also that some quality or qualities of his mental process are *different*" (Tart, 1969). The main focus of psychologists who are interested in ASCs is typically empirical and scientific. How many such states exist? How can they be reliably classified and differentiated (taxonomic questions)? What are the conditions or stimulus situations that predictably bring them about? What effects do they have on human physiology and behavior? What phenomenological experiences do they engender in the experiencing subject, and how do these differ from the contents of ordinary, waking consciousness? Can we discern any patterns, regularities, lawfulness among such experiences and their effects? The effort to find answers to these and similar questions is what characterizes this rapidly growing field. No attempt will be made to review them all here except to show how certain findings have already provided additional information concerning the human quest for self-transcendence.

To do so, we need to take a look at the taxonomic problem. This is a structural phenomenological question, and the standard reference here is to the work of Stanley Krippner (1972).

### Classification of altered states

Krippner has identified 20 differing states of consciousness: the first 19 are altered states in reference to the last, normal waking consciousness. They are thought to be semiautonomous with some overlap and can be categorized as follows.

1. *Dreaming state*—characterized chiefly by rapid eye movements (REM) and the absence of slow brain waves on the electroencephalogram (EEG).
2. *Sleeping state*—absence of REM and emerging patterns of slow, high-amplitude brain waves.

3. *Hypnagogic state*—characterized by vivid imagery at the onset of the sleep cycle.

4. *Hypnopompic state*—when such imagery occurs at the end of the sleep cycle.

5. *Hyperalert state*—a waking state characterized by intense concentration and increased vigilance, usually in moments where survival is at stake or as a reaction to certain drugs.

6. *Lethargic state*—characterized by a pronounced slowing down of mental activity, as, for example, in profound depression or induced by hypoglycemia or fatigue.

7. *State of rapture*—characterized by intense positive or pleasurable feelings and emotions, sometimes induced by, for example, orgiastic rituals.

8. *State of hysteria*—marked by intense negative and destructive emotions (subjectively evaluated as such), as in violent mob action, fear, or anger.

9. *State of fragmentation*—characterized by a lack of integration of important segments of the personality, as in psychosis, multiple personality, or other dissociative states.

10. *Regressive state*—a state of consciousness clearly inappropriate for any individual's chronological age, as under certain forms of hypnotic, age-regression instructions.

11. *Meditative state*—characterized by an altered, expanded mode of perception, involving a sense of unity or self-transcendence, heightened sensory perception, strong affect, and timelessness. Such states are self-induced usually through the practice of certain learned techniques and remain largely under the control of the subject. So-called mystical experiences are often characteristic of the meditative state.

12. *Trance state*—as in hypnosis, characterized by heightened suggestibility, alertness, and concentration on a single stimulus.

13. *Reverie.*

14. *Daydreaming state.*

15. *Internal scanning.*

16. *Stupor*—characterized by greatly reduced ability to perceive incoming stimuli.

17. *Coma*—marked by a complete inability to perceive incoming stimuli.

18. *Stored memory*—usually an aspect of a trance state in which a past experience is vividly reenacted or remembered.

19. *"Expanded" conscious state*—altered modes of perception, at times similar to those found in the meditative state, but induced by psychedelic drugs and therefore not under the control of the subject.

20. *Normal waking consciousness.*

Most of these states have not as yet been extensively studied, with the exception of sleep and dreaming, hypnosis, psychotic states, psychedelic or expanded-conscious states, and meditative or mystical states (Pelletier & Garfield, 1976). Fortunately, research on the latter three categories is of particular relevance to the topic of self-transcendence.

For a detailed presentation and analysis of the research on altered states, with particular emphasis on the above-mentioned categories, the reader is referred to the helpful book *Consciousness East and West* by Kenneth Pelletier and Charles Garfield (1976) cited above. I will content myself here with a brief summary of their discussion and conclusions.

These authors suggest that acute, psychotic episodes, psychedelic states, and deep meditation states can be viewed as lying on a continuum. The former two are more episodic and transitory, less under the control of the subject, induced by a combination of as yet unclearly understood biochemical and interpersonal variables. From a phenomenological perspective, one thing seems clear: all three states generally include an overwhelming experience of self-transcendence. The normal experience of social reality becomes severely disrupted and the individual is flooded with a sense of the mystery of Reality, a sense of awe, wonder (and at times terror) which is notably lacking in normal waking consciousness. (Salvatore Maddi has presented a suggestive hypothesis concerning the physiological mechanisms and their modification through the learning involved in early social intercourse that mediates this slowly developing social construction of reality [Maddi, 1968].)

*Psychotic states.* Acute psychosis is, of course, a serious problem, particularly in cultures like our own in which it is simply considered a disease. Since we have no other categories by which to explain it, it is almost always a degenerative, terrifying experience, seldom leading to an integrative reconstitution of personality functioning. This is not the case in all cultures. While the schizophrenic breakdown process seems to be a universal, transcultural phenomenon, some cultures have apparently devised explanatory categories that more easily lead to a breakthrough. In such instances, the individual becomes, for example, a revered shaman, and his insights are treasured and incorporated into the cultural web of meaning (Eliade, 1964).

There are exceptions in our own culture also. The counter-cultural approach in Western psychiatry has suggested a similar possibility, particularly in cases of acute psychosis (Menninger, 1959; Bateson, 1961; Kaplan, 1964; Laing, 1967; Silverman, 1970). These authors point at least to the potential, admittedly seldom realized, of a *regenerative* psychosis, and John Weir Perry (1974; 1976), a Jungian psychiatrist, has suggested a set of categories (and a method of treatment) from Jungian theory which might help facilitate such an outcome.

*Psychedelic states.*   Pelletier and Garfield's analysis of the research on psychedelic drugs (LSD, marijuana, psylocibin, mescaline, peyote, and the like) results in somewhat similar conclusions. Prolonged use of these drugs to induce altered states is generally debilitating and self-destructive *in our culture.* (In certain Mexican and North American Indian cultures, which surround such use with religious categories of explanation, this is seldom the case [Weil, 1972].) And even in our own society, where research has been conducted in a supportive environment with positive expectations (rather than under laboratory conditions designed to establish their psychoticlike effects), the states produced are generally reported to have been highly positive and beneficial.

Subjects under such conditions report their experiences as pleasurable, free of anxiety, frequently involving an exhilarating sense of unity with other people and the world at large, a sense of humility and awe. Ego integrity is generally maintained, the future is eagerly anticipated, and there is heightened sensory awareness with strong positive affect (quite unlike the fearful affect which accompanies the similar heightened awareness found in psychotic states). Interestingly, subjective accounts of these experiences have been found to be virtually indistinguishable from those reported by mystics (Grof, 1970).

Though the authors conclude that even an essentially negative drug experience seldom has the long-range and totally disabling effects characteristic of schizophrenia, they agree with Weil in supporting the greater efficacy of meditative techniques for producing experiences of self-transcendence (and thereby fuller self-realization).

The superiority of the traditional meditative disciplines lies in their ability better to prepare the individual for such experiences and to aid him or her in integrating them by offering time-tested methods of induction and categories of understanding, usually religious, which are simply unavailable to the drug culture. This is particularly true in our own society, where such chemical substances are considered illegal and dangerous. However, we are not alone in this conviction:

> In fact, every major religion and system of meditation stresses the avoidance of drug-induced altered states. . . . It is significant that the meditative disciplines have evolved predominantly from the Indian, Chinese, and Japanese cultures, where there are significant amounts of psychoactive drugs, such as hashish and opiates, available to the general population. These aforementioned cultures have come to recognize that drugs are an ineffective means of attaining altered states and yet have not inextricably confused the means with the experiences themselves. (Pelletier & Garfield, 1976, pp. 115–116)

***Meditative states.*** This brief review of transpersonal psychology with its focus on altered states of consciousness has already led to a startling possibility—the possibility that our normal, waking consciousness and the experience it involves of an isolated self viewing the rest of the world from its lonely outpost is no more than an artifact, an illusion created by social convention—and apparently a predominantly Western illusion at that (Smith, 1978).

Apparently also, it is an illusion that is rather rapidly and uniformly overcome in almost any ASC, sometimes with destructive but at other times with regenerative, very healing consequences. This latter outcome seems to be especially characteristic of meditative or mystical states, though these too, as the literature of mysticism cautions us, can have destructive consequences for the well-being of unprepared and unguided devotees (Kelsey, 1976). This is reason enough to explain the surge of interest in this category of ASCs by transpersonal psychologists over the last two decades.

We have already adverted to the fact that every major religious system, East or West, has emphasized the role of meditation or contemplation as *the* strategy for producing the desired changes in consciousness. Other means have also been employed: orgiastic rituals, severe ascetical practices, ritual prayer or chants, psychoticlike hallucinations and visions, dreams, and even drugs; but meditative disciplines are the most universally used and generally favored strategies for bringing about the desired liberation from social maya.

The type of meditation best calculated to produce such effects can be termed *deep meditation* and often requires years of training and practice to achieve. All forms of meditation involve "a profound state of passivity accompanied by an apparently paradoxical state of complete awareness" (Pelletier & Garfield, 1976, p. 115). There are obvious parallels here to the descriptions of B-cognition provided by Abraham Maslow and to the passive versus active mode of conscious functioning in Arthur Deikman's model of bimodal consciousness (Deikman, 1971).

Even the more superficial transient forms, which have recently become so popular in the West, have been shown to produce beneficial physiological and psychological effects (Wallace & Benson, 1972). These effects are different from those produced in dreaming and deep sleep and apparently help to offset the stress and tension produced in the normal waking state in additional positive ways.

Two fundamental (and opposite) methods are used to induce the meditative state: focusing attention on a particular object, physiological process (such as breathing), or on a mantra; or expanding attention to increase one's perception of *all* internal or external stimuli. Paradoxically, both methods seem capable of aiding the subject to overcome his or her usual process of selecting and categorizing or prejudging the stimuli to be perceived. The outcome is usually a detached state of watchfulness, a *passive* observation of conscious phenomena in which the meditator begins to experience "a state of being more basic and distinct from both his thoughts and attention. It is this ASC that has been called variously *nirvana, satori,* or *transcendental awareness*" (Pelletier & Garfield, 1976, p. 136)."

The extensive review of empirical research on meditative states provided by these authors will not be repeated here except to note that it covers a wide array of physiological correlates (functional phenomenological research) and qualitative descriptions of such states (structural phenomenological accounts). Comparisons to the more positive structural content of other ASCs are especially striking from the vantage point of self-transcendence:

> According to psychiatrists Walter N. Pahnke and William A. Richards (1966), the fundamental aspects of all of them are (1) an experience of undifferentiated unity; (2) states of insight into depths of truth unplumbed by the intellect; (3) transcendence of space and time; (4) sense of sacredness characterized by awe; (5) deeply felt positive emotion; (6) paradoxical experiences, such as being reborn through death; (7) alleged ineffability, resulting in difficulty in communicating about the experience; (8) transiency, since all such states are relatively brief; and (9) positive changes in attitude and/or behavior. (Pelletier & Garfield, 1976, p. 120)

From this brief survey of transpersonal psychology, we can conclude that it bears much promise for shedding further light on the humanistic theme of self-transcendence. Andrew Weil (1972) has even suggested the existence of a universal, deep-seated human need to seek out altered states of consciousness, correlative to this need for contact on the transpersonal level.

This research on the "frontiers of consciousness," to use John W. White's apt term (1972), has more recently focused on the physiological substrates of ASCs. In particular, these concern the function of the reticular activating system (RAS) in serving as a gating mechanism for incoming stimuli (allowing some to pass through to the cortex while suppressing others). Salvatore Maddi (1968) had already suggested that this function of selectivity, mediated by the reticular formation of the "old brain" just above the spinal cord, is very much influenced by early social learning. Apparently, its usual functioning is significantly changed by the conditions that produce subjectively experienced altered states of consciousness.

A second line of current research focuses on the bilateral functioning of the right and left hemispheres of the cortex itself. The pioneer studies in this field were conducted by Roger Sperry, Michael Gazzaniga, and others on split-brain patients (Sperry, 1968; Sperry, Gazzaniga, & Bogen, 1969; Gazzaniga, 1970). These were patients suffering from severe epilepsy, which was relieved by a surgical procedure that effectively disconnected the two hemispheres of the brain by cutting through the central commissure. Following the operation, experiments were performed which clearly established the fact that the two hemispheres subserve quite different types of functioning (e.g., the left hemisphere, which contains the speech center in right-handed subjects, subserves the performance of verbal tasks and logical analysis; the right hemisphere, nonverbal tasks, such as spatial orientation and intuitive knowledge).

These findings have since been confirmed and extended by other forms of psychological experimentation not involving such drastic surgical intervention (Ornstein, 1972). In keeping with Deikman's model of bimodal consciousness (1971), the suggestion is now being advanced that the conditions used to induce some ASCs, such as hypnotic and deep meditative states, may well involve a shift in bilateral dominance, in most cases from left to right hemisphere involvement. Robert Ornstein and others are currently suggesting that we need to strike a better balance between the two in order to maximize the potential inherent in human consciousness. The intuitive modes of thought of the East and the logical modes of analysis of the West might thereby be combined to produce a synthesis which would overcome the imbalances found in each. This prospect is certainly exciting enough to warrant further investigation. And here, I might add, we see the functional phenomenological approach at its best.

## SELF–TRANSCENDENCE AND RELIGION

Subjective accounts of experiences undergone in deep meditative states of consciousness are strikingly similar, even across cultures. They appear to involve a transcendence of our usual *egocentrism*, while maintaining the integrity of the self. The *interpretation* of these experiences, however, varies from culture to culture. The question remaining is how far psychology can go toward the validation of such interpretations. While we need to keep our scientific and philosophical wits about us, there comes a point, in my estimation, where mere psychologizing (or philosophizing) fails. It is at this point that we enter the realm of religious understanding and theology. Some authors, even among humanistic psychologists, would admittedly part company with me here. Abraham Maslow, to the end of his life, maintained the proposal that psychology would some day supplant religion in supplying us with a universally satisfying view of the transcendent meaning of life (Maslow, 1971). The question is: When is that point reached? How far can psychology go toward validating the answers proposed either by itself or by different religious systems?

While admitting from the start that I do not pretend to have *the* answer to this difficult question, I have been struck by some observations made by the late Ernest Becker in his powerful book *The Denial of Death* (1973). Ingeniously combining insights from the writings of the neoanalyst Otto Rank, the existential religious philosopher Soren Kierkegaard, and current existential analysts, Becker carefully and rather convincingly sets out the proposition that much of human behavior, individual and social, can be traced to our untiring efforts to transcend the terror of death. This is the worm at the core of the apple, the constant dread that gnaws at our vitals as soon as we awaken to self-consciousness. It arises from the existential paradox of the human condition: the fact that we are half animal and half symbolic creatures.

> Man is literally split in two: he has an awareness of his own splendid uniqueness in that he sticks out of nature with a towering majesty, and yet he goes back into the ground a few feet in order blindly and dumbly to rot and disappear forever. (Becker, 1973, p. 26)

The inevitable result of this terrifying paradox, according to Becker, is that "everything that man does in his symbolic world is an attempt to deny and overcome his grotesque fate" (1973, p. 27).

We repress the knowledge of death, deny our fear of it, develop individual and social stratagems to transcend death itself through myths of heroism and various forms of immortality. Above all, we construct *causa sui* (self-caused or self-activated) projects, attempts to achieve a sense of self-sufficiency, through becoming creators in our own right, through our offspring, our works, or the myths we create to sustain our illusions. (Becker was professionally a cultural anthropologist, an astute student of the ways in which various cultures attempt to convey ultimate meaning to their members through heroic mythic-ritual complexes.) We need these illusions to live by, or we go mad. The psychotic is overwhelmed by the terror of death; the neurotic erects elaborate defenses against the ultimate chaos; the normal individual lives the "vital lie" supplied by his or her culture; the creative artist at least manages to fashion a meaningful expression of the basic dilemma.

While we desperately need such illusions in order to escape madness and utter despair, some illusions are better than others. (It is important to note here that Becker uses this term in its original meaning, as the "play" of the imagination.) The criterion to be used here is how close or how far removed the illusion is from the acknowledgement of the fact of death, the fact, as Kierkegaard expressed it, of our innate *creatureliness*.

It is in the application of this criterion that Becker is at his bitingly best:

> Modern man is drinking and drugging himself out of awareness, or he spends his time shopping, which is the same thing. As awareness calls for types of heroic dedication that his culture no longer provides for him,

society contrives to help him forget. Or, alternatively, he buries himself in psychology in the belief that awareness all by itself will be some kind of magical cure for his problems. But psychology was born with the breakdown of shared social heroisms; it can only be gone beyond with the creation of new heroisms that are basically matters of belief and will, dedication to a vision. (Becker, 1973, p. 28)

A bit later on he states: "the only way to get beyond the natural contradictions of existence [is] in the time-worn religious way: to project one's problems onto a god-figure, to be healed by an all-embracing and all-justifying beyond" (1973, p. 285).

For this, he claims, we need to make the Kierkegaardian "leap of faith" or, as some theologians would prefer to express it, be graced by the *gift* of faith from a benevolent Creator. And the further implication of this statement is the most controversial of all: some religions, *from a psychological standpoint*, are better illusions than others, according to the same criterion mentioned above. We are not sufficient unto ourselves, nor is Nature sufficient unto itself to provide the solution we yearn for. The nature that we perceive through our senses or their technological extensions is as much a creature as we are, subject to decay and death through the law of entropy. It follows then that any purely immanentist view (such as Taoism?) which equates the Absolute with Nature, however it is conceived, is not as satisfying a solution to our dilemma as one which posits the existence of a transcendent Creator who graces us both (nature and humanity) with existence and meaning. As Becker says, "Religion takes one's very creatureliness, one's insignificance, and makes it a condition of hope. Full transcendence of the human condition means limitless possibility unimaginable to us" (1973, p. 20).

This, then, is the best illusion; a solution which grounds our existence in absolute transcendence while placing on us the responsibility to develop our human potential to the best of our capacity. Psychology can and indeed must serve to strip away the lesser illusions, forcing us to face and embrace the dilemma of human existence. In spite of some efforts to the contrary, it cannot provide the ultimate answer. For that we need *contact*, at the transpersonal level, with a transcendent Other. Transpersonal psychology can even show us, through its renewed emphasis on meditative states, how to prepare the ground for the ultimate solution by helping us overcome the egocentrism of the socially constructed self. Beyond that, it cannot go. We stand before the mystery of faith.

Becker assumes the best illusion is a play of imagination that is primarily irrational. He sees no problem here. Perhaps indeed there is none. I would simply point out that his penetrating analysis is far from being irrational itself. There remain, it appears to me, strong cognitive and rational elements in the preparation for the ultimate juxtaposition of psychology and religion. The boundary is clearly drawn.

According to Becker then, the role of psychology is both preparatory and pragmatic: to unmask the pretensions that follow upon repression of the basic existential dilemma and to critique the solutions proposed. William James, the founder of American psychology (and of the philosophy of pragmatism), had suggested a similar criterion for judging the validity of religious experiences: Do they work? Do they lead to a fuller, richer human existence, marked by reverence for life, compassion and respect for all beings, personal serenity, and transcendence of purely social conventions (James, 1929)? Becker would agree, adding the note that such experiences, to be valid, must not deny the basic human condition, or they will prove ultimately self-defeating. The most promising solution for him would have the following elements:

It will find us. We are not capable of finding it ourselves.

Paradoxically, it will demand that we be true to ourselves: that we will fashion our own existence, accept responsibility for our own actions, and thus avoid succumbing to infantile dependence. As Pierre Teilhard de Chardin once put the same thought: "God did not come to diminish the magnificent responsibility and splendid ambition that is ours: *of becoming our own self* (1960, p. 39)."

Finally, it will ask that, having done so, we submit what we have fashioned to the transcendent Other, the Creator of all existence, in an act of humility and surrender.

# 10 Person-Centeredness: In Research and Therapy

The great 17th-century French philosopher, Blaise Pascal, once remarked:

> Man is only a reed, the feeblest reed in nature, but he is a thinking reed. There is no need for the entire universe to arm itself in order to annihilate him: a vapour, a drop of water, suffices to kill him. But were the universe to crush him, man would yet be more noble than that which slays him, because he knows that he dies, and the advantage that the universe has over him; of this the universe knows nothing. (Rawlings, 1946, p. 35)

This passage beautifully articulates a highly characteristic conviction of humanistic psychologists: the human person, man or woman, is a unique phenomenon in nature, and he or she is so precisely because of the attribute of self-reflective awareness. As we have seen, existential psychologists are particularly strong in their insistence on the singular importance of this astonishing evolutionary development. For them, person alone ex-*ists*, stands apart from mere being through self-knowledge and conscious experience. All other things in the universe simply *are*, or possess being.

As a direct corollary flowing from this crucial distinction, existentialists—and other humanists as well—do not hesitate to ascribe a unique value to human life, a sense of its superiority over all other forms, a sense of wonder, awe, and even reverence when confronting the core mystery of personhood. However this development is explained, scientifically, philosophically, or theologically, by accident of evolution or purposeful design, this centering on the value and dignity of personhood more than any other theme establishes the *humanistic orientation* of this whole approach.

Three of the other themes explored in this work are of particular importance in contributing to the person-centeredness of the humanistic-existential movement because of their practical consequences: the phenomenological approach toward their subject matter, their convictions concerning the existence of an actualizing or growth tendency within the human organism, and their emphasis on the possibility of a degree of self-determination or personal freedom in the conduct of human affairs. In presenting the person-centered emphasis in humanistic psychology, I will examine the implications of these contributions to research and psychotherapy in some detail and add an extensive account of the radical person-centered approach advocated by Carl Rogers and his associates. Then, in the following chapter, I will present a brief survey of the impact of this emphasis on other areas of human living beyond the discipline of psychology itself.

## PHENOMENOLOGICAL APPROACH

The phenomenological approaches presented in Chapter 4, whether structural or functional, share one thing in common: they all depend for their effectiveness on entering the subject's private world of conscious experience, his or her internal frame of reference, or personal *Dasein*, in order to understand, describe, or explore it from within. For the scientific investigator or therapist who engages in such an effort, several consequences seem inevitably to follow:

1. *The effort itself is person-centered.* A phenomenological approach by definition is essentially an exploration of this individual subject's experience and view of reality. It is basically idiographic. One's purpose may well be to discern some common or universal elements in such individual accounts of experience or some functional relationships between such elements and other variables within or outside its range, but such data must necessarily emerge from the given focus on individual experience. (Rogers, for example, has often been quoted as saying: "That which is most personal is also most general.") The patterns, when discovered, arise from within the subject and could never be ascertained apart from the person-centered focus utilized by the investigator unlike the results of other, more objective methods.

2. The adoption of a phenomenological approach as applied to several different subjects leads quickly to a *vivid realization of the uniqueness of the individual,* his or her idiosyncratic *Dasein*, or Being-in-the-World, and concomitantly, of the richness and vast diversity of

human experience. Even when common patterns do emerge, they are inevitably tempered by this stamp of uniqueness. Depressed individuals may indeed be alike, as Minkowski has pointed out, in experiencing the future as closed to them and empty of meaning and in ruminating endlessly and guiltily over the past. And yet each experiences his or her depression uniquely, with varying degrees of pain and intensity and self-disgust and over incidents and circumstances that belong exclusively to his or her own life-context. Human experience can never be cloned.

3. If it is to be at all successful, the effort to apply the phenomenological method in order to grasp and reconstruct a particular subject's *Dasein* necessarily involves some sort of *caring encounter* with that individual not usually found in the more traditional objective approaches. Not only is the process person-centered, therefore, but *interpersonal* as well. This added dimension strikingly differentiates the phenomenological approaches from other methods of investigation. Traditional experimental methods in psychology deliberately proscribe this type of involvement with the subject, opting instead for the ideal of impersonal detachment on the part of the investigator in the interests of scientific objectivity.

There is no question that such an impersonal mode of investigation will simply not do in phenomenological studies. A certain delicacy of feeling, a certain respect and caring for the individual must necessarily be communicated if we are to expect him or her to reveal to us the more intimate, perhaps even frightening and shameful, aspects of conscious experience. Such revelations are shared only in an atmosphere of warmth and safety for the one so revealing. Coldness or aloofness on the part of the investigator or helper simply cuts off the flow of communication or, worse yet, leads to distorted and inauthentic messages designed to fend off further intrusion. Certain interpersonal skills are therefore required of the phenomenological investigator that are alarmingly absent from the training of most academic psychologists.

This observation may seem at first glance to be irrelevant to the concerns of traditional experimental psychology. However, experimental psychologists do often work with human subjects, a fact that has led many humanistic authors to question the validity of some of the results obtained and reported by them, even in so-called objective investigations. Jourard, for example, once proposed the hypothesis that the responses given by human subjects in the typical psychological experiment might be primarily an artifact of the impersonal mode of relationship between subject and experimenter traditionally prescribed for such investigations.

In the context of their research on self-disclosure, he and his students began "to explore the possibility of replicating typical psychological experiments, first in the impersonal way their designers conducted the studies and then in the context of greater openness and mutual knowing between the psychologist and his subjects" (p. 109). Initial results did show a significant difference in reaction to a simple word-association test linked to the experimenter's rated experience of the relationship between himself and the subjects studied and some dramatic increases in subject self-disclosure when the investigators engaged in mutual dialogue with their subjects (Jourard, 1967, pp. 113–115).

## Experimenter bias

I would not want to give the impression that the relationship between the experimenter (or the experimental situation) and the subject has been a neglected topic in traditional psychological circles. Social scientists have devised highly sophisticated methods to neutralize the social-desirability variable (the tendency of subjects to present a positive image of themselves) in the construction of questionnaires and interview schedules (Edwards, 1957). Experimental psychologists are quite aware of the influence of experimenter bias, uncovered by Orne (1962) and by Rosenthal (1963, 1966), which is the tendency of subjects, unconsciously at times, to comply with a researcher's expectations of their behavior and thus spuriously to confirm the hypotheses of the study.

However, I tend to agree with Amedeo Giorgi's (1970) critique of the typical response to these discoveries. Commenting on some standard suggestions (Plutchik, 1968) for controlling experimenter bias (minimizing contact between experimenter and subject, double-blind procedures, replication by different investigators), Giorgi argues that none of these methods really solves the problem. From a phenomenological viewpoint, one cannot remove the presence of the experimenter from such investigations. One can only change the *mode* of that presence from a personal to an impersonal one (or from an actual, physical presence to a fantasied one). These differences may be quite critical, not only for psychology, but for all the human sciences.

This is not to deny that the neutrality of the observer may be the best possible approach in certain situations but simply to question its absolute validity under any and all circumstances or its characterization as a nonpresence. Double-blind procedures, for example, have proved invaluable in isolating and neutralizing the so-called placebo effect in drug studies (though perhaps, as Jourard suggests [1971], we need also to know more about this effect itself: why it works and under what conditions). But for those many instances in which full subject cooperation is vital to the experimental procedure, Giorgi argues strongly for a fully engaged attitude from experimenter and subjects alike (1970, pp. 189–90).

## The cooperative approach

This would involve, from the experimenter, a thorough account of his or her biases and assumptions in designing the research and reporting the results, and from the subjects a report of how the experimenter and the situation itself affected them. Such procedures boldly reintroduce subjectivity into the experimental situation but not in the pejorative sense so often used by the traditionalists. Giorgi's point is well taken: make explicit what is frequently implicit and unacknowledged. The further consequence is that replication, so often touted as an ideal, but unobserved in practice, becomes obviously more necessary to provide the requisite controls for whatever is uncovered by this more honest approach.

Finally, to return to my point that a phenomenological approach inevitably leads to a person-centered attitude toward the subjects being investigated, I quote from Giorgi's call for a "nonmanipulative paradigm" in human research. After suggesting that research designs remain open-ended "so that the final closure can be made by the subject himself," through his or her more spontaneous participation and truly collaborative efforts, Giorgi states:

> In short, if one truly believes that humans should not manipulate other humans, then it seems to be absurd to try to build a human science on the basis of a paradigm that violates this essential point. Obviously here we are referring only to the direct or indirect manipulation of other humans and not to the manipulation of the physical environment. (1970, p. 204)

Perhaps an example may help to clarify the implications of these somewhat theoretical observations. A doctoral student proposes to study the physiological effects of the aging process on certain perceptual skills of the elderly. He openly adopts the position, shared by many researchers, that such skills are not irretrievably lost because of senility but have simply become dormant through lack of need and use and might be recovered through practice. A double-blind procedure is proposed whereby neither the psychologists conducting the experiment and testing nor the subjects themselves will be aware of the purpose of the experiment. Typical standardized methods of presentation and testing are so designed that the experimental situation will not vary for the subjects involved except to control for order of presentation effects. In sum, he develops a beautifully designed experiment from the traditional viewpoint.

The experiment could then be replicated with a matched group of elderly subjects with the following differences: (a) experimenters and subjects would both know what the experiment was designed to prove; (b) an appeal would be made for the subjects' full cooperation on the basis that the research might well establish that they were capable of better functioning than even they themselves might suppose; (c) the atmosphere surrounding the experiment be made as emotionally supportive as possible with special and obvious attention paid to the comfort of the elderly participants. Results of this approach could then be compared in traditional statistical ways to results obtained from the impersonal double-blind procedure. My hypothesis would be that the subjects in the first experiment would find it difficult to respond at full potential to the impersonal procedures to which they would be exposed. The replication would test whether a more person-centered approach is better able to tap a potential already hypothesized as existing. It certainly could not supply one if it is indeed lacking.

Our discussion to this point has focused on the possibility, as yet mostly unrealized, of applying a person-centered approach to the human subjects of psychological experimentation in order to enhance present methods of investigation. A further comment seems apropos: *letting the phenomenon*, as the phenomenologists are so fond of saying, *speak for itself*.

What this implies is a methodology which encourages our human subjects to reveal themselves not only through the necessarily limited channels of the instruments designed to capture and quantify the variables of particular interest to the researcher but also, more broadly, in any form of expression the subjects might choose for themselves. Such an approach can be highly heuristic in leading the investigator to further understanding and to the generation of new hypotheses for later exploration. Its promise lies in taking advantage of the privileged position in which we find ourselves when working with human subjects: access not only to their externally observable behavior, but also to the conscious meanings that underlie it. This too requires a special skill from the investigator, involving a slightly different person-centered nuance. Robert Kirsch, in a review of the latest volumes of Robert Coles's monumental work, *Children of Crisis* (1977), describes it well:

> That perception [of man and the world obtained from his subjects by creating an atmosphere in which they felt quite free to express themselves] is another way of seeing and sensing, not the only way, but in equal contrast to the icy and misleading quantification and—equally, I think—many attempts at empathy and compassion. There are all kinds of ways. Certainly a good piece of advice came from a Pueblo Indian grandmother who told Dr. Coles:
> "When you go to our children, try to become a friendly tree that they will want to sit near. Enjoy them. Forget yourself. If we could all forget ourselves a bit more—then our children would feel free to be a bit more themselves. Sometimes we get too close to our children; we scare them with—*ourselves*. They can't become themselves. It is *them* we should try to know." (Kirsch, 1978, p. 11)

Coles himself, in following this method, frequently found his original preconceptions being overturned to be replaced by new insights arising from the spontaneously proffered verbal and other expressive forms of communication through which his subjects had been encouraged to reveal themselves. His approach is uniquely person-centered and deserving of much broader application.

Professional psychologists have exercised far greater initiative than their more academic colleagues in applying a person-centered approach to their work in the fields of psychotherapy and human relations. There exists by now a large body of research on the role of the therapist or consultant and the type of engagement with clients or systems that leads to constructive change, much of which documents the effectiveness of implementing such a stance. This will be discussed in greater detail in the final section of this chapter. I wish here merely to note that current research, particularly in psychotherapy, simply takes these findings for granted, incorporates them, and is now moving toward the study of the interaction of these personalistic variables with specific client problems, on the one hand, and strategies of intervention applied by the helper or consultant, on the other (Garfield & Bergin, 1978; Lazarus, 1976).

## THE PRINCIPLE OF SELF–ACTUALIZATION

Another of the themes discussed in this work, the almost universal assumption of an actualizing or growth tendency in human and other living organisms, contributes perhaps the strongest influence of all to the humanists' person-centered emphasis. The principle of self-actualization arising from this postulate provides us with a criterion for adjustment which is radically person-centered rather than sociocentric. It has had far-reaching consequences for both the practice of psychotherapy and the reformulation of personality theory itself. The origins and meaning of this construct have been detailed in Chapter 6. I wish here to emphasize its revolutionary implications for the viewpoint it gives us on the age-old problem of the relationship between the individual and society.

### Applications to psychotherapy

Adherence to one or another version of the principle of self-actualization has to date most obviously and dramatically affected the practice of psychotherapy. Anthony Sutich, on the basis of Goldstein's theory of the organism, issued an early call for a growth-centered orientation in the field:

> The end-product of several growth experiences, coupled with the development of the necessary orientation context, is the growth-centered attitude. This attitude expresses what may be called a superior level of

emotional maturity, and is an effective and efficient basis for an indefinite number of additional insights and growth-experiences. . . . Finally, it means the voluntary or free acceptance of self-actualization (Goldstein, 1939) or the full-valued personality as the overall objective of counseling and/or other relevant techniques and relationships. (1969, p. 85)

During the same period, Carl Rogers (1942, 1951) had begun to develop his client-centered approach on a similar theoretical foundation, thereby establishing the charter for modern counseling psychology. These and similar efforts were later described as "Taoistic therapies" by Abraham Maslow:

The data I turn to first [to answer the question: can science discover the values by which men live] are the accumulated experiences of dynamic psychotherapy, starting with Freud and continuing up to the present day in most therapies that have to do with discovering the identity, or the Real Self. I would prefer to call them all the "uncovering therapies" or Taoistic therapies in order to stress that they purport to uncover (more than to construct) the deepest self which has been covered over by bad habits, misconceptions, neuroticizing, etc. (1966, p. 124)

Ernest Rossi, in an article entitled "Game and Growth: Two Dimensions of our Psychotherapeutic Zeitgeist," carries forward the distinction between growth-centered and more traditional adjustment approaches to psychotherapy and addresses the problems this implies for current practitioners:

The basic idea of this paper is that psychotherapists are struggling to define, develop, and integrate two very different dimensions in their work with human beings. In the game dimension one is generally concerned with the individual's relation to the outside world and his ways of coping with it. . . . In the growth dimension, on the other hand, one is more concerned with the individual's experience of his inner world and his relation to it. (1969, p. 239)

Rossi goes on to analyze the problems confronted by therapists as they shift back and forth between these two dimensions and attempt to integrate them.

One source of this tension, in my experience, is the polarity between the universal and the singular. Possessing a certain amount of expertise in the field of human relations, the therapist brings to the helping task a wealth of knowledge and information about normal and abnormal psychology, psychodynamics, and the criteria of good mental health. His or her temptation is to play the role of expert, checking what is heard or observed against this background, diagnosing and prescribing as accurately and knowledgeably as possible. Working from this mode, however, the therapist tends to sacrifice the individual to the universal. The goal becomes indeed one of adjustment: fitting the individual's experience into a larger framework; stretching the client, as gently and painlessly as possible, onto the Procrustean bed of the norm. The client may come away with a genuine growth experience from this process, but there is considerable danger that his or her potential for a uniquely creative, particularized integration or solution will be lost in the shuffle.

This is the other side of the polarity: the belief that there exists within the individual an actualizing tendency unique to his or her specific organism as it interacts with the particular environment within which it operates. That somehow, in the deepest sense and perhaps unconsciously for most of us, I know best what is "good for me," how best to integrate the unique potential that differentiates me from all other individuals, and that therefore represents my unique contribution to the mosaic of society or humanity as a whole.

Such assumptions seem to demand a different mode of interaction from the therapist, a more person-centered mode in which the therapist serves primarily as a *catalyst or facilitator,* intervening in such a way as to enable the client to come to terms with and free those processes which block the smooth functioning of his or her own actualizing tendency. It is this mode which characterizes the newer, growth-oriented, Taoistic, "uncovering" therapies. The approach favored by Carl Rogers, as I shall show, radically embraces this side of the polarity. My own experience indicates that a synthesis is possible, involving a more *collaborative* approach. Remaining basically person-centered in orientation and dependent on the client's own creative potential for integration, the therapist attempts to apply the universal to the particular where appropriate. This is accomplished by gradually introducing the therapist's broader knowledge, *as it fits the client's experience and readiness,* to the task of unblocking the client's own resources.

This suggestion is in reality not far removed from the Rogerian position. In admitting his own antipathy toward a mode of encounter group leadership in which leaders uniformly guide members through a set of prescribed exercises, Rogers indicates how such exercises can occasionally be used in a client-centered way. Confronting a particularly apathetic group, he once suggested that the group form an inner circle and an outer one, with the persons in the outer circle attempting to articulate the feelings of the individuals in front of them. The suggestion was ignored, and the group went on as though it had never been made.

> But within an hour, one man picked up the central aspect of this device and used it, saying, "I want to speak for John and say what I believe he is *actually* feeling." At least a dozen times in the next day or two, others used it—but in their own spontaneous ways, not as a crude or stiff device (Rogers, 1970, p. 56). This shows how *knowledge* of different exercises can feed into the realness and spontaneity that is the essence of a person-centered group. (Rogers, 1977, p. 23)

## REEMPHASIS ON SELF–DETERMINATION

This last passage and the point that it illustrates lead directly to the consideration of a third humanistic theme contributing to a person-centered approach: the reemphasis on self-determination. In Chapter 7, the following dimensions of that theme were explored.

1. The experience of the self as *proactive* not merely reactive, capable through self-awareness of fashioning a creative response to the intrapersonal and environmental determinants of behavior.
2. The *developmental* character of personal freedom, proceeding from the inevitable conditioning mechanisms so prevalent in early childhood to the possibility of greater self-determination as the capacity for reflexive consciousness matures.
3. The *three-dimensional requirement* for the emergence of true self-determination: the maturational development of reflexive consciousness, growing awareness of the resources and restrictions present in one's unique environment or existential world, and increasing appropriation of the vertical or depth dimension of self-awareness.

The experience cited by Rogers provides an apt illustration of how this process functions. By providing an occasion for mutual sharing of experience in the safe, accepting interpersonal climate of the group, a certain amount of progress had presumably been made toward greater self-awareness. An impasse is reached. The leader suggests a method or technique for resolving it but does not impose himself further on the freedom of the members. In so doing, he enlarges the "horizon of consciousness" of the resources available to them but lets it go at that. Later one of the members makes use of the suggestion, creatively adapting it to a new situation. Other members take it up, spontaneously fashioning it to the needs of the moment, and the impasse is resolved.

There is a revealing reciprocity in this illustration between person-centeredness and self-determination. One of the reasons why Rogers has formulated and clung to his radical person-centered approach is his abiding belief in the capacity of individuals creatively to construct their own best solutions to life's problems, provided all the data of experience are available to awareness in the fullness of their impact. He sees himself as providing the occasion, in an individual or group setting, for that process of appropriation to occur. His faith in the person's capacity for self-determination, under these enforced conditions and at the individual's own pace, seems to be one of the principal factors in facilitating the growth of truly self-determining behavior, and that outcome in turn reinforces the respect for the individual which underlies his person-centered approach. A deep respect for the other's freedom, limited though that freedom may be at the moment, is one of the attitudes that seems to facilitate enlargement of the zone of free personal activity.

# A RADICAL PERSON–CENTERED APPROACH

The best articulated and most representative example of the humanistic theme of person-centeredness, in all respects, is to be found in the work of Carl Rogers and his associates, over a span of some 50 years, in the development of the client-centered movement. In this section I will briefly trace the elaboration of Roger's thought from its earliest beginnings to the present from the perspective of the gradual merging of the three humanistic themes mentioned previously in this chapter.

*1. Nondirective therapy.* During the earliest phase of his work, functioning as a clinical psychologist with disturbed children and their parents in Rochester, New York, during the 1930s, Rogers developed his own unique methods of counseling. They proved to be at considerable variance with the diagnostic and dynamic methods (principally Freudian) in which he had been trained at Columbia University. Tentatively at first and later with greater confidence as he found some of his own ideas supported by the American disciples of Otto Rank—Jessie Taft, Frederick Allen, and Virginia Robinson—he formulated his own original nondirective approach to counseling. Invited to teach his new methods at Rochester University, he later accepted a full professorship at Ohio State University in 1940, and there published his first major work, *Counseling and Psychotherapy* (1942).

The essence of nondirective therapy, up to this point, lay in the development of a highly practical and innovative phenomenological approach to clients and a developing faith in the ability of clients, as a result of this approach, to mobilize their own personal resources toward the solution of their problems.

This period was characterized by the development of methods in which therapists were trained to become empathic listeners, skilled in entering the private world of the client through the use of what came to be known as the "reflective" or "understanding" response. Counseling was presented as a process in which the therapist was to be experienced as a warm and caring, nonjudgmental alter ego or reflecting mirror for the client, avoiding any response which might be characterized as merely supportive, evaluative, or judgmental, probing for further information, or interpreting to the client what the therapist *thought* he or she might mean on a deeper, psychodynamic level previously unknown to the client (Porter, 1950). Simple reflection of the client's statements in the therapist's own terms but accurately matching the depth of feeling and conscious content of what the client had said came to be the preferred norm of therapist intervention. The emphasis in this initial period was on the development and implementation of such nondirective techniques, always under the proviso that they could not be expected to work unless the therapist genuinely accepted, at least as a working hypothesis, that the client under such circumstances would find within himself or herself the resources necessary for problem solution.

This early nondirective therapy was also marked not only by a noteworthy deemphasis on the more prevalent directive or guidance-oriented interventions of the therapist, but also by a concerted effort to keep the therapist's own personality as far as possible out of the interaction. He or she was simply expected to function as a reflecting, though warm and caring, mirror of the client's own perceptions and conscious experience, what Rank (1936) had previously termed *an assistant ego*. Through this means, it was hoped among other benefits, that the transference and counter-transference problems so typical of traditional psychoanalysis might be neatly sidestepped.

In perhaps an oversimplified summary, it was as if the therapist were saying to the client: "You do not understand yourself in this situation perhaps because you have not been able to focus successfully on all the facts that enter into it for you. I am here to help you obtain such a focus. Make *me* understand. Correct me if I do not seem to do so. I will not judge you or simply reassure you, or lead you in directions you do not wish to go, or interfere with my own ideas about what might have gone wrong for you and why. I simply want to *understand*. If you can make *me* understand, you will too. The picture will become clearer for you, and then you yourself will know what to do."

The apparent simplicity of this approach was, of course, deceiving. The prevailing concepts of psychotherapy were so different that trainers and students alike found it difficult to implement in practice. But another innovation began and encouraged by Rogers, helped greatly to overcome these initial difficulties and led in turn to further advances and changes in methodology. This was the emphasis on making the therapy process scientifically public for the first time through the use and transcription of electrical recordings of entire cases. The first such case was published in Rogers's own book (1942). This was followed by the *Casebook of Non-directive Counseling* (Snyder, 1947) in which five cases were presented, most of them verbatim, published by one of Rogers's students at Ohio State. Further extensive materials were made available to interested researchers by Rogers and his colleagues at the University of Chicago Counseling Center, where Rogers had moved in 1945 and where he remained for 12 years. The availability of such complete case accounts proved especially valuable to Rogers and his own staff in the generation of hypotheses for further research on his emerging self theory and on the process of psychotherapy and constructive personality change itself (Seeman, 1949; Rogers & Dymond, 1954).

**2. *Client-centered therapy.*** Rogers's later work at Ohio State and the first years at the University of Chicago culminated in the publication of the book *Client-centered Therapy* (1951). In this work we see his first attempts at developing a scientific theory of personality, his own *self theory*, based upon his experiences in psychotherapy and research conducted on the materials collected up to that point. The term *nondirective therapy* is still used in this volume but becomes increasingly supplanted in later publications by its title, *client-centered therapy*.

The self theory here presented is still dependent upon the earlier phenomenological premises and methods, but a new concept emerges as increasingly central: the notion of the actualizing tendency toward growth and self-regulation as the basic tendency or drive of all living organisms. Supported in his own convictions again by a Rankian notion, the "will-to-health" (Rank, 1936), and by the work of Goldstein, Angyal, Maslow, Lecky, Snygg and Combs, and others (Rogers, 1951, p. 481), Rogers presents his own developing phenomenological theory of the self with a major emphasis on this construct. It provides the theoretical base he needs to underpin his own practical experience of the basic trustworthiness and positive potential for constructive change inherent within the human organism.

The process of psychotherapy remains relatively unchanged in this work, but very quickly thereafter the variables involved become more sharply defined and honed by research. A bit more emphasis is placed on the influence of the therapist's personality in the 1951 work in that it is hypothesized that the therapist must be "congruent" (i.e., better adjusted than the client in the areas of conflict experienced by the latter, for maximum constructive change to occur). This now becomes one of the major variables considered by Rogers in a landmark article published in 1957 and entitled "The Necessary and Sufficient Conditions of Therapeutic Personality Change."

Briefly, these conditions are described as *empathy* (the ability to understand the client's internal frame of reference and successfully to communicate such understanding to the client); *unconditional positive regard* (the communication of a nonpossessive, nonjudgmental warmth and caring for the client); and *congruence* on the part of the therapist (the ability to own and understand his or her own reactions to the therapeutic situation and, on that basis, to act nondefensively toward the client). This latter condition, as we shall see, evolves later into the notion of therapist *genuineness* in a much more personal encounter with the client, but the principal emphasis of *Client-centered Therapy* is on the development of Rogerian self theory.

This trend culminates in 1959 with the most sophisticated presentation of his personality theory, in a volume edited by the systematic psychologist, Sigmund Koch (1959, pp. 184–256). *Client-centered Therapy* also contains the first published accounts, in book form, of the application of Rogerian methods to fields other than one-to-one counseling: education, through student-centered teaching; play therapy, with the use of nonverbal materials; counseling groups, and the application of group methods to leadership and administration, and to the training of therapists themselves.

This period was also marked, as mentioned previously, by the application of new phenomenological research methods, notably Stephenson's Q-technique, to hypotheses concerned with the validation of Rogers's self theory and the processes of constructive therapeutic change (Rogers & Dymond, 1954).

Basic aspects of Rogerian self theory have been discussed elsewhere in this work. As far as constructive personality growth is concerned, Rogers broadens his vision beyond the field of psychotherapy to include any helping relationship. In sum, he seems to be saying at this point: People will change and grow in constructive ways when their own basic actualizing tendencies in that direction are released in a consistent interpersonal relationship with another who clearly communicates to them a nonpossessive, caring acceptance of them as persons worthy of trust and respect; in a deep, empathic understanding of their private world of existence; and in a nondefensive posture in himself or herself toward the problem situation in which clients find themselves enmeshed.

**3. *Emphasis on encounter.*** In 1957, Rogers and several of his associates moved to the University of Wisconsin where, for a period of six years, they engaged themselves in a challenging research project involving the application and modification of the client-centered approach to a group of hospitalized chronic schizophrenics. Significant shifts in both research emphases and in client-centered practice occurred as a direct result of contact with this hard-core group of mental patients. Research geared to the validation of Rogers's self theory had already faded into the background in the later years at the University of Chicago in favor of studies on the therapist attitudes suggested by Rogers as facilitating client improvement (Halkides, 1958; Barrett-Lennard, 1959; 1962).

This emphasis was continued and refined at Wisconsin through the development and application of more advanced relationship inventories (Van der Veen, 1970; Truax & Mitchell, 1971) to measure the conditions of therapist empathy, warmth or caring, and congruence. In addition, new process scales were developed and validated in an attempt to measure more objectively the changes in client experiencing that resulted from therapeutic intervention (Rogers & Rablen, 1958; Rogers, 1961; Tomlinson & Hart, 1962). Eugene Gendlin, one of Rogers's associates at both universities, contributed significantly to the development of this trend (Gendlin, 1961, 1962, 1963) and the results of this research emphasis proved to be of special importance for Rogers in the formulation of his concept of the fully functioning person (which was presented in Chapter 8 on the theme of authenticity). Interesting initial accounts of the thinking involved in the project with schizophrenics can be found in *Person to Person* (Rogers & Stevens, 1967), published in the same year as the more technical final report (Rogers, Gendlin, Kiesler & Truax, 1967).

The title of the book, *Person to Person*, represents the most significant shift in the practice of client-centered therapy resulting from this experience: the new emphasis on *encounter* between therapist and client. It was quickly discovered, in working with this more withdrawn and comparatively unmotivated group of patients, that the relative passivity of the therapist, characteristic of the earlier nondirective phase, had to be abandoned in favor of a more active stance. This did not mean that the therapists found themselves becoming more directive toward their clients. Rather, they found themselves increasingly sharing more of their own feelings, reactions, and genuine caring for them, generally in a nonimposing way, in the face of client resistances and prolonged silences. This often proved effective and led to a reevaluation of the concept of therapist "congruence" toward one of "realness" or "genuineness" in a more actively shared here-and-now encounter with the other.

The flavor of this new approach can be garnered from the following statement by Rogers:

> In this respect [his emerging conviction that therapy has more to do with the *relationship* than with techniques, theory or ideology] I believe my views have become more, rather than less, extreme. I believe it is the *realness* of the therapist in the relationship which is the most important element. It is when the therapist is natural and spontaneous that he seems to be most effective. (Rogers & Stevens, 1967, p. 185)

He goes on to recount how in this project sharply different therapists achieved good results in quite different ways: some were more confronting and impatient, others more gentle and obviously warm in their approach. What seemed to matter was that the therapists who were successful presented themselves (in the judgment of the raters) spontaneously and openly, as they were in the moment of encounter.

In the same volume, Eugene Gendlin summarizes well this new shift in emphasis. Reviewing Rogers's (1957) three hypothesized conditions thought to be necessary and sufficient for constructive therapeutic change—empathy, unconditional positive regard, and congruence—he found the last condition to be of most importance in work with schizophrenics. Previous formulas, including earlier emphasis on "reflection of feeling," proved ineffective. Empathy remained crucial, but therapists found themselves engaging in a wider range of behaviors in responding to these clients.

> To "be himself" has also meant that the therapist has become more expressive. The therapist much more often expresses his own feelings, his experiencing of the moment. . . . The therapist need not wait pas-

sively till the client expresses something intimate or therapeutically relevant. Instead, he can draw on his own momentary experiencing and find there an ever present reservoir from which he can draw, and with which he can initiate, deepen, and carry on therapeutic interaction even with an unmotivated, silent, or externalized person. (Gendlin, 1967, pp. 121–22)

Gendlin also found himself enlarging the concept of congruence (changed now to realness or genuineness) to include letting the client see his occasional weaknesses: admitting, when such instances occur in the interaction, that he has made a mistake, done the wrong thing, or failed to understand. These and other aspects of experiencing presented to the client are always shared in a nonimposing way ("This is what *I* am experiencing or perceiving at the moment"), with no implication that the client is necessarily experiencing the same thing or is responsible for causing the therapist's reactions.

Here we see clearly emerging, in this concept of nonimposition, the third theme of our perspective: a thoroughgoing respect for the client's personal freedom and capacity for self-determination. What were the results?

> Later, the research evidence confirmed that those therapists who were more able to be genuine than others (as well as empathic and caring), had clients who made significantly more positive gain in therapy and more clients who operated at higher process levels. This confirmation has influenced client-centered therapists in general to enlarge their concept of genuineness to a more active, intuitive self-reporting. (Meador & Rogers, 1973, p. 155)

In further support of this position, it was found that patients whose therapists offered relatively low levels of these characteristics during therapy exhibited deterioration in personality and behavior (Truax & Mitchell, 1971).

In 1964 Rogers moved to La Jolla, California, as a Resident Fellow of the Western Behavioral Sciences Institute and, since 1968, of the Center for Studies of the Person, which he helped establish. Here he and his associates applied their new discoveries to a more normal population through the development of what has come to be known as the *basic encounter group*. The reader is referred to the book *Carl Rogers on Encounter Groups* (1970) for an account of the structure and functioning of these small groups and the potency of their effects on individual participants.

The success and popularity of the encounter-group movement, which initially was applied to groups of relative strangers in the still-existing La Jolla Summer Program in human relations training, led quickly to a client-centered approach to institutional change in a number of divergent settings: education (Rogers, 1969), marriage and newer partnership lifestyles (Rogers, 1972), and community-building in families, religious institutions, and work settings (Coulson, 1973). Current projects emanating from the Center for Studies of the Person also involve the humanizing of medical education and the doctor-patient relationship, business and management consultation, women's groups, life-transition workshops, and the application of the person-centered approach to transcultural and intercultural groups in many countries of Western Europe, Central and South America, and Asia. Most of the research now being done is of an evaluative nature, as is to be expected from the applied approach. Betty Meador (1971), for example, in a research study using the previously developed process scale, found that participation in such an intensive small group experience tends to facilitate therapeutic movement.

**4. *Revolutionary implications.*** Throughout the many years of experience in the application of the client-centered approach to these diverse settings, Rogers and his associates have, with rare exceptions, remained true to their central assumptions concerning human nature. Membership and participation in the intensive small group remains voluntary. Respect for the individual's right to pace himself or herself within the group experience remains a strong characteristic of the style of facilitation. Gimmicks, by which leaders routinely run members through preset group exercises, are minimized both theoretically and practically (Coulson, 1972). The belief in the individual's inherent right and capacity for self-direction and growth remains the hallmark of the Rogerian person-centered approach throughout all the other changes it has undergone. Only recently, as was previously mentioned, have the revolutionary implications of this radical person-centeredness become obvious to Rogers himself. A recent work (Rogers, 1977) spells out in detail his awareness of the political impact of the attitudes he has persistently championed.

This statement should not be taken to imply that person-centeredness as a theme is restricted to this particular humanistic author. Fritz Perls, founder of Gestalt therapy, preferred the small group setting for the facilitation of therapeutic growth. His version of the encounter group depends more upon the use of role-playing, fantasy and dream materials, and nonverbal exchanges and is much more directive than the Rogerian style of leadership. But Perls was also quite critical of attempts to bypass respect for the individual's process in efforts to force personal growth.

> We are entering the phase of the turner-onners: turn on to instant cure, instant joy, instant sensory-awareness. We are entering the phase of the quacks and the con-men, who think if you get some break-through, you are cured. . . . I must say I am *very* concerned with what's going on right now. . . .

A technique is a gimmick. A gimmick should be used only in the extreme case. We've got enough people running around collecting gimmicks, more gimmicks and abusing them. (Perls, 1971, p. 1)

And in his autobiography, he stated:

This is one sphere where I cannot find fault with myself. I would not be where I am without my sensitivity, timing and intuition. Even when I carry out group experiments, they are so constructed as to take into account the place where each one is at that moment. (Perls, 1969, p. 190)

## A NEW ECO–PSYCHOLOGY

What seems to be emerging here are the beginnings of a humanistically based *eco-psychology*. The implications are clear: given the individual's unique potential for constructive growth and irreplaceable contribution to society's welfare, we must look for the means to facilitate that process in every possible instance. Not to do so is to run the risk of appalling waste and loss of the creative impulse that resides, however modestly, in every human person. Given the problems that face us today, such wastefulness of human resources is a luxury we can no longer afford. To this end, it is small wonder that humanistic psychologists in growing numbers are progressively turning their attention to the larger social issues of our day and to the rehumanization of those social institutions that seem bent on the exercise of power and control over their members.

Elizabeth Leonie Simpson points to this trend in a recent volume of readings in humanistic psychology (Nevill, 1977). Referring to a collection of opinions on the future direction of humanistic psychology gathered by James Bugental (1967) in an earlier work, she writes:

This was an impressive and inspiring list, but its omission was dramatic: only one author saw humanistic psychology put to work in social planning and governmental practices, as well as in individual change. . . . In the past humanistic psychology has been utilized in education, research, industrial management, race relations, community organization, and family relations, as well as psychotherapy (Richards & Welch, 1973). Its future will be even more comprehensive. It will include a deepening and accelerated emphasis on the application of humanistic insights to social issues. (Simpson, 1977, p. 82)

And, in the same volume, Edwin Barker concludes:

*Experiencing respect* for the intrinsic worth of others *as they are* has been thought of as "only" a religious attitude. And yet, it is fast becoming clear that there is no chance for a civil social environment, an adequate economic order, an orderly succession of power, even, possibly, our physical survival, without a change toward valuing all human beings as ends in themselves and not as means to other ends. This has not been felt to be a political, utilitarian, instrumental, practical attitude, and certainly not a "scientific," "realistic," one. Our task is to change that. (Barker, 1977, pp. 97—98)

In its advocacy of the theme of person-centeredness, humanistic psychology values nothing for the human person "beyond freedom and dignity." In the next chapter, I will indicate how the person-centered approach has been and continues to be extended to the broader arena of social systems and issues.

# 11 Eco-Psychology: Impact on Social Systems

In the preceding chapter, my discussion of the contributions of humanistic psychology was limited to the discipline of psychology itself. There it was shown that paradigms in general psychology are slowly shifting. New methods are developing or are being proposed for the conduct of experimental research with human subjects that will hopefully provide more reliable information about standard topics as well as open new, more relevant fields of investigation.

(This search for new paradigms is by no means restricted to psychology. For the past year, the author has been a member of an informal group of social scientists and philosophers of science who have been comparing notes across disciplines in the human sciences. I have been struck by the fact that many of my colleagues in sociology, anthropology, economics, and political science are experiencing many of the same concerns about the limitations of current models of investigation in their respective fields. They too are concerned about supplementing the usual external, naturalistic observations of human behavior with innovative means for studying the effects of human *agency* in their respective domains.)

The impact of humanistic theory, as we saw, is currently much more evident in the area of professional psychology, in clinical counseling training and practice. This is not surprising in view of the fact that so many of the founders of humanistic-existential psychology have been identified with that branch of the discipline. Humanistic psychotherapy is well established in its own right, and many of its tested techniques have been incorporated into other approaches, including the application of the newer behavioral therapies (and vice versa). This influence has also extended beyond traditional psychotherapy and counseling settings to the whole field of paraprofessional training and community psychology (Tageson & Corazzini, 1974). Most forms of *human relations training,* an integral part of such programs, freely incorporate the learning of the relationship skills of effective listening, empathic communication, and other phenomenological approaches that were originally developed in the context of client-centered and other humanistic therapies (Egan, 1975).

But the story does not end here. Fueled by growing concern over the ability of social institutions to facilitate or more frequently inhibit the actualization of individual human potential, humanistic psychology has increasingly turned its attention to this broader arena. My purpose in this chapter is to provide a brief sampling of the contributions of humanistic psychology toward the rehumanization of some of these powerful social institutions. For a fuller account, the reader is referred to the growing number of books of readings that have appeared in conjunction with this movement in recent years (Severin, 1965; Bugental, 1967; Sutich & Vich, 1969; McWaters, 1977; Nevill, 1977; Welch, Tate, & Richards, 1978; Jourard & Landsman, 1980). What I wish to convey here is a sense of the broad scope of this influence in contemporary society.

No claim is being made that humanistic psychology has initiated all the movements so influenced, nor have the contributions documented here always been successful. Frequently, as we shall see, they have been met with considerable resistance and opposition for reasons that will become clear in the telling.

## THE HUMAN POTENTIAL MOVEMENT

One new social institution that has emerged as a popular offshoot of humanistic psychology is the *growth center,* the embodiment of the *human potential movement.* Following the prototype founded at Esalen in California by Michael Murphy, which exercised such widespread influence in the 1960s, growth centers have been established in almost every major population center in the United States. Since these are financially self-sustaining institutions, their number has varied widely, depending on the demand for their services and the managerial acumen of their organizers. In 1973, for example, William Schutz estimated their number at between 150 and 200, not counting the enormous number of workshops offered throughout the country by individual entrepreneurs in some particular method of personal growth or by institutes developed to promote a particular method of psychotherapy (Schutz, 1973).

Typically, as John Mann (1979) reports in an excellent discussion of the human potential movement, the growth center is designed to provide an organizational setting where a potpourri of such methods are offered to the interested consumer. He or she is free to choose from a rather wildly eclectic assortment of offerings ranging from ongoing encounter or consciousness-raising groups to weekend or evening workshops in various means of personal exploration and expression, such as hatha yoga, Zen meditation techniques, sensory awareness exercises, rolfing (a form of deep massage), dance, the martial arts, bioenergetic exercises, and the like.

Workshop leaders may or may not be professionally certified or licensed psychologists or other professionals. The only requirement is that they can establish the possession of some particular expertise or training of potential interest to consumers. Though lectures are frequently offered, the major emphasis is on providing an *experiential* form of learning or expansion of consciousness.

Customers are presumed to be persons who, though normal by the usual criteria of socialization, are somehow dissatisfied with their current existence and are seeking something more out of life. Psychotherapy for the mentally disturbed is not the aim—such persons are routinely referred for treatment elsewhere, though screening methods apparently vary from center to center. In this, the customer of the growth center represents a rough parallel to his or her Eastern counterpart who, already successfully socialized, wishes to embark on a way of liberation. The difference, of course, is obvious, in that the Eastern seeker is committed to years of arduous training in one particular discipline of enlightenment. The Western searcher is free to sample a wide variety of such offerings and may or may not choose to pursue one path or method in depth.

This has led to charges of superficiality against the growth center approach, charges that are met by the response that it is too early to close out accounts on what is best suited to facilitate the optimal development of human potential and that such cross-fertilization of methods provides an exciting natural laboratory, free of cultural restraints and interpretations, for experimenting with a fuller range of such activities and efforts. Mann himself, though obviously an advocate of the human potential movement, suggests a further problem related to the self-selection factor so characteristic of the growth center consumer:

> However, it would be naive to suggest that a person is automatically drawn to what he necessarily needs. The opposite may be true. . . . To

the extent that HP practices are highly focused on one or two approaches [by the consumer], the selection process represents an important issue. If people refer themselves, will they have the insight and courage to do what is good for them as distinct from what feels good? (Mann, 1979, p. 521)

Though the author goes on to suggest that this may not be a serious problem, the notorious lack of outcome evaluation studies on the programs offered by growth centers (an admittedly difficult task) leaves the question dangling.

Mann further documents a shift within the growth center and human potential movements from an early emphasis on group-encounter methods to an increasing focus on the inner person and transpersonal or mystical experience. The "me decade" of the 1960s (Wolfe, 1976), he claims, with its "encounter ethic" of total self-expression, was replaced in the 70s by a new religious awakening. While the emphasis remained on self-expression, this new thrust served "to raise the level of the personal search for fulfillment to a cosmic plane" (Mann, 1979, p. 507) roughly paralleling the correlation established in previous chapters between the humanistic themes of self-actualization and self-transcendence and the recent surge of interest in transpersonal psychology.

We turn now to another development within the broader framework of humanistic psychology itself. While some humanists have turned their attention to the exploration of what might be termed one's *inner space*, others have focused their efforts outward to the powerful social institutions that so heavily influence the development of the human person for good or for ill. In the process, a new humanistic eco-psychology is being developed which takes very seriously indeed the interaction of person and environment in a more holistic manner. This new emphasis, in my estimation, is also very promising toward providing another needed corrective to the naively optimistic, rather exclusive, focus on self-actualization which marked the early beginnings of the humanistic-existential movement, particularly in its more popularized versions. A brief survey of such contributions follows.

## HUMANISTIC MANAGEMENT

Thanks to the influence of Karl Marx, it is by now a truism to claim that economic institutions profoundly affect the well-being of all members of society. This is clearly obvious where physical or material well-being is concerned. Economic institutions, by definition, concern themselves with the provision, production, management, and distribution of the material resources we all require for sheer survival, as well as for the gratification of the vast array of human needs. What is often overlooked (though certainly not by Marx) is that such institutions are also the principal vehicles through which we seek to actualize our highest aspirations: to create, to engage in meaningful work, to find a responsible role to play in society, to exercise and express what we believe to be our unique talents and capabilities.

Among other things, Marx was a humanist in his scathing denunciations of the depersonalizing effects of the industrial revolution and of the cruel, dehumanizing excesses of 19th-century capitalism. We need not agree with his solutions to share his concerns about the problem. Which leads us to the question: Is a humanistic capitalism possible? (Harman, 1978). Or more specifically, can the management of modern corporate enterprises be geared both to the goals of the organization (efficient, profit-making production of goods and services) and to the goals of the individual, whether worker, manager, owner, or consumer (ultimately, their self-realization).

From the first, humanistic psychologists were called upon to address this problem by business leaders who had become acquainted with this new trend in psychological circles (industrial psychology was already a well-established discipline). In fact, this is apparently the first arena outside of clinical and academic psychology in which humanistic theories and techniques were to be applied. In 1947, T-group (for training-group) methodology was established at the newly founded National Training Laboratory in Bethel, Maine.

## T-groups

T-groups are basically a form of human relations training for managers. The philosophy behind them was much influenced by the person-entered approach then being developed by Carl Rogers and his associates (Leavitt, 1965). (Rogers himself served as a consultant for the Western Electric Corporation during this period.) The method used was (and is) the small encounter or sensitivity group. Managers from all over the country, initially strangers to one another, gather at NTL for these intensive group experiences that last from a few hours to up to 14 days. Leaders (or trainers) are usually psychologists who use a nondirective approach in leading these unstructured groups. The only task or agenda of the group is for the members to come to know one another as deeply as possible, to share experiences, personal values and goals, and emotional reactions to one another; to confront the conflicts that evolve as they relate to one another and the leader who refuses to lead, to grow in consciousness of their own relationship style and its effects on others by giving and receiving feedback in the group setting.

The ultimate aim of T-group methodology is to increase interpersonal effectiveness, to alert managers to the human dimensions of organizational functioning, and to encourage a more participative managerial style—all designed to improve organizational functioning by merging individual with organizational needs and goals (Bradford, Gibbs, & Benne, 1964). The method proved to be very popular. Thousands of managers throughout North America, Europe, and Asia have undergone the T-group experience, generally under the auspices of the National Training Laboratories (the original NTL now operates from several centers) and its offshoot, the Western Training Laboratories. Extensive research conducted during the 1960s has led to mixed evaluations of the effectiveness claimed for this approach, though some positive outcomes have been noted (Campbell & Dunnette, 1968; Cooper & Mangham, 1971).

### From T-groups to organization development

One of the principal difficulties encountered in the initial development of T-group methodology arose from the "stranger group" approach to managerial training. Managers returning to their own organizations often encountered resistance from subordinates and superiors alike as they enthusiastically attempted to implement a more person-centered approach. This phenomenon led logically to the next step: a more holistic focus on the organization itself, conceived as a system of interacting elements or units. Humanistic theorists and researchers, including several NTL fellows, began devoting their efforts to the study of such systems and to the development of intervention strategies better calculated to effect change in the desired direction.

On the theoretical front, Douglas McGregor of the Massachusetts Institute of Technology published his widely quoted work *The Human Side of Enterprise* (1960) in which he contrasted the traditional managerial approach (Theory X) to a more humanistic one (Theory Y) based upon Maslow's need-hierarchy. In his view, traditional procedures are based upon faulty assumptions concerning human nature. Managers, distrustful of the motivation of workers (workers are viewed as inherently lazy, irresponsible, resistant to change, unconcerned about the needs of the organization, and so on), exercise tight controls over subordinates, assume a very authoritarian approach, and delegate little or no responsibility to others. Theory X, therefore, satisfies only the physiological and safety needs and to a lesser extent the social needs of the worker.

McGregor argued instead for the application of a more comprehensive theory of management, which would take into account the emergent ego-needs and needs for self-actualization that Maslow claimed follow upon the gratification of physiological, safety, and social needs. Theory Y proposes a participative management approach in an effort to mobilize more fully the resources of the individual worker. Management is still seen as responsible for organizing production to meet economic objectives; but it also should attempt to meet the workers' needs for some autonomy, some direction of their own behavior, some responsibility in the decision-making process.

McGregor viewed worker passivity, apathy, and resistance to organizational needs as a response to traditional managerial distrust and suspicion, not as inherent characteristics of human behavior. Innovative ideas that he put forth included decentralization and delegation of authority, job enlargement (to give the worker more scope for his or her own creativity), and *self-targeting*, a method of performance appraisal where subordinates are held responsible for setting targets or objectives for themselves, and where they play a significant role in the evaluation of their own performance. By this means, McGregor felt, the company would be able to take advantage of the workers' own needs for prestige and self-fulfillment, and both would benefit.

Abraham Maslow published his own influential work, *Eupsychian Management*, in 1965, applying his hierarchical motivational theory to business and other organizations, a formulation which again challenged classical economics theory concerning the motivation of workers and managers alike. This work was translated into Japanese two years later and has apparently been very influential in supporting the holistic, family approach to corporate management and worker life so characteristic of Japanese industry.

(One rather amusing but insightful observation made by Maslow [1971] is that workers will never be satisfied, given the unending array of human needs: new higher needs emerge as lower ones are gratified. But one can gauge the health of an organization by attending to the quality of workers' gripes, which Maslow classified as "grumbles" or "metagrumbles." Grumbles occur when workers are dissatisfied with salary schedules and working conditions [physiological, survival, safety needs]; metagrumbles when they gripe about not having enough responsibility or scope for their own creativity [self-actualization needs].)

On the research front, Beatrice and Sydney Rome (1967), under contract to the Air Force, developed a computer-simulation laboratory technique (the Leviathan project) that enabled them to establish experimentally the superiority of a humanistically oriented social organization for effective task performance. Jack and Lorraine Gibb, under contract from the Office of Naval Research, made systematic observations of T-groups in *natural* settings, including management teams, and reported promising results (Gibb & Gibb, 1967).

From these and many similar efforts there arose a form of process consultation and a set of change strategies that collectively fall under the rubric of *organization development* (OD). Humanistic in orientation but all-embracing in its efforts to meet both the developmental needs of workers and managers and the task requirements of the organization itself, this more comprehensive approach developed rapidly in the decades of the 60s and 70s. It was given helpful direction and impetus by the analytic work of Robert Blake and J. S. Mouton (1965, 1968).

*The managerial grid.* The concept they introduced was that of the managerial grid, by which they were able to plot all executive or managerial styles on a grid of two dimensions: concern for production and concern for people. Using a nine-point rating scale on both dimensions, a particular manager's style is plotted to represent his or her effectiveness in light of these two concerns. Thus, the 9,1 executive is high on task efficiency but very low in concern for human satisfaction. A 9,9 represents, in their view, the ideal manager, one who is capable of maximizing both productive efficiency and worker satisfaction. This ideal is best met under conditions of *team management:* "high task achievement from committed people who have a common stake in the firm's purposes, with good relationships of trust and respect. Production is achieved by the integration of task and human requirements into a unified system" (Kelly, 1974, p. 676).

Blake and Mouton went on to apply the managerial grid concept to the training of management in six specific phases. The details of their system need not concern us here since it has been superseded by further developments. T-group methodology, however, continues to function as a central strategy in OD but is now more frequently utilized in the natural setting of the organization itself. For further information on OD, the reader is referred to a number of works by its leading proponents (Bennis, 1970; Argyris, 1976, 1978; Schein, 1980). An edited volume on *Humanizing Organizational Behavior* (Metzer & Wickert, 1976) testifies to the current state of OD by including information on the incorporation of the newer behavioral methods toward the goal indicated in its title.

## HUMANISTIC EDUCATION

Schooling, or the formal educational establishment, is indisputably one of the most powerful institutions for furthering the socialization process in modern industrial society. It is charged with the task of providing the young with the requisite skills and training, intellectual and vocational, both for effective citizenship and for participation in our highly specialized economy. There is good reason to believe that, next to the family, the school is the most potent socializing force in the development of what William Glasser has called a success or failure identity (Glasser, 1969).

## Some historical notes

As pointed out before, humanistic psychologists have not been blind to the fact that social institutions have enormous impact on the process of self-actualization. Quickly and instinctively, they turned their attention to the educational system or, just as frequently, were consulted by educators already imbued with humanistic values and ideals for whatever assistance they could provide. As a result, the movement that came to be called humanistic education gathered considerable momentum in the decades of the 60s and 70s.

Arthur Combs, who had previously coauthored a classic work in phenomenological psychology, soon after turned his attention through his teaching and research at the University of Florida to teacher preparation from a humanistic standpoint (Combs, 1965). George B. Leonard of the Esalen Institute published his popular, controversial, and utopian book *Education and Ecstasy* (1968). Many innovative projects were funded during this period. The Ford-Esalen Project for Innovation in Humanistic Education, funded by the Ford Foundation, produced a report on its confluent education program (Brown, 1968) to be followed shortly by reports on the psychological education projects sponsored by the Harvard Graduate School of Education (Alschuler, 1969; Sprinthall & Mosher, 1970; Mosher & Sprinthall, 1971). Both involved efforts to integrate affective and motivational components into classroom teaching along humanistic lines.

Carl Rogers's influential book *Freedom to Learn* appeared in 1969, the same year as Glasser's *Schools Without Failure*, and he gives an account of two projects undertaken by his staff in his most recent work, *A Way of Being* (1980). (The interested reader may wish to consult the extensive bibliography prepared by John Canfield and Mark Phillips of the Center for Humanistic Education, University of Massachusetts at Amherst, for further information on various books, films, tapes, games and simulations, and other resources currently available in this field.)

In a previous article (Tageson, 1973), which grew out of my experience as a participant in the Aurora Project conducted at the University of Notre Dame, I attempted to pinpoint the contributions of humanistic psychology to education as centering around the theme of holism. The point made there was that humanistic psychologists accept the classical definition of learning as a change of behavior resulting from interaction with the environment. Environment for the humanist, however, becomes preeminently the *interpersonal* environment in which the learner finds himself or herself. Human learning always takes place in such an interpersonal environment, and its affective components play an important part in determining whether cognitive learning takes place or not.

The humanistic view is, once more, a holistic one. Learning involves the *whole* person. Educators at times seem to presume that learning occurs in an affective vacuum: pure mind speaking to pure mind. So-called cognitive learning, in the humanistic view, cannot be treated as though it were somehow independent of the whole person. Teaching itself is a form of "inter-personal" communication, and so the humanist stresses the importance of the teacher as the most influential variable in the educational process. This emphasis is evident from a cursory review of the literature previously cited. In it the teacher is often termed the *facilitator* of learning, the one who constructs and conducts the learning communty. Always assuming the teacher has been adequately prepared intellectually in the subject matter to be taught, he or she *as person* is seen as the most important variable in the learning process.

According to this view learning, which depends on interaction with the environment, takes place most successfully when the environment is *stimulating and benevolent*. When the environment is instead basically punitive, dull, or uninteresting, then behavior is inhibited, and little or no learning occurs (except, as the behaviorists remind us, avoidance learning). This puts the teacher squarely into the picture again. At least where school learning is concerned, it is the teacher's considerable task to create such a benevolent and stimulating environment. He or she does this best by the quality of their personal relationships with each student.

There is a growing body of research to support this contention. Rosenthal's study, *Pygmalion in the Classroom* (1968), had already documented the effect that a teacher's prior beliefs concerning student potential have on student achievement and intellectual growth. More recently, a very broad-based study involving 3,700 hours of classroom instruction from 550 elementary and secondary school teachers in the United States, England, Canada, the Virgin Islands, and Israel, revealed a clearly significant correlation between the facilitative conditions provided by teachers and the academic achievement of students. The facilitative conditions studied were derived from Rogers's person-centered theory and included empathy (the attempt to understand the personal meaning of students' school experience), positive regard (shown by the various ways in which teachers indicated respect for students as persons), and congruence (the extent to which teachers were genuine in relationships with students). Comparable facilitative conditions had, of course, already been shown to be related to outcomes in therapy: their presence was related to positive outcomes; their absence to deterioration of functioning (Rogers, Gendlin, Kiesler, & Truax, 1967).

In this comprehensive educational study (Aspy & Roebuck, 1974), results were parallel. Students of teachers high in the facilitative conditions tended to show the greatest gains in academic learning, whereas some students of low-level teachers tended to show some deterioration from previous levels of performance. Other correlations, all in the predicted direction, were found with increased creative problem solving, positive student self-concepts, student-initiated behavior, fewer disciplinary problems, and lower rates of absence from school.

## Organization development in education

Under the influence of considerations such as these, much of the early literature in humanistic education predictably focused on the necessary overhaul of teacher-preparation programs and on the in-service training of teachers already in the field (Combs, 1968). It quickly became evident, however, that this was too narrow a focus. Predictions made in earlier articles (Lawson & Tageson, 1971; Tageson, 1973) that the cooperation of administrators would also have to be assured for such innovative practices and interventions to have any chance for success proved to be quite correct.

Our own experience with school superintendents, principals, and disgruntled teachers who wished to implement more student-centered methods but felt balked by the system was soon reinforced by reports from other investigators (Rogers, 1977). In the study previously cited (Aspy & Roebuck, 1974), for example, it was found that the gains achieved were most likely to occur under situations in which facilitative teachers were backed up and supervised by similarly facilitative principals. Rogers also comments on this interaction in detailing the results of follow-up studies conducted on the two projects under his direction (Rogers, 1977, 1980).

Several investigators have suggested a promising remedy for this problem: the use of an *organization development* approach. This involves an assessment of the condition of the entire system in advance of any intervention and, where feasible, the subsequent application of strategies designed to insure the support of all elements involved (Schmuck & Miles, 1971; McCabe, 1973; Sciortino & Madden, 1973). Where the educational system is concerned, such an approach involves not only students and teachers, but administrators, school boards, and parents as well. Detailed suggestions and accounts of the successful use of such a strategy can be found in the book *A Humanistic Psychology of Education* by Richard and Patricia Schmuck (1974).

## The affective matrix

The aim of humanistic education is to identify and facilitate the actualization of the unique potential which exists in the individual student at whatever level of development in the educational system. The good, humane teacher, principally responsible for creating the learning community, remains the focus for primary intervention. But good teachers also require strong support systems to aid in unleashing whatever creative potential they may have toward reaching this goal. Not just the best in technological resources are required, though these are important as well, but also the emotional support of peers, administrators, parents, and the community at large, generated by a climate of shared values and goals in an atmosphere of mutual trust and respect. This is what I have called the *affective matrix* of the educational enterprise, and it must be constantly attended to if success is to be achieved in rehumanizing what is often otherwise a very depersonalizing system.

The effort must begin, of course, with the institutions responsible for the training of teachers or better with the community of administrators, instructors, and student teachers that make up such institutions. Arthur Combs has been one of the leading pioneers in this venture and has developed detailed proposals for carrying it out, down to the methods of observation that student teachers are trained to use in uncovering the *personal meanings* of the school experience to the pupils whom they are required to observe in the classroom setting (Combs, 1968).

The next step is to address the system itself into which the student teacher will graduate. Here, as both experience and research show, the preferred method is a multilevel approach incorporating the techniques of organization development cited above and in the section on humanistic management. Typically, this involves the attempt to create an atmosphere of mutual respect and acceptance by providing occasions during which small groups of administrators, teachers, parents, and students can consistently meet, preferably with professionally trained group leaders at first, to discuss (a) their deepest values and convictions concerning the educational process, themselves, and their relationships to each other; and (b) the tasks they share in common. (During the Aurora Project at Notre Dame, the former were called *developmental groups*; the latter, *task-oriented groups*. Both were felt to be necessary for the creation of an effective learning community.)

The conviction underlying this approach is that when all members of the system mutually search out ways to make the school more person-centered, schooling then becomes the humane experience it ought to be: a true learning community in the kind of benevolent and stimulating environment in which the values of humanism are not so much taught as constantly experienced. The aim is simply to establish the positive affective matrix in which all the available resources are brought to bear in the service of the student's self-actualization; the development of his or her unique potential.

Such an approach quickly branches out to include the whole educational process: curriculum, hardware and technology, the process of

supervision (Doyle, 1972), and auxiliary services. Once such an atmosphere is developed and promoted, such matters can be safely left to
the experts within the system. This attitude is itself an essential part of
the definition of humanistic education.

## HUMANISTIC MEDICINE

Medicine is a major social institution that touches human life at its
most critical points: birth, death, and, particularly, those frightening
moments in between when, through accident, injury, or illness, we are
forcefully reminded of the fragility of our existence. Here understood as
the entire complex of health care services and organizations, the institution of medicine has begun to react to the dehumanizing trends that
have unwittingly accompanied the enormous technological improvements of recent years.

Rick Carlson and Dale Garell (1978) provide a helpful historical
overview of these recent developments, dividing them into four major
periods.

1.  *The era of public health* during the 1800s, when enormous
improvements were made and applied to whole populations in the
areas of sanitation, nutrition, immunization against contagious diseases, and improved living and working conditions. During this period,
medicine itself was practiced without the benefit of later scientific
improvements as a sort of cottage industry in which individual physicians did the best they could with the limited resources at their disposal.

2.  *The rise of science and technology,* a period following the public
health era in which attention was focused on specific disorders untreat-
able by public health measures. Spanning the last 50 years or so, this
period has been marked by major advances in the understanding and
treatment of disease entities, improvements in surgical techniques,
pharmacology, immunization, and genetic interventions. As a result,
the practice of medicine became more and more specialized. Health
care became disease-oriented, increasingly hospital-based, and depart-
mentalized. Bureaucratic management techniques were introduced
which extended medical care to more and more people but ironically at
the expense of the personal touch that characterized previous doctor-
patient relationships.

3.  *The delivery system approach.* This last development had led to
a growing emphasis, since the mid-60s, on the delivery of this new
product: medical care services. Health is no longer the patient's responsibility. When illness or injury strikes, the individual enters an awesome assembly line, manned by an army of technicians and specialists,
to be diagnosed, treated, cured, and returned to the environment from

which he or she came. And all of this is marketed, promoted, and underwritten by huge, bureaucratic insurance companies, and increasingly by the government. The process is efficient but highly depersonalized: a mirror of the society in which we live. The strains endemic to such a system are increasingly being felt: by medical personnel themselves, who have the highest rates of suicide, alcoholism, and other drug abuse in our society; and by the patients, who are becoming dissatisfied with the impersonality of the system and their own abdication of power over the care of their health.

4. *Emerging alternatives.* These developments led, in the decade of the 1970s, to an increasing interest within the field of medicine itself and among the general public in new paradigms for the understanding and delivery of health care along more humanistic lines. No one wishes to forego the tremendous advances of the recent past. The aim of these movements, however, is in the direction of returning some responsibility for maintenance of health to patients themselves; to treat patients as whole persons, body, mind, and spirit, rather than diseased organ systems; to increase the effectiveness of healers along all these dimensions; and to rehumanize the delivery system itself.

Variously called humanistic medicine, holistic medicine, or holistic health care, these approaches are all characterized by a return to the theme of holism so strongly emphasized by humanistic psychology (see Chapter 5). Holistic health care has become a major program in many growth centers. Wellness clinics have sprung up throughout the country to help the public become more aware and cope more effectively with the stresses and strains that have given rise to a host of new diseases, the so-called diseases of civilization: hypertension, obesity, coronary disease, alcoholism, drug abuse, automobile and other accidents. Lifestyles are examined and change is encouraged, relaxation and meditation techniques are taught, groups are formed to develop the interpersonal skills required for more satisfying relationships with others.

Holistic medical clinics (Jourard, 1971) are being developed where patients can not only receive medical treatment but engage with others in similar explorations of disease-producing lifestyles and the responsible management of one's own health. Natural childbirth methods, with involvement of both parents in the birth process, have become increasingly popular as a way of emphasizing the personal meaning of this important human event. And at the other end of the spectrum of life, hospices have been founded to provide a haven for the terminally ill, where they can prepare for death with dignity in an atmosphere of human concern.

Within the medical profession itself, new developments toward a more humanistic medical practice are being introduced. Family practice is being given greater emphasis and status as a specialization within medical training. And in some instances, medical educators have called upon humanistic psychologists to help physicians and other medical personnel who are in training to learn better skills for communicating with patients and relating to them on a more personal level, as well as to aid in forming their own support groups for dealing more effectively with the stresses induced by medical practice itself. The Rogerian-oriented Center for Studies of the Person in La Jolla, California, for example, has been conducting an ongoing project called Human Dimensions in Medical Education for the past several years and is also conducting and evaluating experimental programs in selected Veterans Administration hospitals. (For a list of similar projects, see Miller, 1978, p. 359.)

## HUMANISTIC PSYCHOLOGY AND THE LAW

The application of humanistic psychological theory and practice to the field of law is mostly, at present, a subcurrent, but a growing one. Areas in which it has been applied include legal education, law enforcement, and corrections.

### Legal education

The functions that lawyers perform in our society are broad and varied, encompassing the entire field of human rights. While often advocates (an adversarial role), lawyers are even more frequently *counselors*, a term traditionally applied to them. They spend "more time in their offices, in person-to-person encounters counseling troubled individuals, than in any other single area" (Freeman, 1971, pp. 1–2). In the opinion of many legal educators, preparation for this function has been sorely deficient. By way of remedy, several law schools have added humanistically oriented skill development courses in counseling and human relations to their curricula.

Thomas Shaffer, former dean of the Notre Dame Law School, was one of the first to see and address this need and, in his publications, has documented this growing trend (Shaffer, 1971, 1973). The model he himself proposes is truly client-centered, participatory, and aimed at increasing client self-determination. The lawyer, at least in his or her role as counselor, is seen as a resource person and facilitator, quite similar to the function we saw ascribed to the teacher in the model of humanistic education.

### Law enforcement

Stephen Woolpert (1980) provides a helpful summary of recent efforts to apply humanistic theoretical models and correlative training methods in the field of law enforcement, with particular emphasis on police management and officer training procedures. In the latter case, the humanistic approach emphasizes, in addition to objectified training, a variety of experiential learning techniques, such as simulation, encounter, and self-disclosure. Programs using this mode include:

1. *Crisis intervention training:* for improved handling of domestic disturbance calls (which, Woolpert reports, account for roughly one fourth of the deaths and assaults suffered by police in the line of duty), potential suicides, terrorism, interviews with distraught victims, and effective crowd control.

2. *Sensitivity training programs* for police recruits. Simulated conflict situations are here presented in which recruits are observed and given supportive and helpful feedback by fellow officers and superiors to help them deal with their own reactions, to learn effective methods of conflict resolution, and thereby to reduce "the likelihood that police actions will precipitate the very violence they seek to prevent" (Woolpert, 1980, p. 73).

3. *Neighborhood team policing:* a program whereby a collaborative group of detectives and patrolmen are assigned responsibility for a particular area of a community and given considerable authority for determining their own methods of operation, assignments, and scheduling.

4. To these might be added recent *efforts to improve community-police relationships* through a variety of encounter-group formats facilitated by professionals and pioneered by humanistic psychologists.

While evaluations of such programs have generally confirmed their positive effects, Woolpert (1980), in reviewing this literature, points to a problem we have already noted in our discussion of humanistic management and education. Humanistic programs cannot be expected to succeed if simply grafted onto existing managerial systems that are not themselves humanistically oriented. This is especially true in the case of police management, which has traditionally followed a highly authoritarian, military organizational model. As in education, the tensions that result can only be destructive and divisive because of the basic incompatibility of these approaches (Boss, 1978).

Woolpert therefore proposes a familiar solution: the application of the organization development approach, derived from humanistic theory, to police management itself. Reviewing several case studies where this has been attempted (Zurcher, 1971; Weisbrod, Lamb, & Drexler, 1974; Boss, 1979), he concludes:

> Among the specific results reported are increased job effectiveness and work satisfaction, an expansion of self-awareness and interpersonal understanding among the staff, and an improved organizational climate.
>
> Thus, a managerial philosophy must exist which recognizes the complementary, synergistic relationship between individual and organiza-

tional needs. This makes it possible for specific policies and programs to contribute to the simultaneous growth of employees and clients. Such programs, moreover, can succeed without sacrificing efficiency and technical competence. In the absence of such a managerial philosophy, however, the chances of success decline rapidly. (Woolpert, 1980, p. 76)

## Corrections

Humanistic psychologists, together with their behavioral colleagues, are relative newcomers to the field of corrections and rehabilitation of criminal offenders. Thomas Szasz (1963) and other counter-cultural psychiatrists (Torrey, 1974) have, from a theoretical standpoint, compellingly argued against the application of a medical "disease" model to criminal behavior. Their position on issues of personal freedom and responsibility on which they base their principal arguments is remarkably similar to that taken in the present volume and would probably be endorsed by most humanistic psychologists.

Perhaps the most noteworthy instance in which techniques originated by humanistic psychologists have been applied is in the area of substance abuse. Encounter-group methods, more strongly confrontational than found in most growth centers, are typically used in the residential and outpatient treatment of drug offenders. And residential treatment centers themselves are frequently organized and run in such a way as to emphasize and reinforce the development of personal responsibility (Kolton, 1973; Simon, 1978). William Glasser's reality therapy, which has strong humanistic overtones, was first developed and successfully employed with juvenile offenders (Glasser, 1964), and Paul McCormick (1973) reported outcomes favorable to transactional analysis over behavior modification with a similar group of offenders.

## HUMANISTIC PSYCHOLOGY AND RELIGION

The issue of self-transcendence has led many humanistic and transpersonal psychologists to a renewed and very positive interest in the whole domain of religious experience. This topic and its implications for psychology and religion has already been explored at some length in Chapter 9 of this book.

The history of efforts to apply humanistic psychological theory and methods to institutional religion has yet to be written. William Coulson, Douglas Land, Bruce Meador, and the present author were instrumental in establishing the Group for Psychology and Religion as a project of the Rogerian Center for Studies of the Person in California in the mid-60s. Workshops incorporating encounter-group methods were offered throughout the western states at the invitation of several religious communities of men and women in an effort to enhance community building along more humanistic, less authoritarian lines.

An account of the aims and methods developed by this group together with an estimate of the effectiveness of their interventions can be found in Coulson (1973). This project was later expanded into the more broadly based La Jolla Summer Program by Coulson, Meador, and Land for the training of group leaders for other settings as well as for religious institutions.

## MARRIAGE, FAMILY, AND CHILDREN

The social institution primarily responsible for the acculturation of the members of any given society has been, is, and probably always will be the family. While in our society at least, family living patterns have undergone some truly radical changes in the recent past, this basic function has not been seriously altered. The changes referred to are familiar enough: an increasing divorce rate leading to serial marriages and a growing number of blended families (his children, her children, their children); single-parent families; families in which parents pursue independent careers (recent estimates of the number of "traditional" families in the United States in which father is the sole breadwinner range from only 6 percent to 17 percent).

Humanistic psychology is not, of course, responsible for creating these shifting patterns, though its often misunderstood ethic of self-realization may have contributed somewhat to the dissolution of certain marriages. Several humanistic psychologists have, however, addressed the problems endemic to modern marriage, family life, and parenting in such a shifting social climate, both theoretically and practically.

The late Sidney Jourard, for example, while remaining open to the possibility that people may indeed grow in maturity through divorce and remarriage, acutely analyzed the modern myths that surround the institution of marriage in our day (e.g., if I find the right person, we will live happily ever after, with no basic changes occurring in ourselves or in the relationship as we first experienced it). He argued forcefully for the position that marriage offers an unparalleled opportunity for mutual growth, provided both partners commit themselves to constant dialogue and personal self-disclosure as the inevitable changes occur (Jourard, 1978). Otherwise, he feared, we run the danger of perpetuating the myths by merely seeking the "right" partner (who will not change) over and over again. So common is this trend, he felt, that the stable, enduring, committed marriage for a lifetime is in danger of becoming an alternative lifestyle.

Carl Rogers (1972) makes a similar point in his book *Becoming Partners: Marriage and its Alternatives.* Modern marriage, to be successful in facilitating the growth of both partners to fuller personhood, must involve a commitment to an ongoing *process* not merely a static contract.

A nondefensive openness to the other's ongoing experience as well as one's own in mutual dialogue may well enrich the lives of both partners, as he illustrates in his own case and through interviews with other couples. Both authors caution us that such a process can be exceedingly painful at times, though well worth the effort involved.

At the opposite end of the scale, the pathological consequences of a rigid, homeostatic, defensive style of communication on *family life* have been well documented by a number of researchers (Laing & Esterson, 1964; Jackson, 1968; Satir, 1964, 1972). The burgeoning field of family systems theory and therapy (Guerin, 1976) has a well-developed humanistic sector among its proponents. Besides developing innovative therapeutic methods for engaging severely dysfunctional families (Bell, 1976; Whitaker, 1976), this group has increasingly concerned itself, in typical humanistic fashion, with the facilitation of healthier, growth-enhancing relationships among the more normal population of married couples and families.

Most family theorists subscribe to the notion that the marital system, the relationship between husband and wife, is at the core of the family system. The married couple is the architect of the family structure: what goes on (or does not go on) between them is felt to be responsible for the health or the pathology of the system as a whole. Facilitating the healthy growth of the marital system is therefore the strategy of choice.

Marriage encounter groups, sponsored by religious organizations as well as by growth centers, have become increasingly popular means for accomplishing this purpose. Couples' communication workshops, embodying a more formal educational format, have also proved to be effective vehicles for promoting deeper, more satisfying relationships (Miller, Nunnally, & Wackman, 1976, 1978). Both methods borrow heavily from techniques originated by humanistic psychologists.

The difficult task of parenting has not been neglected by humanistically oriented practitioners. Rudolf Dreikurs's approach (Dreikurs & Soltz, 1964), derived from Adlerian principles, is widely used in many nursery schools and parent-training programs. And Thomas Gordon (1974) has developed and disseminated his widely used Parent Effectiveness Training program (PET). For the treatment of the severely disturbed child, there is existential child therapy, developed by Clark Moustakas (1973).

## POWER TO THE POWERLESS

A number of oppressed groups have caught the attention of a growing number of social activists within the humanistic movement. Persons in these groups share one common characteristic: their growth toward self-actualization is severely inhibited by oppressive and dehumanizing cultural norms and practices. Once again, no claim is being made that the liberation movements that have arisen so dramatically among their ranks have been led by humanistic psychologists. But the fact remains that the leaders of these movements have often consciously appropriated the theoretical language and practical techniques of humanistic psychology in order to justify and promote their cause.

By way of example: consciousness, as we have seen, is the central issue in humanistic psychology. The expansion of awareness through the various techniques devised for that purpose is the key to self-determination and an authentic existence. Consciousness-raising is the stated objective of all such methods. And the consciousness-raising group is one of the principal tools employed by liberationists to make people aware of the oppressive conditions under which they labor—the first step toward transcending them. Dorothy Nevill (1977), a humanistic psychologist, and Theodora Wells (1977), a prominent business consultant, are among a group of authors who discuss the issue of *feminism* in the light of humanistic psychology. Elizabeth Rave (1978) has recently encouraged greater participation by humanistic psychologists in the battle against *racism*, and George Tate (1978), a black psychologist, has written on the parallels between humanistic psychology and the efforts of black psychologists to establish new paradigms for understanding the black experience.

A notable contribution toward a solution of the problem of *ageism* has recently been made by the SAGE (Senior Actualization and Growth Exploration) Project. First established in the San Francisco Bay Area in 1974 by Gay Luce, Eugenia Gerrard, Ken Dychtwald, and a group of like-minded humanistic psychologists, psychiatrists, and other therapists, this project has attempted to overcome prevailing stereotypes and prejudices against the elderly. In particular, they have addressed themselves to the stereotype that the aging are too rigid, too set in their ways, to profit from interventions designed to promote psychological change and growth. In both institutional settings and in core groups of unimpaired or minimally impaired older adults, they have shown just the opposite. The SAGE approach is holistic, focusing on physical, mental, and spiritual health simultaneously. Techniques are adapted from Eastern and Western exercises utilized by the human potential movement to promote self-actualization. The initial success was so encouraging that the SAGE staff has involved itself in the training of some 20,000 health professionals working with the elderly and has aided the development of more than 100 similar programs throughout the country (Dychtwald, 1981). Research on this approach and methodology has confirmed its effectiveness in lowering stress, heightening self-esteem, and increasing coping skills and several other key psychosocial variables in the elderly participants of the core groups (Dychtwald, 1978).

In response to this situation, Dychtwald has established the National Association for Humanistic Gerontology (NAHG) to serve as a network organization and clearinghouse for the stimulation of projects and ideas embodying a humanistic approach to the rapidly developing specialty of gerontology. It is his stated hope that such an approach will continue to generate more positive images of aging "by demonstrating that people over 60 can grow and transcend the often negative expectations of our culture" (Dychtwald, 1981, p. 50).

## HUMANISTIC POLITICAL SCIENCE

"Power to the powerless," the slogan adopted as the title of the previous section, and "power to the person," which aptly summarizes the person-centered theme of humanistic psychology (see Chapter 10), carry obvious political implications. After all, political systems have been defined as "any persistent pattern of human relationships that involves, to a significant extent, power, rule, or authority" (Dahl, 1963, p. 6). Therefore, where power is reinvested in individuals, where individuals are encouraged to trust their own inner locus of evaluation, to take responsibility for their own actions, to guide their behavior by an inner gyroscope rather than by purely external norms, to transcend commonly accepted definitions of self, we are obviously dealing with power shifts that are nothing short of revolutionary. And yet this is what humanistic psychology, from one perspective, is all about. This above all explains why attempts to rehumanize social institutions, whether in the economic sphere, education, medicine, law, religion, or the family, so often encounter such fierce resistance.

In spite of all this (or perhaps just because such unexpected and violent opposition had first to be repeatedly experienced), the political implications of humanistic psychology have only recently been recognized and addressed. Carl Rogers himself, the founder of the person-centered approach that has been applied to so many areas of human interaction, from therapy to international relationships, confessed that the political impact of his thinking had not even occurred to him until three years prior to the publication of his book on personal power, subtitled "Inner Strength and its Revolutionary Impact" (Rogers, 1977). In this work he documents the shifts in power that occur wherever the person-centered approach is seriously adopted, as well as the antagonisms that inevitably arise from those whose power base is thereby threatened. His analysis leaves him optimistic but cautiously so.

Walt Anderson, a political scientist who has considerable personal acquaintance with humanistic psychology and the human potential movement, suggests the need for *political science* itself to adopt the new paradigmatic approach of the third force in modern psychology (Anderson, 1973, 1977, 1978). He finds severely wanting the images of human nature and the supposed sources of political behavior (narcissism, greed, lust for power, irrational motivation) which currently dominate the thinking of most political scientists. Not, Anderson claims, that these images and sources of political motivation do not at times correspond to reality. But they represent a stunted, even pathological view of human nature. And this nothing-but approach, this paradigmatic view borrowed from classical economics and from Freudian and behavioral psychology, is creating strains for the discipline of political science which are finally beginning to surface.

> Thus academic political science was taken completely off guard by the protest movements of the 1960s and the liberation movements of the 1970s and still has trouble dealing with evidence of idealistic behavior or seriously considering the possibility that any really fundamental change can or will take place in American society. (Anderson, 1978, p. 433)

He argues instead for the more comprehensive views of Abraham Maslow (1970), Charles Hampden-Turner (1971), and other humanists (Bugental, 1971; Matson, 1978) on the psychological and social development of human beings, views that stress the prepotency of lower needs but insist also on basic human capacities and desires for higher levels of development. From such a stance, he believes, we can begin to develop a *politics of growth*: political systems which have as their aim the fullest possible development of human potential. After illustrating what this might mean in matters of current public policy (e.g., welfare), he concludes: "Our new vision of the possibilities of human existence becomes a set of guidelines for building a human community" (Anderson, 1978, p. 437).

Earlier in the same article he anticipates a criticism of humanistic psychology (which we will encounter again in the final chapter of this book). So far, he maintains, the emphasis has been on individual, personal growth. Implicit in this is the assumption that social change can occur only incrementally (i.e., when a sufficiently large number of individuals have undergone the type of growth experiences offered by the human potential movement). He questions this assumption and favors instead an expansion of the social action approach, exemplified throughout this chapter, which attempts to change the functioning of larger social structures more directly.

# 12 Epilogue: Critique and Future Directions

> Science is rooted in what I have just called the whole apparatus of common sense thought. That is the datum from which it starts, and to which it must recur. . . . You may polish up common sense, you may contradict it in detail, you may surprise it. But ultimately your whole task is to satisfy it.
>
> Alfred North Whitehead

Common sense dictates that we cannot have a complete science of human psychology without taking into account that attribute which distinguishes us from all other living organisms: the mystery of human consciousness. We are self-conscious animals. That is our glory and some would say our curse. We have seen how the discipline of psychology began with the study of consciousness itself but from a faulty paradigm borrowed from the natural sciences. When that failed, it sought to ignore consciousness completely by focusing on behavior alone. The purpose of this book has been to demonstrate how humanistic-existential psychology has attempted to restore the empirical study of consciousness to center stage, its rightful place within the discipline if the demands of common sense are indeed to be satisfied.

That effort has met with modest success within the establishment of psychology itself. No modern textbook in general psychology can afford to ignore it, and there are by now several well-established "schools" of humanistic-existential psychotherapy (Yalom, 1980). But so far, as I attempted to show in the preceding chapter, the impact of the humanistic movement has been more keenly felt in areas outside the discipline of psychology. Given the broad sweep of social systems and issues to which humanistic psychologists have addressed themselves, how pervasive has this influence been? Has this approach to psychology appealed to the common sense of the populace at large, and if so, to what extent?

## CULTURAL REVOLUTION

A recent lengthy article by Daniel Yankelovich (1981), previewing his book which, as of this writing, had not yet appeared in print, provides some truly startling answers to these questions. Yankelovich, a psychologist who is president of the social research firm of Yankelovich, Skelly, and White, Inc., extensively documents what he terms a true cultural revolution in the making. Summarizing a vast amount of survey data collected over the past few decades by his own firm and other respected social science research organizations, Yankelovich concludes that a number of major shifts have occurred in the web of shared meanings which define American culture.

He believes these cultural shifts, though they gathered considerable momentum in the period of economic affluence following World War II, to be irreversible. They are obviously on a collision course with the straitened economic circumstances and the upsurge of conservatism in politics and economics that mark the beginning of this decade, but they have a life of their own apart from these institutions of society. They have to do with the ways in which we collectively define the very purpose and nature of our lives.

The major shift that Yankelovich charts over recent decades is a movement away from the self-denying work ethic of the past to an ethic of self-fulfillment, which he seems to ascribe to the popular appeal of the human potential movement and humanistic psychology. (He devotes a whole section of his article to the influence of Abraham Maslow and the latter's theoretical emphasis on self-actualization.) Pinpointing the recent shift in answers to interview and questionnaire items that operationally define this self-fulfillment ethic, Yankelovich estimates that the vast majority of Americans (some 80 percent) now subscribe to it. Sixty-three percent of us subscribe to it in its weak form, mixing the search for expressive self-fulfillment with commitment to more traditional values of hard work and sacrifice; 17 percent to its strong form, the my-growth-at-all-costs segment of the population. He concludes from his data that only a minority of Americans (20 percent, consisting mostly of men and women over 50 who live primarily in the rapidly diminishing rural areas of our country) still cling to the traditional values in their entirety.

In analyzing this sweeping grass-roots phenomenon. which he likens to a cultural earthquake with all the connotations of insecure footing and tumbling structures which that image conveys, Yanke-lovich is quick to criticize the strong form of the self-fulfillment ethic. Attributing it (wrongly, I think) to Maslow, he defines it as the self-focused effort to gratify, first and foremost, all one's personal needs as quickly as they arise, often to the detriment of one's commitments and responsibilities to others. He points out (rightly, I think) the basic hedonism and inherent contradictions of such a position. Human needs are infinite. Such excessive egocentrism, at whatever level of the need-hierarchy it is exercised, is ultimately self-defeating. The author recounts many anecdotes, some rather pathetically amusing, of this type of feverish pursuit of self-fulfillment. It leads inevitably, he feels, to a sense of isolation, a loss of the rich rewards of true intimacy (which demands a certain degree of self-sacrifice and compromise). And it leads also, he suspects, to the fierce backlash of groups like the Moral Majority, who fear the effects of this new lifestyle on the moral integrity of the nation.

The unexpected onslaught of economic hard times also threatens the new lifestyle of these "strong-formers." The gratification of material needs was one of its principal components. We are entering a long period of belt-tightening which, for this group, can only lead to frustration and confusion. The world has indeed been turned upside down.

## Toward a broader ethic

Yankelovich makes it clear that he does not disagree with the *goals* of the self-fulfillment ethic but only with the *means* used to achieve them by the strong-formers. (The reader of this book should be aware by now that I, along with many of my humanistic colleagues, would heartily endorse that sentiment.) He seems more in agreement with the methods used by the weak-formers, who mix adherence to certain traditional values (responsibility to family and society, and so on) with goals of creative self-expression and personal fulfillment.

Some strong-formers will benefit from their life experiments and learn better methods for achieving their goals. Economic hardship alone will force many to abandon their exclusive concern with "the inner journey." Weak-formers can be expected to continue their own life experiments, the attempt to integrate the best of the old values with the best of the new, those which enhance the attainment of self-fulfillment. Their very numbers (almost two thirds of the American public) assure the continuation of this trend. The world may be turned upside down, but it will never turn back to the old ways of construing the American Dream.

It is impossible in this brief account to repeat all the statistical evidence that Yankelovich marshalls in support of these preceding statements. To give just one example: the author combines survey data from several sources to conclude that the norms concerning whether a married woman should work outside the home have been reversed in a single generation and, further, that the reason for this is not just economic necessity.

> Indeed, an impressive 67 percent of women who work say that they do so for reasons of self-fulfillment as well as for economic reasons. The majority of women today, including those who work for pay *and* those who stay at home, state that their ideal of the woman who is truly fulfilling herself is someone who can manage a career as well as a home. (Yankelovich, 1981, p. 72)

Yankelovich concludes his analysis by affirming his belief, roughly paralleling the themes developed in the present volume, that the ethic of self-commitment which characterized the cultural shift of the past few decades will be incorporated into a new, broader ethic: an *ethic of commitment*. He cites evidence, admittedly somewhat sparse at present, to show that such an ethic may be evolving from two kinds of commitment: toward the development of deeper and closer personal relationships and a growing hunger for real community; and toward an increasing commitment to "sacred/expressive" values over purely material/instrumental ones. By *sacred* he wishes to encompass both religious and secular forms, the latter referring to a reverence for all living and natural things, an ecological outlook that attempts to live life in harmony with nature. The new ethic will involve, in a word, *self-transcendence* (see Chapter 9), recognizing that true self-fulfillment "can be realized only through a web of shared meanings that transcend the conception of the self as isolated physical object" (1981, p. 89).

## THE ROLE OF THE UNCONSCIOUS

There is no doubt in my own mind that the pop version of humanistic psychology does stress what Yankelovich calls the strong version of the self-fulfillment ethic, the me-first attitude so forcefully expressed in the Gestalt Prayer ("I do my thing, and you do your thing . . .") attributed to Fritz Perls (1969). This is indeed unfortunate, and I have attempted to show in this volume that a close examination of the thought of leading humanistic authors provides no justification for such an interpretation. It does persist, however, and it is justifiably attacked by many current critics.

Another such critic is James Hillman (1975). His slashing attack on humanistic psychology (along with behaviorism) deserves special mention if only because he is the most original thinker in the field of archetypal psychology since Carl Jung. In his stimulating work *Revisioning Psychology*, Hillman puts forth the unique proposition that our behavior is not primarily a function of environmental contingencies (the behavioral position), or of our subjective *conscious* interpretations of reality (the phenomenological position), but of our *images* or *fantasies* of the real world. Emotionally charged, deeply rooted in the collective archetypal unconscious, these images or fantasies are what guide and determine our conduct. We are not ordinarily conscious of them, but they are accessible through our dreams and other expressions of human imagination. This is, of course, in complete accord with the position of most depth psychologists that our daily actions are primarily influenced by unconscious determinants.

What differentiates Hillman and other Jungians from most depth psychologists is their assumption of the existence of a transpersonal realm of *psychic reality*, which transcends the life and psyche of the individual. In a sense, we are all possessed by the gods and demons (daimones) of this psychic world. Soul-making, the real purpose of psychology, according to Hillman, occurs when we begin consciously to appropriate and integrate this confusing cast of characters who vie for attention in the unconscious depths of our personality.

Imagination, then, is the key to self-actualization for Hillman and other archetypal psychologists. And symbols are the language of imagination. Certain symbols have archetypal significance (i.e., they arise from the collective unconscious of the race and are given expression in a culture's myths or fairy tales, as well as in certain dream symbols). They are not, therefore, simply fictions or subjective products. They embody the collective experience of humankind as it confronts the dilemmas of human existence throughout the ages, and they therefore contain much wisdom. In one sense, myths make us to be what we are; we do not make myths. We act out, for the most part unconsciously, the themes of the stories contained in our myths.

In Jungian analytical practice, archetypal dream symbols, products of active imagination, and other imaginative expressions, are linked with these larger mythical themes by a process of *amplification* (Kaufmann, 1979). In this way, the themes that have unconsciously determined the life of the analysand are gradually made conscious, and the process of integration of their often conflicting motifs, the process of individuation itself, can begin. The subject of analysis now has, at his or her conscious disposal, the "wisdom of the unconscious."

Hillman is especially caustic in his criticism of what he too believes to be the self-fulfillment ethic of humanistic psychology. He is right on target in criticizing this "strong" form of the humanistic ethic, its overemphasis on following one's subjective feelings, the dominance of what he calls the Hero myth of egocentric consciousness. But part of my endeavor has been to show that this is a false reading of leading humanistic authors. Their trust in the wisdom of the *total* organism goes far beyond simply trusting one's own subjective feelings, though the latter are often crucial barometers toward understanding one's current personality functioning. In principle at least, trust in the wisdom of the organism has much in common with trust in the wisdom of the unconscious. Humanistic psychologists begin with conscious experience but, as we have seen, are quite concerned with *expanding* that consciousness to include other facets of personal functioning. Nor do they ignore imagery. Gestalt therapists and transpersonal psychologists have been quite innovative in employing dream interpretation, imagistic techniques, and other right-brain activities to uncover these other facets.

I have already discussed (in Chapter 5) some emerging humanistic notions on the role and concept of the unconscious. Many transpersonal psychologists in particular remain open to the Jungian concept of the collective unconscious; others do not. It is my personal conviction that the phenomena reported by *all* depth psychologists need to be incorporated into humanistic theory and practice more satisfactorily than they currently are. This remains an unresolved area and a direction for the future.

## The problem of evil

Hillman is equally critical of humanistic psychology, and in particular its American branch, for what he considers to be its overoptimistic, rosy-spectacled view of human nature and its overemphasis on potentially unlimited, positive human growth. He insists that there are destructive, violent, death-dealing forces at work within psychic reality, as well as constructive, life-enhancing tendencies. He may be right. American humanists do tend to be more optimistic, pragmatic, and progress-oriented than even their European counterparts in the existential-analytic branch of the movement. Our own shores have been left relatively untouched by the upheavals that have afflicted European society during the past century alone. We are just beginning to face the limits of the myth of unimpeded progress that has characterized our own version of civilization.

But there is more to it than this. Hillman is here confronting the age-old problem of evil and its origins. He is even critical of Judeo-Christian monotheism on this score, as, to a much lesser extent, was Jung himself (1958). However, this certainly remains a highly debatable issue, another area for future theoretical and practical evaluation within humanistic psychology.

I personally find Hillman's own solution a bit curious. He seems to feel that ancient Greco-Roman myths are the best source for potential resolution of this problem and focuses almost exclusively on this literature. There are other myths from other cultures as well which address this crucial question. And if John Dunne (1973), a leading theologian and founder of narrative theology, is correct, there may even be a progression in the history of mythology, from the ancient Babylonian epic of Gilgamesh, through the Greeks and Romans, to medieval Judeo-Christian sources, and up to the present time that represents differing but progressively more enlightening human views on the problems of death and evil. Dunne also wants us to become aware of "the story we are in" so that we may make a more conscious choice of the direction we wish individually to take. He, like Jung, believes in a progression of religious understanding and, though remaining a Christian, is more cosmopolitan than Hillman in the respect that he pays to other cultural views.

## THE ISSUE OF VERIFICATION

Even if Hillman and other commentators are correct in asserting that myths are much more than purely subjective fabrications of imagination, their interpretation is often quite subjective. This poses a serious problem concerning the *verification* of statements made about them, a problem that obviously has not yet been resolved. That undoubtedly is an issue for scholars outside the field of science. But humanistic psychology, as we have repeatedly seen, has also been criticized by the scientific community on the issue of verification. I trust that enough has been said throughout this volume to establish the viability of empirical structural and functional phenomenological approaches in the investigation of issues of concern to humanistic psychologists.

In the structural area, methods need to be sharpened and better controls and replications instituted along the lines suggested by van Kaam (1966) and Giorgi (1970). In addition, recent verification methods developed by the stage-theorists in developmental psychology might serve as useful models, as Child (1973) suggests.

In the functional area, Price and Barrell (1980) have recently proposed a promising model for the psychometric scaling of experiential variables, and Rychlak (1977) has offered (and illustrated in practice) an excellent paradigm for rigorous experimental research in humanistic psychology: begin with humanistic theoretical assumptions concerning the origins of human behavior and derive from these a set of methodological variables that can be subjected to strict canons of scientific verification. Rogers and his associates, as we have seen at many points, pioneered this area along with Kelly and his students. Rogers was even more active in promoting evaluative research, both process and outcome, on his own humanistically oriented approach to psychotherapy, and Aaron Beck (1976) and his colleagues are presently active in evaluating the results of their humanistic cognitive therapy.

However, to quote another old logical adage: "*ab posse ad esse non valet illatio"* ("from the mere possibility of an event, one cannot argue to its existence"). Child's criticism is still valid. With the exception of the instances noted above and a very few others, there has been a relative dearth of empirical research in humanistic psychology. There are undoubtedly good reasons for this state of affairs: the antiestablishment status and attitudes of many humanistic psychologists; the fact that many are clinicians too engaged in the exigencies of their practices to have any energy left for the application of research skills learned in their training; even the conviction (prominent among Gestalt and other experiential therapists) that no appropriate methods exist for investigating or validating the complex variables they assume to be responsible for human behavior.

There are, however, encouraging signs of change. Research paradigms in cognitive, developmental, and social psychology now routinely include multioperational methods (i.e., measurements of subjectively perceived changes in response to experimental manipulations or naturally occurring events along with the more traditional behavioral observations). This is a clear convergence with humanistic concerns. And a growing number of young researchers continue to derive variables directly from humanistic-phenomenological assumptions and submit them to experimental investigation.

To give one such instance: George Howard and his colleagues (1979, 1980, 1981) at the University of Houston have recently completed and published a series of experiments on *response-shift bias.* The results they obtained cast considerable doubt on the effectiveness of traditional pre/post measures for evaluating changes in subjects who are exposed, e.g., to workshop experiences in assertiveness training or leadership skills. They argue directly from phenomenological theory that the *lived experience* of the workshop itself may well change the standards by which subjects evaluate themselves at the end, creating a response-shift bias. In effect, subjects no longer evaluate themselves by the standards they use in responding to the initial self-report measure, the traditional pretest. Howard et al. (1979) note that when response-shifts occur, even true experimental designs are incapable of providing an unbiased estimate of treatment effects.

In order to operationalize this theoretical construct, Howard and his associates add a *retrospective pretest measure* to the traditional ones. During the postintervention session, subjects are asked to respond to each item on the self-report measure twice. First they report how they perceive themselves to be at present, the usual postintervention assessment. Immediately after answering each item in this manner, they are requested to answer the same item again, only this time in reference to how they now perceive themselves to have been *just before the workshop was conducted,* an assessment which they label the *Then* measure. The difference between Pre and Then self-report ratings becomes the measure of response-shift. Howard (1981) reports the following results in experiments using this measure:

> In five of the 12 studies to date where direct comparisons between Pre/Post and Then/Post approaches could be made, the Then/Post analysis yielded a drastically different set of conclusions regarding the effectiveness of the intervention from the Pre/Post approach (in every case the Pre/Post assessment was overly conservative—that is, claiming no treatment effect where the treatment effect did indeed exist).

Further analysis revealed that in no study were Pre/Post measures superior or even equivalent to the Then/Post approach in reflecting *behavioral* indications of change. In several cases correlations of the latter approach with such behavioral indicators were significantly greater. Efforts were also successfully made to rule out other suggested explanations of the effects obtained (social desirability, memory distortion, and the like).

Now at Notre Dame, Howard is continuing his research program on this construct as well as addressing other topics: comparison of self-report to behavioral measures as indices of change, and the research subject as a participant observer along lines suggested by Giorgi and others.

## FURTHER DIRECTIONS FOR THE FUTURE

Several directions for the future development of humanistic psychology have already been suggested in this chapter: continued movement toward an ethic of self-commitment and greater social concern; a more satisfactory incorporation of the phenomena uncovered by depth psychologists; and greatly increased attention to the issue of verification. This last point is of particular importance to the continued viability of humanistic psychology in the academic and professional community of psychologists.

In the academic community, present trends point to an increasing acceptance of humanistic concerns in research on human behavior. Subject-contributed variables have gained the attention of a growing number of researchers in cognitive, developmental, and social psychology, and in social learning theory. Recent developments in structural modeling approaches in the field of statistics are providing new methodological tools for this purpose (Kenny, 1979). These advances enable researchers to pair subject-contributed variables with manipulable ones in traditional experimental situations. The intriguing advantage claimed for these newer methods over former correlational procedures is that *causal* inferences can now be drawn concerning the relative contributions of both types of variables.

Research on formal humanistic paradigms has been slower in developing, but such efforts, where they do occur, are gradually becoming accepted for publication in the more respected professional journals. The movement here is toward *convergence* of interest and a greater acceptance of the need for complementary approaches and methods to the study of human behavior.

In the professional community, the movement is toward greater *collaboration* between humanists, behaviorists, and other schools of psychotherapy. Ricks, Wandersman, and Poppen (1976) have provided considerable documentation of such collaborative efforts, particularly in the case of humanists and behaviorists. They conclude that training in psychotherapy should include exposure to analytic, behavioral, and humanistic theories and methods in order to serve the best interests of the varied types of clients who seek professional help. Arnold Lazarus (1976) and Leonard Krasner (1977), two prominent behaviorists, do not hesitate to appropriate humanistic methods in their own professional approach. Krasner, in particular, has pointed to the shared values and concerns of both movements: a concern for the freedom of the individual from aversive controls, a shared rejection of the disease model of psychopathology, and a common goal of increased self-regulation of behavior. Many humanists, from their own standpoint, have sought training in cognitive and behavioral psychotherapeutic methods to further their own humanistic goals. While none of these approaches may be strictly reducible to any of the others, all share equally humanitarian goals. Ironically, humanistic psychologists seem to be trailing the field in only one respect: the deep concern, pioneered by one of the principal founders of this movement (Rogers, 1942), to subject the psychotherapeutic process wherever possible to good quality empirical research.

Overall, however, the empirical study of human consciousness is finally reclaiming its rightful place in the discipline of psychology. Whitehead's plea for common sense is being heard.

# References

Abramson, H. A. (Ed.). *Problems of consciousness*. New York: Josiah Macy, Jr., Foundation, 1954.

Adler, A. *The neurotic constitution*. New York: Dodd, Mead, 1926.

Adler, A. [*The practice and theory of individual psychology*] (P. Radin, Trans.). New York: Harcourt Brace Jovanovich, 1927.

Adler, A. *The individual psychology of Alfred Adler*. New York: Basic Books, 1956.

Adler, A. *What life should mean to you*. New York: Capricorn Books, 1958.

Adler, A. *Superiority and social interest: A collection of later writings* (H. L. Ansbacher & R. R. Ansbacher, Eds.). Evanston, Ill.: Northwestern University Press, 1964.

Alexander, F. *Psychosomatic medicine*. New York: W. W. Norton, 1950.

Allers, R. [*The psychology of character*] (E. B. Strauss, Trans.). New York: Sheed & Ward, 1931.

Allport, G. W. *Personality: A psychological interpretation*. New York: Holt, Rinehart & Winston, 1937.

Allport, G. W. *The use of personal documents in psychological science*. New York: Social Science Research Council, 1942.

Allport, G. W. *Becoming: Basic consider-*ations *for a psychology of personality*. New Haven, Conn.: Yale University Press, 1955.

Allport, G. W. *Pattern and growth in personality*. New York: Holt, Rinehart & Winston, 1961.

Alschuler, A. S. The origins and nature of psychological education. *Educational Opportunity Forum*, 1969, *1*, 1–16.

Anderson, W. *Politics and the new humanism*. Pacific Palisades, Calif.: Goodyear Publishing, 1973.

Anderson, W. Psychology, politics, and human development. In B. McWaters (Ed.), *Humanistic perspectives: Current trends in psychology*. Monterey, Calif.: Brooks/Cole Publishing, 1977.

Anderson, W. Politics and the new humanism. In I. D. Welch; G. A. Tate; & F. Richards (Eds.), *Humanistic psychology: A source book*. Buffalo, N.Y.: Prometheus Books, 1978.

Andrews, J. E. *The effect of word meaning on the affective learning styles of ascendent and submissive subjects*. Unpublished master's thesis, Purdue University, 1972.

Angyal, A. *Foundations for the science of personality*. New York: Commonwealth Fund, 1941.

Ansbacher, H. L. Goal-oriented individual psychology: Alfred Adler's theory. In

A. Burton (Ed.), *Operational theories of personality.* New York: Brunner/Mazel, 1974.

Argyris, C. *Increasing leadership effectiveness.* New York: John Wiley & Sons, 1976.

Argyris, D., & Schon, D. A. *Organizational learning: A theory of action perspective.* Reading, Mass.: Addison-Wesley Publishing 1978.

Aspy, D. N., & Roebuck, F. N. From humane ideas to humane technology and back again many times. *Education,* 1974, 95, 163–171.

Assagioli, R. *Psychosynthesis: A manual of principles and techniques.* New York: Viking Press, 1965.

Bakan, D. *Disease, pain, and sacrifice: Toward a psychology of suffering.* Chicago: University of Chicago Press, 1968.

Bandura, A. *Principles of behavior modification.* New York: Holt, Rinehart & Winston, 1969.

Banikiotes, P. G., & Neimeyer, G. J. *Construct importance and rating similarity as determinants of interpersonal attraction.* Unpublished paper, University of Notre Dame, 1980.

Bannister, D., & Mair, J. *The evaluation of personal constructs.* New York: Academic Press, 1968.

Barker, E. N. Human priorities. In D. D. Nevill (Ed.), *Humanistic psychology: New frontiers.* New York: Gardner Press, 1977.

Barrett-Lennard, G. *Dimensions of perceived therapist response related to therapeutic change.* Unpublished doctoral dissertation, University of Chicago, 1959.

Barrett-Lennard, G. Dimensions of therapist response as causal factors in therapeutic change. *Psychological Monographs,* 1962, 76 (Whole No. 562).

Bateson, G. (Ed.). *Perceval's narrative: A patient's account of his psychosis.* Stanford, Calif.: Stanford University Press, 1961.

Beck, A. T. *Cognitive therapy and the emotional disorders.* New York: International Universities Press, 1976.

Becker, E. *The denial of death.* New York: Free Press, 1973. Copyright © 1973 by The Free Press, a Division of Macmillan Publishing Company, Inc.

Bell, J. E. A theoretical framework for family group therapy. In P. Guerin (Ed.), *Family therapy: Theory and practice.* New York: Gardner Press, 1976.

Bennis, W. G. (Ed.). *American bureaucracy.* Chicago: Aldine, 1970.

Benoit, H. *The supreme doctrine: Psychological studies in Zen thought.* New York: Pantheon Books, 1955.

Berg, I. A. Deviant responses and deviant people: The formulation of the deviation hypothesis. *Journal of Counseling Psychology,* 1957, 4, 159.

Berger, P. L. *Invitation to sociology: A humanistic perspective.* New York: Doubleday, 1963.

Berger, P. L., & Luckmann, T. *The social construction of reality.* New York: Doubleday, 1966.

Bhaskar, R. *The possibility of naturalism: A philosophical critique of the contemporary human sciences.* Atlantic Highlands, N.J.: Humanities Press, 1979.

Binswanger, L. Quoted by Eugen Kahn in H. M. Ruitenbeek (Ed.), *Psychoanalysis and existential philosophy.* New York: E. P. Dutton, 1962, p. 204.

Binswanger, L. [*Being-in-the-world: Selected papers of Ludwig Binswanger*] (J. Needleman, Trans.). New York: Basic Books, 1963.

Blake, R. R., & Mouton, J. S. *The managerial grid.* Houston: Gulf Publishing, 1964.

Blake, R. R., & Mouton, J. S. *Corporate excellence through grid organization development.* Houston: Gulf Publishing, 1968.

Blakney, R. B. *The way of life: A new translation of the Tao Teh Ching.* New York: New American Library, 1955.

Block, J. The assessment of communication: Role variations as a function of interactional context. *Journal of Personality,* 1952, *21,* 272–286.

Block, J., & Bennett, L. The assessment of communication: Perception and transmission as a function of the social situation. *Human Relations,* 1955, *8,* 317–325.

Boss, M. [*Psychoanalysis and daseinsanalysis*] (L. B. Lefebre, Trans.). New York: Basic Books, 1963.

Boss, W. The effects of leader absence on a confrontation team-building design. *Journal of Applied Behavioral Science,* 1978, *14,* 469–478.

Boss, W. It doesn't matter if you win or lose, unless you're losing: Organizational change in a law enforcement agency. *Journal of Applied Behavioral Science,* 1979, *15,* 198–220.

Bradford, L. P.; Gibb, J. R.; & Benne, K. D. (Eds.). *T-group theory and laboratory method.* New York: John Wiley & Sons, 1964.

Breger, L., & McGaugh, J. L. Critique and reformulation of "learning-theory" approaches to psychotherapy and neurosis. In T. Millon (Ed.), *Theories of psychopathology and personality: Essays and critiques* (2d ed.). Philadelphia: W. B. Saunders, 1973.

Bridgman, P. W. *The logic of modern physics.* New York: Macmillan, 1927.

Brill, A. A. Determinism in psychiatry and psychoanalysis. *American Journal of Psychiatry,* 1938, *95,* 600.

Brown, B. *Now: The human dimension. A report of the Ford-Esalen project for innovation in humanistic education.* (Monograph 1). Big Sur, Calif.: Esalen Institute, 1968.

Brown, R., & Herrnstein, R. J. *Psychology.* Boston: Little, Brown, 1975.

Browne, L. (Ed.). *The world's great scriptures.* New York: Macmillan, 1961.

Buber, M. [*I and thou*] (W. Kaufmann, Trans.). New York: Charles Scribner's Sons, 1970.

Bugental, J. F. T. *The search for authenticity.* New York: Holt, Rinehart & Winston, 1965.

Bugental, J. F. T. (Ed.). *Challenges of humanistic psychology.* New York: McGraw-Hill, 1967.

Bugental, J. F. T. The humanistic ethic— The individual in psychotherapy as a societal change agent. *Journal of Humanistic Psychology,* 1971, *11*(1), 11–25.

Bühler, C. Human life as a whole as a central subject of humanistic psychology. In J. F. T. Bugental (Ed.), *Challenges of humanistic psychology.* New York: McGraw-Hill, 1967.

Bühler, C. Human life goals in the humanistic perspective. In A. J. Sutich & M. A. Vich (Eds.), *Readings in humanistic psychology.* New York: Free Press, 1969.

Bühler, C., & Allen, M. *Introduction to humanistic psychology.* Monterey, Calif.: Brooks/Cole Publishing, 1972.

Campbell, J. P., & Dunnette, M. D. Effectiveness of T-group experiences in managerial training and development. *Psychological Bulletin,* 1968, *70*(2), 73–104.

Carlson, R., & Garell, D. Humanistic health care: The evolution of the medical system. In I. D. Welch; G. A. Tate; & F. Richards (Eds.), *Humanistic psychology: A source book.* Buffalo, N.Y.: Prometheus Books, 1978.

Carpenter, F. *The Skinner primer: Behind freedom and dignity.* New York: Free Press, 1974.

Castaneda, C. *A separate reality: Further*

*conversations with Don Juan.* New York: Simon & Schuster, 1971.

Chaudhuri, H. Yoga psychology. In C. Tart (Ed.), *Transpersonal psychologies.* New York: Harper & Row, 1975.

Child, I. L. *Humanistic psychology and the research tradition: Their several virtues.* New York: John Wiley & Sons, 1973.

Choisy, M. Psychoanalysis and Catholicism. *Cross Currents,* 1951, *3,* 84.

Chomsky, N. *Language and mind* (2d ed.). New York: Harcourt Brace Jovanovich, 1972.

Clark, J. V., & Culbert, S. A. Mutually therapeutic perception and self-awareness in a T-group. *Journal of Applied Behavioral Science,* 1965, *1,* 180–194.

Coles, R. *Eskimos, Chicanos, Indians* (Vol. 4; *Children of crisis).* Boston: Little, Brown, 1977.

Combs, A. W. *The professional education of teachers.* Boston: Allyn & Bacon, 1965.

Combs, A. W. Humanistic goals of education. In I. D. Welch; G. A. Tate; & F. Richards (Eds.), *Humanistic psychology: A source book.* Buffalo, N.Y.: Prometheus Books, 1978.

Combs, A. W., & Snygg, D. *Individual behavior: A perceptual approach to behavior* (Rev. ed.). New York: Harper & Row, 1959.

Cooper, C. L., & Mangham, I. L. *T-groups: A survey of research.* New York: Wiley-Interscience, 1971.

Coulson, W. R. *Groups, gimmicks, and instant gurus.* New York: Harper & Row, 1972.

Coulson, W. R. *A sense of community.* Columbus, Ohio: Charles E. Merrill Publishing, 1973.

Coulson, W. R., & Rogers, C. R. (Eds.). *Man and the science of man.* Columbus, Ohio: Charles E. Merrill Publishing, 1968.

Crumbaugh, J. C. Cross-validation of Purpose-in-Life Test based on Frankl's concept. *Journal of Individual Psychology,* 1968, *24,* 74–81.

Crumbaugh, J. C., & Maholick, L. T. An experimental study in existentialism: The psychometric approach to Frankl's concept of noogenic neurosis. *Journal of Clinical Psychology,* 1964, *20,* 200–207.

Culbert, S. A. Trainer self-disclosure and member growth in two T-groups. *Journal of Applied Behavioral Science,* 1968, *4,* 47–73.

Curran, C. A. *Personality factors in counseling.* New York: Grune & Stratton, 1945.

Dahl, R. *Modern political analysis.* Englewood Cliffs, N.J.: Prentice-Hall, 1963.

Dalbiez, R. [*Psychoanalytical methods and the doctrine of Freud*] (Vol. 2, F. T. Lindsay, Trans.). New York: Longmans, Green, 1941.

Deikman, A. Bimodal consciousness. *Archives of General Psychiatry,* 1971, *25,* 418–489.

Deikman, A. *Personal freedom: On finding your way to the real world.* New York: Grossman Publishers, 1976.

Dollard, J., & Miller, N. E. *Personality and psychotherapy.* New York: McGraw-Hill, 1950.

Doyle, W. Human functions in teaching. *Notre Dame Journal of Education,* 1972, *3,* 126–139.

Dreikurs, R., & Soltz, V. *Children: The challenge.* New York: Duell, Sloan & Pearce, 1964.

Duck, S. W. *Personal relationships and personal constructs.* London: Wiley, 1973.

Duck, S. W. Inquiry, hypothesis, and the quest for validation: Personal construct systems in the development of acquaintance. In S. W. Duck (Ed.), *Theory* and practice in interpersonal attraction. London: Academic Press, 1977.

Duck, S. W. The personal and the interpersonal in construct theory: Social and individual aspects of relationships. In P. Stringer & D. Bannister (Eds.), *Constructs of sociality and individuality*. London: Academic Press, 1979.

Dunne, J. S. *Time and myth*. New York: Doubleday, 1973.

Durlak, J. A. Relationship between individual attitudes toward life and death. *Journal of Consulting and Clinical Psychology*, 1972, *38*, 463.

Dychtwald, K. The SAGE Project: A new image of age. *Journal of Humanistic Psychology*, 1978, *18*(2), 69–74.

Dychtwald, K. Services for the elderly. *Journal of Humanistic Psychology*, 1981, *21*, 39–56.

Egan, G. *The skilled helper*. Monterey, Calif.: Brooks/Cole Publishing, 1975.

Eliade, M. *Shamanism*. Princeton, N.J.: Ballinger, 1964.

Erikson, E. H. *Identity and the life cycle*. New York: International Universities Press, 1959.

Estes, W. K. New perspectives on some old issues in association theory. In N. J. Mackintosh & W. K. Honig (Eds.), *Fundamental issues in associative learning*. Halifax, Canada: Dalhousie University Press, 1969.

Feldenkrais, M. *Body and mature behavior*. New York: International Universities Press, 1949.

Feldenkrais, M. *Awareness through movement: Health exercises for personal growth*. New York: Harper & Row, 1972.

Frank, J. *Persuasion and healing: A comparative study of psychotherapy*. Baltimore: Johns Hopkins University Press, 1961.

Frankl, V. E. [*Man's search for meaning: An introduction to logotherapy*] (I.

Lasch, Trans.). New York: Washington Square Press, 1963.

Frankl, V. E. [*The doctor and the soul: From psychotherapy to logotherapy*] (2d ed.; R. & C. Winston, Trans.). New York: Alfred A. Knopf, 1965. Copyright © 1955, 1965 by Alfred A. Knopf, Inc. Reprinted by permission of Alfred A. Knopf, Inc.

Frankl, V. E. Self-transcendence as a human phenomenon. In A. J. Sutich & M. A. Vich (Eds.), *Readings in humanistic psychology*. New York: Free Press, 1969.

Frankl, V. E. *The unconscious God*. New York: Simon & Schuster, 1975.

Frankl, V. E. *The unheard cry for meaning: Psychotherapy and humanism*. New York: Simon & Schuster, 1978.

Freeman, H. A. The role of lawyers as counselors. In T. Shaffer (Ed.), *Legal counseling handbook*. Notre Dame, Ind.: University of Notre Dame Press, 1971.

Freud, S. [*Introductory lectures on psychoanalysis*] (J. Riviere, Trans.). London: Allen & Unwin, 1921.

Freud, S. *The ego and the id*. London: Hogarth Press, 1927.

Freud, S. [*The basic writings of Sigmund Freud*] (A. A. Brill, Trans.). New York: Modern Library, 1938.

Freud, S. [*Collected papers*] (Vol. 4; J. Riviere, Trans.). London: Hogarth Press, 1950.

Freud, S. *Beyond the pleasure principle*. Standard Edition (Vol. 18). London: Hogarth Press, 1955. (Originally published, 1920.)

Freud, S. *Civilization and its discontents*. Standard Edition (Vol. 21). London: Hogarth Press, 1961. (Originally published, 1930.) (a)

Freud, S. *The ego and the id*. Standard Edition (Vol. 19). London: Hogarth

Press, 1961. (Originally published, 1923.) (b)

Freud, S. *The psychopathology of everyday life.* Standard Edition (Vol. 6). London: Hogarth Press, 1966. (Originally published, 1901.)

Fromm, E. *Man for himself.* New York: Holt, Rinehart & Winston, 1947.

Galster, J. M. *Affective factors in paired-associate acquisition and tachistoscopic recognition of faces and names.* Unpublished master's thesis, Purdue University, 1972.

Gazzaniga, M. S. *The bisected brain.* New York: Appleton-Century-Crofts, 1970.

Gendlin, E. T. Experiencing: A variable in the process of therapeutic change. *American Journal of Psychology,* 1961, 15, 223–245.

Gendlin, E. T. *Experiencing and the creation of meaning.* New York: Free Press, 1962.

Gendlin, E. T. Experiencing and the nature of concepts. *The Christian Scholar,* 1963, 46, 245–255.

Gendlin, E. T. Subverbal communication and therapist expressivity: Trends in client-centered therapy with schizophrenics. In C. R. Rogers, B. Stevens et al. (Eds.), *Person to person: The problem of being human.* Lafayette, Calif.: Real People Press, 1967.

Gendlin, E. T. Experiential psychotherapy. In R. J. Corsini (Ed.), *Current psychotherapies* (2d ed.). Itasca, Ill.: F. E. Peacock Publishers, 1979.

Gibb, J. R., & Gibb, L. M. Humanistic elements in group growth. In J. F. T. Bugental (Ed.), *Challenges of humanistic psychology.* New York: McGraw-Hill, 1967.

Giorgi, A. *Psychology as a human science: A phenomenologically based approach.* New York: Harper & Row, 1970.

Giorgi, A.; Fischer, W. F.; & Von Eckartsberg, R. (Eds.). *Duquesne studies in phenomenological psychology.* Pittsburgh: Duquesne University Press, 1971–.

Glasser, W. *Reality therapy.* New York: Harper & Row, 1965.

Glasser, W. *Schools without failure.* New York: Harper & Row, 1969.

Goldstein, K. *The organism: A holistic approach to biology derived from pathological data in man.* New York: American Book, 1939.

Goldstein, K. *Human nature in the light of psychopathology.* Cambridge, Mass.: Harvard University Press, 1940.

Gordon, T. *P.E.T.: Parent effectiveness training.* New York: Peter H. Wyden, 1970.

Grof, S. The use of LSD in psychotherapy. *Journal of Psychedelic Drugs,* 1970, 3, 52–62.

Guerin, P. J. (Ed.). *Family therapy: Theory and practice.* New York: Gardner Press, 1976.

Halkides, G. *An experimental study of four conditions necessary for therapeutic personality change.* Unpublished doctoral dissertation, University of Chicago, 1958.

Hall, C. S., & Lindzey, G. *Theories of personality.* New York: John Wiley & Sons, 1957.

Hall, C. S., & Lindzey, G. *Theories of personality* (2d ed.). New York: John Wiley & Sons, 1970.

Hampden-Turner, C. *Radical man.* Cambridge, Mass.: Schenkman, 1971.

Harman, W. W. Humanistic capitalism: Another alternative. In I. D. Welch; G. A. Tate; & F. Richards (Eds.), *Humanistic psychology: A source book.* Buffalo, N.Y.: Prometheus Books, 1978.

Hartman, R. The science of value. In A. H. Maslow (Ed.), *New knowledge in human values.* New York: Harper & Row, 1959.

Havighurst, R. J. *Developmental tasks and education* (2d ed.). New York: Longmans, 1952.

Heidegger, M. [*Being and time*] (J. Macquarrie & E. S. Robinson, Trans.). New York: Harper & Row, 1962.

Herrnstein, R. J. The evolution of behaviorism. *American Psychologist, 1977, 32,* 593–603. (a)

Herrnstein, R. J. Doing what comes naturally: A reply to Professor Skinner. *American Psychologist, 1977, 32,* 1013–1016. (b)

Hilgard, E. R. *Introduction to psychology* (3d ed.). New York: Harcourt, Brace & World, 1962.

Hilgard, E. R., & Bower, G. H. *Theories of learning* (3d ed.). New York: Appleton-Century-Crofts, 1966.

Hillman, J. *Re-visioning psychology.* New York: Harper & Row, 1975.

Horney, K. *The neurotic personality of our time.* New York: W. W. Norton, 1937.

Horney, K. *New ways in psychoanalysis.* New York: W. W. Norton, 1939.

Horney, K. *Self-analysis.* New York: W. W. Norton, 1942.

Horney, K. *Neurosis and human growth.* New York: W. W. Norton, 1950.

Howard, G. S. Response-shift bias: A problem in evaluating interventions with pre/post self-reports. *Evaluation Review,* 1980, 4, 93–106.

Howard, G. S. *Dare we develop a human science?* Unpublished paper, University of Houston, 1981.

Howard G. S., & Dailey, P. J. Response-shift bias: A source of contamination of self-report measures. *Journal of Applied Psychology,* 1979, 64, 144–150.

Howard, G. S.; Dailey, P. J.; & Gulanick, N. A. The feasibility of informed pretests in attenuating response-shift bias. *Applied Psychological Measurement,* 1979, 3, 481–494.

Howard, G. S.; Maxwell, S. E.; Weiner, R.;

Boynton, K.; & Rooney, W. Is a behavioral measure the best estimate of behavioral parameters? Perhaps not. *Applied Psychological Measurement,* 1980, 4, 340–351.

Howard, G. S.; Millham, J.; Slaten, S.; & O'Donnell, L. Influence of subject response-style effects on retrospective measures. *Applied Psychological Measurement* (in press).

Howard, G. S.; Ralph, K. M.; Gulanick, N. A.; Nance, D. W.; & Gerber, S. K. Internal validity in pretest-posttest self-report evaluations and a re-evaluation of retrospective pretests. *Applied Psychological Measurement,* 1979, 3, 1–23.

Howard, G. S.; Schmeck, R. R.; & Bray, J. H. Internal invalidity in studies employing self-report instruments: A suggested remedy. *Journal of Educational Measurement,* 1979, 16, 129–135.

Howe, E. G. *Motives and mechanism of the mind: An introduction to psychopathology and applied psychology.* London: Lancet, 1931.

Hull, C. L. *Principles of behavior.* New York: Appleton-Century-Crofts, 1943.

Hull, C. L. *A behavior system: An introduction to behavior theory concerning the individual organism.* New Haven, Conn.: Yale University Press, 1952.

Husserl, E. [*Ideas: General introduction to pure phenomenology*] (W. R. Boyce Gibson, Trans.). New York: Macmillan, 1931.

*International encyclopedia of unified science* (2 vols.). O. Neurath; C. Carnap; & C. Morris (Eds.). Chicago: University of Chicago Press, 1970.

Jackson, D. (Ed.). *Therapy, communication and change.* Palo Alto, Calif.: Science & Behavior Books, 1968.

James, W. *The varieties of religious experience: A study in human nature.* New York: Modern Library, 1929.

Jaspers, K. *Allgemeine psychopathologie.* Berlin: Springer, 1913.

Jaspers, K. [*General psychopathology*] (J. Hoenig & M. W. Hamilton, Trans.). Chicago: University of Chicago Press, 1963.

Jourard, S. M. *Personal adjustment: An approach through the study of healthy personality.* New York: Macmillan, 1958.

Jourard, S. M. Experimenter-subject dialogue: A paradigm for a humanistic science of psychology. In J. F. T. Bugental (Ed.), *Challenges of humanistic psychology.* New York: McGraw-Hill, 1967.

Jourard, S. M. *Disclosing man to himself.* New York: D. Van Nostrand, 1968.

Jourard, S. M. *The transparent self: Self-disclosure and well-being* (Rev. ed.). New York: D. Van Nostrand, 1971. (a) Copyright © 1971 by Van Nostrand Reinhold Company. Reprinted by permission.

Jourard, S. M. *Self-disclosure: An experimental analysis of the transparent self.* New York: John Wiley & Sons, 1971. (b)

Jourard, S. M. Marriage is for life. In I. D. Welch; G. A. Tate; & F. Richards (Eds.), *Humanistic psychology: A source book.* Buffalo, N.Y.: Prometheus Books, 1978.

Jourard, S. M., & Landsman, T. *Healthy personality: An approach from the viewpoint of humanistic psychology* (Rev. ed.). New York: Macmillan, 1980.

Jung, C. G. [*Modern man in search of a soul*] (R. F. C. Hull, Trans.). New York: Harcourt, Brace Jovanovich, 1933.

Jung, C. G. Answer to Job. In *Psychology and religion: West and east* (Collected Works, Vol. 11). Princeton, N.J.: Princeton University Press, 1958. (Originally published, 1952.)

Jung, C. G. *The archetypes and the collective unconscious* (Collected Works, Vol. 9). Princeton, N.J.: Princeton University Press, 1959. (Originally published, 1940.)

Kaplan, B. (Ed.). *The inner world of mental illness.* New York: Harper & Row, 1964.

Kaplan, H. S. *The new sex therapy: Active treatment of sexual dysfunctions.* New York: Brunner/Mazel, 1974.

Kasamatsu, A., & Hirai, T. An electroencephalographic study of the Zen meditation (zazen). *Folio Psychiatrica Neurologica Japonica,* 1966, *20,* 315-336. Reprinted in C. Tart (Ed.), *Altered states of consciousness.* New York: John Wiley & Sons, 1969.

Kaufmann, Y. Analytical psychotherapy. In R. J. Corsini (Ed.), *Current psychotherapies.* Itasca, Ill.: F. E. Peacock, Publishers, 1979.

Keen, E. *A primer in phenomenological psychology.* New York: Holt, Rinehart & Winston, 1975.

Kelly, G. A. *The psychology of personal constructs: A theory of personality* (2 vols.). New York: W. W. Norton, 1955.

Kelly, J. *Organizational behaviour: An existential-systems approach* (Rev. ed.). Homewood, Ill.: Richard D. Irwin, 1974.

Kelsey, M. T. *Encounter with God.* Minneapolis, Minn.: Bethany Fellowship, 1972.

Kelsey, M. T. *The other side of silence: A guide to Christian meditation.* New York: Paulist Press, 1976.

Kempler, W. Gestalt therapy. In R. J. Corsini (Ed.), *Current psychotherapies.* Itasca, Ill.: F. E. Peacock Publishers, 1973. Excerpted material reproduced by permission of the publisher, F. E. Peacock, Inc., Itasca, Illinois.

Kenny, D. A. *Correlation and causality.* New York: John Wiley & Sons, 1979.

Kinget, G. M. *On being human: A systematic view.* New York: Harcourt Brace Jovanovich, 1975.

Kirsch, R. A man who listens to—and learns from—children. In *West View, Los Angeles Times*, February 26, 1978, p. 11.

Koch, S. Psychology and emerging conceptions of knowledge as unitary. In T. W. Wann (Ed.), *Behaviorism and phenomenology: Contrasting bases for modern psychology*. Chicago: University of Chicago Press, 1964.

Koch, S. (Ed.). *Psychology: A study of a science* (Vol. 3; *Formulations of the person and the social context*). New York: McGraw-Hill, 1959.

Kolton, M. The humanistic treatment philosophy of innovative drug programs. *Journal of Humanistic Psychology*, 1973, *13*(4), 47–56.

Krasner, L. The future and the past in the behaviorism-humanism dialogue. *American Psychologist*, 1978, *33*, 799–804.

Krippner, S. Altered states of consciousness. In J. White (Ed.), *The highest state of consciousness*. New York: Doubleday, 1972.

Kruglanski, A. W. On the paradigmatic objections to experimental psychology. *American Psychologist*, 1976, *31*, 655–663.

Kuhn, T. S. *The structure of scientific revolutions*. Chicago: Univeristy of Chicago Press, 1962.

Kuhn, T. S. *The structure of scientific revolutions* (2d ed. enl.). Chicago: University of Chicago Press, 1970.

Laing, R. D., & Esterson, A. *Sanity, madness and the family*. London: Tavistock Publications, 1964.

Laing, R. D. *The politics of experience*. New York: Pantheon Books, 1967.

Latner, J. *The Gestalt therapy book*. New York: Julian Press, 1973.

LaValle, M. Gestalt: The process of being. Unpublished paper, University of Notre Dame, 1977.

Lawson, C. A., & Tageson, C. W. Quality education: A view from the top. *Notre Dame Journal of Education*, 1971, *2*, 221–232.

Lazarus, A. (Ed.). *Multimodal behavior therapy*. New York: Springer, 1976.

Leavitt, H. J. Applied organizational change in industry. In J. G. March (Ed.), *Handbook of organizations*. Chicago: Rand McNally, 1965.

Lecky, P. *Self-consistency: A theory of personality*. New York: Island Press, 1945.

Leonard, G. B. *Education and ecstasy*. New York: Delacorte Press, 1968.

Lewin, K. [*A dynamic theory of personality: Selected papers*] (D. K. Adams & K. E. Zener, Trans.). New York: McGraw-Hill, 1935.

Lewin, K. *Principles of topological psychology*. New York: McGraw-Hill, 1936.

Lowen, A. *Physical dynamics of character structure*. New York: Grune & Stratton, 1958.

Lowen, A. *Love and orgasm*. New York: Macmillan, 1965.

Lowen, A. *The betrayal of the body*. New York: Collier, 1967.

Lowen, A. *Pleasure: A creative approach to life*. New York: Coward, McCann, 1970.

Lowen, A. *The language of the body*. New York: Collier, 1971.

Lowen, A. *Depression and the body: The biological basis of faith and reality*. New York: Coward, McCann, 1972.

Lowen, A. The body in personality theory: Wilhelm Reich and Alexander Lowen. In A. Burton (Ed.), *Operational theories of personality*. New York: Brunner/Mazel, 1974.

Maddi, S. R. The existential neurosis. *Journal of Abnormal Psychology*, 1967, *72*, 311–325.

Maddi, S. R. *Personality theories: A com-*

parative analysis. Homewood, Ill.: Dorsey Press, 1968.

Maddi, S. R. Personality theories: A comparative analysis (4th ed.). Homewood, Ill.: Dorsey Press, 1980.

Mann, J. H. Human potential. In R. J. Corsini (Ed.), Current psychotherapies (2d ed.). Itasca, Ill.: F. E. Peacock Publishers, 1979.

Marcel, G. [Homo viator: Introduction to a metaphysic of hope] (E. Craufurd, Trans.). Chicago: Henry Regnery, 1951.

Maslow, A. H. A theory of human motivation. Psychological Review, 1943, 50, 370–396.

Maslow, A. Motivation and personality. New York: Harper & Row, 1954.

Maslow, A. H. Religions, values, and peak-experiences. Columbus, Ohio: Ohio State University Press, 1964.

Maslow, A. H. The psychology of science: A reconnaissance. Chicago: Henry Regnery, 1966.

Maslow, A. H. Eupsychian management: A journal. Homewood, Ill.: Irwin-Dorsey, 1965. Japanese translation, Tokyo: Charles E. Tuttle Co., 1967.

Maslow, A. H. Toward a psychology of being (2d ed.). Princeton, N.J.: D. Van Nostrand, 1968.

Maslow, A. H. Comments on Dr. Frankl's paper. In A. J. Sutich & M. A. Vich (Eds.), Readings in humanistic psychology. New York: Free Press, 1969.

Maslow, A. H. Motivation and personality (Rev. ed.). New York: Harper & Row, 1970.

Maslow, A. H. The farther reaches of human nature. New York: Viking Press, 1971.

Matson, F. W. Humanistic political science: And humane politics. In I. D. Welch; G. A. Tate; & F. Richards (Eds.), Humanistic psychology: A source book. Buffalo, N. Y.: Prometheus Books, 1978.

Matson, F. W. Humanistic theory: The third revolution in psychology. In I. D. Welch; G. A. Tate; & F. Richards (Eds.), Humanistic psychology: A source book. Buffalo, N. Y.: Prometheus Books, 1978.

May, R. (Ed.). Existential psychology. New York: Random House, 1961.

May, R. Intentionality: The heart of human will. Journal of Humanistic Psychology, 1965, 5, 202-209.

May, R. Love and will. New York: W. W. Norton, 1969.

May, R.; Angel, E.; & Ellenberger, H. F. (Eds.). Existence: A new dimension in psychiatry and psychology. New York: Basic Books, 1958. Copyright © 1978 by Basic Books, Inc. By permission of Basic Books, Inc., Publishers, New York.

McCabe, S. P. Organizational functioning and effective humanistic education. Counseling and Values, 1973, 17, 97–104.

McCormick, P. TA and behavior modification: A comparison study. Transactional Analysis Journal, 1973, 3(2), 10–14.

McFarland, K. K. The influence of reinforcement value and school achievement on a "pictorial-verbal" learning task. Unpublished master's thesis, St. Louis University, 1969.

McGregor, D. M. The human side of enterprise. New York: McGraw-Hill, 1960.

McWaters, B. (Ed.). Humanistic perspectives: Current trends in psychology. Monterey, Calif.: Brooks/Cole Publishing, 1977.

Mead, G. H. Mind, self, and society. Chicago: University of Chicago Press, 1934.

Meador, B. D. Individual process in a basic encounter group. Journal of Counseling Psychology, 1971, 18, 70–76.

Meador, B. D., & Rogers, C. R. Client-centered therapy. In R. J. Corsini (Ed.), Current psychotherapies. Itasca, Ill.: F. E. Peacock Publishers, 1973.

Meador, B. D., & Rogers, C. R. Person-centered therapy. In R. J. Corsini (Ed.), Current psychotherapies (2d ed.). Itasca, Ill.: F. E. Peacock Publishers, 1979.

Meier, A. Frankl's will to meaning as measured by the Purpose-in-Life-Test in relation to age and sex differences. Unpublished dissertation, University of Ottawa, 1973.

Menninger, K. Man against himself. New York: Harcourt Brace Jovanovich, 1938.

Menninger, K. Toward a unitary concept of mental illness. In B. H. Hall (Ed.), A psychiatrist's world. New York: Viking Press, 1959.

Metzer, H., & Wickert, F. R. (Eds.). Humanizing organizational behavior. Springfield, Ill.: Charles C Thomas, 1976.

Miller, J. G. Unconsciousness. New York: John Wiley & Sons, 1942.

Miller, S. A new humanism in medicine. In I. D. Welch; G. A. Tate; & F. Richards (Eds.), Humanistic psychology: A source book. Buffalo, N.Y.: Prometheus Books, 1978.

Miller, S.; Nunnally, E. W.; & Wackman, D. B. A communication training program for couples. Social Casework, 1976, 57(1), 9–18.

Miller, S.; Nunnally, E. W.; & Wackman, D. B. Alive and aware. Minneapolis, Minn.: Interpersonal Communication Programs, 1978.

Minkowski, E. La schizophrenie. Paris: Payot, 1927.

Minkowski, E. Le temps vecu. Paris: d'Artrey, 1933.

Misiak, H., & Sexton, V. S. Phenomenological, existential, and humanistic psychologies: A historical survey. New York: Grune & Stratton, 1973.

Mosak, H. H. Adlerian psychotherapy. In R. J. Corsini (Ed.), Current psychothera-

pies (2d ed.). Itasca, Ill.: F. E. Peacock Publishers, 1979.

Mosak, H. H., & Dreikurs, R. Adlerian psychotherapy. In R. J. Corsini (Ed.), Current psychotherapies. Itasca, Ill.: F. E. Peacock Publishers, 1973.

Mosher, R. L., & Sprinthall, N. A. Psychological education: A means to promote personal development during adolescence. The Counseling Psychologist, 1971, 3(4), 3–82.

Moustakas, C. E. Children in play therapy. New York: J. Aronson, 1973.

Mowrer, O. H., & Kluckhohn, C. A dynamic theory of personality. In J. McV. Hunt (Ed.), Personality and the behavior disorders (Vol. 1). New York: Ronald Press, 1944.

Murphy, G., & Murphy, L. Asian psychology. New York: Basic Books, 1968.

Murphy, L. Extent of Purpose-in-Life and four Frankl-proposed life objectives. Unpublished dissertation, University of Ottawa, 1967.

Murray, H. A. Explorations in personality: A clinical and experimental study of fifty men of college age. New York: Oxford University Press, 1938.

Neimeyer, G. J.; Banikiotes, P. G.; & Ianni, L. E. Self-disclosure and psychological construing: A personal construct approach to interpersonal perception. Social Behavior and Personality, 1979, 7, 161–165.

Neimeyer, G. J. Personal construct systems in the development and deterioration of interpersonal relationships. Unpublished paper, University of Notre Dame, 1980.

Nevill, D. D. Feminism and humanism. In D. D. Nevill (Ed.), Humanistic psychology: New frontiers. New York: Gardner Press, 1977. (a)

Nevill, D. D. (Ed.). Humanistic psychology: New frontiers. New York: Gardner Press, 1977. (b)

Nuttin, J. [Psychoanalysis and personality: A dynamic theory of normal personality] (Rev. ed., G. Lamb, Trans.). New York: Sheed & Ward, 1962. Copyright © 1953, renewed 1981, by Sheed and Ward, Inc. Reprinted with permission of Andrews and McMeel, Inc.

Orne, M. T. On the social psychology of the psychological experiment: With particular reference to demand characteristics and their implications. American Psychologist, 1962, 17, 776–783.

Ornstein, R. E. The psychology of consciousness. New York: Viking Press, 1972.

Ornstein, R. E. (Ed.) The nature of human consciousness: A book of readings. New York: Viking Press, 1973.

Osgood, C. E.; Suci, G. J.; & Tannenbaum, P. H. The measurement of meaning. Urbana, Ill.: University of Illinois Press, 1957.

Owens, C. M. Zen buddhism. In C. Tart (Ed.), Transpersonal psychologies. New York: Harper & Row, 1975.

Pahnke, W. N., & Richards, W. A. Implications of LSD and experimental mysticism. Journal of Religion and Health, 1966, 5, 175–208.

Parsons, T., & Bales, R. F. Family, socialization, and interaction process. New York: Free Press, 1955.

Pelletier, K. R., & Garfield, C. Consciousness: East and West. New York: Harper & Row, 1976.

Perls, F. Gestalt therapy verbatim. Lafayette, Calif.: Real People Press, 1969. (a)

Perls, F. In and out of the garbage pail. Lafayette, Calif.: Real People Press, 1969. (b)

Perls, F. The Gestalt approach and eyewitness to therapy. Palo Alto, Calif.: Science & Behavior Books, 1973.

Perls, F.; Hefferline, R. F.; & Goodman, P. Gestalt therapy: Excitement and growth in the human personality. New York: Julian Press, 1951.

Perry, J. W. The far side of madness. Englewood Cliffs, N.J.: Prentice-Hall, 1974.

Perry, J. W. Roots of renewal in myth and madness. San Francisco: Jossey-Bass, 1976.

Perry, W. Conjectures on sociality. In F. Fransella (Ed.), Personal construct psychology. New York: Academic Press, 1978.

Plutchik, R. Foundations of experimental research. New York: Harper & Row, 1968.

Polanyi, M. Personal knowledge. Chicago: University of Chicago Press, 1958.

Pope, K. S., & Singer, J. L. (Eds.). The stream of consciousness. New York: Plenum Press, 1978.

Porter, E. H., Jr. An introduction to therapeutic counseling. Boston: Houghton Mifflin, 1950.

Price, D. D., & Barrell, J. J. An experiential approach with quantitative methods: A research paradigm. Journal of Humanistic Psychology, 1980, 20(3), 75–95.

Rank, O. Will therapy. New York: Alfred A. Knopf, 1936.

Rank, O. [Will therapy and truth and reality] (J. Taft, Trans.). New York, Alfred A. Knopf, 1945.

Rave, E. Humanistic psychology and white racism. In I. D. Welch; G. A. Tate; & F. Richards (Eds.), Humanistic psychology: A source book. Buffalo, N.Y.: Prometheus Books, 1978.

Rawlings, G. B. B. (Ed.). Pensées of Pascal. New York: Peter Pauper Press, 1946.

Reich, W. The function of the orgasm. New York: Orgone Institute Press, 1944.

Reich, W. Character analysis. London: Vision Press, 1948.

Richards, R., & Welch, I. D. Sightings: Essays in humanistic psychology. Boulder, Colo.: Shields Publishing, 1973.

Ricks, D. F.; Wandersman, A.; & Poppen,

P. J. Humanism and behaviorism: Toward new syntheses. In A. Wandersman; P. J. Poppen; & D. F. Ricks (Eds.), *Humanism and behaviorism: Dialogue and growth.* New York: Pergamon Press, 1976.

Roazen, P. *Freud and his followers.* New York: Alfred A. Knopf, 1974.

Rioch, M., et al. *NIMH pilot project in training mental health counselors: Summary of first year's work.* Unpublished paper, NIMH Adult Psychiatry Branch, Washington, D.C., 1960.

Rogers, C. R. *Counseling and psychotherapy.* Boston: Houghton Mifflin, 1942.

Rogers, C. R. Divergent trends in methods of improving adjustment. *Harvard Educational Review,* 1948, *18,* 209–219.

Rogers, C. R. *Client-centered therapy.* Boston: Houghton Mifflin, 1951.

Rogers, C. R. The necessary and sufficient conditions of therapeutic personality change. *Journal of Consulting Psychology,* 1957, *21,* 95–103.

Rogers, C. R. A theory of therapy, personality, and interpersonal relationships, as developed in the client-centered framework. In S. Koch (Ed.), *Psychology: A study of a science* (Vol. 3, Formulations of the person and the social context). New York: McGraw-Hill, 1959.

Rogers, C. R. The process equation of psychotherapy. *American Journal of Psychotherapy,* 1961, *15*(1), 27–45. (a)

Rogers, C. R. *On becoming a person.* Boston: Houghton Mifflin, 1961. (b)

Rogers, C. R. The concept of the fully functioning person. *Psychotherapy: Theory, Research, and Practice,* 1963, *1*(1), 17–26.

Rogers, C. R. Toward a science of the person. In T. W. Wann (Ed.), *Behaviorism and phenomenology: Contrasting bases for modern psychology.* Chicago: University of Chicago Press, 1964.

Rogers, C. R. *Freedom to learn.* Columbus, Ohio: Charles E. Merrill Publishing, 1969.

Rogers, C. R. *Carl Rogers on encounter groups.* New York: Harper & Row, 1970.

Rogers, C. R. *Becoming partners: Marriage and its alternatives.* New York: Delacorte Press, 1972.

Rogers, C. R. *Carl Rogers on personal power.* New York: Delacorte Press, 1977. Copyright © 1977 by Carl Rogers. Reprinted by permission of Delacorte Press.

Rogers, C. R. *A way of being.* Boston: Houghton Mifflin, 1980.

Rogers, C. R., & Dymond, R. F. (Eds.). *Psychotherapy and personality change.* Chicago: University of Chicago Press, 1954.

Rogers, C. R.; Gendlin, E. T.; Kiesler, D. J.; & Truax, C. (Eds.). *The therapeutic relationship and its impact: A study of psychotherapy with schizophrenics.* Madison, Wis.: University of Wisconsin Press, 1967.

Rogers, C. R., & Rablen, R. A. *A scale of process in psychotherapy.* Unpublished manuscript, Center for Studies of the Person, La Jolla, Calif., 1958.

Rogers, C. R., Stevens, B., et al. *Person to person: The problem of being human.* Lafayette, Calif.: Real People Press, 1967.

Rogers, C. R., & Wood, J. K. Client-centered theory: Carl R. Rogers. In A. Burton (Ed.), *Operational theories of personality.* New York: Brunner/Mazel, 1974.

Rome, B., & Rome, S. Humanistic research on large social organizations. In J. F. T. Bugental (Ed.), *Challenges of humanistic psychology.* New York: McGraw-Hill, 1967.

Rosenthal, R. On the social psychology of the psychological experiment. *American Scientist,* 1963, *51,* 268–283.

Rosenthal, R. *Experimenter effects in behavioral research.* New York: Appleton-Century-Crofts, 1966.

Rosenthal, R., & Jacobson, L. *Pygmalion in the classroom.* New York: Holt, Rinehart & Winston, 1968.

Rossi, E. L. Game and growth: The dimensions of our psychotherapeutic zeitgeist. In A. J. Sutich & M. A. Vich (Eds.), *Readings in humanistic psychology.* New York: Free Press, 1969.

Rolf, I. *Structural integration.* New York: Viking Press, 1972.

Rychlak, J. F. Reinforcement value: A suggested idiographic, intensity dimension of meaningfulness for the personality theorist. *Journal of Personality,* 1966, *34,* 311–335.

Rychlak, J. F. *A philosophy of science for personality theory.* Boston: Houghton Mifflin, 1968.

Rychlak, J. F. Is a concept of "self" necessary in psychological theory, and if so why? A humanistic perspective. In A. Wandersman; P. Poppen; & D. Ricks (Eds.), *Humanism and behaviorism: Dialogue and growth.* New York: Pergamon Press, 1976. Reprinted by permission.

Rychlak, J. F. *The psychology of rigorous humanism.* New York: Wiley-Interscience, 1977.

Rychlak, J. F. *Discovering free will and personal responsibility.* New York: Oxford University Press, 1979.

Rychlak, J. F. Concepts of free will in modern psychological science. *The Journal of Mind and Behavior,* 1980, *1,* 9–32.

Rychlak, J. F.; Carlson, N. L.; & Dunning, L. P. Personal adjustment and the free recall of materials with affectively positive or negative meaningfulness. *Journal of Abnormal Psychology,* 1974, *83,* 480-487.

Rychlak, J. F.; McKee, D. B.; Schneider, W. E.; & Abramson, Y. Affective evaluation in the verbal learning styles of normals and abnormals. *Journal of Abnormal Psychology,* 1971, *77,* 11–16.

Rychlak, J. F., & Tobin, T. J. Order effects in the affective learning styles of overachievers and underachievers. *Journal of Educational Psychology,* 1971, *62,* 141–147.

Salmon, P. A psychology of personal growth. In D. Bannister (Ed.), *Perspectives in personal construct theory.* New York: Academic Press, 1970.

Sarbin, T., & Adler, N. Commonalities in systems of conduct reorganization. Paper presented at the California State Psychological Association, San Diego, January 1967.

Sartre, J. P. [*No exit*] (S. Gilbert, Trans.). New York: Alfred A. Knopf, 1947.

Satir, V. *Conjoint family therapy.* Palo Alto, Calif.: Science & Behavior Books, 1964.

Satir, V. *Peoplemaking.* Palo Alto, Calif.: Science & Behavior Books, 1972.

Schein, E. H. *Organizational psychology* (3d ed.). Englewood Cliffs, N.J.: Prentice-Hall, 1980.

Schmale, A. H. Relation of separation and depression to disease. *Psychosomatic Medicine,* 1958, *20,* 259–277.

Schmuck, R. A., & Miles, M. B. (Eds.). *Organization development in schools.* Palo Alto, Calif.: National Press Books, 1971.

Schmuck, R. A., & Schmuck, P. A. *A humanistic psychology of education.* Palo Alto, Calif.: National Press Books, 1974.

Schultz, D. *Growth psychology: Models of the healthy personality.* New York: D. Van Nostrand, 1977.

Schutz, W. C. *Joy.* New York: Grove Press, 1967.

Schutz, W. C. *Here comes everybody.* New York: Harper & Row, 1971.

Schutz, W. C. Encounter. In R. J. Corsini (Ed.), *Current psychotherapies.* Itasca, Ill.: F. E. Peacock, Publishers, 1973.

Sciortino, P. T., & Madden, D. Person-organization pairing. *Counseling and Values*, 1973, *17*, 118–125.

Seeman, J. A study of the process of non-directive therapy. *Journal of Consulting Psychology*, 1949, *13*, 157–168.

Severin, F. (Ed.). *Humanistic viewpoints in psychology*. New York: McGraw-Hill, 1965.

Shaffer, T. (Ed.). *Legal counseling handbook*. Notre Dame, Ind.: University of Notre Dame Press, 1971.

Shaffer, T. *Counselors at law*. Notre Dame, Ind.: University of Notre Dame Press, 1973.

Sih, P. (Ed.). *Tao Teh Ching*. New York: St. John's University Press, 1961.

Silverman, J. A paradigm for the study of altered states of consciousness. *British Journal of Psychiatry*, 1968, *114*, 1201–1218.

Silverman, J. When schizophrenia helps. *Psychology Today*, September, 1970, 63–65.

Simon, S. Synanon: Toward building a humanistic organization. *Journal of Humanistic Psychology*, 1978, *18*(3), 3–20.

Simpson, E. L. Humanistic psychology: An attempt to define human nature. In D. D. Nevill (Ed.), *Humanistic psychology: New frontiers*. New York: Gardner Press, 1977.

Skinner, B. F. *Walden Two*. New York: Macmillan, 1948.

Skinner, B. F. *Science and human behavior*. New York: Macmillan, 1953.

Skinner, B. F. *Beyond freedom and dignity*. New York: Alfred A. Knopf, 1971. Copyright © 1971 by Alfred A. Knopf, Inc. Reprinted by permission of Alfred A. Knopf, Inc.

Skinner, B. F. *About behaviorism*. New York: Alfred A. Knopf, 1974.

Skinner, B. F. Herrnstein and the evolution of behaviorism. *American Psychologist*, 1977, *32*, 1006–1012.

Smith, M. B. *Social psychology and human values*. Chicago: Aldine, 1969.

Smith, M. B. On self-actualization: A trans-ambivalent examination of a focal theme in Maslow's psychology. *Journal of Humanistic Psychology*, 1973, *13*(2), 17–33.

Smith, M. B. Perspectives on selfhood. *American Psychologist*, 1978, *33*, 1053–1063.

Snygg, D., & Combs, A. W. *Individual behavior: A new frame of reference for psychology*. New York: Harper & Brothers, 1949.

Sperry, R. W. Mental unity following surgical disconnection of the cerebral hemispheres. *The Harvey Lectures*, Series 62. New York: Academic Press, 1968.

Sperry, R. W.; Gazzaniga, M. A.; & Bogen, J. E. Interhemispheric relationships: The neocortical commissures—syndromes of hemispheric disconnection. *Handbook of clinical neurology* (Vol. 4). New York: John Wiley & Sons, 1969.

Sprinthall, N., & Mosher, R. Psychological education in secondary schools. *American Psychologist*, 1970, *25*, 911–924.

Stephenson, W. *The study of behavior: Q-technique and its methodology*. Chicago: University of Chicago Press, 1953.

Sullivan, H. S. *Conceptions of modern psychiatry*. Washington, D.C.: W. A. White Foundation, 1945.

Sutich, A. J. Statement of purpose. *Journal of Transpersonal Psychology*, 1969, *1*.

Sutich, A. J. The growth-experience and the growth-centered attitude. In A. J. Sutich & M. A. Vich (Eds.), *Readings in humanistic psychology*. New York: Free Press, 1969.

Sutich, A. J., & Vich, M. (Eds.). *Readings in humanistic psychology*. New York: Free Press, 1969.

Szasz, T. S. *Law, liberty, and psychiatry*. New York: Macmillan, 1963.

Tageson, C. W. *The relationship of self-perceptions to realism of vocational choice.* Washington, D.C.: Catholic University Press, 1960.

Tageson, C. W. Our split-level personalities. *Way,* 1963, *19*(2), 38–45.

Tageson, C. W. The problem of personal freedom in contemporary psychology. *Notre Dame Journal of Education,* 1971, *2*(2), 123–131.

Tageson, C. W. Humanistic education. *Counseling and Values,* 1973, *17*(2), 90–97.

Tageson, C. W., & Corazzini, J. G. A collaborative model for consultation and paraprofessional development. *Professional Psychology,* 1974, *5*, 191–197. (a)

Tageson, C. W., & Corazzini, J. G. The paraprofessional in the minority community. *Counseling and Values,* 1974, *18*(3), 193–198. (b)

Tageson, C. W.; Koval, J.; & Bartlett, W. *Study of church vocations.* Detroit: National Center for Church Vocations, 1974.

Tart, C. (Ed.). *Altered states of consciousness: A book of readings.* New York: John Wiley & Sons, 1969.

Tart, C. States of consciousness and state-specific sciences. *Science,* 1972, *176*, 1203–1210.

Tart, C. (Ed.). *Transpersonal psychologies.* New York: Harper & Row, 1975.

Tate, G. A. The healthy personality and the black experience. In I. D. Welch; G. A. Tate; & F. Richards (Eds.), *Humanistic psychology: A source book.* Buffalo, N.Y.: Prometheus Books, 1978. (a)

Tate, G. A. Humanistic psychology and black psychology: A study of parallels. In I. D. Welch; G. A. Tate; & F. Richards (Eds.), *Humanistic psychology: A source book.* Buffalo, N.Y.: Prometheus Books, 1978. (b)

Teilhard de Chardin, P. *The divine milieu.* New York: Harper & Brothers, 1960.

Teilhard de Chardin, P. *The phenomenon of man* (2d ed.). New York: Harper & Row, 1965.

Tiger, L., & Fox, R. *The imperial animal.* New York: Dell, 1974.

Tillich, P. *The courage to be.* New Haven, Conn.: Yale University Press, 1952.

Tolman, E. C. *Purposive behavior in animals and man.* New York: Appleton-Century, 1932.

Tolman, E. C. Cognitive maps in rats and men. *Psychological Review,* 1948, *55*, 189–208.

Tomlinson, T. M. *Three approaches to the study of psychotherapy: Process, outcome, and change.* Unpublished doctoral dissertation, University of Wisconsin, 1962. (a)

Tomlinson, T. M., & Hart, J. T., Jr. A validation study of the process scale. *Journal of Consulting Psychology,* 1962, *26*, 74–78. (b)

Torrey, E. F. *The death of psychiatry.* Radnor, Pa.: Chilton Book Company, 1974.

Tournier, P. *The meaning of persons.* New York: Harper & Brothers, 1957.

Truax, C. B., & Mitchell, K. M. Research on certain therapist interpersonal skills in relation to process and outcome. In A. E. Bergin & S. L. Garfield (Eds.), *Handbook of psychotherapy and behavior change.* New York: John Wiley & Sons, 1971.

Valle, R. S., & King, M. (Eds.). *Existential-phenomenological alternatives for psychology.* New York: Oxford University Press, 1978.

van den Berg, J. H. *A different existence.* Pittsburgh: Duquesne University Press, 1972.

van den Berg, J. H. *Divided existence and complex society.* Pittsburgh: Duquesne University Press, 1974.

Van der Veen, F. Client perception of therapist conditions as a factor in psychotherapy. In J. T. Hart & T. M. Tomlinson (Eds.), *New directions in client-centered therapy.* Boston: Houghton Mifflin, 1970.

van Kaam, A. *Existential foundations of psychology.* Pittsburgh: Duquesne University Press, 1966.

van Steenberghen, F. [*Epistemology*] (L. Noonan, Trans.). New York: J. F. Wagner, 1970.

Walker, A. M.; Rablen, R. A.; & Rogers, C. R. Development of a scale to measure process changes in psychotherapy. *Journal of Clinical Psychology,* 1960, 16, 79–85.

Wallace, R. K., & Benson, H. The physiology of meditation. *Scientific American,* February 1972, 85–90.

Wann, T. W. (Ed.). *Behaviorism and phenomenology: Contrasting bases for modern psychology.* Chicago: University of Chicago Press, 1964.

Watson, J. B. *Behaviorism.* New York: W. W. Norton, 1925.

Watts, A. *Psychotherapy East and West.* New York: Pantheon Books, 1961. Copyright © 1975 by Pantheon Books, a division of Random House, Inc.

Weil, A. The natural mind. *Psychology Today,* October 1972, 51–97.

Weisbrod, M.; Lamb, H.; & Drexler, A. *Improving police department management through problem-solving task forces: A case study in organization development.* Reading, Mass.: Addison-Wesley Publishing, 1974.

Welch, I. D.; Tate, G. A.; & Richards, F. (Eds.). *Humanistic psychology: A source book.* Buffalo, N.Y.: Prometheus Books, 1978.

Wells, T. Psychology of woman. In B. McWaters (Ed.), *Humanistic perspectives: Current trends in psychology.*

Monterey, Calif.: Brooks/Cole Publishing, 1977.

Wexberg, E. *Individual psychology.* London: Allen & Unwin, 1929.

Whitaker, C. The hindrance of theory in clinical work. In P. Guerin (Ed.), *Family therapy: Theory and practice.* New York: Gardner Press, 1976.

White, J. *The highest state of consciousness.* New York: Doubleday, 1972.

Whitehead, A. N. *Science and the modern world.* New York: Macmillan, 1948.

Wilhelm, R. [*The I ching; or, Book of changes*] (3d ed.; C. F. Baynes, Trans.). Princeton, N.J.: Princeton University Press, 1967.

Williams, R. J. The biological approach to the study of personality. In T. Millon (Ed.), *Theories of psychopathology and personality: Essays and critiques* (2d ed.). Philadelphia: W. B. Saunders, 1973.

Wilson, E. O. *Sociobiology.* Cambridge, Mass.: Harvard University Press, 1975.

Wolfe, T. *Mauve gloves and madmen, clutter and vine.* New York: Farrar, Straus & Giroux, 1976.

Wolfe, W. B. *How to be happy though human.* London: Routledge & Kegan Paul, 1932.

Woolpert, S. Humanizing law enforcement: A new paradigm. *Journal of Humanistic Psychology,* 1980, 20(4), 67–81.

Wylie, R. C. *The self-concept* (Rev. ed.; Vol. 1). Lincoln: University of Nebraska Press, 1974.

Yalom, I. D. *Existential psychotherapy.* New York: Basic Books, 1980.

Yankelovich, D. New rules in American life: Searching for self-fulfillment in a world turned upside down. *Psychology Today,* April 1981, 35–91.

Yarnell, T. D. Purpose-in-Life-Test: Further correlates. *Journal of Individual Psychology*, 1971, *27*, 76–79.

Zavalloni, R. [*Self-determination: The psychology of personal freedom*] (V. Biasiol & C. W. Tageson, Trans.). Chicago: Forum Books, 1962.

Zilboorg, G. *Mind, medicine, and man.* New York: Harcourt, Brace, 1943.

Zimbardo, P. G. *The cognitive control of motivation.* Glenview, Ill.: Scott, Foresman, 1969.

Zurcher, J. Team management/team policing. *Police Chief*, 1971, *38*, 54–56.

# Index

## A

Act psychology, 54
Actor, person as, 18–19
Adler, Alfred, 8, 9, 24, 135, 139, 168, 182
  creative self, 151, 152–53, 182
  finalism, 116
Affective assessment, 66–69
Affective matrix, 337–39
*Agape*, 47–48, 151
Ageism, 246
Aggression, 79, 82–83, 109, 149–50
Allen, Frederick, 218
Allers, Rudolf, 145
Allport, Gordon, 33, 61, 82, 86–87, 88, 114
Alpha waves, 103
Altered states of consciousness, 12–16, 48,
    103, 142
  classification, 198–200
  defined, 14–15
  meditative, 202–4
  psychedelic, 199, 201
  psychotic, 200–201
  Rogers on, 191
Amplification, 253
Anderson, Walt, 247–48
Anxiety, and self-actualization, 122, 154
Aquinas, Thomas, 29, 124
Archetypes, 13, 154, 252–54
Aristotle, 29, 132
  teleology, 108, 110–11, 116, 119, 136, 142
*Asian Psychology* (Murphy and Murphy),
    15–16
Assagioli, Roberto, 14, 48, 99–100
Assistant ego, 219
Association for Humanistic Psychology, 93
Augustine, 29
Authenticity, 42–44, 142, 146–47, 157; *see
    also* Health, psychological *and* Self-
    actualization
  theories
    Frankl, 43, 160, 163, 167–71
    Gestalt school, 172–78, 182

Authenticity—*Cont.*
  theories—*Cont.*
    Maslow, 164–67, 182
    Nuttin, 157–61, 172, 182
    Rogers, 178–82
Autonomy; *see* Self-determination

## B

B-cognition, 159–60, 165–67, 189–90, 202
B-values, 47, 159–60, 165–67, 169, 189–90
Bakan, David, 90
Bandura, Albert, 109, 131
Barker, Edwin, 225–26
Barrell, J. J., 255
Baruk, Henri, 11
Beck, Aaron, 255
Becker, Ernest, 120, 205–7
Becoming, human state as, 121–22, 142
*Becoming Partners: Marriage and its Alterna-
    tives* (Rogers), 244–45
Behaviorism, 4–8, 9, 11, 74, 77, 153, 248, 258;
    *see also* Skinner, B. F.
  consciousness, 8, 39, 102, 129
  determinism, 126–31, 133, 136
  learning, 5–6, 43, 109, 127–29, 130–31
  limitations, 6–8
  psychological health, 147–49
  radical pessimism, 39
  reductionism, 35, 79, 80, 81–82, 83, 84–
    85
Being
  compared to becoming, 121–22
  compared to existence, 208
Being-in-the-world, 99, 136–37, 157, 209
Benoit, Hubert, 15
Berger, Peter, 76
*Beyond Freedom and Dignity* (Skinner), 17,
    47
Bhaskar, Roy, 75
Binswanger, Ludwig, 11, 32, 59, 91, 99
Bioenergetics, 92
Biographical techniques, 87–88

Biological differences, and individual development, 157
Biology, and teleology, 108
Blacks, 68–69, 246
Blake, Robert, 234
Blakney, R. B., 195
Bonaventure, 29
Boss, Medard, 11, 59
Brain-injured patients, studies of, 34–35, 112
Brain physiology, and altered states of consciousness, 203–4
Brentano, Franz, 54
Bridgman, P. W., 5
Brill, A. A., 135
Buber, Martin, 46
Buddha, 192–93
Buddhism, 193, 194, 195
Bugental, James, 27, 43, 84, 225
Bühler, Charlotte, 86–88, 110

**C**

Cancer, 90
*Carl Rogers on Encounter Groups* (Rogers), 223
Carlson, Rick, 239
Carnap, Rudolf, 75
Carpenter, F., 143, 144
Caruso, Igor, 11
*Casebook of Non-directive Counseling* (Snyder), 219
Castaneda, C., 193
Categorical imperative, 132–33
*Causa sui* project, 205
Center for Studies of the Person, 223, 224, 241, 243
Chardin, Pierre Teilhard de, 84, 207
Child, Irvin, 70–71, 255, 256
*Children of Crisis* (Coles), 213
Choisy, Maryse, 134
Chuang-tzu, 195, 196
*Civilization and Its Discontents* (Freud), 79
Client-centered therapy, 49–50, 61, 96–97, 112–13; see also Rogers, Carl
  applications, 223–24
  and authenticity, 179–82
  conditions for, 220, 222, 236
  origins in nondirective therapy, 218–19
  process scale, 180–82, 221
  therapist in, 220, 221–23
*Client-centered Therapy* (Rogers), 219–20
Coles, Robert, 213–14
Combs, Arthur, 235, 238
Commitment, ethic of, 252
Communications workshops, 245
Computers, 27–28
Conditioned reflex, 4, 5–6, 25–26, 35; see also Behaviorism
Conditions of worth, 96–97

Confluence, 174, 176–77, 178
Confucianism, 193, 195
Confucius, 195, 196
Congruence, 220, 222–23, 236
Conscience
  Freudian theory, 133, 151, 164
  intrinsic, of Maslow, 115, 163–64
Consciousness; see also Altered states of consciousness and Unconscious
  dialectical nature, 27–29, 66, 139–40
  early studies, 2–4
  as embodied, 88–89
  as focus of humanistic psychology, 6, 10, 48
  higher form of, in Eastern thought, 197
  holistic approach, 35–36
  immediate givens, as knowledge basis, 20–21, 57
  and intentionality of May, 137–39
  levels of, 19–26, 36, 85, 116–19, 157–61
    psychophysiological, 21, 159
    psychosocial, 21–22, 159–60
    transpersonal, 22, 160, 184–87
  needs and drives arising from, 22–25, 84, 157–59, 184–87
  passive theory of cognitive functioning, 27–28
  phenomenological analysis, 57–58
  scientific study of, 7–8, 20, 55–56, 101
  and self-actualization, 40–41, 116, 119, 121
  and self-determination, 18, 136–38
  and telosposivity, 139–41
  uniqueness of, 1–2, 18, 32–33, 45, 51, 249
*Consciousness East and West* (Pelletier and Garfield), 200
Consciousness-raising groups, 246
Constructive ideal of personality, 26, 158
Cooley, Charles, 137
Copernicus, 29
Corrard, Eugenia, 246
Coulson, William, 243, 244
*Counseling and Psychotherapy* (Rogers), 218, 219
Creative self, 152–53
Crisis intervention training, 242
*Critique of Practical Reason* (Kant), 132
*Critique of Pure Reason* (Kant), 132
Culture
  and human needs, 23–25
  and thirst for Absolute, 186
Curran, Charles, 88

**D**

D-cognition, 165
Death
  instinct, 82, 181
  terror, 205–7
Defense mechanisms, 133–34
Deikman, Arthur, 197, 202, 204

*Denial of Death, The* (Becker), 204–7
Depth psychology, 8–10, 11, 43, 48–49, 77,
    253; *see also* Freud, Sigmund, and
    Freudian theory
Depression, 58, 178, 210
Descartes, René, 3, 7–8, 88, 130, 142
Destructive tendencies, and self-actualization,
    121
Determinism, 41, 44; *see also* Self-determina-
    tion
    behaviorism, 126–31, 133, 136
    Freudian theory, 27, 132–6
    and natural science paradigm, 125–26
    shift away from, 123–25
    soft, in humanistic psychology, 136–45
Dewey, John, 137
Dialectical transcendence, 139; *see also*
    Consciousness
Disease, holistic analysis of, 88–90
Dreaming state, 198, 200, 202
Dreikurs, Rudolf, 245
Drives; *see also* Needs
    and Frankl's will to meaning, 120, 167, 171
    Freudian theory, 23–24, 78–79, 82–83
    Hull's reduction theory, 5–6, 81–82, 106–7,
        130–31
    humanistic analysis, 83–84
    and needs, 106–7
Drug-induced states, 199, 201
Dunne, John, 254–55
Dyadic effect, 98
Dychtwald, Ken, 246, 247
Dynamic listening, 32

**E**

Eastern thought, 99, 192–97, 229
Eating, and levels of consciousness, 36, 117
Eco-psychology, 225–26, 230
Economic institutions, and humanism,
    230–31
Education, humanistic, 234–39
*Education and Ecstasy* (Leonard), 235
Efficient cause, 110, 114
Ego; *see also* Consciousness
    Eastern thought, 193, 194–95
    ego-analysts, 135–36
    Freudian theory, 109, 135
    Jungian theory, 154–56
    humanistic psychology, 136–37
Ego-analysts, 135–36, 150
*Ego and the Id, The* (Freud), 83
Ego-ideal, 134, 151
Egocentrism, 204, 251
Einstein, Albert, 139–40
Emotions, 66–67, 92, 129
Empathy, in Rogerian therapy, 220, 222, 236
Encounter groups, 49, 50, 181, 223–25, 230,
    243, 245

Erikson, Erik, 87, 135–36
Esalen Institute, 93, 228, 235
*Eupsychian Management* (Maslow), 233
Evil, 38–39, 40, 190, 196, 254–55
Existential analysis, 24, 32, 58, 186
Existentialism, 45, 57–58, 99, 168
Expanded consciousness state, 199, 200
Experience
    as basis of science, 53
    in Gestalt theory, 3–4, 172
Experimentation
    double-blind procedures, 211, 212, 213
    person-centered versus impersonal ap-
        proach, 210–14
    replication, 211, 212–13
    verification, 70–71, 255–57

**F**

Family, 244–45
Fechner, Gustav, 2–3, 82
Feelings, on client-centered therapy scale, 180
Feldenkrais, Moshe, 93
Feminism, 246
Final cause, 107, 110–11, 140–41; *see also*
    Self-determination
Ford-Esalen Project for Innovation in Human-
    istic Education, 235
Formal cause, 110
Frank, Jerome, 90
Frankl, Viktor, 11, 13, 14, 23, 85
    antireductionism, 84
    authenticity, 43, 160, 163, 167–71
    logotherapy, 171, 188
    self-determination, 137, 142, 144
    self-transcendence, 47, 170, 187–88, 190
    will to meaning, 14, 40–42, 47, 120,
        167–71, 183, 187–88
Free-functioning, 174–78
Freedom; *see* Self-determination
*Freedom to Learn* (Rogers), 235
Freud, Sigmund, and Freudian theory, 164,
    188, 215, 248; *see also* Depth psychology
    *and Psychoanalysis*
    *agape*, 47–48, 151
    authenticity, 44
    drives, 23–24, 78–79, 82–83
    homeostasis, 109, 116
    illusion of freedom, 41, 127, 132–36, 138
    methodology, 54, 74
    pessimism, 39
    psychological health, 149–51
    reductionism, 35, 78–79, 80, 82–83, 84–85
    unconscious, 8–9, 90–91, 103, 109–10, 117,
        129, 133, 135
    will to pleasure, 109, 149–50, 151, 168
Fromm, Erich, 24, 164
Fully-functioning person, 43, 144, 178–82,
    190–91, 196, 221

Functional phenomenology; *see* Phenomenology

**G**

"Game and Growth: Two Dimensions of our
Psychotherapeutic Zeitgeist," (Rossi), 215
Garell, Dale, 239
Garfield, Charles, 14, 15, 200, 201
Gendlin, Eugene, 102, 120, 180, 187, 221,
222–23
Geology, hypothetico-deductive method in, 61
Gestalt theory, 3–4, 33–34, 35, 254, 256; *see
also* Perls, Fritz
authenticity, 172–78, 182
definition of self, 173
neurotic styles, 174–78
therapy, 92, 93, 173–74, 181
*Gestalt Therapy* (Perls, Hefferline, and
Goodman), 46
Gibb, Jack and Lorraine, 233
Gift of self, 159–60, 163
Giorgi, Amedeo
experimental method, 211, 212, 255
science paradigms, 54–55, 69, 73, 74
Glasser, William, 234, 235, 243
Goldstein, Kurt, 10, 220
actualizing tendency, 37, 106, 113
study of organism, 34–35, 37, 214
God, existence of, 132–33
Gordon, Thomas, 245
Group for Psychology and Religion, 243–44
Growth centers, 194, 228–30, 243
Grumbles, 233
Guilt, and self-actualization, 122, 164, 170–71

**H**

Hampden-Turner, Charles, 248
Hartmann, Heinz, 135
Harvard Graduate School of Education, 235
Havighurst, R. J., 87
Hegel, Georg, 29
Health, physical, 10, 88–89, 239–41
Health, psychological; *see also* Authenticity
*and* Self-actualization
Adler's theory, 151, 152–53, 182
behaviorism, 147–49
Freudian theory, 149–51
humanistic theories, 43, 239–41
Jungian theory, 151, 153–56, 160, 182
and self-determination, 141–42
Heidegger, Martin, 11, 57–58, 136
Heisenberg principle, 76
Hero myth, 155, 205–6, 253
Herrnstein, Richard, 127
Hilgard, E. R., 123, 125
Hillman, James, 252–55
Hobbes, Thomas, 80

Holism, 33–36, 37, 106, 172
and Bühler's life cycles, 86–88
and disease, 88–90
Eastern thought, 192
and learning, 235–36
and Nuttin's consciousness levels, 85–86
and self-transcendence, 99–100
and unconscious, 90–99
Holistic medicine, 239–41
Homeostasis, 37, 40, 108–9
rejection by humanistic psychology, 114,
115, 116–17, 120–21
Homokineticism, 122
Horney, Karen, 24, 112, 122
Howard, George, 256–57
Howe, Eric G., 135
Hull, Clark, 5, 81–82, 106–7, 108–9, 130–31
Human Dimensions in Medical Education
project, 241
Human potential movement, 194, 228–30
Human relations training, 228
*Human Side of Enterprise, The* (McGregor),
232
*Humanism and Behaviorism: Dialogue and
Growth* (Wandersman, Poppen, and
Ricks), 68
Humanistic psychology; *see also specific
topics*
authenticity, 156–57
criticism, 252–57
general characteristics, 10–12
and psychology paradigm, 55
and self-determination, 110, 136, 145
and social issues, 225–26, 227–28
*Humanistic Psychology of Education, A*
(Schmuck and Schmuck), 237
*Humanistic Psychology and the Research
Tradition* (Child), 70
*Humanizing Organization Behavior* (Metzer
and Wickert), 234
Hume, David, 57
Husserl, Edmund, 57, 58
Hypnosis, 199, 204
Hypothetico-deductive approach to scientific
investigation, 60–61

**I**

Id, 83, 135, 142, 149–50
Identism, 3
Images, and archetypal unconscious, 253,
254
Inborn motivational dynamics, 127
Individuation process, 154–56
Induction, and consciousness, 27
Inner nature, 114–15
"Inner Strength and its Revolutionary
Impact," (Rogers), 247
Intellectual awareness, 173–74

Intentionality; *see also* Self-determination
  and life cycle, 87
  self as center of, 40
  and self-determination, 137–39, 145
*International Encyclopedia of Unified
  Science,* 80
Interpersonal relationships, in client-centered
  therapy, 181
Interviews, 87–88, 97–98
Intrinsic conscience, 115, 163–64
Introjection, 174–75, 178
Introspectionism, 54, 56, 72, 103

**J**

James, William, 12, 13, 207
Jaspers, Karl, 11, 58
Jourard, Sidney, 11
  analysis of disease, 10, 89–90
  impersonal and personal modes of investi-
    gation, 210–11
  marriage, 244
  self-disclosure theory, 10, 32, 97–99, 181,
    210–11
Jung, Carl, 8, 9, 90, 135, 196, 200–201, 252,
    254, 255
  archetypes, 13, 154, 192
  authenticity, 151, 153–56, 182
  collective unconscious, 13, 25, 153, 252–53
  individuation process, 142, 153–56, 160
  superconscious self, 14, 99–100
  transcendent function, 153, 156
  and transpersonal psychology, 13, 14,
    15–16

**K**

Kaam, Adrian van, 69, 255
Kant, Immanuel, 28–29, 57, 66, 116
  dialectical transcendence, 139
  freedom and morality, 132–33, 136
Keen, Ernest, 69
Kelly, George, 64–65, 180, 255
Kempler, Walter, 27, 172–74
Kierkegaard, Soren, 45, 57, 205, 206
Kirsch, Robert, 213
Knowing, Rogers's levels of, 31
Koch, Sigmund, 6–7, 71, 75, 126
Kohlberg, Lawrence, 71
Krasner, Leonard, 258
Krippner, Stanley, 198
Kris, Ernst, 135
Kuhn, Thomas, 29, 52–56

**L**

La Jolla Summer Program, 244
Laing, R. D., 11, 43
Land, Douglas, 243, 244

Language, 10
  learning, in behaviorist theory, 128, 129
  structure, and dialectical nature of con-
    sciousness, 140
Lao-tzu, 195, 196
Last Gestalt, 173, 191
Latner, Joel, 120, 173, 191
Law, and humanistic psychology, 241–43
Lazarus, Arnold, 258
Learning
  behavioristic theory, 5–6, 43, 109, 127–29,
    130–31
  humanistic theory, 235
Leonard, George B., 235
Lewin, Kurt, 34
Libido, 82
Life
  as open system, 105–6
  teleological explanations, 108
Life cycles, 86–88
Life instinct, 82
Literatures of freedom and dignity, 17–18
Lockean paradigm, 136; *see also* Science
Locus of evaluation, 43–44
Logical learning theory, 65–69
Logical positivism, 4–5, 6, 18–19, 57, 73,
    125
Logotherapy, 171, 188
*Love and Will* (May), 137
Lowen, Alexander, 92–93
Luce, Gay, 246

**M**

McGregor, Douglas, 232–33
Maddi, Salvatore, 200, 203
Male role, and self-disclosure, 98
Management, humanistic, 231–34
Managerial grid, 234
Mandala, 156
Mann, John, 229–30
Marcel, Gabriel, 46
Marx, Karl, 230–31
Marxism, 18
Maslow, Abraham, 4, 11, 27, 124, 138, 248
  authenticity, 164–67, 182
  hierarchy of needs, 84, 86, 161–63, 166,
    232–33, 250, 251
  holism, 35
  management, 233
  nadir experiences, 170
  peak experiences, 32, 47, 71, 99, 163, 164,
    176, 189, 195
  science, 52, 70–71, 76, 204
  self-actualization, 13–14, 39, 43, 113–16,
    117, 161–67, 189
  self-transcendence, 170, 188–90
  Taoistic therapies, 196, 215
Materialism, 80, 84, 109, 197

May, Rollo, 11, 33, 59
  self-actualization, 39, 121–22
  self-determination, 41, 137–39, 142
  unconscious, 91
Maya, 193
"Me decade," 230
Mead, George Herbert, 197
Meador, Betty, 223, 224
Meador, Bruce, 243, 244
Meaning fulfillment, 170–71, 187
Medicine, humanistic, 239–41
Meditation, 103, 194, 197, 199, 200, 201–4
Metagrumbles, 233
Metapathologies, 166–67
Mind-body dichotomy, 2–3, 88–90
Minkowski, Eugene, 58, 60, 210
Morality, basis of, 132–33
Moustakas, Clark, 245
Mouton, J. S., 234
Murphy, Gardner, 15–16, 71
Murphy, Lois, 15–16
Murphy, Michael, 228
Murray, Henry, 61, 107
Mysticism, 36, 192, 194–95, 199, 200, 202–4, 230
Myths, and archetypal unconscious, 253, 254–55

N

National Association for Humanistic Gerontology (NAHG), 247
National Training Laboratory, 231, 232
Natural childbirth, 240
"Necessary and Sufficient Conditions of Therapeutic Personality Change, The" (Rogers), 220
Needs; see also Drives
  and consciousness, 22–25, 84, 157–59, 184–87
  and drives, 106–7
  Maslow's hierarchy, 84, 86, 161–63, 166, 232–33, 250, 251
  Nuttin's levels, 157–59, 184–87
  for personal regard, 96–97
Neimeyer, Greg, 64
Neurosis
  contact-boundary, in Gestalt theory, 174–78
  and death terror, 205
  Freudian theory, 138
  noogenic, 85, 166, 170–71, 186–87
  obsessive-compulsive, 140
  and self-knowledge, 97
Nevill, Dorothy, 246
Nietsche, Friedrich, 57
Nirvana, 203
No Exit (Sartre), 46
Nondirective therapy, 218–19; see also Client-centered therapy

Noumenon, 132
Nuttin, Joseph, 11
  authenticity, 157–61, 172, 184
  consciousness, levels of, 19–26, 36, 85, 116–19, 157–61
  constructive ideal of personality, 26, 158
  gift of self, 159–60, 163
  holism, 84, 85–86
  self-actualization, 38, 41, 44, 85–86, 116–19, 157, 163, 172
  self-transcendence, 45–46, 86, 184–87
  unconscious, 33, 94–95, 98

O

Oedipal phase, 133, 150–51
Open systems, 26, 105–6
Openness to self, 39
Operants, 128
Operationism, 5–6, 7, 125; see also Behaviorism
Oppressed groups, 245–47
Organization development (OD), 233–34, 237, 238
Orne, M. T., 211
Ornstein, Robert, 14, 15, 204
Osgood, C. E., 63

P

Pahnke, Walter N., 203
Pain, Disease, and Sacrifice (Bakan), 90
Paranormal phenomena, 191; see also Altered states of consciousness
Parent Effectiveness Training (PET) program, 245
Participating experience, 87–88
Pattern and Growth in Personality (Allport), 86–87
Pavlov, Ivan, 4
Peak experiences, 32, 47, 71, 99, 163, 164, 176, 189, 195
Pelletier, Kenneth, 14, 15, 200, 201
Perception, 3–4, 6, 33–34; see also Consciousness
Perls, Fritz, 11, 196, 252; see also Gestalt theory
  self-actualization, 43, 86, 120, 224–25
  self-transcendence, 46, 190, 196, 197
Perry, John Weir, 200–201
Person to Person (Rogers and Stevens), 221–22
Person-centeredness, 48–50, 208–9; see also Client-centered therapy
  phenomenological approach, 209–14
  and self-actualization, 214–16
  and self-determination, 217
Persona, 155
Personal construct theory, 64–65

Personality adjustment, and self-concept/self-ideal, 62–63
*Persuasion and Healing* (Frank), 90
Phenomenology, 6–7, 19, 32–33; *see also* Science
  origins, 57–59
  and person-centeredness, 209–14
  structural and functional, 59–61, 101, 255
    examples of functional, 61–69
    radical and moderate positions, 69–75
Physics, prediction in, 76
Piaget, Jean, 71, 143, 148
Placebo effect, 89, 211
Plato, 29
Polanyi, Michael, 86–87
Police management, humanistic, 241–43
Political science, humanistic, 247–48
Poppen, P. J., 258
Positivism, 4–5, 6, 18–19, 57, 73, 125
Price, D. D., 255
Projection, in Gestalt theory, 174, 175–76, 178
Protopoint, 28
Psychedelic states, 199, 200, 201
Psychoanalysis, 8–9, 11, 41; *see also* Depth psychology *and* Freud, Sigmund, and Freudian theory
*Psychoanalysis and Personality* (Nuttin), 19
Psychology
  meaning of, 2
  measurement, role of, 69–70, 73
  natural science paradigm in, 53–56
  and philosophy, 56–59
  verifiability, 70–71, 255–57
Psychology of Being, 47
*Psychology as a Human Science* (Giorgi), 54
*Psychology of Rigorous Humanism, The* (Rychlak), 68
Psychopathology
  behavioristic analysis, 149
  and conditions of worth, 96–97
  as focus of depth psychology, 9–10
  holistic analysis, 88, 89
  and self-disclosure, 97
*Psychopathology of Everyday Life, The* (Freud), 9, 133–34, 135
Psychophysical awareness, 173–74
Psychophysical parallelism, 3, 88
Psychosis, 199, 200, 205
Psychosynthesis, 14
Psychotherapy, 124, 229
  client-centered; *see* Client-centered therapy
  and Eastern thought, 194
  and life cycle research, 88
  person-centered approach, 209–10, 214
*Psychotherapy East and West* (Watts), 15–16, 192
Public health programs, 239
Purpose-in-life test, 188
*Pygmalion in the Classroom* (Rosenthal), 236

**Q–R**

Q technique and Q sort, 32, 62–63, 221
Racism, 246
Rank, Otto, 112, 135, 182, 205, 218, 219, 220
Raye, Elizabeth, 246
Reality principle, 150
Reality therapy, 243
Reductionism, 3–4, 11; *see also* Holism
  behaviorism, 35, 79, 80, 81–82, 83, 84–85
  biological, 78–80, 81
  Freudian theory, 35, 78–79, 80, 82–83, 84–85
  and holism, 35, 36
  linguistic, 101–2
  mathematical, 80, 100–104
  quantification as, 69
Reich, Wilhelm, 92
Reinforcement learning, 5–6, 127–28, 130–31; *see also* Behaviorism
Reinforcement value (RV), 67–68
Religion, 186, 188, 252
  and death terror, 204–7
  Eastern thought, 190, 192–97, 201
  and evil, 254–55
  and humanistic psychology, 243–44
Repression, 14, 86, 92, 117
Response-shift bias, 256–57
Reticular formation, and transcendent state, 203
Retroflection, 174, 177–78
*Revisioning Psychology* (Hillman), 252–53
Richards, William A., 203
Ricks, D. F., 258
Robinson, Virginia, 218
Rogers, Carl, 11, 66, 88, 175, 231, 247; *see also* Client-centered therapy
  actualizing tendency, 37–39, 43–44, 95–97, 111–13, 115, 116, 120, 152, 221
  authenticity, 178–82
  education, 235, 237
  fully-functioning person, 43, 144, 178–82, 190–91, 196, 221
  knowledge, 31
  marriage, 244–45
  methodology, 61–63, 70, 73, 102, 104, 255
  person-centered approach, 76, 112–13, 209, 216, 236
  self, theory of, 219–20
  self-determination, 41, 137, 138, 144, 217
  self-transcendence, 46, 190–91, 196, 197
  unconditional positive regard, 46, 159–60, 179, 221, 222, 236
  unconscious, 93, 95–97, 98
Role Construct Repertory Test (Rep Test), 64–65
Roles, and individuation process, 154
Rolf, Ida, 93
Rome, Beatrice and Sidney, 233

Rosenthal, R., 211, 236
Rossi, Ernest, 215
Rychlak, Joseph, 116, 125, 148, 255
  cognitive functioning model, 27–29, 127
  logical learning theory, 65–69, 111
  science paradigms, 70, 126, 136
  telosponsivity, 139–41

## S

Sartre, Jean-Paul, 45, 46, 168
Satori, 203
Schizophrenia, 58, 68, 88, 150, 181, 200, 201
  and client-centered therapy, 221–23
Schmuck, Richard and Patricia, 237
Scholastic tradition, 111
School administrators, 237, 238
*Schools without Failure* (Glasser), 235
Schultz, D., 166, 167
Schutz, William, 93, 228–29
Science; see also Phenomenology and
    Psychology
  and cognitive need, 185
  and consciousness, 7–8, 20, 55–56, 101
  and determinism, 125–26
  hypothetico-deductive approach, 60–61
  and mystical phenomena, 192
  paradigms in, 52–56, 73–74, 125, 136
  and positivism, 4–5
  prediction and control, 76–77
  quantification, 60–61, 69–70, 73
  redefinition, 73, 74
  and social control, 18
  and teleology, 107–11
*Science in the Modern World* (Whitehead),
  55
Scotus, John Duns, 29, 124
Secondary reinforcement, 81–82
Self; see also Consciousness and Ego
  communication of, in client-centered
    therapy, 181
  emergence of, 155–56
  Gestalt theory, 46, 173–78
Self-actualization, 26, 36–41, 43
  individual life cycles, 87–88
  oppressed groups, 245–46
  person-centered approach, 214–16
  theories
    Frankl, 40–42, 47, 120
    Maslow, 13–14, 39, 43, 113–16, 117,
      161–67, 189
    May, 39, 121–22
    Nuttin, 38, 41, 44, 85–86, 116–19, 157,
      163, 172
    Perls, 48, 86, 120, 224–25
    Rogers, 37–39, 43–44, 95–97, 111–13,
      115, 116, 120, 152
Self-actualizers, 13–14, 115, 161, 164, 165,
  188–89

Self-concept, in Rogerian therapy
  and real self, 178–79
  and self-ideal, 62–63
Self-consciousness; see Consciousness
Self-determination, 25–26, 41–42, 48; see also
    Determinism
  and consciousness, 17–18, 25–26, 74–75
  developmental view, 42, 142–45, 217
  and person-centeredness, 127
  and psychological health, 141–42
  theories
    Frankl, 137, 142, 144
    Freud, 41, 127, 132–36, 138
    Kant, 132–33
    May, 41, 137–39, 142
    Rogers, 41, 137, 138, 144, 217
    Rychlak, 139–41
    Skinner, 17–19, 25, 74, 77
*Self-determination: The Psychology of
Personal Freedom* (Zavalloni), 123
Self-disclosure, 10, 32, 97–99, 181, 210–11
*Self Disclosure: An Experimental Analysis of
the Transparent Self* (Jourard), 98
Self-fulfillment ethic, 250–52, 253–54
Self-reflexivity, 28; see also Consciousness
Self-targeting, 233
Self-transcendence, 14, 45–48, 99–100,
  183–84
  and altered states of consciousness,
    198–204
  and Eastern thought, 192–98
  and religion, 186, 188, 190, 201, 204–7
  theories
    Frankl, 170, 187–88, 190
    Latner, 191
    Maslow, 170, 188–90
    Nuttin, 45–46, 86, 184–87
    Rogers, 46, 190–91, 196, 197
Senior Actualization and Growth Exploration
  (SAGE) project, 246
Sensation, 3–4, 33–34
Sensitivity groups, 231
Sensitivity training, 242
Sexuality
  Freudian theory, 23–24, 79, 82, 109, 149–50
  and narcissism, 187
  nonsatisfaction compared to repression,
    158, 159
Shaffer, Thomas, 241
Simpson, Elizabeth Leonie, 225
Skinner, B. F., 6, 7, 81, 88; see also Behavior-
  ism
  autonomy and determinism, 17–19, 25, 74,
    77, 126–31, 133, 136
  self-transcendence, 47
  uses of conditioning, 17–19, 147–48
Sleeping state, 198, 200, 202
Social ego, 193
Social institutions, 225–26, 235, 247–48

Social interest, 152
Social learning theory, 148; see also Behaviorism
Socialization
    behavioristic analysis, 148
    and education, 234
    and ego development, 150–51
    and metaphysical ideas, 193, 197
    and self-determination, 38–39
    and unconscious, 94–97
Socrates, 29
Space program, 78, 83–84, 185
Spinoza, 135
Steenberghen, Fernand van, 19–20, 75
Stephenson, William, 32, 62
Straus, Erwin, 58–59
Structural phenomenology; see Phenomenology
Sublimation, 83, 84–85, 149, 151, 159
Suffering, and self-actualization, 169–70, 190
Sullivan, Harry Stack, 24
Super, Donald, 63
Super meaning, 188
Superconscious sphere, 14, 99–100
Superego, 132–33, 134, 142, 151, 164
Supreme Doctrine: Psychological Studies in Zen Thought, The (Benoit), 15
Sutich, Anthony, 12–13, 214–15
Szasz, Thomas, 243

**T**

T-groups, 231–32, 233, 234
Taft, Jessie, 218
Tageson, C. W., 63, 235
Tao Teh Ching, 195
Taoism, 190, 192, 193, 194–97, 206
Taoistic therapies, 196, 215, 216
Tart, Charles, 14, 15–16, 73, 103, 192, 197, 198
Teachers, and humanistic education, 236–38
Teleology, 107–11; see also Self-determination
Telic decentralization, 90
Theory X and Theory Y management, 232–33
Thorndike's law of effect, 128
Tillich, Paul, 120
Tolman, Edward, 109
Tournier, Paul, 11, 142
Trance state, 199
Transcendent function, 156
Transcendent values, 168–69
Transcendental awareness, 203
Transparent Self, The (Jourard), 89, 98
Transpersonal Psychologies (Tart), 15
Transpersonal psychology, 12–16, 48, 198–204
Transpersonal Self, 14

**U**

Unconditional positive regard, 159–60, 179, 221, 222, 236
Unconscious
    and behaviorism, 129
    body as repository of, 92–93
    collective, 13, 25, 153, 252–54
    as dimension in personal freedom zone, 144–45
    dynamic, in Freudian theory, 8–9, 29, 90–91, 93, 103, 109–10, 117, 129, 133, 135
    humanistic psychology, 33, 90–99
    intimate conscious of Nuttin, 93–95, 158
    Rogerian theory, 93, 95–97, 98
    and self-disclosure, 97–99
    and transcendent function, 156
University of Chicago Counseling Center, 219, 221
University of Wisconsin, 181, 221
Use of Personal Documents in Psychological Science, The (Allport), 86–87

**V**

Values, transcendent, 168–69
Varieties of Religious Experience, The (James), 12
Verbal community, 128–29
Verification, 70–71, 255–57
Von Gebsattel, Viktor, 58, 60

**W**

Walden Two (Skinner), 17, 39
Wandersman, A., 258
Watson, John, 5
Watts, Alan, 15–16, 48, 192, 194, 195–96
Way of Being, A (Glasser), 235
Way of Life, The, 195
Weil, Andrew, 203
Wells, Theodora, 246
Western Behavioral Sciences Institute, 223
Western Training Laboratories, 232
Wexberg, E., 152
White, John W., 203
Whitehead, Alfred North, 55, 249, 258
Will, 124; see also Determinism and Self-determination
Will to health, 220
Will to meaning, 14, 40–42, 47, 120, 167–71, 183, 187–88
Will to pleasure, 109, 149–50, 151, 168
Will to power, 168
Women, work attitudes of, 251–52
Wood, J. K., 181
Woolpert, Stephen, 241–43
Work ethic, 250

Wu-wei, 196
Wundt, Wilhelm, 4, 54

**Y**

Yankelovich, Daniel, 250–52

**Z**

Zavalloni, Roberto, 123–24, 134, 138, 145
Zen, 193, 229
Zilboorg, Gregory, 134–35
Zone of personal freedom, 143–45

This book has been set VIP, in 10 and 9 point
Melior, leaded 2 points. Chapter numbers and
titles are 30 point Helvetica. The overall size
of the type area is 30 by 47½ picas.